The Reminiscences of Doctor John Sebastian Helmcken

THE REMINISCENCES
OF
DOCTOR JOHN SEBASTIAN
HELMCKEN

Edited by Dorothy Blakey Smith
with an introduction by W. Kaye Lamb

Published in co-operation with the
Provincial Archives of British Columbia

UNIVERSITY OF BRITISH COLUMBIA PRESS

The Reminiscences of Doctor John Sebastian Helmcken
© The University of British Columbia 1975

This book has been published with the help of a grant from the Humanities Research Council of Canada, using funds provided by the Canada Council, and a grant from the Leon and Thea Koerner Foundation for the illustrations.

Canadian Shared Cataloguing in Publication Data

Helmcken, John Sebastian, 1824-1920.
    The reminiscences of Doctor John Sebastian Helmcken

    1. Helmcken, John Sebastian, 1824-1920.
2. British Columbia - History - Sources.
I. Smith, Dorothy Blakey, 1899-   ed.
II. Title.
F   610'.92'4
[LC: F1088.H44
ISBN 0-7748-0038-0

International Standard Book Number 0-7748-0038-0
Printed in Canada

CONTENTS

ILLUSTRATIONS

PHOTOGRAPHIC CREDITS

Plates 1, 5, 6, 8, 11, 12, 13, 14, 15, 16, 17, 18, 19, 20, 22, 23 appear courtesy of the Provincial Archives of British Columbia and Mr. Ainslie J. Helmcken provided Plate 24. Plate 2 is from a map in Special Collections, the University of British Columbia Library. Plate 3, from the frontispiece of the centenary booklet of St. George's School, 1905, was provided by Pastor Dietrich Altmann. Plate 4 is from the collection of the Guildhall Library, London, and Plate 7 was provided by the Department of Medical Illustration and Photography, Guy's Hospital Medical School, London. Plate 21 is from the collection of the City Archives, Vancouver.

ACKNOWLEDGEMENTS

Thanks are due in the first instance to Mr. Ainslie J. Helmcken, Archivist of the City of Victoria, who early in 1973 drew the attention of the University of British Columbia Press to Dr. John Sebastian Helmcken's "Reminiscences" of 1892 and supplied a working transcript of the manuscript in the Provincial Archives. Mr. Helmcken's personal acquaintance with his grandfather has been a great advantage: with patience and good humour he has furnished many details of family information, as well as allowing access to photographs in his own collection and that of the City Archives.

Mr. Willard E. Ireland, Provincial Librarian and Archivist at the time the project was undertaken, and his successors, Mr. Allan Turner, Provincial Archivist, and Mr. James G. Mitchell, Legislative Librarian, have given their full co-operation; and the members of their staffs, especially in the Provincial Archives, have been unfailingly helpful in checking specific details and in supplying copies of maps, paintings, and photographs. At the University of British Columbia, Miss Frances Woodward and Mrs. Anne Yandle of the Special Collections in the Library also gave assistance; Mrs. Barbara Gibson, Woodward Library, verified the textual readings of JSH's medical comments; and Mr. R. C. Beaumont, Department of German, furnished a reasonable interpretation of a letter containing significant family information, written to Dr. Helmcken in German script — and in atrociously bad German.

Dr. W. Kaye Lamb, formerly the Provincial Archivist, then the Librarian of the University of British Columbia, and finally the Dominion Archivist and National Librarian, has placed Dr. Helmcken in perspective in his Introduction and has also given me confidence that no gross editorial error could evade his extensive knowledge of the political history of the period. Dr. Margaret A. Ormsby, formerly Head of the Department of History, the University of British Columbia, read the manuscript of the book in its early stages and has been, as always, most generous in her encouragement and help.

In piecing together Dr. Helmcken's life before he came to Fort Victoria in 1850, I have been greatly assisted by Mr. Godfrey Thompson, F.L.A., the City Librarian of the Guildhall Library, who sent me information and maps concerning Whitechapel in JSH's boyhood, and by Mrs. A. Boulton, whose painstaking research into parish registers, census returns, and other civic records produced valuable information concerning the Mittler and Helmcken families. Pastor Dietrich Altmann of the present German Lutheran St. George's Church made available material on the history of the church and its school, and Dr. W. E. Fredeman, Department of English, the University of British Columbia, spent some of his own very limited research time in examining the records relating to the Helmcken family there. Miss J. M. Farmer, Wills Librarian of Guy's Hospital Medical School, allowed access to the early records in her keeping, and Mr. C. F. Forbes, Humanities Division, the University of British Columbia Library, checked with the utmost patience and accuracy the records covering J. S. Helmcken's period of attendance there. Mr. Thomas Cope of Litchfield Way, London, who has made a special study of early British railways, gave me fully documented information concerning the railways in Victorian London used by the Helmcken family.

A number of other people have very kindly answered, or have done their utmost to answer, specific questions put to them. Some of this help is acknowledged in the appropriate footnotes below; but mention should also be made of Dr. D. G. W. Edwards, the Pacific Forest Research Centre, Victoria; Mrs. Margaret 'Espinasse; Miss H. R. Humphrey; Dr. J. Beattie MacLean; Mrs. Marjorie Pettigrew, resident custodian, Helmcken House; Mrs. A. F. Rendle and Mrs. C. L. Craig, Victoria Medical Society; and Dr. Stuart R. Tompkins.

My final debt of gratitude is to Dr. Jane C. Fredeman, senior editor of the University of British Columbia Press, with whom I have now been associated for two pleasant years in the struggle to bring some sort of order out of Dr. Helmcken's "Reminiscences." Her highly intelligent observations both on the text itself and on the editorial appendages have been of the utmost value. For any errors in fact or form that have escaped her mercilessly accurate eye the responsibility must now be mine alone.

Victoria, British Columbia   Dorothy Blakey Smith
October 1975

INTRODUCTION

In December 1910 Dr. John Sebastian Helmcken retired as physician to the provincial jail in Victoria. R. E. Gosnell, realizing that this was no ordinary occasion, seized upon it to point out that Helmcken's retirement was that of a man who had "lived and occupied an official position throughout the entire political life" of British Columbia. He had held this particular post since 1851—ever since a jail had existed in the province—a period of sixty years. But this neither indicated the full length of his public service nor suggested its breadth. In 1850 Helmcken had received the first appointment made by the first governor of Vancouver Island, and he was active in colonial assemblies and councils from the time the first assembly came into existence in 1856 until the last meetings of the Executive Council of British Columbia in 1871, just before the united colony became a province of Canada. It is hardly an exaggeration to say that he had been involved in virtually every important political decision made during the crown colony period. "If old men could remember everything," Gosnell wrote, "he is the only man living who could sit down and write the whole history of British Columbia from personal knowledge."[1]

Gosnell was probably unaware that eighteen years earlier, in 1892, Helmcken had gone so far as to jot down the extensive reminiscences here published. While incomplete, in parts fragmentary, and subject to errors of memory such as afflict us all, they nevertheless contain a wealth of comment and anecdote that throws much light on the decades that saw the broad outlines of an extensive civilized community emerge from a wilderness.

A few years after Confederation, in 1878, H. H. Bancroft spent a month

[1] R. E. Gosnell, "Doctor Helmcken," *Man to Man Magazine*, January 1911, p. 28.

in Victoria gathering material for his *History of British Columbia*. Helmcken, of course, was an obvious source of information. In the *History* Bancroft gives this vivid impression of him:

> Short and slightly built, with a huge head, always having on it a huge hat, balancing itself upon his shoulders; with deep, clear, intelligent eyes, in which there was self-confidence and critical discrimination, but no malice; with a wide-spreading and well-projecting mouth, holding in it the ever-present cigar, and given to much laughter; with a kind heart that gave the lie to many of his words and actions—there has never been a man in British Columbia who, with an exterior so impenetrable by a stranger, has for so many years maintained the respect and confidence of the community, who made more friends, or performed more acts of unparaded charity, than John Sebastian Helmcken.[1]

This account is friendly and appreciative, but Bancroft evidently did not find it easy to extract information from Helmcken; the reserve with strangers to which he refers got in the way. As a result he did not record accurately certain events in which Helmcken played a part. The latter's comment in the reminiscences was brief and scathing: "Bancroft tells lies." This was unfair both to Bancroft and to his *History*, which is a work of substantial value in spite of its deficiencies; but it may well have been Bancroft's inaccuracies that prompted Helmcken to put pen to paper. It can scarcely have been a coincidence that the first of four reminiscent articles contributed to year-end issues of the Victoria *Colonist* appeared in December 1887, only a few months after the *History of British Columbia* was published. Others followed in New Year's Day issues in 1889, 1890, and 1891; and it was in May 1892 that Helmcken finally sat down to write his reminiscences in a more or less systematic way.

They fall naturally into two parts. In the first he describes his early life in London and his travels before he arrived in Victoria in 1850. The second consists of his recollections of events in the Colony of Van-

---

[1]H. H. Bancroft, *History of British Columbia* (San Francisco: The History Company, 1887), p. 243. For another glimpse of Helmcken as Bancroft saw him, see Bancroft's *Literary Industries* (San Francisco: The History Company, 1890), pp. 538-39.

couver Island and (after 1866) in the united colony of British Columbia until Confederation. At that point they break off abruptly; there is scarcely a word about the last forty-nine years of his very long life.

Helmcken was born in London, of German descent. His father had been unfortunate; employed first in a large sugar refinery, he had later become licensee of the White Swan, a public house popular with the sugar workers. Hard work in the hot atmosphere of the refinery had ruined his health, and a decline in the sugar trade had affected the White Swan adversely. Helmcken knew his father only as "a good kind upright man, but ... always ailing, too broken to be active." He died when John Sebastian was fifteen.

The mother was the mainstay of the family. Clearly a remarkable personality, she was, in Helmcken's phrase, "everything to everybody ... a stout strong robust determined energetic woman, nice looking ... always at work from morn till night. ..." Work and strict discipline were the rules of the household, and as a consequence the son acquired a habit of industry and a willingness to undertake tedious and unpaid chores that were later to account in no small degree for his influence in political affairs.

Helmcken was raised in Whitechapel, within a mile of the Tower of London. The neighbourhood had seen better days but was far from being a slum, though there were sordid areas nearby. Visiting them in later years John Sebastian came to realize that poverty could be caused by poor management—by the frittering away of resources—as well as by the lack of money. In this respect his home was an object lesson; somehow his mother managed to raise her family of eight children in reasonable comfort on a slender income, derived presumably from the White Swan, of which she was licensee for twenty-five years after her husband's death.

Helmcken was the eldest of her four sons and seems also to have been much the ablest. His mother, recognizing his ability, gave him the best schooling she could afford. When he was thirteen or fourteen her friendship with Dr. Graves, the family doctor, who lived across the street, became important. Graves had a great admiration for Mrs. Helmcken, who had assisted him in the difficult days when he was establishing his practice. Both he and his wife took a liking to young John Sebastian, and the result was a suggestion that he should be employed as an errand boy to deliver medicines in the evening at a wage of half a crown a week. In the reminiscences Helmcken recounts in detail the way in which this first engagement led to an apprenticeship in pharmacy, later to be succeeded by a full-fledged medical apprenticeship. Four years of lectures and study at Guy's Hospital followed, and Helmcken's account of lectures, general hospital conditions, and practical training in the 1840's is a remarkable description of the then state of many aspects of medicine and medical education. His habit of industry stood him in good stead. He worked hard, had no money to pay for amusements that might have distracted him, and had his reward in the high standing, medals, and prizes that he won at the end of each of the four sessions at Guy's.

In the spring of 1847 he was admitted as a Licentiate of the Apothecaries' Society and in March 1848, before his twenty-fourth birthday, he passed the qualifying examinations and became a Member of the Royal College of Surgeons. It was a moment of quiet triumph for both mother and son. Other successful candidates spent a night on the town to celebrate; this Helmcken could not afford to do: "I having no money perhaps to spend, returned home and shewed Mother my certificate. Poor Mother, how she cried—how pleased was she—and so we both enjoyed ourselves in common!"

In the spring of 1847, at the end of his third session at Guy's, Helmcken had felt "fagged and restless" and had seized an opportunity to make a voyage to York Factory, on Hudson's Bay, as ship's doctor in the Hudson's Bay Company supply ship *Prince Rupert*. Arrangements for the voyage brought him into touch with the company's secretary, Archibald Barclay, and this contact was to determine his future. A year later, after qualifying at the Royal College of Surgeons, he was still anxious to see more of the world, and Barclay introduced him to Richard Green, a prominent shipowner, who arranged for him to serve as doctor in the passenger ship *Malacca*. Her voyage was intended to be to Bombay and return, but it was extended to Singapore, Hong Kong, and Canton, and lasted eighteen months. Home again in September 1849, Helmcken had to make a longer-term decision about his future. His intention had been to establish a practice in London, but he had become aware of the long years of effort and small income this would involve. When Archibald Barclay offered him the post of doctor at the Hudson's Bay establishment at Fort Vancouver, from which his nephew, Forbes Barclay, was retiring, Helmcken decided to accept. Only five weeks after the *Malacca* docked he sailed in the Company's ship *Norman Morison* on the five-month voyage to Fort Victoria. When she anchored in Esquimalt Harbour on 24 March, 1850, Helmcken could consider himself something of a traveller, for he had spent more than twenty-seven of the previous thirty-three months on three sea voyages that between them had totalled more than 45,000 miles.

He came to Fort Victoria just as the Colony of Vancouver Island was coming into existence. Richard Blanshard, the first governor, had arrived only a fortnight before him. Creation of the colony had been prompted by the Oregon boundary settlement with the United States in 1846. This established an international boundary that followed the 49th parallel westward to the Gulf of Georgia, then dipped southward to include the whole of Vancouver Island in British territory. Anticipating such a settlement, the Hudson's Bay Company had already built Fort Victoria at the southern tip of the island, and by the time Blanshard arrived had transferred to it most of its western headquarters' activities. The old headquarters, at Fort Vancouver, on the Columbia River, was now marooned deep in the United States. An influx of American settlers had dashed British hopes of retaining possession of the mainland as far south as the Columbia, and some feared that a similar influx might imperil the newly won British sovereignty in Vancouver Island. A visible official presence was thus very necessary. As virtually every white inhabitant of the island was connected with the Hudson's Bay Company, it seemed sensible to use the Company, initially at least, as the means of setting up the colony. Accordingly, early in 1849, a Royal Grant ceded the Island to it for colonization purposes and set forth in general terms the conditions that were to govern settlement. But it was also deemed essential to give the colony an official government, and this was superimposed on the authority of the Company, which the Royal Grant had already made responsible for managing most of the colony's affairs. It was an arrangement that obviously invited friction between the two and the Company had expected to prevent this, and to enjoy complete control, by having Chief Factor James Douglas, its able and experienced senior officer at Fort Victoria, appointed governor. But political considerations in England made this impracticable, and Blanshard had been appointed in his stead.

There seems to have been some expectation that Helmcken would serve as Blanshard's secretary, but he never functioned as such. Helmcken remarks that he and Blanshard "never became friends—he evidently did not care for me." Nevertheless he must have made a good impression, for he received the first appointment made by the governor. About two months after Helmcken arrived Douglas had sent him as company surgeon to Fort Rupert, at the northern end of Vancouver Island, where for a time coal mining prospects appeared to be good. Helmcken describes the difficulties with the miners and others that arose there and that prompted Blanshard to appoint him a magistrate to deal with them. The governor explained his reasons for his choice in an interesting despatch to the Colonial Office: "Mr. Helmcken has only recently arrived in the Colony from England, he is therefore a stranger to the petty brawls that have occurred, and the ill feelings they have occasioned between the Hudson's Bay Company and their servants; from this and from my knowledge of his character I have great confidence in his impartiality. . . ."[1] Impartial he may have been, but adjudicating disputes between the Company and its servants was an invidious duty for one in its employ, and Helmcken shed the office at the first opportunity.

At Fort Rupert Helmcken had his first important dealings with the native population. While he was there the Indians killed three sailors from a merchant ship, and he displayed both courage and restraint in his attempts to arrest the murderers. In his many later dealings with the Indians, they seem to have recognized instinctively his innate good will and wish to be fair. Even at Fort Rupert, in very difficult circumstances, he had not found the chiefs wholly unfriendly, and forty years later he would testify that no Indian had ever done him an injury.

When he returned to Fort Victoria in December 1850, he found that two changes were impending that were to be of great moment to him personally. First, Douglas had decided that he was to be medical officer there, instead of going to Fort Vancouver to replace Forbes Barclay as originally intended. Secondly, as was inevitable, friction had developed between Douglas and Blanshard. The governor was unwell, discouraged, and profoundly unhappy; the colony was not developing at all in the way he had expected. He had tendered his resignation and by September 1851 Douglas would become governor, as the Company had wished in the first place.

Helmcken welcomed both developments because he was anxious to become James Douglas's son-in-law. On one of his first visits to Fort Victoria he had chanced to see Cecilia, Douglas's eldest daughter, "flitting about," he records, "active as a little squirrel, and one of the prettiest objects I had ever seen. . . ." For a time Douglas seems not to have been enthusiastic about the match, but after character references had been secured from Mrs. Helmcken and Dr. Graves, he consented to the marriage, which took place in December 1852. Indeed, the date of the ceremony was actually advanced some months at Douglas's request.

---

[1]Blanshard to the Colonial Secretary, 10 July 1850 (Vancouver Island, Governor Blanshard, Despatches to London, 1849-1851, Provincial Archives of British Columbia).

He was about to leave on an expedition that involved grave personal risk and was glad to be able to leave behind a son-in-law who could assist with family affairs if the worst happened.

His marriage made it unlikely that Helmcken would ever leave Victoria. The couple lived next door to the Douglases, and no thought of taking Cecilia elsewhere seems ever to have occurred to him. His service with the Hudson's Bay Company was to extend for many years beyond the five-year term of his first appointment, and when it finally ended he would settle down to private practice in what had then become a community of considerable size.

With a measure of justification Blanshard had blamed the Hudson's Bay Company for the slow development of the colony; its enthusiasm for settlement had never been great. But the chief causes were the discovery of gold in California and a cumbersome and costly land policy. The gold rush offered an almost irresistible lure that enticed sailors to desert their ships, company servants to abscond, and many of the few colonists who did come to the island to head southward at the first opportunity. Both the Colonial Office and the Company had been most anxious to avoid indiscriminate immigration, and they had decided that land should be available only by purchase and at the relatively high price of one pound an acre. With free land available to settlers in nearby American territory, it is not surprising that there was no great rush of buyers. In the first five years of the colony's existence the only significant signs of progress were the founding of Nanaimo, where extensive deposits of good coal had been discovered, and the farms being developed by a few dozen individuals, most of them connected with the Company, and by the Puget's Sound Agricultural Company, a Hudson's Bay subsidiary. At the end of 1854 the total adult white population of Vancouver Island was still no more than 426.

Helmcken's entry into politics was precipitated by a decision made by the law lords in London. They ruled suddenly that Douglas and his small council, appointed initially by Blanshard when he was about to leave the island, lacked power to legislate. Out of the blue, in the spring of 1856, Douglas therefore received instructions from the Colonial Office to arrange immediately for the election of an assembly. The prospect filled him with dismay; he pleaded that he had "a very slender knowledge of legislation" and was "without legal advice or intelligent assistance of any kind."[1] But he duly arranged for an election, which was held early in July. He had difficulty in securing candidates for some of the seats, and Helmcken was persuaded to run in Esquimalt and Victoria District, where he was elected by acclamation. In a somewhat flowery address on the hustings—the earliest political speech of which we have record in British Columbia—he declared that he had determined to quit his "hitherto quiet and unobtrusive life, to launch upon the stormy ocean of politics, and to brave the restless sea of public opinion." Later, referring to his own small stature and huge head, he added: "I am, it is true, a little man, but with a head large enough, and I hope it contains sufficient sense to know what may be for your interest, what for your detriment."[2]

Helmcken was to be much more deeply involved in the affairs of the assembly than he expected, for at the first session, held on 12 August, he was chosen Speaker, a position he was to hold in successive assemblies as long as the colony of Vancouver Island existed. Though he always protested that he found the speakership burdensome and only continued to serve as a public duty, he was actually well suited for it by temperament. He was somewhat of a lone wolf — a man who had many friends but few if any intimates. In a small community this lack of commitment helped him to be and to appear to be impartial. His habit of industry and willingness to work were further assets. For some time most of the chores connected with the assembly, from sweeping out the meeting place to drafting minutes and documents, fell to his lot. He was not without his problems. Neither he nor any of the other members had had any experience of government, and in the beginning he had to improvise proceedings as well as he could. He had some private doubts about democracy—doubts held much more strongly by Douglas, who once remarked that he distrusted representative government and was convinced that it could not be carried on "without recourse directly or indirectly to bribery and corrupting influences."[3] But Helmcken contrived to make the system work, and Douglas underestimated him when complaining that he was "without intelligent assistance."

Over a period of ten years Helmcken was Speaker of three successive

---

[1] Douglas to the Colonial Secretary, 22 May 1856 (Vancouver Island, House of Assembly, *Minutes . . . August 12th, 1856 to September 25th, 1858*, ed. E.O.S. Scholefield, Archives Memoir no. 3 [Victoria: King's Printer, 1918], PABC).

[2] The address is printed in full in Alexander Begg, *History of British Columbia* (Toronto: W. Briggs, 1894), pp. 205-7.

[3] Quoted in Margaret Ormsby, "Sir James Douglas," *Dictionary of Canadian Biography* 10 (Toronto: University of Toronto Press, 1972), p. 244.

assemblies, each with distinctive characteristics and problems. In the first, which sat from 1856 to 1859, family, Company, and official matters were frequently closely intertwined. The problem of the colony's finances is the best example. According to the terms of the Royal Grant, the Hudson's Bay Company was to pay the colony's civil and military expenses from a trust fund, money for which was to be derived from land sales and royalties on coal and timber. Revenues had been much lower than expected, and Douglas was having great difficulty in providing such elementary necessities as roads. He hoped the assembly would supplement the trust fund by levying taxes, but this it firmly declined to do. Five of the seven members were or had been connected with the Company, and they might have been expected to stand in some awe of Douglas, who continued to serve as the Company's chief officer as well as governor of the colony; but they were also landowners who would feel the weight of taxation, and they shared the general opinion of the community that the Company should meet all expenses and look to the British government, if need be, to make good any deficit. As Speaker of the Assembly and the governor's son-in-law, Helmcken was in a position of special delicacy, but he did not allow his personal relationship with Douglas to influence his rulings from the chair.

The problem was given a new twist in 1858. For some time the Committee of the Hudson's Bay Company in London had felt that Douglas was no longer giving adequate attention to its affairs, and in 1857 it had sent Alexander Grant Dallas to Victoria to assist him, a move that Douglas did not relish. In spite of his feelings, he permitted Dallas to marry his daughter Jane in March 1858, just a month before the rush to the Fraser River gold mines overwhelmed Victoria and completely transformed the local scene. Changes then occurred rapidly. Douglas, while continuing to be governor of Vancouver Island, was given the additional appointment of governor of the new mainland colony of British Columbia, but on condition that he sever his connections with the Hudson's Bay Company. Dallas succeeded him as officer in charge of the Company's western operations.

The general feeling had been that the Company had not been doing enough for the colony of Vancouver Island; Dallas took the view that under Douglas it had been doing far too much. A new alignment was thus formed, with Douglas and the Assembly, presided over by son-in-law Helmcken, on the one side and the Hudson's Bay Company, now headed by son-in-law Dallas, on the other.

The second assembly was elected in January 1860 and existed until 1863. Helmcken, who considered it "a first rate house," was the only one of the thirteen members who had sat in the previous legislature. Its position was much more comfortable, for the Crown had ended the colonization arrangement with the Hudson's Bay Company and had assumed full control of Vancouver Island; the troublesome dual government of earlier days was thus abolished. The gold rush was at its height and Victoria in particular was growing rapidly and enjoying a period of great prosperity. These were also the last years of the reign of James Douglas, who would be knighted and retire from both his governorships early in 1864.

He had two successors — Arthur Edward Kennedy on Vancouver Island and Frederick Seymour in British Columbia. Kennedy had had administrative experience in Africa and Australia, but he had not had dealings with an elected legislature. He was soon in difficulties with the Island's third assembly, and once again the issues were financial. Kennedy made derogatory remarks about the Assembly in his despatches to the Colonial Office (the council, he alleged, was "mainly occupied in the correction of mistakes, or undoing the crude legislation of the Lower House"),[1] but it is clear that Helmcken presided over it with considerable skill and fought the governor to a standstill. Helmcken scarcely mentions the episode in his reminiscences, no doubt because the two and a half years that the third assembly existed and in which Kennedy held office were overshadowed by the huge question mark that was hanging over the future of Vancouver Island. The gold rush was declining rapidly, Victoria's prosperity was collapsing, and the colony was in dire financial straits. The only ready solution seemed to be union with the mainland colony, which it was hoped would result in substantial reductions in administrative costs. When this was first proposed, the Island was ready to agree, but only on its own terms; as the state of its economy worsened, it was compelled to accept union unconditionally, and the merger took effect on 19 November 1866.

Douglas had ruled the mainland single-handed, without the assistance of a council or assembly, but just before his retirement he had constituted a Legislative Council; nine of its members were appointed, but five were elected. When Vancouver Island joined British Columbia, it lost its assembly but became entitled to elect four members to the united colony's council. Not surprisingly, Helmcken was one of the number.

In this new capacity he had a freedom to participate in debate and in political manoeuvring that he could not enjoy as a Speaker; of this he

---

[1]Kennedy to the Colonial Secretary, 21 March 1865 (Vancouver Island, Governor Kennedy, Despatches to London, 25 March 1864—19 March 1866, PABC).

took full advantage, and he soon became an influential member of the council. Two highly important and controversial matters were dealt with in the next few years, and as a result of his activities Helmcken's reminiscences and other papers tell us more about the discussions they prompted than any other source.

The first was the location of the capital of the united colonies. Neither British Columbia nor Seymour, its governor, had been enthusiastic about the union, which had in effect been imposed by the British government. Foreseeing that the capital question would be raised, Seymour had stated his views on the matter to the Colonial Office while the union was still only under discussion: "in seeking union with British Columbia," he had written, "Vancouver Island relinquishes all claim to the possession within her limits of the seat of Government. New Westminster has been chosen as the capital of British Columbia, and it would not be fair to the reluctant Colony to deprive her of the Governor and staff of officers."[1]

But Seymour had reckoned without Helmcken. In March 1867, only weeks after his election, he moved a resolution, passed by the council by a vote of thirteen to eight, urging that the capital be moved to Victoria. As Seymour showed no sign of accepting the recommendation, Helmcken and a small but determined group of Victorians mounted a campaign in its support. "I worked like a madman," he recalls in his vivid and at times almost gleeful account of the controversy. He enlisted the help of Dallas and others in England, including admirals and other senior naval officers who had visited Esquimalt and had pleasant recollections of the hospitality they had enjoyed in nearby Victoria. It was an effective lobby and it produced results. A year after Helmcken's resolution had been passed, Seymour informed the council that the Colonial Office had instructed him to "consider the public convenience as the main guide in the selection of a seat of government," and added: "I am commanded to come to a decision without further delay, and I desire to avail myself . . . of your assistance in so doing. . . . I shall be glad if you will come to a division on the subject."[2] Personally, Seymour still favoured New Westminster. This was well known, and even after all the controversy the question had caused, he seems to have had a naive expectation that his

---

[1]Seymour to the Colonial Secretary, 17 February 1866 (*Papers relative to the Proposed Union of British Columbia and Vancouver Island*, 1866 [Cmd. 3667, 1st series], PABC).

[2]Seymour's address to the Legislative Council, 21 March 1868 (British Columbia, Legislative Council, *Journals* [New Westminster, 1868], p. 42).

wishes in the matter would be followed. But Helmcken had done his work well and the council decided in favour of Victoria by a vote of fourteen to five. The change in capital was proclaimed on 25 May 1868.

By that time the second issue—Confederation—was much to the fore. In his reminiscences Helmcken denies emphatically, and quite correctly, that he was ever in favour of annexation by the United States, though for a time he feared that it might be forced upon British Columbia by circumstances. In 1867, the same year the eastern provinces achieved Confederation, the Americans purchased Alaska and, according to Helmcken, "boasted they had sandwiched British Columbia and could eat her up at any time!!!" It was obvious that the colony could not continue to exist for long as a separate entity; Helmcken doubted the practicability of joining Canada, and annexation appeared to be the only alternative. His doubts about Confederation were twofold. First, he did not think that Canada would be willing, and it might not be able, to offer trading arrangements and cash subsidies that would be adequate to solve British Columbia's financial and commercial problems. Secondly, the union would be meaningless without ready means of communication between East and West, and he was not convinced that Canada could or would build a railway across the continent.

The whole aspect of matters changed suddenly in 1869. Seymour, whose views on Confederation had been typically lukewarm and vacillating, died while on a visit to the northern coast. He was succeeded promptly by Anthony Musgrave, a much abler and more positive character, who arrived with private instructions to further the cause of Confederation in any way he could. The purchase of Alaska and a mild agitation in favour of annexation, mostly in Victoria, had alarmed the British government, which was anxious to retain its foothold on the Pacific Coast. To expand Confederation westward promised to be an effective countermove, and arrangements were completed with the Hudson's Bay Company to acquire its proprietary rights in Rupert's Land and to transfer the whole of the vast western territories to Canada. This removed the physical barrier to union; instead of being two thousand miles away, the western border of the Dominion suddenly coincided with the eastern boundary of British Columbia.

Because of his doubts, Helmcken had opposed Confederation as being premature; he had been re-elected to the Legislative Council in November 1868 on an anti-Confederation ticket. Musgrave was attracted by Helmcken, and as opposition centred in Victoria, the governor realized that he was a key figure in the controversy. Although Helmcken admits that prejudice entered into his attitude, Musgrave perceived that it was based primarily on a hard-headed appraisal of what appeared to be the facts of the case. He felt that the appraisal was unduly pessimistic and did not despair of persuading Helmcken to modify his stand. His first step was to take him into camp; in December 1869 he persuaded him to accept membership in the select Executive Council. His next was to point out to him that in a letter opposing Confederation published in the Victoria *Chronicle* he had inadvertently suggested the use of an inflated population figure as a basis for the calculation of subsidies—the stratagem that went far to make union financially practicable. About the same time Helmcken's friend J. W. Trutch, chief commissioner of lands and works, began to insist that a railway through the mountains was not the impracticable project Helmcken feared it would prove to be. The result of all this was a gradual modification of his attitude, and in the end he was responsible in great part for formulating the terms of union that British Columbia would present to Ottawa, terms which were followed closely in the final agreement. In other words, as Musgrave suspected, Helmcken was not opposed to Confederation providing the conditions were satisfactory.

But the notable debate of March 1870 on Confederation in the Legislative Council, a verbatim report of which has fortunately survived, showed that his pessimism was far from being dispelled. He was still worried about annexation: "it is impossible to deny the probability of the less being absorbed by the greater; and it cannot be regarded as improbable that ultimately, not only this Colony, but the whole of the Dominion of Canada will be absorbed by the United States." The terms of Confederation would have to make union worth while economically: "No union between this Colony and Canada can permanently exist, unless it be to the material and pecuniary advantage of this Colony to remain in the union." Sentiment would play no part: "no union on account of love need be looked for . . . Love for Canada has to be acquired by the prosperity of the country, and from our children." He was still sceptical about the railway: "it is absurd for us to ally ourselves with a people with whom we have, and can have, no communication."[1]

These views were expressed on the first day of the debate. By the end of it, a fortnight later, Helmcken was ready to favour Confederation if the terms that had been hammered out were accepted in Ottawa.

---

[1]British Columbia, Legislative Council, *Debate on the Subject of Confederation with Canada*, reprinted from the *Government Gazette Extraordinary* of March 1870 (Victoria: King's Printer, 1912), pp. 8, 13.

Musgrave's next move was to persuade him to be a member of the three-man delegation that was to go to Ottawa and negotiate with the Dominion government. The other members were Trutch and R. W. W. Carrall, one of the councillors from a mainland constituency.

The journey to Ottawa by way of San Francisco and the recently completed Union Pacific dispelled one doubt; the Americans had proven that it was practicable to build a railway through the mountains, and if money were forthcoming presumably Canada could do the same. And the negotiations at Ottawa quickly revealed that Canada was willing not only to build a Canadian transcontinental but to be generous in financial matters as well. The course of the discussions can be followed in some detail, thanks to Helmcken's day-to-day diary—the only record of the proceedings known to exist and one of the most historically valuable items in his papers. The reminiscences add interesting details, particularly regarding the relative status of Trutch and the other two members of the delegation. Trutch, Helmcken relates, "was to be the front and general of the whole affair . . . so from the word go, we were not on an equal footing, and soon discovered this at Ottawa. Trutch was everything and everybody. . . ." With characteristic generosity he adds: "it mattered little in reality, as we all had to stick to the Terms." Nevertheless, it is clear that he was hurt by the total lack of any public mark of appreciation of his efforts after his return to Victoria: "no notice was taken of the delegates—no vote of thanks even given them—positively nothing. It is true some half a dozen bankers and so forth gave Trutch a dinner, but neither Carrall nor I were invited."

Trutch's performance at Ottawa probably had much to do with his appointment as British Columbia's first lieutenant-governor. He appreciated Helmcken's qualities if the public did not, and he approached him with a view to having him head the first provincial government. Helmcken declined, as he had determined to leave political life and devote himself to his medical practice. For this there were two reasons. In 1863 he had been raised to the rank of chief trader in the service of the Hudson's Bay Company, but the Company underwent an extensive reorganization at the end of the decade, and the post was abolished in 1870. The same year the Company appointed him surgeon at Victoria, but the stipend was only a thousand dollars a year. Personal as well as financial circumstances had changed. Helmcken's wife died in 1865; she had borne him seven children, four of whom survived infancy, and the youngest of these was only nine in 1871. An adequate income was essential, and he wished to be close to home.

In July 1871, after he refused Trutch's invitation, Helmcken received a letter from Sir John Macdonald, prime minister of Canada, urging him to reconsider. "Trutch," wrote Macdonald, "was greatly disconcerted by the intimation from you that you had given up politics, and his feeling of dismay at your retirement has extended to my colleagues and myself. We hope that you will reconsider that determination."[1] But Helmcken was adamant, and in August in a letter that deserves quotation at some length he reviewed the reasons for the decision:

> I would do much for British Columbia; for twenty years I served her faithfully without receiving or desiring fee or reward, my position in the Hudson's Bay Co's service affording me an income sufficient to supply my few simple and inexpensive wants.—The future troubled me not. Had I devoted myself during that period to my profession and avoided politics I might easily have made and saved sufficient to enable me now to serve my country. I did not do so. Owing to radical changes in the Hudson's Bay Company my position in their service has been dispensed with. Deprived thus of my income, and my property not having increased in value, I am now compelled to seek a livelihood outside the service.
>
> I agree with you "that political life is not conducive either to domestic comfort or pecuniary gain, still some one must undertake the task and make the sacrifice."
>
> I have already made the sacrifice and, were I childless, would not hesitate to take the risk again under the present more lucrative regime, but not being so, I dare not run the risk of sacrificing my little ones. They must have their porridge. I must provide it. It becomes a question then whether I shall do so by following the medical or political profession:—there cannot be any combination of the two. The practice of medicine, which I like, will always afford me an income, there being always the unfortunate sick. Political practice on the other hand affords a very precarious income. Were I to give up my profession and become the adviser of the Governor and then find myself after a longer or shorter interval displaced, what means would I have for my support? None. My practice and office both gone.
>
> You must excuse me troubling you with domestic matters. You

---

[1]Macdonald to Helmcken, 17 July 1871, Macdonald Correspondence, Helmcken Collection, PABC.

will see they compel or at least induce me to follow a course not in accordance, I regret to say, with your wishes. Much as I would like to serve you and assist Governor Trutch in the way you mention, I dare not do so, and believe me, it causes me no inconsiderable pain to say this. The desire to quit political life, however, is not a sudden whim or caprice; my visit to Ottawa undertaken at the urgent request of many, assuredly not for selfish purposes, postponed putting into effect the determination made at least two years ago. The union of B.C. with Canada having been consummated and an entirely new political system having been introduced into the former—a system that I always opposed—the time seems most natural and opportune for my quitting the political change, independently of the other reasons.

In a later paragraph he displays both his modesty and his marked distaste for responsible government, which was being introduced in British Columbia as a result of the union with Canada. One suspects, indeed, that that distaste may well have been the determining factor in his decision to retire:

I have always been an overrated man. Of my ability and capacity to carry on the Government I entertain very grave doubts. Educated under a very different system to that now introduced, I feel that I cannot change to suit the alteration and indeed loathe the very idea of having to become obsequious, if nothing more degrading, to keep a number of supporters together. In my profession the patients are my slaves—in the political profession I would become the slave.[1]

Macdonald made one further attempt to enlist his services; in October, through Trutch, he offered Helmcken a senatorship, but this too was declined. Helmcken was to have only one other contact with politics. Trutch, who had been the most vigorous advocate of including a transcontinental railway in the terms of union, had a great desire to play a part in its construction through the mountains. Early in 1873, when work was

[1]Helmcken to Macdonald, 23 August 1871, Macdonald Papers, Public Archives of Canada.

scheduled to begin shortly, Trutch expected to be appointed to an engineering post and planned to resign as lieutenant-governor. Henry Nathan, Member of Parliament for Victoria, was aware of this and urged Helmcken to be his successor.[1] Whether or not he would have accepted we do not know, for the famous Pacific Scandal intervened, Macdonald was forced to resign, and the company that was to build the railway collapsed.

Helmcken scarcely mentions the post-Confederation years, which he devoted to his medical practice. In addition to the post of physician to the jail, he served for a time as coroner, and his appointment as surgeon for the Hudson's Bay Company continued until 1885. That year the British Columbia Medical Society was formed; Helmcken became its president, and his son, James Douglas Helmcken, who had recently completed his medical course and had returned to Victoria to practise, was its secretary. The society's chief aim was the setting of adequate standards, and its efforts resulted in the Medical Act of 1886. Under its authority the Medical Council of British Columbia came into existence, and, very appropriately, the first name entered upon the register it established was that of John Sebastian Helmcken.

Little recognition has been given to the considerable part Helmcken played in the provision of care for the sick in Victoria. The incident that led to the opening of the first hospital is well known: one morning in 1858 a sick man was abandoned on the doorstep of the Rev. Edward Cridge, the colonial chaplain. Cridge cared for him in his home, but by the end of November he and others, including Helmcken, had organized a hospital in a vacant cottage that had been made available for the purpose rent free. The next year the government erected a building on the Indian reserve and the Royal Hospital came into existence. A female ward was added in 1863, but the site on the reserve was not proving salubrious and a Female Infirmary was built on Pandora Street in 1864. Helmcken had been serving for some time as president of the board of directors of the Royal Hospital, and it became apparent to him that major benefits would result if the two institutions could be merged. This

[1] See John T. Saywell, "Sir Joseph Trutch," *BCHQ* 19 (1955) : 89.

was first considered seriously in 1869 and was carried into effect in 1872.[1] The same year, in keeping with his determination to concentrate on his medical practice, Helmcken insisted on resigning as board president; "his private affairs," he explained, "were of such a pressing nature that he could no longer discharge the arduous duties connected with the hospital."[2]

He had been active in the support of other hospitals as well. In 1860 the substantial French community in Victoria had founded La Société Française de Bienfaisance et Secours Mutuels (better known locally as the French Benevolent Society), which built its own hospital in 1865 and deserves to rank as a pioneer health insurance scheme. Helmcken seems not to have served as its physician in charge, but he evidently assisted it in other ways, for on New Year's Day 1876 the Society presented him with a silver goblet (now in Helmcken House) in acknowledgement of "gratuitous services" he had rendered for some time past. The society continued in existence until 1891, when it, too, merged with the Royal Hospital, which had been incorporated in 1890 under its present name of Royal Jubilee Hospital.[3]

In August 1875 Helmcken had laid the cornerstone of Victoria's third hospital, St. Joseph's (now Victoria General Hospital), founded by the Sisters of St. Ann. He had been friendly with the Sisters ever since their first appearance in Victoria in June 1858, and on their fiftieth anniversary, in 1908, he was asked to give the address at the opening of a new wing of St. Joseph's.

Helmcken made no more than a modest income from his practice, in great part because he was reluctant to collect from the poor and those who were better off did not always pay their bills. He remarks that when he was in the Assembly his constituents seemed to expect free service! His patients were devoted to him, amongst other reasons because he was always ready to respond to a call, no matter what the hour. "Many a night," his daughter stated, "I have seen him go off on foot in a storm, with his lantern, his gum boots, and greatcoat, to attend some poor ailing soul. . . . In later years came a horse and buggy. When

---

[1] See "The Journal of Arthur Thomas Bushby," ed. Dorothy Blakey Smith, *BCHQ* 21 (1957-58): 133n.
[2] Victoria *Colonist*, 27 March 1872.
[3] See Willard E. Ireland, "The French in British Columbia," *BCHQ* 13 (1949): 78-84.

people saw Julia with her feet in the ditch, cropping grass, they knew that 'the good doctor' as he was called, was nearby."[1]

Julia also figures in Emily Carr's description of Helmcken, perhaps the most interesting impression of the man that has come down to us. The time of which she writes would be the early 1880's.

When Victoria was young specialists had not been invented—the Family Doctor did you all over. You did not have a special doctor for each part. Dr. Helmcken attended to all our ailments— Father's gout, our stomach-aches; he even told us what to do once when the cat had fits. If he was wanted in a hurry he got there in no time and did not wait for you to become sicker so that he could make a bigger cure. You began to get better the moment you heard Dr. Helmcken coming up the stairs. He did have the most horrible medicines—castor oil, Gregory's powder, blue pills, black draughts, sulphur and treacle.

Jokey people called him Dr. Heal-my-skin. He had been Doctor in the old Fort and knew everybody in Victoria. He was very thin, very active, very cheery. He had an old brown mare called Julia. When the Doctor came to see Mother we fed Julia at the gate with clover. The Doctor loved old Julia. One stormy night he was sent for because Mother was very ill. He came very quickly and Mother said, "I am sorry to bring you and Julia out on such a night, Doctor." "Julia is in her stable. What was the good of two of us getting wet?" he replied.

My little brother fell across a picket fence once and tore his leg. The doctor put him on our dining-room sofa and sewed it up. The Chinaboy came rushing in to say, "House all burn up!" Dr. Helmcken put in the last stitch, wiped his needle on his coat sleeve and put it into his case, then stripping off his coat, rushed to the kitchen pump and pumped till the fire was put out.

Once I knelt on a needle which broke into my knee. While I was telling Mother about it who should come up the steps but the Doctor! He had just looked in to see the baby who had not been very well. They put me on the kitchen table. The Doctor cut slits in my knee and wiggled his fingers round inside it for three hours hunting

---

[1]Quoted in J. H. MacDermot, "J. S. Helmcken," *Canadian Medical Association Journal* 55 (1946) : 9. The daughter is not identified.

for the pieces of needle. They did not know the way of drawing bits out with a magnet then, nor did they give chloroform for little things like that.

The Doctor said, "Yell, lassie, yell! It will let the pain out." I did yell, but the pain stayed in.

I remember the Doctor's glad voice as he said, "Thank God, I have got all of it now, or the lassie would have been lame for life with that under her knee cap!" Then he washed his hands under the kitchen tap and gave me a peppermint.[1]

Dr. Honor Kidd has examined Helmcken's case books for this period. They prompted this comment: "As for the type of medicine he practised—it appears the doctor had come a long way from the pains-taking and careful investigations of his patients that he carried out at Guy's Hospital in his student days." Citing one entry she adds: "The casual diagnosis and the therapy both seem a little fearsome to-day." But his patients remained faithful to him. "Perhaps," Dr. Kidd writes, "John Sebastian Helmcken was not a good doctor, even by the standards of the times; his methods were rough and ready, and his diagnosis often arrived at by trial and error; but if medical success be judged by the esteem, confidence and love of patients, then Dr. Helmcken was out-standing in his profession."[2]

In the winter of 1884-85 he suffered a severe attack of typhoid fever, and he seems to have been less active thereafter. By 1890 the main burden of the Helmcken practice had been assumed by his son. His visits to the jail were the last of his medical activities, and they continued until 1910, when he was eighty-six years old. For another ten years he lived on quietly in the house he had built in 1852 and had occupied for sixty-eight years, and there he died on 1 September 1920, having seen an incredible transformation not only in British Columbia but in his own profession. In his youth he had dealt with the sick and the dead under conditions of hygiene that make it difficult to understand how anyone could have survived; he experienced the introduction of anaesthetics and antiseptics and lived to see the X-ray a standard item of equipment in any hospital worthy of the name.

[1] Emily Carr, *The Book of Small* (Toronto: Oxford University Press, 1942), pp. 199-200.
[2] Honor M. Kidd, "Pioneer Doctor John Sebastian Helmcken," *Bulletin of the History of Medicine* 21 (1947): pp. 454, 457.

Helmcken deprecated any suggestion that he was writing history; he insisted that he was offering no more than "personal recollections" of people and events of an earlier day. The value of his narrative is obvious, but its preservation and publication were never a foregone conclusion. It is in this connection that I have been asked to end this introduction with a personal recollection of my own.

Helmcken's youngest daughter, Edith Louisa (Dolly), was born in 1862 and was not yet three years old when her mother died. She lived with her father until her marriage to William Ralph Higgins in 1889, and after her husband's death in 1896 she returned to her father's home. When he died in 1920 she had spent fifty-two of her fifty-eight years in his company. She was completely devoted to him and, after his death, to his memory.

I met her first in 1934, shortly after I was appointed Provincial Librarian and Archivist. I had already heard about the reminiscences, and a member of the family warned me that Mrs. Higgins intended to leave instructions in her will that her father's house should be torn down and his manuscripts destroyed. She could not bear the thought that the house might be allowed to deteriorate into a slum and that the reminiscences might fall into unsympathetic hands.

After our first meeting I saw her fairly frequently, and we became friends. On my walk to the office I passed the house, which is almost in the shadow of the Parliament Buildings, and from time to time she invited me to lunch. I usually arrived armed with a question that could probably be answered by consulting the reminiscences. She would bring out the five volumes, hunt for the relevant passage, and read it to me. Then, one memorable day, she handed me a volume and suggested that I should read it myself. Even a brief glance was sufficient to show that the reminiscences comprised an historical narrative of quite exceptional interest; the problem I faced was how to ensure that Mrs. Higgins did not carry out her expressed intention of leaving directions that they should be destroyed.

At last I determined to pay her a special visit. I told her that I wished to talk about the preservation of the reminiscences, that I would expect no comment from her; I should simply state my case and leave. This I did. I pointed out that by and large the people who were remembered, or whose contribution to the development of the country was known and properly appreciated, were those about whom adequate documentation was available. Thus she held in her hands much of what the future could know about her father; to destroy the reminiscences would be in a considerable measure to destroy his memory. Having said my say I went away, leaving her sitting quietly, looking out the window, her hand in her lap, resting on one of the five manuscript volumes.

To the best of my knowledge the idea of destroying the volumes was never raised thereafter, and Mrs. Higgins's will gave no instructions about the reminiscences. Neither did it make any reference to the house, which I had mentioned to her on various occasions. I had told her that I considered it unthinkable that a building of such historic interest—the oldest structure in British Columbia now existing in substantially its original state—would be allowed to go to rack and ruin. After her death in 1939, at the age of seventy-seven, I asked the Hon. John Hart, minister of finance, to visit the house with me. Though additions had been made to it on two occasions, the house as first built in 1852 had not been disturbed. This was the first time I had seen Dr. Helmcken's bedroom, which we found exactly as he had left it nearly twenty years before; his clothes were hanging neatly in the cupboard; the shirt he would have put on the next morning was ready to hand. Mr. Hart was charmed and impressed and negotiations soon began between the government and the estate that resulted in the acquisition of the house in July. The outbreak of war in September delayed plans for a time, but Helmcken House opened to the public as an historical museum in August 1941.

The house and its contents have been preserved, as far as possible, as they were in Helmcken's day. Together with the reminiscences, the correspondence, and other papers now in the Helmcken Collection in the Provincial Archives, Helmcken House will long call to mind the private life and public services of one of the most interesting personalities who played an important part in the life of British Columbia in early days.

W. Kaye Lamb

A NOTE ON THE TEXT

The Helmcken Collection in the Provincial Archives of British Columbia contains a number of items catalogued as the "Reminiscences" of John Sebastian Helmcken. The present publication confines itself to a holograph begun on 27 May 1892 with the words "Well here goes.—" The manuscript is contained in five notebooks of uniform size (approximately 22½ by 17½ cm.), the first bound in black American cloth, the others with marbled covers. The paper is lined, and except in one instance (vol. V, pp. 111-12) Helmcken has written only on the recto of the leaf. He has left blank several leaves at the beginning of each volume, as well as other leaves at various stages of the narrative, apparently where he felt that a particular topic required further development. The actual manuscript runs to 609 pages, which Helmcken himself has numbered by volume, although the narrative is continuous and there are no title-pages either for the individual volumes or for the manuscript as a whole. The handwriting is not always easy to decipher: though Helmcken wrote in ink, he used a rather coarse pen-nib, and, in addition, the manuscript is obviously a first draft which he wrote at some speed and made no attempt to revise. Again, at several points during his narrative he is at pains to emphasize that many of his memories are purely personal and domestic and that he is not writing history as such, but merely setting down his own recollections of the historical events in which he happened to be involved.

It appeared therefore that the manuscript itself hardly demanded an inexorable fidelity to the author's text. On the other hand, to have brought Helmcken's spelling, punctuation, grammar, idiom, and sentence structure into strict conformity with modern usage would have required a good deal of editorial emendation, even re-writing. Such interference with the manuscript would inevitably have infuriated the scholar, checked the spontaneous flow of the old Doctor's memories, and dissipated for scholar and general reader alike the charm of what is essentially a period piece — a personal memoir which at the same time illuminates a number of facets of the social and political life of England, Vancouver Island, and British Columbia more than a century ago. The present text is accordingly a compromise, designed to preserve the individual quality of the manuscript without putting too many obstacles in the way of a modern literate reader. It tries to reproduce exactly what Helmcken wrote, provided that the sense is clear and that the stylistic details do not make for unduly difficult reading.

Wherever Helmcken has left a blank in his manuscript, presumably because a name or a date had slipped his memory, the fact has been noted and a conjecture added if possible. Where he has left out a word (an omission which occurs most frequently as a leaf is turned), a conjecture has been added in square brackets.

In the matter of spelling, obvious slips of a hasty pen, such as *hobbeled* or *orgain*, have been silently corrected; but spellings which were in good nineteenth-century use, such as *controul* or *musquito*, have been retained. Helmcken's spelling of personal names is often phonetic. At the first instance of an incorrect spelling the correct form has been added in square brackets; thereafter it appears without comment. A similar practice has been followed for place names, except that spellings standard in Helmcken's day, such as *Esquimault* or *Hudson's Bay* (for the body of water) have been retained. Indian names present a special problem. Since "strictly speaking, there is no one 'correct' English spelling of an Indian name,"[1] Helmcken's own spelling has been retained, followed in square brackets by a form which appears to have the sanction of anthropologists today. The capitalization of the manuscript is extremely erratic and, in accordance with Victorian style, far more extensive than is acceptable today. Capitals for proper nouns and adjectives have been regularized, and the Victorian practice of capitalizing particular institutions or offices, as in *the Senior Surgeon of the Hospital* or *the Master of the School*, has been retained. Apostrophes to indicate the possessive case have been supplied. Helmcken's use of abbreviations and contractions is not consistent, and forms such as *St*, *Co*, and *Govt* have therefore been regularized as *Street*, *Company*, and *Government* except in such frequently used combinations as *HBCo* or *HMGovt*. Helmcken indicates

---

[1]Wilson Duff, "The Indians of British Columbia," *The Indian History of British Columbia: Volume I. The Impact of the White Man*, Anthropology in British Columbia, Memoir no. 5 (Victoria: Queen's Printer, 1964), p. 10.

the names of ships and the titles of books only by a sporadic use of quotation marks. For the convenience of the reader ship's names and book titles have been italicized throughout.

The punctuation of the manuscript is highly inconsistent, often lacking altogether, and dependent on the dash to an extent far greater than modern usage allows. Nevertheless, in order to maintain the informal flow of the narrative, it has been retained as far as possible. Quotation marks have been added to indicate direct speech and removed where they appeared superfluous. Otherwise, Helmcken's punctuation has been emended only where the meaning is not clear or where a too steady succession of dashes might have rendered the reader breathless and annoyed. Helmcken was born in London in 1824 and hence was educated in the period when English puncutation was still wavering between two theories of pointing: the elocutionary or breath-pause theory and the syntactical theory by which after 1850 or so it was largely replaced.[1] His manuscript gives the effect of the speaking voice, and affords but little illustration of punctuation designed after the modern manner to bring out the logical structure of a sentence. Then too, Helmcken's parents and grandparents were German; in his early social and religious life he was bilingual; and he was educated at a school where he was "drilled" in both German and English. It is hardly surprising therefore that writing in his old age (he was nearly sixty-eight when he began these reminiscences) he still retains some details of punctuation, such as the comma between two sentences or with a restrictive clause, that are Germanic rather than English.[2]

As far as it was possible to determine the author's intention, the paragraphing of the manuscript has been retained. In the body of the page the paragraphs are clearly indicated, but when Helmcken turns over a leaf he sometimes leaves blank a line or part of a line, yet commences a new page without indentation. In these cases it has been assumed that a paragraph was intended, unless the sense of the passage clearly demands no break. An occasional lengthy passage in which there is no break in the handwriting, though there is in the sense, has been divided into paragraphs for ease in reading.

The manuscript makes frequent reference, usually by surname only, to numerous members of the wide circle of Helmcken's friends and

[1]See Park Honan, "Eighteenth and Nineteenth Century English Punctuation Theory," *English Studies* 4 (1960) : 92-102.
[2]See Ann Eljenholm Nichols, "Punctuation Problems for Speakers of Germanic Languages," *Language Learning* 12 (1962) : 195-204.

acquaintances, many of whom are of interest in the history of British Columbia. Biographical footnotes have therefore been added to the text. They are intended to provide a brief identification, in context, of the person named and to direct the reader if possible to a source of further information. Despite Helmcken's protests that it was "not [his] intention to write history" and that these are "only personal recollections," his manuscript has already been widely used as a primary source by historians of the period and it will no doubt continue to serve the same purpose. Certain bibliographical footnotes have accordingly been added in an attempt to set the historical record straight, especially where Helmcken's memory would appear to have failed him. The remaining footnotes are designed to clarify the text for the general reader, to whom this manuscript of 1892 is now presented in its entirety for the first time.

CHRONOLOGY

1817	17 September	Claus Helmcken marries Catherine Mittler in Christ Church, Spitalfields, London
1824	5 June	John Sebastian Helmcken born in Brick Lane, Whitechapel, London, their fourth child and eldest son
c.1825		Claus Helmcken becomes the licensee of the White Swan public house at No. 36, Great Alie Street, Whitechapel
1825	13 February	JSH is baptized in Christ Church, Spitalfields
1828	midsummer term	JSH is enrolled at St. George's German and English School in Little Alie Street
c.1831		The family moves to No. 36, Great Alie Street
1837 or 1838	spring or summer?	JSH becomes an errand boy for William Henry Graves, M.R.C.S., of No. 4, Alie Place
1839	25 March	JSH leaves St. George's School
	summer?	JSH is apprenticed to Dr. Graves as a chemist and druggist
	7 September	JSH's father Claus dies
1841		The apprenticeship is cancelled and JSH is articled to Dr. Graves as a medical pupil
1844	2 October	JSH registers at Guy's Hospital for the winter session of 1844-45
1845	April	Wins first prize for Practical Chemistry and second prize for Materia Medica
	13 May	Registers for the summer session of 1845
	25 August	Registers for the winter session of 1845-46

1846	April	Wins "Dr. Barlow's Testimonial," awarded by the Clinical Society, and an "Honorary Medical Certificate" for the winter session of 1845-46
	Summer	Works in Dr. Golding Bird's "children's wards"
1846	Autumn	Goes on a walking tour to the Isle of Wight and Southampton
	October	Registers for the winter session of 1846-47
1847	January	Awarded dressership in surgery for three months
	April	Admitted as Licentiate of the Apothecaries' Company and wins one of the two "Pupils' Physical Prizes" awarded
	7 June	Sails from Gravesend for York Factory as surgeon in the HBC ship *Prince Rupert*
	29 October	*The Prince Rupert* returns to Gravesend
	4 November	JSH registers for the winter session of 1847-48
1848	January	Awarded dressership in surgery under Mr. Bransby Cooper for three months
	March	Admitted as a Member of the Royal College of Surgeons
	26 May	Sails from Gravesend for Bombay and Canton as surgeon in the *Malacca*
1849	5 January	JSH's grandfather Sebastian Mittler dies
1849	15 September	Arrival of the *Malacca* at the East Indian Docks is reported
	12 October	JSH receives HBC appointment as surgeon and clerk for a term of five years
	18 October	Sails from Gravesend for Vancouver Island in the *Norman Morison*
1850	24 March	The *Norman Morison* arrives at Esquimalt
	May	JSH arrives at Fort Rupert as HBC surgeon
	22 June	Governor Richard Blanshard issues JSH a commission as magistrate at Fort Rupert
	22 July	Chief Factor James Douglas refuses to accept JSH's resignation from the HBC
	December	JSH is called back to Fort Victoria to attend Governor Blanshard and remains as surgeon there

1851		Douglas replaces Blanshard as Governor of Vancouver Island but retains his post as chief factor with the HBC
		JSH is made surgeon to the jail in the bastion of the Fort
1852	27 December	Marries Cecilia, eldest daughter of James Douglas
1853	29 October	Claude Douglas [or Douglas Claude] Helmcken is born (baptized 11 December)
1854	17 January	Claude Douglas dies
1855	19 March	Catherine Amelia [Amy] Helmcken is born
1856	2 July	JSH is elected as member of the Legislative Assembly of Vancouver Island for Esquimalt and Victoria District
	12 August	The first Legislative Assembly of Vancouver Island is convened, and JSH is elected Speaker, a post which he holds until the union of the colonies of Vancouver Island and British Columbia in 1866
	September	Margaret Jane [Daisy] Helmcken is born (baptized 9 March 1858)
1857	17 February	JSH is presented with a silver tea service by the grateful colonists of Vancouver Island
1858	2 February	James Douglas Helmcken is born
	11 March	Margaret Jane dies
	2 August	The mainland colony of British Columbia is created
	September	James Douglas is appointed governor of British Columbia on condition that he sever his connection with the HBC
1859	23 December	Henry [Harry] Dallas Helmcken is born
1860	11 January	JSH is elected as member for Esquimalt and Metchosin District
1862	7 February	Elected president of the Royal Hospital
	24 June	Edith Louisa [Dolly] Helmcken is born
1863	13 April	JSH is appointed chief trader HBC
	22 July	Re-elected as member for Esquimalt and Metchosin District
1865	January or February?	Cecil Roderick Helmcken born

	4 February	Cecilia (Douglas) Helmcken dies
	27 February	Cecil Roderick Helmcken buried
1866	19 November	The Act for the Union of Vancouver Island and British Columbia is proclaimed
	13 December	JSH is elected to the Legislative Council of British Columbia for District No. 1 (the City of Victoria and the Town of Esquimalt)
1868	3 November	Re-elected to the Legislative Council on an anti-Confederation platform
1869	3 or 5 February	JSH's mother Catherine (Mittler) Helmcken dies
	31 December	JSH is appointed to the Executive Council of British Columbia
1870	8 April?	Appointed surgeon to the HBC establishment in Victoria and his chief tradership is terminated
	21 April	Accepts appointment as one of the three Confederation delegates to Ottawa
	14 May	Leaves Victoria for Ottawa
	3 June	Arrives in Ottawa
	18 July	Arrives back in Victoria
	August or September?	Sends James Douglas Helmcken to school in Jedburgh, Scotland
	14 November	JSH is re-elected to the Legislative Council on a pro-Confederation platform
1871	20 July	British Columbia enters Confederation, and JSH retires from active politics
	August or September?	Sends Harry Dallas Helmcken to school in Jedburgh, Scotland
1872	26 March	Resigns as president of the Board of Directors of the Royal Hospital
1875	21 August	Lays cornerstone of St. Joseph's Hospital
1876	1 January	Presented with an engraved silver cup by the grateful members of the French Benevolent Society
1877	4 December	Catherine Amelia Helmcken marries George Archibald McTavish
1884-85	winter	JSH has a severe attack of typhoid fever
1885	14 January	The British Columbia Medical Society is formed and JSH is elected president

	6 October	JSH's appointment as surgeon to the HBC in Victoria is terminated
1886	6 April	The Act respecting the profession of Medicine and Surgery incorporates the Medical Council of British Columbia
	1 June	JSH is licensed to practise by the British Columbia Medical Council
	September - October	Writes letters to the newspaper concerning a railway to the northern part of Vancouver Island
1887-1891		Writes articles in the Victoria *Colonist* concerning his early experiences in Vancouver Island
1889	24 April	Edith Louisa Helmcken marries William Ralph Higgins
1891	16 December	JSH gives the address at the official opening of the Training School for Nurses at the Royal Jubilee Hospital
1892	27 May	Begins to write the present "Reminiscences"
1896?		The office on Fort Street that JSH has occupied since c. 1858 is replaced by a livery stable
1896		Resigns from the consulting staff of the Royal Jubilee Hospital in protest against the use of the Pemberton bequest for an operating room instead of the maternity ward he had advocated for years
	31 October	W. R. Higgins dies, and his widow goes to live with her father JSH
1903	18 October - 13 December	JSH writes a series of articles in the *Colonist*, most of them entitled "Historical Reminiscences," based on the autobiography of Roderick Finlayson
1908	3 October	Delivers an address at the ceremony marking the opening of the new wing of St. Joseph's Hospital by Premier Richard McBride
1910	31 December	Retires as physician to the jail, with a pension from the provincial government
1920	1 September	JSH dies and his body is cremated in Vancouver

	18 September	His ashes are placed in his wife Cecilia's tomb in Pioneer Square
1938		The British Columbia Historical Association places a memorial tablet at the foot of the family tomb
1939	13 April	Mrs. Higgins dies
	July	The government of British Columbia purchases the Helmcken house and the Helmcken Papers are placed in the Provincial Archives
1941	26 August	Helmcken House is opened as an historical museum
1943	14 March	A plaque to the left of the doorway is unveiled: "Helmcken House built 1852 by Dr. J. S. Helmcken, Pioneer Surgeon and Legislator. Arrived Victoria, 1850. Aided in negotiating Union of British Columbia with Canada, 1870."

"When beginning to write, I had no intention of writing history and indeed do not pretend to do so now, but only personal recollections—so dates may be a little confused occasionally."

John Sebastian Helmcken, 1892

Well here goes. —

May 27th / 1892.

My grandfather of whom I have some recollections came from Mis-
kirch.[1] His father, he said, kept the keys of the city and locked the
gate every night and presumably opened it or them in the morning.
This is all I know about him—whether great or small is unknown.

My grandfather was a handsome man, six feet in height and entered
the French army, but whether from choice or necessity is unknown:
at all events I always supposed for some reason or other, that he ran
away from home, but there is no evidence that he ever distinguished
or extinguished himself there or elsewhere, altho he used to talk about
the King and Queen of France and the Swiss guard to which he may
have belonged, but be this as it may he was an enthusiastic admirer of
Napoleon the First, and when speaking of him would become enthusiastic, draw himself straight in military fashion and looked quite young
again. Attempting to speak French, he made a mess of it for no one
could understand *his* French. This enthusiasm for Napoleon amused
me, then a very little fellow, because it led to fierce disputes between
him and my father, who was a Low German and had fled his country
on account of Napoleon, the conscription and what not—anyhow
his family had been ruined. My grandfather's name was Sebastian
Mittler; a Roman Catholic, and I think received the name of Sebastian,
because he was born or baptized on St. Sebastian's Day, the custom

[1]Presumably the modern Messkirch (on earlier maps spelled Mösskirch), a medieval
town with a seventeenth-century castle, in South Baden some twenty-five miles
from the Swiss border.

of the country, but there is no certainty about this. My earliest recollection is that he lived in Spitalfields, had a tolerably [large?] house and garden, where I once or twice at all events played, for I remember that a large bush of fennel grew there, upon which subsisted numerous large snails with handsome shells, and a plum tree, which never bore fruit, notwithstanding the efforts of gardeners to make it do so, and therefore probably was the more valued, as the sickly generally are: on another occasion I fell down and made a gash in my head, and great was the consternation. Curiously enough I have no recollection of having seen any of their children there, altho there were three daughters, besides my mother—they may have been married. A son did not exist. Of my grandmother, who was also German, I have but a faint recollection, and this only in connection with my cut head— she gave me buttons to play with and candy to eat, and so made me leave off crying. She must have died soon after this. Perhaps for this reason it happened later on, that my grandfather came to live with my parents later on in Ayliff Street.[1] At all events I was a little boy and slept in his room, but not in his bed, for if I had, it was believed he would have lived on my strength; a sort of vampire. He liked his glass of grog at night, and so occasionally took a little too much, and was difficult to get upstairs. On telling him in the morning, he would say, "Me drunk! Mein Gott no: too much lemon in de grog upset my stomach and so mein head! Made me sick and mein head swimmen." Snuff he took by wholesale night and day. He slept quietly, I snored, so he used to awaken me by speech or anything thrown at me, and tell me to shut my mouth. In return for this, I would occasionally steal his snuff box from under his pillow, go back to bed and of course be fast asleep. Not long—and there would be a fumbling and then— "Dat boy again! Jack, where is my snuff box!" but Jack did not hear— his face being under the blankets, and of course snoring. "Jack—mein Gott I'm starving: mein lieber boy, do give me mein box!" Well I would awaken or pretend to and go to his bed, with an innocent question. "Grandpa, what do you want? Oh—that snuff box again. Why here it is; slipped from under your pillow into the bed!" Then he would take a big pinch, and I go back to bed sniggering in the dark. He was a Roman Catholic—a strict one about once a month, and for the

---

[1]In Whitechapel, a district in East London adjacent to Spitalfields. Ayliff is an alternative form of Alie (see below, p. 11). In 1906 Great and Little Alie Streets became simply Alie Street, and they survive under that name today.

intermediate time rather forgetful. However as he was poor this did not matter much to the church and perhaps not much to him either. He had good health but also a wound from an old fractured leg, which bothered him a good deal. In due course he died an old man,[1] but I do not for some reason or other remember this or the time. Of my grandmother I know nothing. She was German I believe, and a Protestant, so as all her children were girls, they were educated as Protestant, had they been boys, the religion of their father would have fallen to their lot.

It often happened that there were fierce disputes between my parents and my grandfather on this score, for the former were almost ultra-Protestants and Lutherans at this. Such disputes usually occurred about once a month, as before said, when my grandfather went to the church at Moorfields[2] for some purpose or other. Of course I heard several of these disputes.

One of his daughters married a worthless fellow called Nixon: they both died leaving a daughter, cared for by Caroline who never married.[3] Another one married—but what her changed name was I do not remember,[4] but they had a daughter named Regina and a monkey, who once stole my apple from my hands and bolted with it into the trees growing I think in the churchyard of St. George's church Ratcliff Highway near which this Aunt and Uncle lived.[5] These Aunts and Uncles are all dead. Of Regina I know positively nothing, but of Miss Nixon I heard and received a letter from some years ago, but where she may be now is altogether unknown.[6]

---

[1]According to his death certificate (General Register Office, London), Sebastian Mittler died on 5 January 1849, aged eighty.

[2]By the beginning of the nineteenth century the great marsh lying to the north of the medieval city had been drained and built upon. Finsbury Circus and Finsbury Square eventually occupied the site of Moorfields.

[3]See below, p. 50n4.

[4]Mary Regina Mittler married Diederich Lankenau on 20 October 1817 (Christ Church, Spitalfields, marriage register).

[5]Ratcliff Highway was a busy thoroughfare running behind London Dock. It achieved an unwelcome notoriety in 1811 through the series of murders which inspired Thomas De Quincey's essay on "Murder Considered as One of the Fine Arts" (1827) and was re-christened St. George Street. On modern maps it appears as The Highway. The church, the Anglican foundation of St. George-in-the-East, was burned out in the 1941 blitz; the churchyard had previously (1886) been converted into a public garden.

[6]Elizabeth Nixon went into domestic service. On 23 November 1866 JSH's mother wrote: "Your cousin Elizabeth as got a situation at Clapham Common as housemaid in a gentleman's family" (Helmcken Collection, Provincial Archives of British Columbia [hereafter cited as HC and as PABC].

Of my father's father and mother and their relatives, I know positively nothing, save probably that they lived in Bremerlee [Bremerlehe] Hanover, whence my father said he came from.[1] My brother Henry, in his wanderjahr, went with a companion to Bremerlehe out of curiosity to find out his relatives there, but no one would take any notice of him, if indeed he ever found any real or supposed relatives at all. My father undoubtedly possessed lands there, but we generally believed that he had given them or his share to a sister, named Ann I believe. Possibly in Germany, property is or was divided among descendants at the death and so my father gave or could not claim his share, he being in England and a British subject. He never once returned to Germany.

When I was a boy, Germans used to become naturalized in batches —it saved expense. In relation to this subject it may be observed, that some of the family are said to spell the name Helmiken and indeed my schoolmaster and the religious teacher said I ought to spell my name in the same manner. They said, the only difference is, that in German writing the c and the i are both the same, save that when it means i it has a dot over it, thus Helmcken or Helmiken. Probably some did not dot their i's or cross their t's—anyhow education may not have been so general as now. Anyhow Helm-i-ken seems more natural and significant than Helm-c-ken—why c and k should be connected in a word is to me a puzzle, still this may have been common under ancient phonography and may have some significance for all I know to the contrary. The i makes Scotch of the name as well as German, for in both Ken means to know, and Helm means a helmet: I always thought a rudder. It matters but little which.

I had three brothers and four sisters.[2] Katherine [Catharine] married and died of renal disease soon after. Mary married a Mr. Fink or Finken, manager of a large sugar refinery at Goodman's Style [Stile]. They had several children. Mrs. Finken died of cancer of the brain, subsequently the family lived at [blank in MS] but I do not know whether Mr. Finken is living or not. Ann married a Mr. Kane and the pair went to Australia, and there [were?] lost sight of altogether. Kane was the sister

---

[1]A town at the mouth of the Weser River in Hanover, marked on an 1835 Arrowsmith map. Later called Lehe, it became part of Wesermunde and is now incorporated with Bremerhaven.

[2]Claus Helmcken and Catharine (later spelled Catherine) Mittler were married on 17 December 1817 (Christ Church, Spitalfields, marriage register), and their eight children were all entered in the register of baptisms of the same church. For further details, see Appendix 1, "A Note on the Helmcken Family."

[*sic*] of Mrs. Kusel whose husband became librarian of London Hospital. Elizabeth married a builder, who had a large lumber yard, but whether she be still living I know not, neither do I know whether she had any children.

My brother Frederick was a builder and lived in Leman Street. Whether he is still living or has any children, I know not. William died a few years ago. Henry I have lost the run of, but he was living in the Mile End Road. I have never seen any of the children of any of these. I think they are all poor, at all events not rich, labouring people, but this is more a matter of surmise than positive knowledge. I suppose my friend Fotherby[1] knows more about them than I do.

Of my father, I recollect but little, save that he was a broken-down man and drank more than was good for him, so he had bad attacks of gout—in fact was always ailing. He left Bremerlehe when a lad, probably on account of military [service?] and the Continental troubles. At all events, he like many other Germans found employment at Messrs. Bowman's the great sugar refiners in Ayliff Street where he rose to some height. Subsequently he was made victualler and kept the White Swan in Ayliff Street very close to the refinery.[2] At this time sugar refining was a very profitable business—the factories immense. The Bowmans had a couple of hundred employees at least, kept an analytical chemist and goodness knows what others besides. The men [who] boarded and lodged in the establishment had beer and spirits served out, at all events on Sundays, when no work was done. They were very orderly and respectable, mostly Lutherans and went to church well dressed on Sundays, mostly to St. George's Church.[3] I was quite a lad when the Free Trade crusade commenced, but the result of this crusade and Free Trade was, the Bowmans like most other sugar refiners were positively ruined, the establishment closed and of course my father went down with them as he had no longer any men to supply.[4] Thus then my father and mother had to work to support eight children, the oldest not being

[1]Dr. Henry I. Fotherby. See below, p. 34.
[2]The sugar refinery of Messrs. Charles and John Frederick Bowman (see Plate 4) was at No. 27, Great Alie Street; the White Swan public house was at No. 36, both premises being on the north side of the street.
[3]i.e., St. George's German Lutheran Church in Little Alie Street. See below, p. 13.
[4]JSH appears to be confused here. The directories show that the Bowmans maintained their factory at No. 27, Great Alie Street until 1852, when they moved to No. 78, Leman Street; and the business was listed in the 1867 directory, nearly thirty years after JSH's father died. Because of the proximity to the docks, sugar refineries flourished in London's East End in the eighteenth and early nineteenth centuries, but after 1819 the selling price of sugar fell steadily, the situation being

more than fourteen years old or so, and a precious hard time they had, altho they never appeared to have, for my mother used to say to be poor and to look poor is to lose all respect from others and themselves. My father had not much energy—he had been powerful and active, but hard work in the hot refinery and other causes combined with the failing refinery business broke him down entirely. The whole responsibility of providing for the family fell on my mother even before my [father] died, which he did when he was 54 years of age, of I believe hepatic dropsy, and was buried in the ground of St. George's Church.[1] He was a good kind upright man, but as I knew him, always ailing, too broken to be active. He never whipped any of us, but occasionally took us to see various places; at length however, the gout prevented him doing even this much, he hobbled about or stuck to his chair. However he used to have hot disputes with my grandfather, for my father hated Napoleon and the French and further was almost as inimical to Roman Catholics, but they usually avoided these subjects and so got on very well together. He generally wound up by saying that a man who spoke French must be a rascal, which did not insult grandfather as the French he spoke no one understood.

My mother,[2] God bless her, was everything and everybody, at least to me and the rest of the family; a stout strong robust determined energetic woman, nice looking, with a florid complexion, blue eyes and always wore a cap with a "front" of ringlets: always at work from morn till night: when sitting she would mend various articles and had my sisters alongside repairing or making also. She took no pleasure in anything but family

---

complicated by the abolition of slavery and the steady growth of a free trade philosophy which culminated in the repeal of the Corn Laws in 1846. According to the bicentenary account of St. George's German Lutheran Church (J. Rieger, "Aus der Geschichte der Deutscher Lutherischer St. Georg-Kirche [1762-1962]," *Der Londoner Bote*, September 1962), by the 1880's only three of the more than thirty sugar refineries which had once employed hundreds of German immigrants were still in operation.

[1]According to his death certificate, Claus Helmcken was fifty-eight, not fifty-four, years of age when he died of dropsy on 7 September 1839 at No. 36, Great Alie Street (i.e., the White Swan). The records of St. George's Church also give his age as fifty-eight at the time of his burial in the churchyard on 15 September 1839.

[2]Catherine (Mittler) Helmcken was born in London c. 1795. After her husband's death she appears to have remained as licensee of the White Swan until c. 1865. She then became part of the household of her son-in-law, Ludwig Fincken (later spelled Finken) at No. 48, Lambeth Street, Goodman's Stile, where she died on 5 February 1869 at the age of seventy-four. JSH preserved her memorial card and the lock of hair she sent to her daughter-in-law Cecilia (Douglas) Helmcken on 12 April 1853 (HC).

affairs and remained in the house for weeks together, having some old friends dropping in occasionally, but never had any set teas or dinners or the like; the pots and pans looked like polished silver, and she looked after them herself: everything had to be, and kept, clean and in order. A pocket, of shepherds-purse shape and extraordinary capacity, hung on her right side, under the dress, and contained an innumerable number of articles; but those that I remember best were a hussiff (housewife), thimbles, sealing wax, a piece of Turkey rhubarb—and the most interesting, a leathern strap, about a foot long, an inch broad, pliable and when applied very tingling: a nice flexible cane hung in a convenient situation and when used whisked like a musquito. These were occasionally used, but when used, there was no mistake about it—they were not playthings. Altho complaining that my father never kept the boys in order, still when he boxed our ears and so forth she resented it, telling him that striking our head and ears would do harm and explaining he should always punish us on those parts posterior where there were no bones! She was most assuredly not severe, but there being four boys, it required perseverance to keep us in order when indoors. In housekeeping most economical: being poor and having to work for money, there were no luxuries, excepting on Sundays—hashes, stews and so forth common—bread and butter for breakfast, with perhaps a little cold meat—we had to eat to live not live to eat, but always had plenty. If we complained, the answer came, it is harder when there is none, and were compelled to eat the fare before leaving table—we all knew this and so said little. Of course we had several German dishes, sauerkraut among the number, and my mother took it into her head to make some, but this turned out a complete failure at which we silently and inwardly rejoiced. I know now that it took no small means to keep eight children in food, clothing &c., but she managed to do it and do it well on very small means—waste there was none—waste not want not the motto—and the frequent, "I hope you may never want for that which you now turn up your nose at." There was only one servant, an Englishwoman, to do the rough and tumble work. Mother would not under any circumstances have an Irishwoman in the house —she considered them deceitful—fair to face and foul behind her back, besides they were usually Roman Catholics, and so capable she said of getting absolution, even if they murdered anyone—in fact with her no Irish need apply. We all had to work as soon as able. Mother had a system—whatever work we had to do, and it certainly was not much, had to be done regularly and at a stated time—if not—well perhaps the strap or other punishment—no play for instance. The girls, who bye the bye never had a taste of the strap or cane, because perhaps they never needed it (!?) had to keep their rooms in order—make their beds—keep their "drawers" and clothes in proper order—but the boys had to blacken their shoes and this was considered a great hardship occasionally, but then the girls were good to us and their thin shoes of little trouble. In these days the people used to wear "pattens," a wooden foot piece with straps across the instep and an iron ring at the bottom keeping the foot piece a couple of inches or so from the pavement—these were used in the wash house and in damp places or rainy weather—sabots never came into use. Mother used to examine all the rooms and drawers to see that everything was in good and proper order. Here let me remark, that Mother did more work than all the girls put together and in this respect resembled the modern mater who scrubs the floor whilst the daughter plays the piano and receives company! The time for bed was ten o'clock at night—the little ones earlier—all up in the morning between six and seven o'clock and sometimes earlier—before breakfast the most of the rough work had been got through with—everything made tidy as Mother used to say. My share at one time was to clean the knives and forks early in the morning—next I was promoted to cleaning boots—then to chopping kindling wood—and so on with little things—but we all received a few pence every week, if we did our work properly. I hated work at home, and thought it very hard, so sometimes I would give my pence to my brother to do the work for me; and yet anywhere else, in the carpenter's or blacksmith's I would work like a trojan! Anyhow the work had to be done, and on one Saturday night, when we all had to be scrubbed with soap and water in a washing tub, the servant told Mother, "Master John has not chopped his wood." "Well," says Mother, "Mary, you know what to do." So Mary took me, gave me a couple of inches of a lighted candle, sent me to the cellar, locking the door behind me. Now I did not like the cellar, there were there black coal, black beetles, black spiders and spiders' webs and everything weird and ghostly —perhaps a rat or so into the bargain. Knowing that my soft tallow candle would not last long, I worked with a will and got out just before the candle expired! Now it was my turn to be scrubbed and the water had become cold and so I cried and cried and cried but it was of no use. I slept soundly after. Bye the bye, the fun and mischief often was to pour cold water on the fellow in the tub—I tell you it is no joke. You see whatever was set us to do had to be done, and so we got used to the discipline and fell into regular and perhaps industrious habits. As to the most of our petty ailments she treated them: a bottle of Epsom salts in peppermint water always stood handy on the shelf—brimstone and treacle of milk came every spring—Mother would stitch up cuts, first washing them with salt water. She would be bled every year and said it did her good, without it she said she was troubled with head-aches and giddiness, nevertheless she was a very healthy woman, the bleeding at all events did her no harm—she used to have a pint taken away and very rich blood it was.

If we did anything very wrong, Mother would keep us in and not punish us immediately, but perhaps tie us to her chair for an hour and [*sic*: *for* or?] two and then the strap or cane—the suspense worse than the cane, but she held it to be wrong to punish when in a state of excitement. Of course we were often unruly in bed in the morning and then sometimes Mother would walk in and give us the strap or cane—it used to tickle then anyhow.

Mother had superstitious notions—believed more or less in dreams and forewarnings, but otherwise a very correct and determined woman —had great force of character. If we were told to do anything—none ever asked why or wherefore, but did it—if not the consequent cane or strap. Obedience and discipline her determination, but we all had lots of play.

Mother and Father were both Lutherans and had a pew in St. George's Church; the Minister, the Revd. Dr. C. E. A. Schwabe,[1] was one of the chaplains to the Queen Dowager, an old very good man who had known my mother many years and I believe baptized [and] confirmed her—but I doubt whether he could have married her—the law being against it.[2] The Clerk or Precentor was Mr. Vorwerg,[3] also an old man; both had held the positions for many years. As before said, Mother had intense antipathies against the Roman Catholic religion—against priests—and everything connected with it. How this came about I know not, but feeling ran high at this time and often shewed itself in the battles

---

[1]Dr. theol. Christian Ernst August Schwabe served as pastor of St. George's Church from 18 August 1799 until his sudden death on 28 February 1843. In 1820 he became the minister of the Prussian Embassy, and he was also appointed chaplain to the Duchess of Kent, mother of Queen Victoria (see *Jubiläums-Bericht zur 100-Jahrfeier der St. Georgs-Schule in London* . . . [London: Siegle, 1905], pp. 19-21; Rieger, "St. Georg-Kirche," p. 3).

[2]Under Lord Hardwicke's Marriage Act of 1753 (An Act for the better preventing of clandestine marriages, 26 Geo. 2, c. 33), it was impossible for anyone to be legally married except by a Church of England clergyman. The Marriage Act of 1836 (6 & 7 Will. 4, c. 85) permitted marriage according to any, or no, religious rites, provided that a certificate from the district registrar was obtained.

[3]He was also the Master of St. George's School. See below, p. 14.

between my mother and grandfather—not a matter of argument but assertion—her great horror was the absolution.

Mother was very particular about the associates of the girls, but even as regards the boys, over whom out of doors she could not have so much controul, she would not allow them to learn or practise on any musical instrument, because she said the instrument would lead them into evil company and the company to drinking and other bad habits. She had a horror of anyone drinking to excess and would not allow it. We had afterwards enough singing in school, but the musical instruments seem to have begun and ended with the Jew's harp! Anyhow in these days being able to play was considered an accomplishment and not a necessity. The mania for the piano is modern. Mother went on the principle to keep all occupied, believing that idleness only led to bad habits and profligacy.— She liked work anyhow—the more the better. Of debt my mother had a horror—if anything were owing she would scrape and scrimp until everything was paid up in full. Honesty in everything was her constitutional principle. Of course there was no extravagance. With this principle there could not be any, where means were very scant. In a subsequent year—but this will come in the bye and bye. I have thus given a sort of picture of my mother a woman of the olden time, and not an uncommon one, who lived only for her children—all self denial.

Now let me put down some random recollections about myself J. S. Helmcken. I was born, so I have been told, in Brick Lane,[1] why called Brick Lane I know not, for it was a terribly busy street as I afterwards found. Tradition states the house was a rag shop or that of a "marine store" dealer, and that my mother took refuge there because I had determined to come into the world in a hurry. I fancy, however, my mother lived there in order to be near her mother at this period. Anyhow there I was born and doubtless a great fuss made, because three sisters had preceded me and I was the first son and heir and so a remarkable fellow—to them. A few years afterwards I saw my birthhouse—a really decent brick building of three stories—but in place of rags, the whole of the front windows were covered with huge [?] posters, with printed letters six or more inches long, with the names of Frost,

---

[1]The Certificate of Baptism dated 22 April 1848 (HC) states that JSH was baptized on 13 February 1825. The same date is given in the register of baptisms of Christ Church, Spitalfields; no date of birth has been found in any contemporary source. Later records indicate 5 June 1824, and this is the date on the family tomb in Pioneer Square, Victoria.

Williams and Jones—the charter—rights of Britons and so forth: in fact it had become a political home—radical at this.[1] I suppose it had relation to the Birmingham riots,[2] and we little boys heard and believed that these men were to be carried to the place of execution on hurdles, and then a horse was to be fastened to each limb and so each culprit torn in quarter and scattered to the four winds of heaven! They had been found guilty of treason &c. &c. I am not aware of there being any general election at the time: tho no doubt the "reform" was agitated. Opposite the house was a splendid view of Spitalfields burial ground and the Church,[3] but I have no recollection of seeing or admiring any works of art there. A market was close by—and an immense brewery two three hundred yards away: weavers lived in the back streets —but the "fields" had disappeared and so had St. Mary Spittall and the Monastery. In fact Brick Lane was an awfully busy thoroughfare from Whitechapel.

However I have not recollection of having lived anywhere, but in Great Alie Street. This was a highly respectable street, the Bowmans, Goodmans,[4] McMurdos [?]—some government offices and a number of houses that at some distant period had been occupied by grand people. Dr. Graves lived exactly opposite our house.[5] There was a blacksmith's shop at the rear and a carpenter's shop no distance off and these were my favorite resorts. The carpenter's shop, belonging to Mr. Branch,[6] had been a stately mansion, with grounds surrounding: the front was still covered with a grape vine, which bore fruit abundantly, but did not always ripen. To nourish this vine and make blood for

---

[1]On 12 July 1839 Parliament rejected the petition calling for the implementation of the six points of the "People's Charter," and some members of the Chartist movement turned to violent action. In November, John Frost and his lieutenants, Zephaniah Williams and William Jones, led an army of Welsh miners against the town of Newport in Monmouthshire, hoping that its capture would be the signal for Chartist risings throughout the country. The attempt failed. The three leaders were arrested and sentenced to transportation.

[2]Chartist speakers continued to defy the ban on meetings imposed by the Birmingham magistrates, and on 4 July 1839 the crowd was broken up by police imported from London, assisted by soldiers.

[3]The Anglican foundation of Christ Church, Spitalfields, Stepney, is still in existence.

[4]P. Goodman is listed in the 1833 directory at No. 16.

[5]William Henry Graves, surgeon, is listed in the 1833 and 1840 directories and the 1841 census as residing at No. 4, Alie Place, off the south side of Great Alie Street. The name was changed to St. Mark's Street in 1906.

[6]Benjamin Branch, carpenter, is listed at No. 41, Great Alie Street in 1840.

the grapes, a couple of buckets of bullock blood used annually to be applied to the roots. The trellis work remained with climbing plants, which were called tea trees and jasmine. There were the four streets —Alie, Leman, Prescott and Mansell,[1] all respectable streets, and named after four [sons-in-law?] or grandsons of Goodman, who had been interested in the West Indies, but the estate or part of it was now in chancery. The Goodmans in my day had some coloured servants—and coachman. At the end of Little Alie Street was a place called Goodman's Stile, I suppose which used to be a stepping place into Goodman's Fields. In the rear of these four streets, was a large quadrangular field, unenclosed and barren, called by us the "Tenter Ground"[2] and here soldiers from the Tower of London used occasionally to be exercised, whilst young Goodman interested himself in breaking in trotting or other horses. This was our playground. On our side the street stood Bowman's sugar refinery, and at the rear of our house, (having a back door leading to it) was a square—surrounded by sugar refineries, belonging to the Bowmans, Cravens and others. Immense buildings occupying acres! These were all ruined by Free Trade. How many times did I play in and about the refineries altho forbidden to do so! I learned all about sugar refining without knowing it. Later on I saw waggon loads of beetroots carried into the buildings. Sugar was to be made from beetroots. The experiments failed and one after the other the refineries shut down. There was a broad yard to our house, paved with flagstones, and huge walls on each side, the walls of other houses or boundary walls. Here was a good place to play ball and what not and a quiet place for mischief too, at least it would have been, had not neighbouring windows overlooked it! Alie Place was a good place too, but Mrs. Graves would not allow play there; that is to say when the boys became boisterous she ordered us all home—and we obeyed; sulkily if you please. The place was nice and quiet anyhow. In Little Alie Street stood St.

---

[1]These four streets survive under their original names today, except that Prescott has lost the final t. Goodman's Stile, mentioned below, also survives, between the east end of Alie Street and Commercial Road.

[2]An open space where weavers placed the wooden frameworks, called tenters, on which cloth was stretched so that it might dry without shrinking. On an 1843 map (see Plate 2) the four streets enclose an open space marked Goodman's Fields. By 1868 the ground had been built over, but its earlier use as a tenter ground was commemorated in the names North, East, South and West Tenter Streets, which survive today.

George's German Church and School[1]—the former old-fashioned, with galleries on each side and above in the corners; a complete church, with the Revd. Dr. C. E. A. Schwabe as Minister. The school was an ordinary schoolroom, with a stove in the centre and plenty light. A graveyard existed immediately at the back of the school and hardly separated from it, save by a diminutive fence. Sunflowers and others grew in it and somehow or other the boys considered it sacred and seldom played there at all. The bricks of the school were furrowed, by the boys sharpening their slate pencils there. The church was heated by a furnace fed from the outside; hot air passing into the church.

Altho this neighbourhood was highly respectable, still at a very short distance was all sorts of disreputable places, common to London. Whitechapel Church was not more than five minutes walk distant; and bye the bye at Goodman's Stile was another sugar refinery, of which Mr. Finken was the manager—sugar refineries everywhere, the employees being Germans.

Mother was very fond of flowers—so she had them growing on the parapet and in the windows. Curiously enough auriculas grew well and so did some other plants—roses and asters for instance and London pride. Mother's auriculas were the envy of many and grew outside her bedroom window. All our bedrooms were at the top of the house— large and well lighted, at least I thought so then.—Communication from bedroom to bedroom was very convenient—and my mother found

[1]St. George's German Lutheran Church was founded in 1762 by wealthy sugar manufacturers to serve the many Germans then employed in the East London refineries. The building was completed in 1763, and in 1846 St. George's was said to be "by far the most frequented of the German churches in London" (John Southerden Burn, *The History of the French, Walloon, Dutch, and other Foreign Protestant Refugees Settled in England from the Reign of Henry VIII to the Revocation of the Edict of Nantes* ... [London: Longman, Brown, Green, and Longmans, 1846], p. 240). Now the oldest German building in Great Britain, it has been declared of historic interest and is in process of repair. Services are still held there by Pastor Dietrich Altmann, who was kind enough to check JSH's comments against his own knowledge and also to provide copies of the centenary booklet of St. George's School (1905) and of Rieger's bicentenary article on St. George's Church. The church building is much the same as in JSH's day, though it is now heated by electricity and the clock that the boys had to wind up with a winch (see below, p. 17) is no more. St. George's German and English School, a charitable institution founded in 1805 under the direction of Dr. Schwabe with seventeen pupils (of whom twelve paid no fees), survived until World War I, but the building JSH knew was replaced in 1877 when the number of pupils was between four and five hundred. The churchyard behind the school, where JSH's father was buried in 1839, was closed by the authorities in 1853, and in 1859 a kindergarten was built on part of the site.

it so! We did not, for when we made too much noise in the morning or had fights with pillows and so forth Mother used to walk in, with her strap and give us jessie. Sometimes when we had done wrong in the day-time, this early morning visit was prearranged. She always kept her promise. I am running on a little too fast and must come back to myself again.

I suppose I was like other little boys full of mischief, and so sent to a girls' school kept by an old Miss Somebody: probably my sisters went there also—but I recollect nothing about it—because there was another "ladies' seminary" kept by the Misses Broughton in Alie Place. However I was soon turned out of or taken away from the girls' school and sent to St. George's German and English School,[1] Vorwerg the Master[2] being a friend of my mother. So having been dressed—made decent and my hair brushed, I set to crying, but this did not hinder my going. Father took me there and left me to cry in the schoolroom all day. After a short time I got used to the discipline and used to go off with alacrity at 9 o'clock in the morning and remain at school until 5 in the afternoon. As schools go now, this would be considered a very poor school indeed, as we were only drilled in English and German, Writing and Arithmetic and Geography.

The school was partly supported by subscriptions, chiefly from Germans—the cost to a scholar being I think about ten shillings per quarter plus books and so forth. There were about eighty boys of all sizes and grades and two ushers, one a paralysed one, but in addition to these there were monitors, boys belonging to the more advanced classes, who were put over the junior ones week and week about— these monitors assisted us and kept order—not by any means a bad system. We had to say our lessons before Mr. Vorwerg in batches and he used to dodge us, because boys would just learn the part that they thought would be theirs in rotation. Examinations every week viva voce—any boy answering a question, that an upper one could not took his place, and so it happened that a boy who at the beginning stood first found in the end himself lower down in rank—something like

---

[1]The records of St. George's School show that JSH was enrolled for the midsummer term of 1828, when he was only four years of age.

[2]In 1808 a new building was erected next to the pastor's house to serve both as a school and as a residence for the teacher, Georg F. Vorwerg. He retired as master of the school in October 1839 but continued as sexton of the church until 1856 (see *Jubiläums-Bericht*, pp. 21 and 23, and the frontispiece showing the buildings in 1821, reproduced in Plate 3).

racing. This system applied to all classes, and to all subjects, so the
boys became pretty sharp, but Vorwerg was old and sometimes very
neglectful: other times just the contrary; but he would have order and
reminded us daily that Order was Heaven's first law! Punishment was
not very common—clops on the hand with a cane or strap—kneel
down on the floor and hold up a brick, sometimes two, or kneel
on a bench and go through the same process—an awful punishment
as anyone may know who chooses to try it. Flogging I only saw but
once, and on this occasion for stealing and lying, yet there always
appeared a rod in pickle tho so seldom used. We were not only
punished for offences in school but also castigated for offences out
of school and school hours altogether, particularly if people outside
or parents or schoolmaster made complaints. These were always enquired into, but woe betide the boy who became a witness, save in
bad cases. It is true we used to fight other schools and used to make
appointments to meet other schools in Bishop Bonner Fields or other
place, and have a regular organized fight—each side having colored
tissue paper masks to represent their side and rank. Of course there
were plenty of bruises and so forth. If complaints were made of the
fights and found warranted, the ringleaders were punished—I saw a
whole dozen of boys made to kneel on a bench—big boys at this, and
the master went along with a long cane thrashing each one in turn.
Of course all the little ones were awe-stricken, but for all this the same
thing would break out again at no distant time. Of rows in the street
there were plenty—in fact we seemed to be an aggressive lot, but were
spoken of as foreigners! Every morning, school opened with prayer and
singing, for we had an organ in the room, and we had to read chapters
in the German Bible, never in the English one. In reading English
Vorwerg would frequently make the boys read some speech of some
great mean[ing?] reported in *The Times*, and to the best of my recollection a good deal of this happened about the time of the agitation
for the emancipation of the slaves in the West Indies.[1] So all the boys
became emancipationists, and people used to come around with petitions against slavery, and every boy who could write signed his name.
It did not matter how many petitions came, each one signed any or
all. Vorwerg used to say the speeches delivered in parliament were the
best English he could give to read—I suppose the truth was that he was
interested in the matter, tho doubtless eloquence was common in the

[1]Slavery was abolished throughout the British colonies in 1833.

Commons at this time—and as public questions create contagion so the boys took the disease and became partisans—emancipationists—reformers and so forth, possibly according to the newspaper and the schoolmaster—tho whether he was a Tory, Whig or a low radical—no doubt being young, we were radicals. Order in school was paramount. I remember a boy, who used to make "stamped paper" by putting a piece of paper on a coin and then rubbing the paper until he had an impression. We used such papers for I O U so many marbles, buttons, tops, pencils and so forth. Vorwerg found this out and tried the culprit in school—he found the boy guilty of counterfeiting and the penalty was death. A stove pipe ran over and across the centre of the schoolroom—he was to be hung to this. Preparations were made for the execution and the boy brought forward. At this all the boys in the school became alarmed, and beseeched the Master to pardon the boy for making and ourselves for using the counterfeit stamps. We did not think it any harm to use them. The Master relented and gave us a lecture about counterfeiting and asserted if we went on in this line, we should soon take to forgery &c. &c. Thus ended this scare. I may here relate an incident that happened to me a few years ago. I wanted a handsome, intelligent, active and industrious French Canadian to sign a receipt. He said he could not write—but if he could he would not be a poor man as he would only have to write a cheque (forging) to get all the money he wanted!!

In connection with the School was the Church. The boys, whose parents wished them to know something about religion, Lutheran or other, went weekly to the vestry, where Dr. C. E. A. Schwabe educated them and gave lessons to learn. The Lutheran Catechism is about as large as the New Testament, giving chapter and verse for all the dogmas or principles laid down. These we had to learn—as also chapters in the New Testament, particularly the Sermon on the Mount. The Minister was an old good sympathetic kind man; not given to punishment, altho he boxed the ears of some occasionally: he was beloved by the boys and his words attended to. The attendance was not compulsory on the whole school. I remember I was a sort of favorite, perhaps not from personal qualities so much as on account of my parents, anyhow I always knew my lessons. Palm Sunday was annually confirmation day. Those who intended being confirmed had pretty hard work for a month or so previously. Questions were written, which we took home and had to answer in writing, and on these writings our success depended. I had to write pages of foolscap—and did it. The first sacrament was on the following Sunday, Easter Sunday.

It was the prescribed duty of certain boys to wind up the church clock once a week—it had a winch. No boy ever went alone! As several went usually together, nice romps we had occasionally in the church, but for all this we felt uncanny in the place, particularly as in the vaults under the entrance to the church, lay buried, some of the enlightened pillars of the church or perhaps ministers &c.[1] I never saw these vaults opened but once—someone had to be buried. A huge flagstone covering the vault had been removed, and descending into the dismal cavern, one saw tiers of leaden coffins, some encased with wood, others where it had rotted off. I did not stop there long—a lantern shed a dismal light—and the air felt cold and I shuddery.

We all were expected to be in church twice every Sunday—and had benches fronting the altar and the Clerk, who was Vorwerg our school-master. Of course we could all sing and so were a sort of choir. During Lent the church was draped in black—pulpit, reading desk and all —and then we had to go to church twice in the week also. At Xmas it was bedecked with rosemary, holly and laurustinus. The services were all in German—the congregation Germans—chiefly from Hanover, at all events Low Germany and comprised among others many German merchants from the City and surroundings.

Taken altogether it was a mighty poor school, but I was a worker. At this time I became a rather sickly boy—said to be from too much school work, but more likely from bad atmospheres—anyhow I was often in the hands of Dr. Graves, who was friendly to my mother for having assisted him in his early endeavours to form a practice—and he was also Surgeon to the Bowmans' Sugar Refinery and some others.

Of course out of school I was—a boy. My delight used to be Branch's carpenter's shop—Branch used to set me to work to chisel out mortices, use the saw or straighten nails! Nails were nails and mostly wrought iron. What games we had in the sawpit and shavings—that is to say when the pit was not being used by the top-sawyer and underman, sawing through a plank, which appeared then big, but which now seems to have been a mere sheet of wood paper.

The blacksmith's shop too delighted me—how I enjoyed the sparks flying from the anvil—the red-hot iron and the welding—but I had no work here—had to stand out of the way.

---

[1]The Rev. Dr. C. E. A. Schwabe was buried there, as was his predecessor G. A. Wachsel, the first minister of St. George's Church (Rieger, "St. Georg-Kirche," p. 3). Pastor Altmann has himself been in the vault and "amongst the rubble and dust saw a few coffins squeezed flat by the lead coffins on top of them."

Altho not allowed to go into the refineries, still I went there, and learned all about sugar refining. All the men knew me and so kept an eye over me as I knew no danger. Many a licking I got for going in, as I always came out dirty—oh so dirty and my shoes sticky from the sugar on and off the floor.

But my greatest passion was gunpowder. It was of no use telling the grocer not to sell or give me any—I got it whenever I had money. I made fiz gigs—trains—crackers and what not on the sly—fired off cannon, which cannon I made out of anything, even holes in the brick walls surrounding the yard. Kegs in the days I am speaking of were hollow. No keg was safe or sacred—they were so good, all I had to do was a [*sic: for* to] file a little hole in the barrel and lo a cannon! Oh these kegs—how many a thrashing I got on your account—every lost keg was put down to my account! Boxes came in for a share, but they used to burst! Of course all this powder business was done on the sly, but there lived two maiden ladies in the next house, the windows of which looked into my yard. I was a terror to these poor women, imagining I would blow the house up—a second Guy Fawkes. Somehow or other they seemed to keep a watch over me and in the midst of my delight would run in and tell my mother—and then—Whew, that strap! I did not like these ladies at all—they never asked me to tea and did not give me any cake! I think half my delight existed in teasing them—we became sworn enemies—I was about 8 or 10 years of age!

I suppose I got through then my younger days like a good many young bears and had to get licked into shape, but altho precious active, I was not a vicious boy, and somehow or other was liked in school and out of school.

We used to have a school festival once a year—summertime, and then we marched to some distant [pleasure ground?] with St. George's banner and flag in front, the boys following in two and two file with a long willow wand in hand and dark blue ribbons attached to our jackets. The last one we marched to White Conduit House in the City Road.[1] As we passed the Green Man (I think) at the corner of Bethnal Green Road, we were, and the band also, regaled with ginger beer or cider, I suppose the landlord was a German, and then we marched

---

[1]An inn well known to eighteenth-century essayists, with extensive pleasure grounds and a cricket pitch where Thomas Lord of "Lord's" was once a groundsman (see Augustus J. C. Hare, *Walks in London* [London: Smith, Elder, n.d.], 1:219; William Kent, *Encyclopedia of London* [London: Dent, 1951], p. 338).

on again hurrahing and making a devil of a row as boys will—there were eighty of us. After arriving at the Conduit House, we had dinner in a fine room in the building—lots of Germans were there. It was my lot to say grace in German, and then how we did eat—and so did the patrons! I remember I was nicely dressed in a shepherd plaid suit and so was my brother Harry. I had been told off to make the motion of the day—I was about a dozen years old. So I was placed on the table and rehearsed my speech and ended amid applause and a shower of sixpences and joeys[1] and one gentleman gave me half a crown. What a mint of money! He was a gentleman!!! This time it was English—Harry had the German speech and met with the like applause and shower. After dinner we played in the tea garden, everybody stuffed us with pottles of "Oboys" cherries[2] and other fruit until we could hold no more. Towards evening there was some theatricals, and singing, but when the sun began to go down, we all had to fall in, and march to the omnibuses[3] which were waiting to take us, banners and band, home, kicking up a row all the way. I guess the people found out who the German boys of St. George's School were! I got home—Mother says, "Look at your nice dress—stained from head to foot and spoiled. Never mind—it's a poor heart that never rejoices."

My boyish days went on without much care or suffering, save from bad health, and so I went through the usual courses of marbles, tops, kites, feeder, rounder, trap and ball[4] and all this sort of thing. Had to walk out with my brothers and sister, who bye the bye never wanted to go home again, and so was troublesome. We were never wrapped up much, but were told to get warm by playing, for Mother said we must be made hardy and not care for a little cold and so we went on, not

---

[1]A slang term for a fourpenny piece.

[2]A pottle is a small wicker basket. A variety of cherry called Bowyer Early Heart is said to have originated in England c. 1815. It is also possible that "Oboys" is JSH's spelling of Hautbois (Great and Little), agricultural villages in Norfolk, a county of many orchards.

[3]The first omnibus in London was seen in 1829: "a handsome machine in the shape of a van, with windows on each side and one at the end ... drawn by three beautiful bays abreast ..." (London *Morning Post*, 7 July 1829, quoted in Kent, *Encyclopedia of London*, p. 391).

[4]A feeder is the player who tosses the ball to the batsman in rounders and similar games; hence, the name of a particular variation. A rounder is usually defined as a complete run at the game of rounders; here, JSH appears to mean the game itself. Trap and ball is presumably trap-ball, in which a ball placed upon one end (slightly hollowed) of a trap is thrown into the air by the batsman striking the other end with his bat, with which he then hits the ball away (OED).

a little heedless of weather altho blue and shivery not unfrequently. I had an attack of whooping cough, which would not go, notwithstanding change of air and all this sort of thing—in fact I became very thin and miserable. One day an old crony of Mother's came in—and among other things in my hearing said, "Of what use is it giving that boy physic? I'll tell you how to cure him. Go into the cellar, get the biggest black spider to be found there, put it into a nutshell—enclose this in a satin bag—hang it around his neck and as the spider rots so will the cough disappear!" My mother laughed, but said to please her friend she would try it as it could not do any harm anyway. So the spider being found and all the rest put in proper shape, the time came for its being put around my neck—but I rebelled—struggled against the application—kicked and then coughed until nearly strangled. Then I was offered a sixpence and some sweeties to induce me to wear the spider, in the nut in the satin bag—and so relenting it was placed accordingly and as it did not bite, it was allowed by me to remain. Some time after the crony reappeared. "Oh," my mother says, "he is well. Now let us look for the spider." Lo and behold there was no spider there, but only a membranous shell—and then the crony said, "Didn't I tell you so? Now don't laugh at me any more!"

How I [*sic: for* Now a?] change had to come over my existence. I have spoken already of the depression and subsequent failure of the sugar refineries, this of course led to depression among others and my parents, business at the refineries became very bad and hard times ensued but Mother was equal to the emergency and economized wherever possible. She never said die.

It so happened that Dr. Graves was attending someone at home, probably my father, when he was going away he saw me and asked Mother, "What are you going to do with this boy?" "Oh, I think he will be a teacher or get into some office, for the Dock Company and merchants in the City and others are constantly making applications at the school for boys for various purposes, when the boy is older he will find plenty, for his master says he is a clever boy, altho he does not show it—he works hard at his lessons." "Well," said the Doctor, "I want someone in the evening just to carry out the medicines. Let me have him—he can continue to go to school just the same." So it was agreed that I should carry around the medicines in a wicker basket with two flaps, no matter what kind of weather it should be, and was to receive I think half a crown per week! I was delighted with the arrangement and fell into the duties for I knew the streets of London very well. I thought it very hard that Mother would not allow me to spend my earnings but make me to [*sic*: *for* made me put] them into the Savings Bank to save the money as she said for a rainy day, which meant for some useful purpose. Mother was and indeed was obliged to be thrifty and so we were taught not to be extravagant and to deny ourselves all but what was moderately necessary—there was neither miserliness nor extravagance—I suppose the old story—spend money—not waste it.

I liked my new place very well: all the faces were familiar and kind to me: in fact I was active and willing and liked and not bad looking either with my dark hair and blue eyes—my hair was a flaxen brown once and then black. Winter came on and then in hail rain snow and blow I trudged my weary rounds with the medicines to all sorts of houses in all sorts of places, to the poor as well as rich for the Doctor had a very large number of patients. Many of the householders would give me a kindly word, but it was hard work and often I would not get home until 10 o'clock at night or later, for often the patients lived at a distance of two or more miles away. However as soon as I got home, Mother would always have a supper ready for me and if wet make me change my clothes—she was proud of her eldest boy, and the Doctor always spoke favorably to her of me, which pleased her and me too. Mr. Healy [Healey] was at this time the only apprentice, lived in the house in Alie Place; his father was a druggist in Hull, Yorkshire.[1] Healey had a lady love to whom he wrote letters and sometimes he would be too late to post his letters in the local office—so he would say, "I will give you sixpence, if you get this letter into the General Post Office before it closes." The General Post Office was in St. Martin's le Grand, a couple of miles nearly from Alie Place, but off I would go on the run and usually got there in time, but on one occasion just when I was about to drop the letter in the box, the whole of the flaps dropped with a bang! This was the usual thing—as the clock struck so the post shut. This was still in a great measure the day of Mail carriages, and often have I seen them start with their four five horses and a bugleman in the boot—everybody made way for them, and also the post boys on horseback.

Healey was very good to me and soon got me to assist him in putting up the medicines—corking the bottles—tying over the corks to make the bottles pretty and wrapping them up nicely, putting the address of

---

[1]Edward Healey, L.S.A., 1845 [*sic*: *for* 1840?], is listed in the 1851 Medical Directory at No. 15, Lister Street, Hull. He was succeeded in the Graves household by Henry I. Fotherby (see below, p. 34); and Fotherby, not Healey, is listed in the 1841 census.

the individual on. By degrees I advanced and folded the powders and selected the pills, for a large assortment of both these were kept ready made. Besides Dr. Graves had a large home practice—he gave advice for nothing during two hours, morning and evening, but the patients had to pay one shilling for their medicine, which Healey had also to put up. So in this way I learned to know something about the lower order of dispensing for there was abundance to do, and I was always willing to help for the sooner the medicines were put up, the sooner I got away. Now it so happened that Xmas after a few months came round and then the New Year. Mrs. Graves chose me to be her lucky boy— that is to say, she had a [superstition?] that a woman or certain kind of man entering first on the first day of the year would bring ill luck.[1] So I was instructed, that as soon as the clock struck twelve, I was to knock at the door, having in my hand some salt—bread and a bundle of matches—the real timber ones with lots of sulphur at the end, for at this time lucifers had not come into use, altho some existed, which we used to draw through sandpaper to strike them.[2] Anyhow after the door was opened I had to enquire for the lady of the house, and giving her bread wish that she might always have plenty—then the salt, that she might be preserved from all evil—and lastly the matches to en- lighten her understanding, wishing at the same time good luck to all in the house. To this some reply was made. I was asked to walk in and welcomed and Mrs. Graves gave me half a crown—cakes and what not—and after a while rejoicing left for home.

Some time after this, when probably I was about fourteen years of age Dr. Graves proposed to my mother that he would make me an apprentice for a couple of years that I might learn dispensing and so forth or in short that I might become a chemist and druggist, which he thought would suit me very well. He said, "Of course he will have to leave school, but this is of less consequence, because he will have nearly every afternoon for himself to read and learn what is necessary. So you can send him to school early in the morning and he can learn his lessons in the afternoon." My father was at this time ill—and soon after died aged I think 54 years, but before he died the

[1]In Scotland and the north of England the "first-foot" on New Year's Day should be a dark man.

[2]The first matches were ignited by dipping an inflammable tip into a bottle of sulphuric acid. In 1827 came the friction match which involved drawing the tip through a piece of folded sandpaper. The lucifer was a friction match ignited on a prepared surface. The next step was the safety match.

deeds were made out and so I became an apprentice.[1] Before however this was done, Mother asked me to consult the Revd. Dr. Schwabe, and he said, "You ought to learn Latin and I would be very glad to teach you, but I am old and live far away (Stamford Hill) but I will give you a letter to Dr. Dauber [Deuber], he is a teacher and lives in Finsbury Square."[2] In due time Dr. Deuber took me to teach—so I had to walk two or three times a week to Finsbury Square at 7 o'clock in the morning no matter what kind of weather it might be. I had to walk a mile, but before starting Mother gave me dry bread and salt to eat, having breakfast waiting when I returned about 8½ o'clock or so—the other children had by this time finished. My chief instruction at Deuber's was Latin—at first he puzzled me in translations by demanding subject, predicate and all this sort of thing, but it did not take long to get used to the Latin grammar, and soon I began to make good progress. Moreover, if I were puzzled Healey would give me a lift, but he was not much at home in the afternoon now, having to attend lectures at the Hospital. After learning the ordinary rules from Valpy's Latin grammar and mastering Caesar and some of the orations of Cicero, Deuber put me into Celsus and other medical but Latin authors.[3] Sometimes he would transfer me to a young German doctor living in the same house, and so we went through Celsus and so forth, he giving me instruction as to the meaning and other matters. Suffice it to say that in course of time, I knew sufficient Latin for my purpose, altho I never liked the language—the Latin poets I refused altogether—first because they were to me very difficult and next I was not a poet and had no love for poetry either then or now! However I did like Scott and Byron

---

[1]JSH is far from precise in his references to the chronology of his life. It would seem that after a year or two as Dr. Graves's errand boy, he was officially apprenticed as a chemist and druggist in the spring or summer of 1839, when he was about fifteen years of age. He left school for good on Lady Day (i.e. 25 March) 1839. His father died in September. This apprenticeship was cancelled when JSH became a medical pupil (see below, p. 26).

[2]The Helmcken Collection contains a letter written to JSH in German on 20 November 1848 from No. 49, Finsbury Square and signed "H. Deuber." The writer thought the situation in Germany looked bad and that the country would soon become a republic: "that alone can save it and liberate it from its tyrants." Cf. Helmcken's comment on p. 24 below: "I now suppose all in this house to have been refugees for some reason or other."

[3]Richard Valpy (1754-1836), headmaster of Reading Grammar School for fifty years, was the author of Greek and Latin grammars in wide circulation. Celsus was the first-century A.D. author of *De Medicina*, said to be the greatest work on general medicine to emanate from the Roman world.

and Johnny Gilpin[1] but these are easily understood and do not soar too high—one cannot follow imaginative poetry—who can Milton? To get up at 6 o'clock on a winter's morning, and have to strike a light with flint and steel and a tinder box, chipping one's fingers not unfrequently is no joke and then go to school on dry bread and salt and no fire to warm a fellow, is no joke, but I did it and possibly did not think it any hardship—for there was an end in view.

Deuber lived in Finsbury Square. The house was kept by an old French aristocrat, still handsome urbane and polite. He taught French. Another taught Music but I did not see him. My friend the other doctor was a medico, who had a practice among Germans, he was a politician too, and gave me copies of German patriotic songs—and so did Deuber. This medico was, I think, a man of "advanced thought or opinions." He puzzled me once by asking me "What is death?" to which I made answer "The cessation of life," but he would not stand this—and I remember how often I asked the question after—"What is death?" and ask the question still. I now suppose all in this house to have been refugees for some reason or other. The divinity used to ask the medico, "What did you think of my sermon yesterday?" "Well I do not think it cost you more than two or at most three cigars— there wasn't much fire in it!" Deuber smoked when composing his sermons, so when excited he smoked many cigars, but when sluggish but few, so the medico judged his sermons, cigars being the currency.

It so happened that about this time Dr. Schwabe died, and the pulpit of the St. George Church became vacant. Deuber tried hard to get the position, but failed, the congregation preferring to get a young preacher from Germany. This new preacher, a very good man whose name I forget brought his sister with him, and after this Vorwerg re-tired and great alterations in the staff and teaching of the school en-sued.[2] Deuber established a church in the Soho—I often went to hear him; his congregation was not very large but respectable. Not long after the news came, that he had eloped to Australia with another man's

---

[1]Possibly a reference to William Cowper's *The Diverting History of John Gilpin.*
[2]Schwabe died on 28 February 1843 (cf. p. 9 above) and was succeeded by Dr. Louis Cappel of Worms, who died in 1882. Under him the kindergarten was founded and the new school building erected. Among the German congregation the school was generally known as the Cappel-Schule (Rieger, "St. Georg-Kirche," p. 3). Nearly four years before Dr. Schwabe died, Mr. Vorwerg had retired and had been succeeded by Heinrich Joachim Daniel Winter (*Jubiläums-Bericht,* p. 23).

wife! What became of the medico and the others in Finsbury Square I know not.

I suppose that when about one half my apprenticeship had expired, Dr. Graves was taken ill—laid down with fever. Mrs. Graves' brother, Dr. Rose[1] attended him, but of course other advice and assistance was called in—great and talented physicians. He was in a very dangerous condition, delirious for some time, so no one but his attendants were allowed to see him. He, however, recovered and after some weeks or months resumed practice. Now during this period Healey had to attend to the indoor patients and a great many of the outdoor patients too, and so it fell to my lot to do all the dispensing and carry out the medicines into the bargain. It was a very anxious time for the whole of us. Previous to this illness, I had been instructed in the art of making thousands of various kinds of pills, tinctures and what not, for Dr. Graves would have all these made according to his own directions on the premises, and he was very particular about it. Dispensing I had had much to do with also, thanks to Healey, but still I was not very proficient and so when Healey was withdrawn, I had to do the best I could and did it—there was no despairing about it. I worked hard not only at this, but running about for various purposes necessitated by the Doctor's and other requirements—in fact anything I could I did cheerfully and met with the approbation of Dr. Rose—to be tired then was unknown—Dr. Graves began to improve and so did we. There was a young lively lady living with Mrs. Graves. She disguised herself one morning and presented herself to Healey as a patient. He saw through her disguise, but asked her no end of questions! In the end she received a prescription to give to me, but as soon as I saw her, I laughed—and this was the end of it as far as I was concerned. She merely put her finger to her lips and left! Mrs. Graves never learned anything of this— if she had—Whew! but the lady did not like to be teased by Healey about it.

In course of time—a long time too, Dr. Graves by degrees attended to his practice again, much to our delight, for we did not like Dr. Rose, but in reality we had no good reason for the dislike—save he was not the same as Dr. Graves, and things did not go on exactly the same.

One day Dr. Graves said to me or rather to my mother, that I had

---

[1]Charles Rose, L.S.A., 1837, of No. 10, Barnes Place, Mile End Road, who in Dr. Graves's will, dated 15 June 1853 (Public Record Office, London), is referred to as his brother-in-law.

been a very good boy during his illness, had made great progress and now if Mother wished and would consent, he would cancel the articles of apprenticeship of the past, and take me as a full apprentice, so that I might become a practitioner like himself.— "What says your son?"

To tell the truth, I was perfectly satisfied to be a chemist and druggist, but visions of keeping carriages and horses, coachman, floated before my eyes, and so I was delighted and grateful to accept the proposal. The question of cost of this education came up, but Mother said, "Never mind my son, you shall be a doctor if you like even if I have to pawn my clothes to pay the cost—we can work at all events." Such was Mother, she would sacrifice herself for her children but I am afraid the children did not appreciate sufficiently the sacrifice until many years after.

The end or beginning of the end of this matter was that kind Dr. Graves said I should be an outdoor apprentice for five years[1]—the usual period; at the end of three years to be allowed to attend the Hospital and lectures. He was to pay me I think ten shillings per week and told Mother that the indentures should cost her nothing as his brother a solicitor at Bath[2] would draw them up for me without cost. My duties and hours would be the same as now and would increase in importance as my education went on. This is actually the way in which I commenced to be a medico and is really due as I said before to the kindness of Dr. Graves. The money I received had to be put in the Savings Bank as usual, and Mother treated me exactly as one of the family— Mother felt very proud of her boy, altho I do not think she made any distinction between me and the rest, but I was the oldest boy, to be a doctor and was the first of my race in England.[3]

Things went on then much the same for the ensuing three years— I did everything, compounded, bled, cupped, applied leeches, administered enemas and anything else I was capable of and in addition carried out the medicines to the various patients' houses.— Of course I was older now and broken in to the exercise. Of bleeding I had

---

[1]In the certificate of character which Dr. Graves supplied at the time of JSH's marriage in 1852, he stated that JSH had been "an articled medical pupil to myself for five years" (HC). He gave no dates. But since JSH entered Guy's Hospital in 1844 (see below, p. 42n3) the indentures were presumably drawn up three years earlier, in 1841. They were apparently cancelled before their expiry (see below, p. 43), but the five-year prerequisite for the M.R.C.S. was made up by JSH's earlier apprenticeship as a chemist and druggist.

[2]John Graves, Solicitor, Bath, is referred to in Dr. Graves's will.

[3]Presumably JSH means the first of his family in England to be a doctor.

enough to do—for Graves bled very freely—of cupping likewise. A Miss Winter afforded me good practice. She was a nervous thin person, not at all bad-looking in the face, but oh, her sides—scarred all over worse than a New Zealand Maori's! Anyhow I used to cup her about every three months for pain in her side. She had been cupped at least fifty times, had on as many as sixty blisters—and had been bled also. She married—and was never troubled with the pain after—never cupped or blistered, but grew fat and had children! However the Doctor attached very great importance to bleeding in some shape or other— counter-irritation and diet with laxatives—particularly magnes. sulph. He had a large practice and was very successful. In any case I think bloodletting has been too much neglected of late, the pendulum gone to the other extreme. I have seen people with severe pain, unable to breathe, as soon as bled get up, breathe easily and walk home comfortably!

It must not be supposed that I was any better than other boys—no doubt I had grumbling times—ill-tempered ones too—and I was passionate but not very sulky—but I had been well disciplined to do as I was told and not to ask questions; if sent on a message, to return immediately &c. &c.; if I did not, the consequences came. As for amusements we had plenty—but they existed chiefly in outings to the country round about London—and few prettier places exist. Kent— Erith—Blackheath—varied by Wandsworth—Epping—Primrose Hill— Highgate—Norwood—St. John's &c. Plenty public institutions—and so forth. To see steamboats come in was a pleasure, for steamboats then were in their infancy[1]—I know my mother would not travel in one or a railway: but whether she ever got over the antipathy, I know not. Anyhow when I wrote to her to come to Vancouver Island, she wrote if I sent Neptune, his carriage and horses, she would not cross the sea—it was sufficient to know that I was well and might soon be home again! I never went home. Railways too were only budding—the Great Western was a wonder, but the Eastern Counties one and subsequently the Brighton were those we usually used.[2] What cars! It seems to me

---

[1]As early as 1815 pleasure trips in a steamboat brought from Glasgow had been organized on the Thames. In 1831 steamers were running daily through the season from the City to Richmond and from the St. Katharine's Docks to various seaside resorts.

[2]The Great Western was opened from Paddington to Maidenhead (23 miles) in 1838 and to Bristol (118 miles) in 1841. The Eastern Counties was opened from Bishopsgate (later from Liverpool Street) to Brentwood (18 miles) in 1840 and to Colchester (51 miles) in 1843. The Brighton was built by three different

now they were of the roughest description—mere benches covered in
—people packed like herrings. Then came the Blackwall R. built
on arches through London, the power used being a traction rope some
four miles long, which used frequently to break—it ran on the surface
of the ground—i.e. the rope did and was two or three inches in diameter—no wire ropes then. Locomotives were not allowed to be used;
being considered too dangerous on account fires. Owing to the eleva-
tion of the R.R. we used to see into rooms as we went along and many
funny sometimes rather revolting sights we saw, as the road passed thro
a very low part of the town.[1]

To church we had to go regularly—had our own pew.— In these
days it was do as I preach and not as I do, for the rector might sometimes be seen drunk on the streets—but poor man he may have been
ill. Anyhow the parish was neglected, but in process of time came the
Revd. Mr. Champneys and a revival took place—there were lots of rows
about church rates too.[2] We were never allowed to go into a dissenting
chapel or meeting house—as to a Roman Catholic one, that was out
of the question altogether. Theatres we were not allowed to visit. As to
the Dissenters—she called them ranters, and they were a nuisance,
blocking up the street gossiping to each other coming out from meeting.
When I look at the Methodists now and compare them with what they

---

companies: the London and Greenwich Railway was opened in 1838; the London
and Croydon, which branched off from the London and Greenwich a mile or so
out of London, opened in 1839; and the London, Brighton and South Coast,
which left the London and Croydon line near the Croydon terminus, was opened
to Brighton in 1841.

[1]The London and Blackwall supplied railway communication between the City
and the East and West India Docks so that passengers might avoid the loop of the
Thames at Greenwich and the crowded navigation of the Pool. Opened from the
Minories in 1840 and from Fenchurch Street in 1841, it made the trip to Blackwall, a distance of three and one-half miles, in seven minutes seven seconds, a
speed of 26.2 miles per hour. It was worked by means of stationary engines at
each terminal winding and unwinding a rope weighing some 40 tons, to which were
attached nine carriages. Each of these could be detached at its proper intermediate station by a guard. The fares were 6d. in a first class compartment and
4d. for standing room in a third class Stanhope compartment holding about
seventy persons. Between the Minories and the West India Dock Road the line
was carried by a brick viaduct 4,020 yards long of 285 arches. In 1849, the year
JSH left England, the London and Blackwall was converted to a locomotive
line of standard gauge.

[2]Although the Helmckens had their own pew in St. George's German Lutheran
Church (cf. p. 9 above), they were still obliged to pay the church rates which
helped to maintain the Church of England in the parish in which they lived.
William Weldon Champneys (1807-75), later Dean of Lichfield, served as rector
of St. Mary's, Whitechapel, 1837-60.

were in my boyhood I am astounded—then they wore the plainest of
clothes and had the plainest of church and the plainest of people—
today they are very much the contrary—indeed it seems that these like
others when they grow fat forget all about the poor they started with,
and the clergy like other clergy think more of getting a good living,
than of ministering to the poor and illiterate. Of what earthly use is
their ministration to the respectable, they knowing as much as the
minister? They belong to the poor properly—and it will be found that
the church of the poor, being the church of the majority, will con-
quer when civil trouble comes again. Anyhow, the clergy all told do
much good and doubtless could they combine [would?] do a great
deal more. At present they are teachers and professors of morals—and
like of old find their chief support in emotional women; with these the
parson almost occupies the place of God, and the church, i.e. building, is idolatrously worshipped like an idolatrous shrine—but why run
away from my subject—my life?

Dr. Graves lived in a nice house at the corner of Alie Place—the
surgery was attached to the house and under the surgery was a paved
yard, where I used to make the infusions, decoctions—melt aloes and
make pills—and walk into the kitchen occasionally, for Mary was a
nice young woman and married James the coachman soon after.

Dr. Graves was a tall thin gentleman, with fine pale distinguishable
face and very nice-mannered—and undoubtedly a gentleman: very particular about his dress—not a speck of dust about him: always wore
very thin-soled boots—the soles having been hammered to this thinness.
As he himself, so were his horses, carriages and servants—all clean and
orderly—so the offices had to be kept so too—the bottles dusted and so
forth. He had a very kind disposition particularly to those he liked—
good to the poor but never ostentatious. His practice chiefly medical,
was very large, both at home and outside. From 9 to 12 A.M. he was
occupied with patients at home—and so from 6 to 8 in the evening—
the afternoons devoted to outside patients. In fact he never seemed
to do anything else than attend to patients—he lived for this and by
this—indeed he had too much to do. It fell to my lot to receive
messages for him, so when a message came in the afternoon, I used to
ask what is the matter and so forth as perhaps Mr. Graves would be
too busy to go. If they said the patient had just been taken ill—I might
consult the Doctor's visiting list and leave a message at a house he was
likely to visit, but if the applicant said, "Oh he has been ill a long
time" but that now it was urgent, I always told them, "You have
had plenty time and ought to have come before 12 o'clock—for all

messages for visits ought to come before this time, so that they may
be seen in order, but as it is I do not think Dr. Graves will be able to
see your sick one today!" Sometimes this did—but sometimes they would
get someone else. I learned to do this with discrimination, for by this
time I knew good patients from bad—and usually I was right. He was
kind and gossipy with Mother, a thing unusual with him, but Mother
had materially assisted him when he first entered practice. One day
there was to be a "grand review" in Hyde Park—so Master asked me if
I would like to go. Of course I would—lots of gunpowder. Well we
went—a carriage and pair, Mrs. & Mr. Graves and some others. We saw
the review, I stood on the rumble carelessly, when about the end, the
big guns went off—music played, drums beat and there was a devil
of a row and smoke. All at once the horses started—they went one
way I the other, falling on my head on the pavement—that is all I
recollect. St. George's Hospital was close bye, so they picked me
[up] and took me there as quickly as they could get out of the crowd,
for they considered me dying—but when going up to the Hospital, I
gave a kick or two and opened my eyes, so they determined to take
me home. Here I was leeched—and cold lotion and physicked, but
laid up for two or three weeks: the insensible part is what I was told.
Mother did not make any fuss, but attended me constantly—no one
else allowed to interfere in this. I injured my shoulder too and this
troubled me for months after.

Mrs. Graves was the daughter of an Admiral Rose,[1] and ought to
have been an admiral herself for she was a martinet and awfully jealous[2]
—I mean a martinet to her servants, who as a rule did not remain
long. A robust woman, as cleanly and neat as the Doctor and saw that
there be no dust in any corner of the room—the handkerchief used to
detect the dust, but she was a good-hearted lady, nevertheless, and particularly kind to me. She abhorred smoking and I believe could smell
a fellow even if he had not smoked for a week, but was a good mother
to the apprentices. Of course I came in for a share of scolding,
but confessedly as a rule deserved it—but she had nothing to do with

[1]Dr. R. J. B. Knight, the deputy head of the Department of Manuscripts at the
National Maritime Museum, Greenwich, reports no trace of an Admiral Rose in
the eighteenth or nineteenth centuries. As he points out, "when ashore naval ranks
often become confused" (cf. "Captain" George Rose, p. 37 below). A daughter,
Ann (Rose) Graves, was born in Hull according to the 1851 census, but neither the
city archivist nor the Central Library in Hull has been able to trace the family.
[2]JSH appears to be using jealous here in the sense of "suspiciously watchful,"
"vigilant or exact in observation," rather than in its more usual meaning.

the offices—this was a blessing anyhow. Religion took her fancy, but it was of an austere kind, and she had some she wished to convert,[1] for by this time a "Church of ease" had been built in the Tenter Ground[2] and Mrs. Graves liked the minister and the church, in fact a pillar. At this time I was quite orthodox—prayers morning and evening, which I am sorry to say to the servants was a bore, and they would play tricks with each other—of which even I was not guiltless. I say again she was always kind to me and had been so when I used to play marbles opposite her door, and was only turned away when my chums made too much noise. A Yorkshire woman, she kept many of the customs of Yorkshire people, so at Xmas I used to shell the white [*sic: for* wheat]—dry it and shell it to make frumenty with; the winnowing was rather a dusty process, but I made up for this when stoning the raisins. Frumenty was a mixture of wheat and raisins and spices and heaven knows what else, like very thick porridge and eaten at Xmas. We all used to eat some of it—and found it pretty indigestible—we were only cockneys! had not the gizzard of a Yorkshireman! Well Mrs. Graves used always to speak about our "Master." Your Master wants this or that and so forth—always "Master," not the Doctor. In the days of apprenticeship, the apprentice had a "Master" and called him so and it had no offensive meaning—he was the master of the business. In this country "boss" is the term used—"Master" is a word for slave owners!!!

Why these kind people should have taken me by the hand and helped me onward would be ungrateful to enquire, but probably it was owing to friendship and feeling for Mother who had so large a family and to their own innate human goodness. As for myself, I am not aware of any peculiar good qualities—I was a puppy—a nice-looking boy with blue eyes, black hair and florid, very obedient—easily disciplined or broken in and faithful as a dog—did my duty, sometimes but not always cheerfully.

At the time of Her Majesty's Coronation [28 June 1838], Mrs. Graves

---

[1]On 13 May 1848, when the newly fledged Dr. Helmcken was preparing to sail for India and China, "his friend Mrs. W. H. Graves" presented him with a copy of *The Anxious Enquirer after Salvation Directed and Encouraged,* by Dr. John Angell James, published by the Religious Tract Society (sixth edition, 1835). This book is now in the possession of his grandson Mr. Ainslie J. Helmcken.

[2]A "chapel of ease" is a subordinate Anglican church, built for the convenience of parishioners who live far from the parish church. St. Mark's, Whitechapel, was opened in 1841, and the present street which bisects the old tenter ground from Alie Street to Prescot Street is named after it.

offered me a place in the carriage to go and see the procession. Then as now, I cared little about shows and pageants, perhaps having seen too many of them. Anyhow I begged off, so someone else took my place and it was agreed that I should take charge of the house. Well, I thought I would have a quiet day and read a novel, to which at this time I was addicted occasionally. In order not to be disturbed, I wrote on a sheet of foolscap (emblematical!) a notice—Dr. Graves had gone to the Coronation so patients would not be seen today and stuck this in a conspicuous place. Stray patients may have read this and so neither knocked nor rang the bell. I had a lovely time, but the party returned unexpectedly early on. I had forgotten to remove the notice, and so the first thing Dr. Graves espied, was the wretched notice! For once he was angry and gave me—fits! I learned afterwards that he thought it a very good joke and laughed heartily, but not before me. Anyhow he did not nurse his anger and the whole thing was soon forgotten.

Here let me say that in the year 1890—a gentleman called at my residence in Victoria. My daughter told him, "Father has just gone, if you follow you may meet him." Well he followed and soon overtook me, calling out "Are you Dr. Helmcken?" "They call me so. What do *you* want?" "Why," says he, "don't you know me?" "No I do not"—took off his hat, showing me a bald head. "Don't you know me now?" "No." "You ought to know me anyhow! Why I am Fred Hodson, your fellow apprentice!"[1] "Oh," says I, "fellows come here and call themselves Lords and all sorts of things falsely, how am I to know whether you be Hodson?" "Why here's my card." "Oh, anybody can get anybody's card—you may have picked this up." "Well," says he, "do you remember the Coronation day—and the notice on the door?" I said, "That is enough—you are Hodson or the devil!" Of course we had a night of it and so forth, but we can only see people as we knew them years gone bye. Neither one knew the other altho they had resided together four years, *forty* [fifty] *years previously.*

Behold me then an outdoor apprentice, a boy of all work. Dispensing —carrying out the medicines in a "doctor's boy" basket-made basket —all doctor's boys' baskets were of a peculiar shape, with flaps and as a rule covered on the top with oilskin or other imperviable stuff, to keep the bottles, pills and powders dry: making pills, tinctures, pills and powders—going to school early in the morning to perfect (!) my

---

[1]Frederick Hodson, M.R.C.S., Eng., 1848; L.S.A., 1848.

Latin and sometimes during the day bleeding, cupping, leeching either in the office or people's residences and as I advanced, so I occasionally saw poor patients—perhaps dressed sores and so forth and so drilled got broken in and what is more liked my profession. It was in this way chiefly that I became acquainted with the slums, beggary, poverty and illness combined—and now a dreadful picture it presents—squalor, dirt, starvation and lots of immorality, but all this seemed a matter of course being constantly visible and present. Of course I could not assist them pecuniarily and in the days I am speaking of parsons paid them no attentions excepting a few to the contrary and there were not many of those charitable combinations of ladies and gentlemen, so common now to relieve the wretched. Of course priests—i.e. Roman Catholics, hardly existed, at least they never came across my path at this time— it is, I am told, very different now—yet there is plenty room for more, tho to remedy the whole is a practical impossibility—until or unless human nature be very much altered. Anyhow amidst all this squalor and other horrors, human hearts were there and each assisted the other to the best of their ability and altho this might have been little in substance it was an enormous amount to them. Indeed it seems to me now that this feeling for a fellow creature exists too in more abundance and more genuine than among the rich—in the latter it is almost conventional, in the former natural. Some people call it "animal," and that they mourn and sorrow like animals—if so it is a pity there is not more of the animal in the rich. Assuredly I saw plenty of drunkenness, but certainly it never struck me that this was so general as it is said to be today—anyhow there was lots of poverty and wretchedness without this adjunct. Of course I thought a few doses of medicine did them a great deal of good and if the patient died—well—it was the will of God! And so these poor people believed—for depend on it they had a religion, at all events were not atheists. I suppose human beings are gregarious animals. Anyhow I think now that I did precious little good —for medicine without care and nursing and food must be worse than useless. Anyhow as I had to do with simple remedies only, they did not much harm anyhow and doubtless sometimes good. Of course I came across queer scenes and people, from play-actors to beggars and what not and like a boy had lots of talks with them which have served me in many things since, anyhow I have never forgotten the misery of poverty and still retain the kindly feeling for the sufferers. In many of these matters, it seemed that apparent poverty was owing to mismanagement. At all events two people working in the same factory or business would domestically be quite different—the house of one would be a scene of squalor, the other neat and tidy—the children of the one ragged and gutter-snipe, the other going to school—and mind both men should be sober and industrious—and the women too, but the one knew how to manage, the other not.

Of course I tumbled among the rich or highly respectable sometimes too—and once had to see Mark Lemon, but did not know his value,[1] but there was one gentleman named Olwyn [?], who lived in Alie Street whom I had to leech occasionally, and he would always talk of the last new opera or play—and then would always ask "Have you seen it yet—do you know so and so?" some celebrated danseuse. This to me a poor doctor's boy! He never had sense or kindness enough to give me a ticket! He was a good fellow, but withal eccentric. The poor actors on the other hand, would have given me plenty—but they could not and a pretty good job for me too.

My indentures were for five years; the details I do not know, for altho read, I have no recollection of them, but I received ten shillings per week, a sort of "board wages" and for other purposes—this money was put into the Savings Bank. Now the first three years were spent in much the same manner as related, but Mr. Healey had passed his examinations—had gone home to Hull, and married the lady on whose letter account I had received sundry sixpences. I never saw this lady—nor Healey again, but before he left I bought a little ornament in the shape of a sword and scabbard on which I had engraved "Forget me not." He had been very kind to me, but evidently I was a hobby-dehoy—the inscription proper would have been—"I will never forget you." He died a few years after my arrival in Victoria and his Memorial Card hung in my office for years; and would be there now, had someone not removed it. Henry Isaac Fotherby took Healey's position:[2] he being the nephew of Dr. Graves and belonged to Lincolnshire. His mother used to send him nice pork pies, particularly at Xmas and he gave me a share of these and other *iktas*[3] in the hamper. After a while Fotherby and I when we became accustomed to each other were fast friends and as you may see from the above was good to me. He assisted me too in my "Latin"—he was pious also and be-

[1]Mark Lemon (1809-70) was the first editor of *Punch*, holding that position from 1841 until his death.

[2]M. B., London, 1847; M.R.C.S., Eng., 1845; L.S.A., 1846. He went into partnership with his uncle, and on Dr. Graves's death in 1853 he inherited the practice (see Graves's will; and Fotherby to JSH, 14 August 1853 [HC]).

[3]A general purpose Chinook word, meaning "things," "goods," indeed almost any personal possession.

longed to a pious family—"Independents"—and as he had afterwards to attend lectures, I had benefit from this also, as well as the *Lancet* and other books of this class, that used to come periodically from a medical society (local) of neighbouring practitioners. Fotherby however, did not confine himself to this entirely, because when he wanted a holiday or a rest, he liked a novel and so did I. I had to go to a circulating library to get the book—deposit a guarantee, and on returning the book paid about two or three pence for the reading, but more if the novel were recent. As I had a great deal of spare time in the afternoon, I indulged in these occasionally too, and if interesting at night also, and I remember the time when reading some tragic story—particularly those in the *Diary of a Late Physician*, that I would be afraid to move off my stool and the gas light seemed to burn blue. I was impressible and curiously enough an exceedingly shy boy—this may seem strange, but in truth, I am even now shy excepting with those I know. There was a row about this book—it was wrong for any doctor to abuse the confidence of his patients and write their history said the critics—and then it turned out that it had not been written by a doctor, but by [Samuel] Warren a living lawyer! who afterwards wrote *Ten Thousand a Year*[1]—which we devoured also. Maryatt, Bulwer, Scott *et hoc genus omne* were devoured in time and some theological books too—but these were not so enticing. But now arose a furore in London—a furore perhaps never seen before or since, the advent of the *Pickwick Papers* by "Boz"—i.e. Charles Dickens.[2] How we used to wait for the day of the monthly number! As the clock struck, I had to post off to Cornhill to get the number, but always had to wait my turn, as there were hundreds as mad as ourselves to get the number as early as possible. How Fotherby gloated over it and how I caught the contagion! It turned out subsequently that Dickens was well known at Guy's Hospital.[3] He was not a student, but mixed with some of the students there (of course before my time)—these of course lived

---

[1]Samuel Warren (1807-77). *The Diary of a Late Physician* appeared in *Blackwood* between August 1836 and August 1837 and in collected form in 1838. *Ten Thousand a Year* appeared in parts between October 1839 and August 1841 and was published as a volume immediately after its conclusion in *Blackwood*.
[2]*The Posthumous Papers of the Pickwick Club* appeared in twelve monthly parts from April 1836 to November 1837 and as a volume in 1837, some time before the commencement of JSH's five-year apprenticeship as a medical pupil, which he appears to be describing here. He may have confused *Pickwick* with one of the novels, also issued in serial form, which succeeded it.
[3]Founded in Southwark by the bookseller Thomas Guy in 1721.

in the Boro[1]—Laut Street &c. Not very long after this, the City was placarded with Toot to Toot &c. This meant the advent of *Punch*[2] which came like a brilliant meteor and keeps up its light and brightness to this day, notwithstanding his many competitors.

After a while "Jerry Beale"[3] was added to the number of apprentices, but for some reason or other he left after a few months, which we did not regret. In his place came a young gentleman from Tredegar Square —a rather refined fastidious creature. He did not remain long—the discipline and work did not suit him or he them, I do not know which. He went and then came Fred Hodson and subsequently just when I left a young man whose name I forget, but who was brought to my remembrance by Mrs. Pinder.[4] Things went on in this style, our "Master" not interfering much with us—indeed it was unnecessary as we all did our duty faithfully—sometimes it is true with a little grumbling— but we had plenty and sometimes more than plenty work to do—at least I had at all events.

About this time Miss Graves,[5] an unmarried sister of Dr. Graves, appeared on the scene and became a resident in Alie Place. She was a good holy woman—thin-visaged, rather skinny—[an?] ascetic one who lived constantly not for this world but the next and whilst here for the church and parson—but I do not think Mrs. Graves and Miss Graves went to the same church, the former being a Churchwoman and the latter a Nonconformist—but as far as I know they did not openly quarrel about this or anything else. Miss Graves was a "dyspep-

[1]The part of Southwark immediately opposite the City is known as "The Borough."

[2]The first number was published on 17 July 1841. The magazine advertisements and handbills announcing the magazine began with the words "Too-to-tooit-tooit" (John W. Dodds, *The Age of Paradox: A Biography of England 1841-1851* [London: V. Gollancz, 1953], p. 49).

[3]In the 1841 census John Beal, aged sixteen, is listed as a surgeon's apprentice in the household of Dr. Graves.

[4]Presumably Anne Marie Henriette Devereux, daughter of Captain John Francis Walter Devereux, who brought his family from England to Victoria in 1863. She married William George Pinder in 1877, and both the Pinders and the Helmckens were members of the Church of Our Lord, the Reformed Episcopal Church in Victoria, established in 1875. "The young man whose name I forget" is probably to be identified with Henry Paul Cuff, listed in the 1851 census as a medical pupil in Dr. Graves's household, but the connection with Mrs. Pinder remains obscure.

[5]"My sister Ann Graves" received an annuity of eighty pounds under the terms of Dr. Graves's will. Dr. Graves's wife was also named Ann; and since only one Ann Graves is listed in the 1841 census, it would appear that Dr. Graves's sister did not join the household until after that date.

tic," suffering very frequently from "heartburn"—a concomitant of this complaint—not the heartburn common to young people. Magnesia relieved the heartburn, and so very frequently in the afternoon Miss Graves would come in and get me to mix her some magnesia and water and perhaps give me good advice. However one day I was wicked, mischievous or bored and so I impudently said to her, "Miss Graves, if you go on this way, when you die, you will turn, not to dust, but to magnesia!" She never spoke to me afterwards, but I have no remembrance of having a lecture from Master or Mistress about this. Somehow or other I had a faculty of making improper and intended-humorous remarks, which sticks to me to this day and which then as now were not well received sometimes, they being misunderstood!—they made bad friends and they called me impudent. I am sure I meant Miss Graves no harm! Poor woman she is dead now—but whether magnesia or dust has never been revealed. If I had known more of chemical changes, I should not have made the mistake. Anyhow it is dangerous to be humorous to an ascetic woman, and always well to avoid such remarks, save to people whom you know will swallow them and laugh. I fancy I acquired this abominable habit from novels and from an eccentric genius, the apprentice of Dr. Keely of Cowvent [Covent] Garden, who used occasionally to come to us, for Keely had been an apprentice with Dr. Graves years previously. Keely died of consumption. He had a very pretty sister, whom I admired—at a distance. The last I heard of Miss Keely was she married and went to New York and her husband engaged in the silk trade. Sweet girl—I think she died in America of consumption.

Bye and bye Mrs. Graves' brother came home from sea (invalided probably) and had a room given him at the top of the house. He was called Captain Rose, of H.M.S. something—had been on the coast of Africa—had been attacked with malarial fever and came home half dead with a diseased liver—the old story.[1] I had frequently to visit him upstairs, make up his medicines and so forth and so we became friendly, for he [had?] but few other visitors. Dr. Graves of course physicked him—put him on proper diet, but allowed neither wine nor alcohol—

---

[1]According to his death certificate, George Rose was not a captain but a "Lieutenant in the Royal Navy." He died of consumption at No. 4, Alie Place on 31 August 1840, aged thirty-eight. He is presumably to be identified with the George Rose who attained the rank of lieutenant on 10 August 1832 and commanded H.M.S. *Fair Rosamond*, Cape of Good Hope and Coast of Africa, from 29 May 1833 to some time between December 1836 and March 1837. He was in command of H.M.S. *Curlew*, on the same station, March-December 1839.

Graves did not take any himself and certainly ordered very little for patients. However one day Captain Rose said, "I do want a drink of beer my boy—can't you bring it?" "No it is contrary to orders, besides the bottle would be discovered"—however he at last persuaded—I relented —and became disobedient—for he said, "Put a drink of beer into a medicine bottle and label it—a wineglassful to be taken three times a day!" I did so, and he had his drink and enjoyed oh so much. Like an ass I did not take the bottle away, so when Master went to see him, he saw the bottle and said, "What's this? I never ordered a wineglassful to be taken &c."—and so the cat came out of the bag—and I got fits for the Doctor was very particular about treatment and would have obedience to his commands.

Anyhow in process of time the poor Captain died—and was kept I suppose the usually adopted week. During this time of solemn silence, a manservant made a noise going up and down stairs and then Mrs. Graves pounced out with solemn visage and told him he was making a noise sufficient to awaken the dead, on which the impudent fellow replied, "If I did waken him, you would be very sorry anyhow"!!!

The three years went on and during this period I saw London and its suburbs—for there can much be seen there for nothing—valuable sights too and what one sees with the eyes as or [*sic*] are lessons ever remembered, whether the lesson came from the British Museum or other institution. Reviews I saw not unfrequently, and at one Her Majesty and Prince Albert in Hyde Park.[1] Her Majesty was a slim pale-faced young lady on horseback, Prince Albert a delicate-looking young man. I saw them very frequently afterwards and in process of time the Royal children, who often were at Buckingham Palace—at the windows too, like other children. At Woolwich were reviews at which real shot and shell were fired across the river. Among the notables remembered were Marshal Soult—Ibraham Pasha[2] and the Duke of Wellington. The house of the latter I went to see after the windows had been smashed by a London mob—and saw the iron shutters over them afterwards. I believe these shutters were never opened after.[3]

---

[1]Victoria had married her cousin Prince Albert on 10 February 1840.
[2]Nicholas Soult (1769-1851), marshal of France, was minister of war (1830-34) and prime minister (1840-44). He was ambassador extraordinary to London in 1838. Ibrahim Pasha (1789-1848) was commander of the Egyptian army under his father, Mehemet Ali, and governor of Cilicia and Syria, 1833-39.
[3]The Duke of Wellington was unpopular with the London mob because of his opposition to the Reform Bill which was finally passed in 1832. The windows of Apsley House were broken on 27 April 1831, although the body of the Duchess,

As I grew older so I suppose I became proud or conceited like any other growing-up cub. I no longer liked carrying the flapped wicker basket, but would put the bottles of medicine, pills and powders in my various pockets. It is true this rumpled them a little and possibly did not look quite so clean and tidy as when they came out of the surgery, but neither the Master (who probably knew nothing about it) nor my fellow apprentices Fotherby and Hodson made any objection and indeed but little could be urged. As far as dress is concerned, I cared very little about this, excepting on Sunday—and then possibly only because I was going to church—but when Graves gave me some of his white trowsers—and they were made of awfully nice stuff—I must needs have them made up, and naturally wore them in very early spring, when the weather was in reality cold, so the little boys used to call out "Ducks want water!" This of course annoyed me, and put an end to the ducks. My hair too would be stiff and would not down—this annoyed me too sometimes; the fact is I did not know how to dress and secondly, if I had known, the money did not exist to meet the desideratum. As I said before, we boys were all brought up to be hardy and so became accustomed to changes of weather—the wonder is, it did not kill some of us, but not one of the eight died, so my mother knew more about it than we did. Anyhow I have since learned in this country that people who live in the open and rough it, are not so much affected with changes of temperature, but much depends on the individual— too much care is as injurious as too little.

By this time I had settled down to routine as far as practicable— lots of work outside and in from school in the morning until 9 or 10 or even later at night, but the afternoons were a "slack period" and were spent in reading and study, save when I was otherwise busy, with pills and tinctures of which enormous quantities were used. I had become in fact a very good "Chemist and Druggist" and made chemical experiments and cold cream lip salve and what not for young ladies and put them into very very [*sic: for* pretty?] porcelain boxes for presents—colored hair oils into the bargain. But on one occasion I must needs try to make musk by means of nitric acid and oil of amber mixed together—the book was not explicit enough—so after a while the mixture exploded and flew over the office and paint, spoiling the latter,

---

who had died three days earlier, was still lying there, and they were broken again on 12 October. Wellington left them unmended and later put up iron shutters, which remained until his own death in 1852.

which had been newly laid on. The place had musk enough in it, so I opened all the windows but it would not down! To cap the climax "Master" came in—he was angry, and gave me a long lecture about the danger of my dabbling in these dangerous experiments. The lecture had a good effect in making me more careful, but at this time I had a sort of craze for practical chemistry, using Parkes[1] and other easy authors.— They stood me in good stead afterwards—but self-knowledge was as nothing when compared with the practical instruction I had afterwards at the Guy's Hospital. Fotherby who now attended the chemical and junior classes at the Hospital, would give me hints, but Hodson knew less about it than myself—in fact he being the junior I had to teach him. There was then a change from three or four years previously, when I knew nothing save how to carry around medicine bottles. We all got on well together, for I knew my position and did not presume much—in fact I was always bashful and about as green as it is possible for a cub to be—I had neither bad habits nor bad company—indeed precious little of the latter, save those in the house and at home. Sometimes Master took me to drive with him—i.e. to keep the horse Jack whilst he went in to see patients—Jack was not a very domestic creature. One day a fellow came along striking the bell of a clock, and calling out "Clocks to mend!"—Jack not liking it backed and would back until he backed into a shop window, and smashed the glass and the front. He was a fine Yorkshire gray, but had a temper, yet was the favorite horse—there were two others. One day we were alarmed at seeing Mrs. & Mr. Graves come home in a dilapidated condition in a hack. Jack had run away on the Mile End Road, a jolly good place to drive, had come into contact with something and pitched Mrs. Graves into a huge vat of water, which stood in front of an inn to water horses—the Governor followed suit!! They were bruised and shaken up and so was the buggy, but the horse remained the favorite. Master never had any horses of his own, but contracted for them with an "inn keeper" who kept one of the old-style and old-fashioned "inns" near Aldgate—I think it was called the Bull—one of the kind that Dickens liked to talk about, and might have had its Sam Weller. James was coachman, and he married the cook—in a hurry—and they were happy afterwards nevertheless and notwithstanding—James was as faithful and industrious as

---

[1]Samuel Parkes (1761-1825), a manufacturing chemist in London, published various manuals of chemistry between 1806 and 1825 for which he was honoured by learned societies.

any man could be and came from a village near Plaistow, where old Cobbley lived. Tom Cobbley used to drive a bull and waggon to London every week and was as well known as the moon! His parents were of the old style of yeoman—an almost extinct race. They were very simple honest and kind. James had been years with Dr. Graves and remained with him until his death, and when this took place it was found that Dr. Graves had left him a pension for life[1]—this shows the character of Dr. Graves. Mrs. Graves had nothing to do with James—and never saw the stables in Buckley [Buckle] Street!

Now there comes a change. Dr. Graves removed from Alie Place to Tower Hill Trinity Square.[2] At this time the ditch around the Tower and the drawbridges existed, and the pump existed which boasted of supplying the best water in the whole of London. I remember when a little boy the great fire at the Tower of London[3]—I saw it—Heavens what crowds of people there were! Afterwards what mementos in the shape of [melted metals?] and so forth. Of course I learned all about the Tower afterwards—the "beefeaters," the drill and so forth, but the most delightful of all, were the drums and fifes going the rounds in the evening—I love drums and fifes still! At this time salutes used to be fired from the Tower on such occasions as Gunpowder Plot—Battle of Waterloo—birthdays and what not. These have been put an end to because the shocks broke numberless windows! The truth is England wanted to be friends with the French and the Roman Catholics. For some reason or other Trinity Square was the great rendezvous in the evening on Guy Fawkes Day—boys and men assembling there, having a little bonfire, and sending off rockets—Roman candles, blue lights, squibs, crackers and so forth by wholesale. In fact it was a carnival, impromptu, thousands went there for fun, always with bad clothes on, for ten to one you would find a cracker banging and jumping about in your pocket, or a cracker or squib fastened to the tail of your coat

---

[1]This passage remains obscure. In Dr. Graves's will, the only legacy to anyone outside the family is an annuity of forty pounds to "my servant William Pope." No William Pope is listed in the household in either the 1841 or the 1851 census, and there is no reference in either census to James [Cobbley?].

[2]Dr. Graves is listed in the directory at No. 4, Alie Place in 1845, but in 1846 the occupant was John Liddle, surgeon (cf. p. 44 below). According to the 1851 census, Dr. Graves was then living at No. 39, Trinity Square, in a precinct of the Tower without the City, in the district of Whitechapel, but it was at No. 40, **Trinity Square** that he died in 1853 (London *Times*, 29 June 1853).

[3]JSH's reference to "melted metals [?]" would appear to indicate that this was the spectacular fire of 1842 in which the Armoury or Great Storehouse was destroyed. But JSH was eighteen years of age at that time, not "a little boy."

and alive at this! Of course Tower Hill was a memorable place, and I suppose this led to its being the place on the Fifth of November—handed down from antiquity—"Pope" day I hear is dying out—what fun we little boys used to have on this day! We knew precious little why we carried the "Pope" with a foolscap on and covered with tinsel—an effigy, but if we happened to meet a lot of Roman Catholic boys—Whoop! There was a fight and if we got off with our "Pope" all right, we cared little for a black eye or a bruise or two! Of course the "Pope" was burned at night—usually hanging him too! The crowd used to look on at the fight and cheer, clap hands and so forth, but occasionally there was a contagious row among the men too. Anyhow people used to give their pennies and so forth, and as England was then more Protestant and did not have priests about the streets, the Protestants had the best of it and the pennies too. The people who fought were Irish and these were by no means popular—Protestants and Catholics could not fully tolerate each other! Possibly the R.C. Emancipation Act[1] had to do with this. Of course what I relate about "Popes" happened when I was a schoolboy—a Lutheran at this. But here we are in Trinity Square—Fotherby, Hodson and your humble servant. The change of place made at first little difference to me save that it made me walk from home there instead of across the street.

The time soon came for me to attend the Hospital—this was allowed. It would have been more convenient for me and my duties to attend London Hospital, but Fotherby having been a student at Guy's, Guy's took my fancy and in fact was thought and no doubt at this time correctly to be the better educational institute.[2] Fotherby who was a hard worker had already become a full-fledged medico, was working now for the M.B. of the University of London—the stiffest of the stiff examinations. He passed with honor.

Well the question now came—where's the money to come from to pay the fees of the Hospital and Medical School, which I think I commenced at the summer sessions.[3] Well, owing to the care of Mother,

[1]Passed in 1829. An Act for the Relief of His Majesty's Roman Catholic subjects (10 Geo. 4, c.7).
[2]The London Hospital was in Whitechapel Road, on the same side of the Thames as JSH's home in Great Alie Street. Guy's was on the south side of the river, across London Bridge (see Plate 2).
[3]JSH registered for the first time on 2 October 1844, for the winter session. A summary of the requirements at that time will be found in *Guy's Hospital 1725-1948*, ed. Hujohn A. Ripman (London: Guy's Hospital Gazette Committee, 1951), p. 62: "To qualify for the examination admitting to the membership of the Royal

I had now a considerable sum in the Savings Bank, so this became available for the purpose and quite sufficient for the time being. At this time too I went to Apothecaries' Hall and passed the "little go"[1]— that is to say Latin and the usual English subjects, but Latin, I think was the only subject of importance, and as usual I had a dispute with the examiner—he said such a word was an adjective—and I maintained it to be an adverb, but had sense enough to acknowledge him to be right and beg pardon. The Latin in this case was a translation of *De Morbo Regio* of Celsus. However, I passed all right, and so dropped Latin then and I think for ever—I doubt whether I have ever bothered with it since and so have really forgotten all I once knew. This passing left me free of this classical incumbrance.

Attendance at lectures after this occupied the greater part of the day, so I really became useless save for the evening—and carrying out medicines, which, having become proud, I no longer liked to do. Dr. Graves then agreed—and perhaps wished that I should be free—and probably the period of my apprenticeship had been satisfied. Of course my "pay," which had become greater now ceased—a rather awkward circumstance, but my money had not yet run out and as I boarded and lodged at home, the expense was not very great. Mother said I should have what was necessary anyhow, and nothing more. So I was a poor student without pocket money. I really at first felt very small among the other better-off students and could not engage in their various clubs and amusements—indeed they soon knew me to be poor and so did not bother me—but never treated me rudely. I worked very hard and as birds of a feather flocked together, became associated with hard-working

---

College of Surgeons, the student must have spent six years in the profession (including three winter and two summer sessions at a teaching hospital) and he was required to attend three courses of lectures in anatomy, two in surgery, two in medicine, two in midwifery, two in chemistry, one in materia medica, and two courses of dissections and anatomy demonstrations." The Pupils' Lecture Book confirms that JSH took the courses listed above and also courses in botany and medical jurisprudence. Until the introduction of the common fee in 1846, the student paid a fee for hospital practice (which varied according to whether he entered as a dresser, a surgical pupil, or a medical pupil) and separate fees for each lecture class. In 1846 the fees were set at "£40 for a year, £40 for a second year, and £10 for every succeeding year of attendance" (*Guy's Hospital Reports*, 2nd series, 5 [1847]). It is not possible to determine from the records the precise sum that JSH paid for his first two years; he seems to have paid £10 for each of the last two; and the total was certainly in the neighbourhood of £100.

[1]This colloquial name for a preliminary examination is still current at Cambridge for the first examination for the B.A. degree.

students, of whom there were a large number, many of whom have since arrived at eminence. Work and study united us and as such we received the respect and approbation of the Professors and I became well known, because at the end of the session I went in for honors and gained the silver medal in Practical Chemistry and something in Materia Medica.[1] This success made me a marked student—what I lacked in money was made up by celebrity. However, now I think working for a prize in any particular subject may be injurious because such work and precious hard work it is leads to neglect of other equally important subjects. However Chemistry and Materia Medica were important and stood me in very good stead then and all my life since. The course of study occupied and could not be less than four years. I had now been broken in and knew the ropes. My chemical craze got me into scrapes at home—often on Sundays I would perform chemical analyses and so forth when the rest were in church. On returning they would find the house filled with sulphuretted hydrogen or some other sweet-smelling abomination! A doctor had taken Graves' house in Alie Place and as the windows of his house were opposite to mine, he used to see me at my devilment, as he supposed, but he was never friendly and I have forgotten who or what he was.[2]

There has been much talk lately of Darwinism. Well I heard the most of this at our botanical lectures for Aikin was a philosopher![3] A

[1]JSH's memory appears to be at fault here. The prize list at the end of the 1844-45 winter session (*Guy's Hospital Reports,* 2nd series, 3 [1845]:324), gives him the first prize for Practical Chemistry and the second prize for Materia Medica. On display in Helmcken House, JSH's original dwelling in Victoria, now an historic site, is a copy of Alfred S. Taylor's *A Manual of Medical Jurisprudence* (London: John Churchill, 1844), inscribed as follows: "Prize for Practical Chemistry, /Awarded April 1845/ to/Mr. J. S. Helmcken/ Ar Aiken/ Alfred S. Taylor / Guy's Hospital/ May 12, 1845." The Provincial Archives has a silver medal (see Plate 6) awarded to JSH "ob solertiam in studiis therapeuticis laudatum 1845." At this time there were "fifteen subjects for which Gold or Silver medals or prizes of instruments or books were provided" (H. C. Cameron, *Mr. Guy's Hospital* [London: Longmans Green, 1954], p. 227). Presumably this silver medal is the "something in materia medica" to which JSH refers, i.e., the second prize.
[2]Dr. John Liddle. See above, p. 41n2.
[3]Arthur Aikin (1773-1854) was a Fellow of the Linnaean Society and a pioneer of the Geological Society, 1807. He published a manual of mineralogy and several papers in the *Chemical Dictionary* and gave a course in chemistry at Guy's from 1821 to 1851. For further information see the article in Samuel Wilks and G. T. Bettany, *A Biographical Dictionary of Guy's Hospital* (London: Ward, Lock, Bowden and Co., 1892), where will be found information on most of JSH's teachers at Guy's.

clever but old and bald-pated man. However, he illustrated the whole theory by plates and so forth. Darwin, with his extraordinary industry, patience, experiments and extraordinary observation went far ahead perfecting the theory. At this time too *The Vestiges of Creation*[1] made its appearance and geology was no longer a very crude prohibited science. Of course the infallible and inspired Bible was brought to bear against the innovations then as now, but we did not suppose the Bible to be a scientific work. Aikin took us on botanical excursions, we travelled mostly the districts between Woolwich and Erith seeking plants, asking questions or having pointed out special things. Aikin was a good walker, but goodness gracious how the flies used to bother his poor head—they made a dead set at him and left us free. The end of the journey usually was Erith—at a very nice little public inn—here we used to feed— and some would take to skittles and so forth and beer, returning by the steamboats in the evening. Aikin was a very clever man—but not a good lecturer for boys—and occasionally we pelted him with paper pellets! Wicked! Aikin and Taylor were our Chemical instructors and also of Medical Jurisprudence. Alfred Taylor achieved a wide world reputation.[2]— Aikin—I know not what he followed—both were enthusiasts in their different hobbies—and they gave me my first prizes.

Now comes on the second session—the work becomes harder and harder—Anatomy—Medicine—Surgery and so forth—but work seems to be my natural bent—I have nothing to do now save my studies.

[Volume II]

Now the second session comes on [1845-46]—the study and work becomes harder and harder, the subjects more numerous—Anatomy, Medicine, Surgery, but as I had now nothing to do but attend to my studies, things were not so bad, for to work I was accustomed. Dr. Barlow was my master and Bransby Cooper ditto,[3] that is to say attached

---

[1]Published in 1844 by Robert Chambers (1802-71), the Edinburgh author and, with his brother William, publisher of *Chambers' Encyclopedia*.

[2]According to *Guy's Hospital Reports*, 2nd series, 2 (1844), the course in chemistry was given by "Mr. A. Aikin & Mr. A. Taylor" during the session commencing 1 October; the course in medical jurisprudence was given by Mr. A. Taylor only, during the summer session commencing 1 May. Alfred Swaine Taylor (1806-80) was professor of medical jurisprudence at Guy's 1831-77 and lecturer on chemistry 1832-70. He was a recognized authority on medico-legal questions and in 1842 published his *Manual of Medical Jurisprudence*. This reached its tenth English edition in 1879 and appeared also in numerous American editions.

[3]George Hilaro Barlow (1806-66) was assistant physician at Guy's 1840-43 and full physician 1843-66. He was the first editor of *Guy's Hospital Reports* and president of the Clinical Report Society. Bransby B. Cooper (1792-1853), the nephew

to them by routine or something. At the end of the session I gained a prize for something[1]—I forget at this moment the subject.

During the summer [of 1845], we had to attend lectures once or twice a week at Chelsea, 8 o'clock in the morning.[2] This was rather steep as we had to walk, the boats not running early enough, nor omnibuses either. After lectures some returned by [*sic*] others adjourned to have a game at billiards or what not, for students of all the schools in London attended, indeed had to attend, these botanical lectures. The gardens were large; nearly all the medicinal plants cultivated therein, so we became acquainted with them at all events, but there was also a botanical garden attached to Guy's where specimens of medicinal plants grew, more however for the professors than students. Dr. Lindley was the Professor and Lecturer at Chelsea—and always pronounced *Hyoscyamus* with a K.[3] Some years after my arrival in Victoria, Mrs. Crease told me Dr. Lindley was her father and that she had drawn many or most of the pictures of plants &c. described in his many botanical works![4] The world is small. In these gardens grew

---

of Sir Astley Paston Cooper, had served as a midshipman and as an army assistant surgeon during the Peninsular Wars before entering the civilian practice of medicine. He was appointed assistant surgeon at Guy's in 1825 and was surgeon to the hospital at the time of his death.

[1]The prize list for the session 1845-46 (*Guy's Hospital Reports*, 2nd series, 4 [1846]: 498) shows that he received "Dr. Barlow's Testimonial," under "Honorary Distinctions awarded by the Clinical Society," and an honorary medical certificate for the winter session 1845-46.

[2]The regular course in botany was a "Summer Course, Daily, at Half-past Eleven [with] Occasional Botanical Excursions." The Chelsea Physic Garden, founded as the garden of the Society of Apothecaries in 1676, was notable for its cultivation of foreign plants. The first cedar of Lebanon to be grown in Britain was planted here in 1683, and cotton seeds from this garden were sent to America in 1732. To reach Chelsea from his home in Great Alie Street, JSH must have had to walk at least five miles.

[3]John Lindley, F.R.S., was professor of botany in the University of London 1829-60 and lecturer on botany to the Apothecaries' Company 1836-53. The British species of the plant mentioned is *Hyoscyamus niger* or henbane, a poisonous narcotic plant. JSH apparently introduced it to Vancouver Island, for Dr. A. R. Benson wrote to him from Fort Victoria, 10 August 1850: "Hyoscyamus I have not got, with the exception of two plants in the garden from your seeds" (HC). For Benson see below, p. 49n1.

[4]Sarah, afterwards Lady Crease (1826-1922), was the wife of Henry Pering Pellew Crease, who was appointed attorney-general of British Columbia in 1861. Some of the water-colour sketches she painted soon after her arrival in Vancouver Island were shown anonymously in the London Exhibition of 1862 and certain of these were used, again anonymously, as the basis of illustrations in R. C. Mayne, *Four Years in British Columbia and Vancouver Island* (London: J. Murray, 1862). The originals are now in the Provincial Archives of British Columbia.

real Cedars of Lebanon—large trees—either the seeds or plants had been brought from the East by the Crusaders or were said to have been brought.

The third session comes on [1846-47] and oh the work! Lectures at 8 o'clock in the morning—Midwifery—and three or four more during the day, dissecting or in the wards the rest of the time. By this time I was a clerk to Dr. Barlow—had to write down every case under his care[1]—at the entrance fully—family history and all—examine the urine, microscopically and otherwise—we had the affix P.B. to our names— Piss Boilers. Making out these reports would keep me often until one or two o'clock in the morning. At the end of the session I received the prize of the Medical Society for the best medical reports.[2]

During the summer [1846] I had Dr. Golding Bird's children's wards (Miriam)[3] and had to report his cases in a similar manner—however it was a pleasure to have the children's wards—the Sister being an elderly lady "who had seen better days." She was real nice. Bird, poor fellow, was a victim of acute rheumatism—crippled all over—with

[1]Some of JSH's case books belonging to his period of study at Guy's Hospital are in the Helmcken Collection. The writing is often illegible and very few entries are dated by year, but they would seem to fall between 24 September 1845 and 23 January 1847. The reports are characterized as "thorough and painstaking" by a modern physician, Honor M. Kidd, *Pioneer Doctor John Sebastian Helmcken* [the William Osler Medal Essay], *Bulletin of the History of Medicine* 21 (July-August 1947) :425.

[2]JSH must be still thinking of Dr. Barlow's Testimonial, awarded to him in 1846, at the end of his second session (see above, p. 46), for in the 1847 prize list Mr. J. Hinton was awarded "Dr. Barlow's Prizes for best Medical Reports," and Mr. D. Hooper was awarded "Dr. Key's Prize for best Surgical Reports."

[3]This reference remains obscure. Golding Bird (1814-54) was lecturer on natural philosophy 1836-53 and assistant physician at Guy's 1843-53, and he did establish a children's ward. But according to Cameron (*Mr. Guy's Hospital*, pp. 136 and 357), it was not until 1848 that he opened a special ward for children in one of the old houses in Sutton Street which was demolished in 1852. It was the custom at Guy's to name the wards after the various virtues or after Biblical characters, but there appears to be no evidence that there was ever a children's ward called Miriam. In 1835 Miriam Ward had eighteen beds for female patients (see the plan of the hospital, ibid., p. 112) ; in 1860 John and Miriam were clinical wards (ibid., p. 201) ; and in modern times, male medical wards (Ripman, *Guy's Hospital*, p. 148). It may be noted however that when the children's ward was closed in 1852 "the cots were then distributed in the various women's wards, ... where the services of women patients could be utilized in their nursing and care" (Cameron, *Mr. Guy's Hospital*, p. 357). It is possible that this same practice was being followed by Dr. Golding Bird before he was able to establish in 1848 a ward restricted to children and that Miriam, if not a children's ward, was a women-and-children's ward as early as 1846. But it must be noted that there appears to be no reference to Miriam in the case books mentioned in note 1 above. JSH's female patients are in wards called Charity or Lydia.

heart disease into the bargain. A brilliant man, with black intelligent eyes—looking very often over his spectacles. He lessoned me too in urine examinations—in fact learned a great deal from him about this disease of the children and other matters. He was friendly and took me one day to see a patient in the ward. By simply staring at her she became cataleptic—and could be put into the most difficult and grotesque positions. After he recovered her, she knew nothing of the matter. I never saw him do this but once. At this time I knew little—tho mesmerism was talked about, accompanied with Dr. Elliottson [Elliotson] and the Miss Okeys who (the latter) turned out to be frauds.[1] If I had known then as much as I do now, she would have been interesting.

Dr. Barlow was a very unassuming man—without brilliancy but great thoughtfulness—rather careless about dress. He took me once to make a post-mortem—the lady had died of peritonitis. Poor woman she was lying on a plank—in a very nicely carpeted room. Barlow believed she died of rupture of something internal—but I know he was particular about appendix vermiformis and ovary. Anyhow I do not know what his realization was, but by some unfortunate occurrence, the body turned over and all the semipurulent fluid, of which there was a large quantity flooded the carpet. I was glad to get out of the house!

[1]John Elliotson (1791-1868), professor of the theory and practice of medicine at the University of London 1831-38 and one of the founders of University College Hospital, began experiments with mesmerism in the hope of relieving the pain of major surgery, for which no anaesthetic had yet been found. In 1838 he gave public demonstrations in mesmerism in the hospital theatre, using as his chief subjects two young girls, his patients, Elizabeth and Jane Okey. Almost at once charges of imposture were made, and the hospital committee requested Elliotson to give no more demonstrations in public. But he continued to experiment on his patients, and the general council then instructed the committee to put a stop altogether to the practice of mesmerism within the hospital. Elliotson at once sent in his resignation. A few years later he established a mesmeric hospital and a journal of mesmeric healing, *The Zoist*. As to whether or not "the Miss Okeys . . . turned out to be frauds" as JSH asserts, the editor of the *Lancet* in 1838 thought so, and his views appear to have been generally accepted by the medical profession, which maintained its intolerance towards mesmerism and "its obstinate rejection of the cumulative evidence of the relief from pain" for a considerable time (Frank Podmore, *Mesmerism and Christian Science* [London: Methuen, 1909], p. 134). On the other hand, George Sandby, *Mesmerism and its Opponents: with a Narrative of Cases* (London: Longman, Brown, Green, and Longmans, 1844), asserts emphatically that "these two sister-patients of Dr. Elliotson were not imposters" (p. 155); and Robert W. Marks, *The Story of Hypnotism* (New York: Prentice-Hall, 1947) considers that Elliotson's "contribution to the scientific extension of hypnotism was enormous. Although he had no insight into its essential nature, he was far ahead of his contemporaries in sensing its therapeutic importance" (p. 73).

Again he took me to a post-mortem of a man who had died of heart disease; the people being very unwilling. Barlow's hobby was heart and chest. A man was put to watch that we did not take anything away; he happened to be away for a minute—perhaps I got him away designedly and then slipped the heart into my hind pocket. After leaving the house I had to cross London Bridge to get to Guy's; on my road, a gentleman stopped me and said, "You must have broken a bottle in your pocket—for it is dripping behind"—this was blood from this heart! I made some answer—had a great fright. How I got to the Hospital, I know not, but I did get there and handed the trophy to Dr. Barlow—the heart was almost as big as that of an ox. Barlow afterwards took me to a meeting of the Medical Society—and when there asked me to give the details of a case—heart of course—but I could not say a word save that I was not accustomed to speaking. So Barlow did it. I say I was always timid and bashful before strangers—could not walk up the aisle of a church without bent head not looking to right or left.

It was during this session that I became acquainted with Benson.[1] Rather a sloven, had been a captain of a vessel, and so nicknamed the Commodore.[2] I remember Bransby Cooper asking Benson to read the report of some surgical case, at the bedside. Benson was not a good reader and Cooper recommended him to mind his stops!

Ash[3] was here also, a hard-working clever man, noted for his short sight, tremendous breadth of shoulder and chest and—short temper. A very sensible companion, well read, when in good humour, but if in a bad one—keep clear.

Richardson from Toronto was here also,[4] and a little notable for

---

[1]Alfred Robson Benson, M.R.C.S., the first medical officer at Fort Victoria (see below, p. 81). For further biographical information see J. T. Walbran, *British Columbia Coast Names 1592-1906* (Ottawa: Government Printing Bureau, 1909).

[2]Cf. JSH to the editor of the *Nanaimo Free Press*, 7 January 1891: ". . . Benson and I were college chums—he was called 'Commodore' and I 'Baron.' We again met in Victoria in March, 1850."

[3]John Ash (c. 1823-86) followed JSH to Victoria in 1862 and was a fellow-member of the Legislative Assembly of Vancouver Island, 1865-66. See below, pp. 192-93, and for further biographical details see the obituary in the Victoria *Colonist*, 18 April 1886.

[4]James Henry Richardson (1823-1910), M.R.C.S., Eng., 1847, was the first graduate in medicine at the University of Toronto and professor of anatomy there for over fifty years. For further details see W. Canniff, *The Medical Profession in Upper Canada* (Toronto: W. Briggs, 1894), pp. 575-77, and the obituary in the Toronto *Globe*, 17 January 1910.

being a Canadian, a hard worker and of a very enquiring mind. He and Dr. Gull[1] were friendly. The three above mentioned, I met in Victoria subsequently, Benson being my predecessor in Victoria. Ash I met in Wells Fargo's during the excitement;[2] he settled in Victoria. Richardson I saw last summer (1891) when he came to visit his son, the Surgeon of the Jubilee Hospital.[3] Nearly half a century before we had been students together—and now each so much changed as to be past recognition at first—but remembered by some peculiar circumstance.

After the summer session [of 1846], I had a vacation, being pretty well used up—and so with a small knapsack started on my journey to Southampton, by taking a new and unfinished steamboat to the Isle of Wight—no comfort and lots of sea-sickness. A couple of students were on board—one a consumptive going to Torquay, then a sort of fashionable place for this incurable complaint. After travelling on foot over the Isle, I took boat to Southampton, where our Aunt Caroline lived.[4] I arrived there penniless, and had not had any breakfast in consequence. The Hotel at Ryde had fleeced me by high charges and so had their runners[?]. I never saw so many pretty women again assembled as those on the pier at Ryde. Well Aunty who lived below Bar,[5] gave me a room, but oh—when night came on, the bugs! They came in regiments from ceiling, wall and floor—how they did bite and when crushed what a horrible fragrance! So I left the candle burning for "they did not like the light"—I was told all old Southampton was over-

---

[1]William Withey Gull (1816-90) entered Guy's as a student in 1837 and after a brilliant scholastic career was attached to the hospital in various posts (according to *Guy's Hospital Reports*, he was lecturer in natural philosophy in JSH's time), until in 1846 he was appointed to the chair of physiology and in 1858 as a full physician to the hospital. Outstanding as a clinical physician, he was created a baronet in 1872 and appointed Physician Extraordinary to the Queen.

[2]Wells, Fargo & Co. established an office in Victoria in July 1858 (*Victoria Gazette*, 17 July 1858), but JSH must mean the Cariboo rather than the Fraser River gold "excitement," for according to Ash's obituary, he did not arrive in Victoria until 1862.

[3]William Augustus Richardson (1861?-1946) was appointed resident medical officer at the Royal Jubilee Hospital when it opened on 20 May 1890 (Herbert H. Murphy, *Royal Jubilee Hospital 1858-1958* [Victoria: Hebden Printing, 1958], p. 44) and held the post with distinction until his departure to seek his fortune in the Klondike (*Colonist*, 30 July 1897).

[4]Caroline Mittler, daughter of Sebastian Mittler and sister of JSH's mother. Subsequently she returned to London and by the time of the 1861 census she was part of the household of her brother-in-law Ludwig Fincken. She died on 8 October 1871, aged fifty-nine years.

[5]Since Bar Gate is the old north gate of the city, it would appear that Aunt Caroline lived between it and the sea. On modern maps the street leading from Bar Gate into the London road is called "Above Bar Street."

run with the same pest. In a day or two I set off on foot for Portsmouth, some eighteen miles away—and arriving there I had a look at the *Victory*, a very small ship even then, but now—Whew!—a nothing. Of course I looked at the plate in the deck, Here Nelson fell, and generally speaking I saw everything there—and this was not very much. Now it was time [to?] return—evening coming on and I meant to return by railway, but lo and behold, by some means or other the money had disappeared and so I had to walk back to Southampton—arriving there at midnight, awfully tired. Aunty was alarmed and supposed me lost or dead, of course. A day or two afterwards I footed it to Winchester—to see colours presented to a regiment. Saw also the inside and out of the Cathedral and wandered about until time to walk home again. In this way I visited all sorts of places here and hereabouts—Netley and afterwards found my way to Salisbury, Brighton and what not mostly on foot. By the time I returned to London I had become active, strong and sunburnt.

At Southampton "Bar" there were two figures of griffins guarding it—some wretch one Sunday morning painted an unmentionable part scarlet. When people got about the streets, there was consternation; and how to get rid of the trouble before people walked to church, so that the disfigurement would not be discovered, was the problem! What device they adopted, I do not know, but everyone knew of the misdeed and avoided the "Bar" even when fig leaves had been applied.

In these days, students, between the summer and winter sessions, would make small parties of two three or four for tramping, in fact tramping was considered the best remedy for recuperation. In this way large portions of England were traversed—her scenery, places of historical interest or what not enjoyed. To walk fifteen or twenty miles in a day became quite an easy matter—i.e. weather permitting. This was generally supposed be a very cheap method of travelling—but experience did not confirm the theory. Anyhow for enjoyment and seeing scenery and so forth, modern travelling conveniences cannot at all compare with tramping—when one is young. People nowadays seem to be globe-trotters quite neglecting the beauties and wonders they have near home. Those who do both will know most—and England will compare very very favourably with other places—England is a garden—and has rough country and mountains enough too.

Now the third session opens[1]—work increases—but what have I to

---

[1]i.e., the winter session which opened on 1 October 1846.

do but work? In this one becomes almost automatic, when there is an object in view—and had not I one! Bransby Cooper becomes my chief—a good kind-hearted man, who gave me one or two lectures about my deportment. I have now to write reports of all cases under their charge—histories past and present—really long ones, in which patients make many confessions. Now I would often be up until one o'clock in the morning, writing out these documents, for they became the statistics of the Hospital. Gas or a common candle served me— with a cup or two of coffee or tea. Off again at 8 A.M. to lecture and so the days went on. Lots of dissecting—no antiseptics then, but every body maggoty and the stench awful, indeed we [be]came so soddened with the smell, that anyone could detect us yards & yards away, and yet we knew it not ourselves! Anyhow I cut myself over and over again, when this occurred I like other students put the cut finger into my mouth, covered the finger was with putridity—but this did not matter. Anyhow I never received any injury from dissecting wounds, but a couple of students died during the session from this cause. I know now and did not know then, neither did anyone else, how dangerous our contaminated bodies were to others—in the wards or elsewhere I am quite certain now that I saw more than one death caused by this.

At this time I had to do also with the post-mortem theatre under Wilkinson King.[1] He was an enthusiast, but phthisical. Here all the surgeons and physicians came to see the end of their cases, to verify their diagnosis and so forth, and so learned much from their conversation. They all insisted on the necessity and desirability of students attending post-mortems—and learn there the errors or correctness of diagnosis.

Addison at this time was undoubtedly the Physician of the Hospital[2] —a very handsome tall robust noble-looking man, whom the students followed as tho he were a God. What he said was law—I never knew him mistaken in diagnosis—and this is what he chiefly cared about. The treatment he would leave to his clerks, first asking them what they would do! He walked through the wards like a noble or king, but was

[1]Thomas Wilkinson King (1811-47) had great intellectual powers but did not live long enough to become famous, for he died of pulmonary disease before he was forty. He was curator of the museum and demonstrator of morbid anatomy at Guy's.

[2]Thomas Addison (1793-1860), the discoverer of "Addison's disease" and author of various important medical works, was assistant physician at Guy's 1824-37 and physician, 1837-60. For many years he was the leading light of Guy's, but he was compelled to retire from the hospital because of threatened brain disease.

a little brusque. Notwithstanding his undoubted talent, I do not think he had a very large practice—why or wherefore I know not—poor man, after I had been here a few years I learned he jumped from a window high above ground, in a fit of insanity and was killed. He was a noble man, but he did give me a scolding. Once I disputed at the *bedside* about the diagnosis. Addison did not say anything, but after his rounds had been gone through, he went as usual to the clinical room to make clinical remarks and it so happened about this particular case, and there in the midst of the lecture before all the students, he gave me such a scolding—not for differing, but for daring to discuss anything at the bedside of the patient—such discussions should always be in private. I blushed and felt very small, but the truth is he was giving the students a lecture as to their behaviour in practice, poor I being the text. A few days after, he invited me and three or four other clerks to breakfast—cold grouse were served—but there wasn't one of us who knew how to carve them—the Doctor laughed at our inability to "dissect" a grouse, and so ordered the serving-man to carve them at a side table. Cooper however gave his clinical assistants nice dinners—and good-natured he was then.

At this time I almost lived in the wards—that is to say when not at lectures—so became well acquainted with the "Sisters," of whom there was one to each ward, living in a couple of rooms at the end thereof. These Sisters taught us a great deal and one student would ask another to lend him a hand in putting up a fracture or dressing a stump &c.—in fact we had to do everything in readiness for the Surgeon or Physician, who would praise or blame as the case required. Hilton, however, was perhaps the most particular.[1] If a bandage were not just so or a wound looked neglected, his clerks got it. He was excellent to be under.

I may here say that at the end of this session I gained the prize for medical clinical reports and at the next session the prize for surgical reports.[2] They cost me no end of time and care, but the time spent on them was well used, as it made me acquainted with disease and causes proximate and remote—besides teaching me the importance

---

[1]John Hilton (1804-78) was appointed assistant surgeon at Guy's in 1844 and succeeded Aston Key as full surgeon in 1849, resigning this office in 1870. His treatise *On Rest and Pain* (1863) is a classic in the field of surgery.

[2]The list of prizes in the *Guy's Hospital Reports* for April 1847 does not contain Helmcken's name in connection with either medical or surgical reports (see above, p. 47n2) ; and from that time until 1859 no prizes were given (Cameron, *Mr. Guy's Hospital*, p. 227). JSH did, however, win a "Pupils' Physical Prize" (see below, p. 58n5).

of observation—but it was very hard work indeed. They did me a world of good and brought me credit also.

At the end of this session I must have gone up for examination at the Apothecaries' Hall.[1] Some used to say the examination was nothing —I found it otherwise. They gave me the anatomy of the intestines— glands and all—lots about Midwifery—placed bottles of chemicals in closed bottles before me and I had to say what they were, and to what uses applied. They wanted to know the acids and salts of manganese —and lots of questions in Materia Medica, Chemistry and Botany. Well it was a pretty stiff examination I thought, but got through pretty decently—anyhow they gave me the "License" for which I paid with pleasure there and then. I had not joined any "crammer's" class for this examination, but had I known what it was like, I certainly should have done so, not for the purpose of being crammed, but to learn to be able to answer questions. Moreover the crammers knew the kind of examinations and educated their pupils accordingly. These were very useful to the tolerably educated, but no crammer could make a wise man out of a fool.

The summer session had now come and I have often thought how foolishly I spent it, but the truth is the whole afterpart of my life has been governed by it. I suppose I felt fagged and restless and so wanted a holiday. It so happened that two medical men were wanted by the Hudson's Bay Co to go in their ships to Hudson's Bay—the patronage of this rested with the Treasurer (Mr. Harrison) of Guy's Hospital,[2] who annually offered them to promising students. Whether I asked for an appointment or whether it was offered I do not remember—anyhow I found myself Surgeon of the Hudson's Bay Co's ship *Prince Rupert* bound on a voyage to York Factory in Hudson's Bay.[3] Captain Hurd [Herd] was the commander and Mr. Reid the 1st officer.[4] This Mr. Reid subsequently came to Vancouver Island in the *Vancouver* with

---

[1]JSH passed this examination in April 1847 (*Guy's Hospital Reports*, 2nd series, 5 [1947]: 208).

[2]Benjamin Harrison the younger (1771-1856) succeeded his father as treasurer of Guy's Hospital in 1797 and held this office until 1848. A benevolent despot, he exerted a tremendous influence on the development of the hospital and was responsible for founding the separate medical school at Guy's.

[3]The sixth HBC ship of that name, launched at the Blackwall Yard of Wigrams and Green in 1841 (Alan Cameron, "Ships of Three Centuries," *The Beaver* [Summer 1970]: 13). For JSH's detailed account of this voyage, see below, pp. 86-102.

[4]For Captain Herd see below, p. 86n4, and for James Murray Reid (1802-68), see Walbran, *British Columbia Coast Names*.

his wife and two daughters, one of whom is now married to Senator W. J. Macdonald.[1] Captain Reid's vessel was lost at Queen Charlotte's Island and having lost his ship had to live and settle in Victoria. Anyhow I went to Hudson's Bay—maybe to save a little money or for adventure—to see the world! But this had better be related hereafter.

The fourth and last session [1847-48] had now arrived and I arrived in rugged health. Well, the same story, work work work from early morn to past midnight. I lived close by the Hospital now—and had to live close too. Midwifery now engaged my attention—in the slums, for we had no lying-in hospital within the walls—poor people used to send for the students, and there was some society for this purpose.[2] In any awkward or dangerous case, the student would send for assistance to the senior clerk and in bad cases for the Professor, in my time Dr. Oldham.[3] What miserable sights met one in the hovels about Bermondsey and the tan-yards! How women did so well in confinement is a wonder—considering the dirt, want of ordinary food and attention, and the fact that the contagiousness of students was not so well known as now. In these cases the poor assisted the poor to the best of their ability and charitable instincts—they neglected their own for their poor neighbour. I now saw all the accidents that were brought to the Hospital—sometimes there would be a flood, particularly when any great gathering—fair—or anything of this kind took place— Derby Day—or excursions and what not. At this time there were three "house surgeons" constantly on hand—these being senior students or young practitioners. These positions were given to deserving students,

[1]William John Macdonald (1829-1916) married Capt. Reid's eldest daughter Catherine on 17 March 1857 (Christ Church marriage register, copy, PABC). He was a member of the Legislative Assembly of Vancouver Island 1860-63; of the Legislative Council of the united colony, 1867-68; and after Confederation one of the three senators appointed to represent British Columbia. For further details see his autobiography *A Pioneer 1851* (Victoria, [1914?]); and Walbran, *British Columbia Coast Names*.
[2]Guy's Lying-in Charity, also called the Extern Lying-in Charity, was founded in 1833 to provide poor women with medical attendance in their own homes during their confinement. It was under the control of a resident physician with two obstetric clerks who were provided with "lodging and commons," and there was also a rotating corps of eight students, on call two hours at a time (*Guy's Hospital Reports*, 2nd series, 6 [1848]: 116-17; Wilks and Bettany, *Biographical Dictionary*, p. 178; and Cameron, *Mr. Guy's Hospital*, p. 3).
[3]Henry Oldham (1815-1902) and John Charles W. Lever (1811-?59) lectured in midwifery during JSH's student career. Actually his certificate in midwifery, 29 April 1848, is signed by Lever as "Lecturer on Midwifery and Physician Accoucheur to Guy's Hospital" (HC).

and one was given to me for three months.[1] We were boarded and lodged in the quadrangle—about four ounces of wine being allowed each individual. The only expense we had was not exactly a matter of choice but of custom. The senior for the month had to provide dessert for dinner and shrimps or something for breakfast, so daily he had to trudge to Billingsgate or to Southwark market to buy the luxuries or get someone to do it for him. Of course the rich laid in good store, but the poor not quite so expensive. During the day we were all engaged on the cases in the Hospital, dressers, doing everything necessary for wounds, fractures and so forth, in fact everything surgical, and we of course had many junior students always around for instruction or assistance—and so they and we learned. In the evening, however, old students used to come up to our (the dressers') rooms, the events of the day being spoken about &c.: some took to cards and so forth, the stakes being small—but heavy enough for me at all events, as I generally lost. The dressers for the week had to provide pipes and beer —long aldermen and beer in pots—nothing else allowed. Lights had to be out at 11 o'clock—the watchman would tap and order lights out, which meant that we covered the windows with green baize to prevent anyone seeing the light from the outside, but if we kept it up too late, the Matron would interfere—and she was law but a good kind law at this.[2] Anyhow at the end of three months most of the dressers were used up—for they had lots of work to do and but little rest—and some dissipation. Edward Cock[3] would come every night to the Hospital and I had to go the rounds with him and have a gossip too—he always carried a pocketful of steel sounds[4] with him and took snuff inordinately, indeed so much, that I have seen him faint over his anatomical lectures. Teddy was an awfully good fellow to the students.

---

[1]According to Cameron (*Mr. Guy's Hospital*, p. 302), the first house surgeon was not appointed until 8 May 1858, and the dressers in the surgical wards who were the forerunners of the house surgeon were furnished with rooms and meals "during their week of residence" (p. 185). JSH appears in the "list of students to whom dresserships have been awarded" in January 1847 and January 1848, and the next group of appointees is listed in April, three months later, as JSH says, not one week later (*Guy's Hospital Reports*, 2nd series, 5 [1847]:210 and 6 [1848]: 199).

[2]Presumably "Mrs. Adams," who held the position from 1839 to 1852 (Cameron, *Mr. Guy's Hospital*, appendix K, "The Matrons of the Hospital," p. 504).

[3]Edward Cock died in 1892 at the age of eighty-seven. The nephew of Sir Astley Cooper, he was a demonstrator of anatomy and assistant surgeon of the hospital 1838-49. He lived for many years in St. Thomas Street close by.

[4]Surgical instruments used for probing parts of the body. The sounds used by JSH are now on display in Helmcken House.

On the opposite side of the quadrangle the Chaplain lived. Maurice by name.[1] He was also our lecturer on Moral Philosophy and such like and considered a clever man. I think this same chaplain afterwards was the preacher at the "Temple" in Lincoln Inn near Temple Bar—at least the Temple Bar that used to be[2]—and became and possibly is now famous. Anyhow somebody married in his, the Chaplain's, house—and poor fools, they spent their honeymoon there, much to the delight of the dressers, who watched their fooleries—for the Chaplain had neglected to draw the blinds!—I will do it here.

Stocker was the Resident Apothecary—i.e. in reality Junior Physician and had been so for years. He had charge of the dispensing and had students for instruction in this branch. Anything happening to the medical patients at night he was called in—a very quiet but clever man. He took, had to take, his rounds every night and often I went with him. He often remarked that the value of opium was too little known in the profession—anyhow he very often prescribed it. All the senior physicians without exception had great faith in him, and Addison remarked, if he were ill, his best and trusted attendant would be John [i.e. James] Stocker.[3]

On the surgical side we had "Teddy" Cock, he lived close by and as beforesaid he would be in the Hospital every night, but if anything serious happened, the Senior Surgeon for the week was sent for, whoever he might be. Key was undoubtedly the Surgeon of the Hospital,[4] surgically he occupied the same position as Addison did medically. These each had a tremendous tale[5] of students following them and listening

---

[1]Frederick Denison Maurice (1805-72) was chaplain at Guy's Hospital from 1836 to 1846, when he resigned his appointment to become chaplain of Lincoln's Inn (one of the four Inns of Court).

[2]Ever since medieval times there has been a gate of some sort at this point to mark the boundary of the City. The triple-gated bar erected by Wren in 1672, adorned with statues and topped with spikes on which the heads of traitors were displayed, was demolished in 1878 as a traffic hazard, but in 1880 the present Temple Bar Memorial, now an almost equal hazard, was erected to mark the site. The old Temple Bar was re-erected in 1888 at Theobald's Park, Herts, near Waltham Cross.

[3]James Stocker succeeded his father as apothecary at Guy's in 1834 and continued in that office until shortly before his death in 1878. During JSH's time he was resident medical officer and secretary of the school, being "authorized to enter Pupils" and "give all requisite information" (*Guy's Hospital Reports*, 2nd series [1844-49]).

[4]Charles Aston Key (1793-1849), a famous surgeon and one of the first to use ether as an anaesthetic, was appointed assistant surgeon in 1821, and from 1824 until his death was full surgeon. He lectured on surgery 1825-44.

[5]Used in the archaic sense of "number, total" (cf. German *Zahl*).

to their observations in the wards. They were both noble men and gentlemen. Key was tall, slender, healthy-looking, with fine features—an elegant operator, and wonderful anatomist—liked by all.

Our Father however was Monson Hills,[1] who occupied some position—he taught the minor branches of Surgery, cupping &c., but was not a professional. He was stout—very neat in dress and was said to have copied Sir Astley Cooper,[2] of whom he told us much. Hills was a man with an amiable presence and a remarkably good-natured face and disposition, it need scarcely be added students had really an affection for him. If an accident were brought in and we were in doubt about a fracture and so forth, we would say, "Where is Hills? He will settle the matter"—he had had so much practical experience. I have his portrait before me now. On the other hand there was an old man-of-war's man—a Cerberus, I forget his name, who kept discipline generally, but he was really a good man—a sort of commander—duty always.

About this time, there existed the Physical Society of Guy's Hospital and a junior branch also belonging to the students,[3] at which any student read a case or a paper—and then it was open for discussion— Wilkes [Wilks]—Habershon—Roper[4] and others who have since become great men, read papers here. They also gave two prizes, one for the best surgical essay and one for a medical one, but the cases related must have been in the Hospital, and the remarks confined to these—no assistance from outside sources tolerated. I wrote an essay on malignant disease of the testicle[5] and signed it Sloth—for the essay was written on a variety of paper, I intending to recopy it, but had

[1]Monson Hills (1792-1853) was cupper to Guy's Hospital and in 1832 published *A Short Treatise on the Operation of Cupping*. He was resident at the hospital and consequently of great assistance to the students, who called him "the Governor" and made him their confidant. The portrait of him to which JSH refers below still hangs in Helmcken House.
[2]Sir Astley Paston Cooper (1768-1841) was surgeon, 1800, and consulting surgeon, 1825, to Guy's Hospital.
[3]The Physical Society of Guy's Hospital was founded in 1771 (Cameron, *Mr. Guy's Hospital*, p. 94); the Pupils' Physical Society was an offshoot founded in 1830 (Ripman, *Guy's Hospital*, p. 46).
[4]S. Wilks, M.R.C.S., April 1847; Samuel O. Habershon, M.R.C.S., June 1847; and George Roper, M.R.C.S., November 1847.
[5]The minutes of a meeting (undated) of the Physical Society during 1846-47 contain Mr. Cock's announcement that "Mr. Helmkin [*sic*] was the successful candidate for the Surgical Prize," his subject being "Disease of the Testis." The list of prizes in 1847 shows JSH as the winner of one of the two "Pupils' Physical Prizes" (*Guy's Hospital Reports*, 2nd series, 5 [1847]:209).

not time. Of course the time came for awarding the prize and Teddy Cock had to do it—the theatre full of students. After some preliminary remarks, he said the prize had been awarded to Sloth—for like the sloth he had stripped the tree of every leaf and left nothing for anyone else. Mr. Sloth will please rise. To the astonishment of many, I did and tremendous applause there was—not because I was popular, for any student would have been treated to a student's applause. I very nearly lost the prize because I had got Dr. Gull to make a drawing for me of a section, showing the malignant cells—this however was over-looked as being unnecessary. This essay cost me no end of reading and hunting up cases recorded in the Hospital reports. I asserted that every patient with malignant disease of the testicle of any standing died whether operated on or not—the disease[?] always being also in the internal glands and moreover there was no sign in the early stages to distinguish it from non-malignant disease, that the only symptom re-corded perhaps bearing on this, that they all felt acute lancinating pain, which is not common to the other.

July 17! [1892]

This small pox and the mental insanity affecting the multitude—the scare, stopped my progress,[1] so I will now begin again. Well then hard work—sixteen hours a day—was my usual allowance, in fact I intended to get my diploma from the Royal College of Surgeons. In due course the

---

[1]Full details of the epidemic of 1892 are given in the "Report of the Commission-ers appointed to enquire into the late epidemic outbreak of small-pox in the Province of British Columbia...," British Columbia, Legislative Assembly, *Sessional Papers*, 6th Parl., 3d. sess., 1893, pp. 507-18. On 17 April 1892 the *Empress of Japan* arrived at Victoria from the Orient with one Chinese in the steerage suffering from smallpox. The 516 Chinese passengers were quarantined at Albert Head, but the ship was allowed to proceed to Vancouver, where the disease later broke out. On 11 July regulations for the suppression of the disease were promulgated, and Dr. John Chapman Davie was appointed Provincial Health Officer. Among the doctors there was great controversy over the respective merits of animal and humanized lymph. Dr. Israel Wood Powell declared firmly that "humanized lymph has had its day" and advised patients to wait for the bovine lymph being imported from Eastern Canada, while JSH was a strong advocate of the arm-to-arm vaccination which "from lengthened experi-ence" he had found safe and effectual. He added: "Wait until tomorrow. Bah! Procrastination in such an emergency is not the motto of J. S. Helmcken" (see their letters in the *Colonist*, 19 July 1892).

time arrived and my name was put down for examination. I did not wish anyone to know about this, seeing that I might be "plucked" and as I had not ten guineas to deposit—the cost of the License or Diploma —I took it into my head to ask Dr. Graves to lend me the amount. He kindly did so without demur. This again shows his good feeling towards and interest in me. Well the evening came. I dressed respectably and I wended my way to the College[1] and [was?] ushered into the room. At 8 o'clock a certain number were called—I was one and entered a large hall with several small tables. The first table I went to was presided over by two professors—the one gave me the anatomy [of] the hand—I had to dissect it, relating from memory all the parts I reached, beginning with the palmar surface first. I was nonplussed at the very beginning—the professor said, "You have forgotten a muscle."— I said nervously, "I do not remember one"—he had his hand flat on the table. He said, "Is there not a muscle here?" "Oh yes, but that is only a skin muscle." "Well—that's all right—now go on" and so I did for five or ten minutes—and then the other professor went to some other anatomy. My quarter of an hour being up, I was transferred to another table—two professors likewise. One gave me hernia in general and then anatomy in particular, and some other matters. My quarter of an hour ended—I was transferred with my paper showing their opinion in hieroglyphics, to another table and so on through a couple or so more—and then the examination being over, sent into the "funking room." Well this room containing little but chairs and a book case—and how to pass an hour was the problem; and shewed the great diversity of character of the students. Some played at athletics—jumping over chairs, leap-frog or anything else—others looked dejected—some laughed and talked— others were silent, but all wondered whether they had passed or not— and all were anxious. We hunted about for "souvenirs" but there was not any but brass-headed nails in the chairs—previous students had left nothing for us. Of course some were very confident, others the reverse, and it turned out that the most confident and playful, were those rejected.

Anyhow presently the usher came in with a list in his hand; reading from it he said, "Will Mr. so-and-so and Mr. so-and-so please to step this way"—nearly one half of the examined, followed him. Those not called now felt a reaction, for they knew very well, that those re-

---

[1]The Royal College of Surgeons, founded in 1745, is still in Lincoln's Inn Fields in central London.

quested to "step this way" had been plucked or perhaps remanded for a written examination. We who remained behind were jolly, knowing full well we had passed our examination and only had to wait for a certificate.[1] This came in a short time and then we were set free between 10 & 11 o'clock at night and then everyone was happy. Some adjourned to have a good supper with the friends waiting for them outside—others went to the theatre or elsewhere, but I having no money perhaps to spend, returned home and shewed Mother my certificate. Poor Mother, how she cried—how pleased was she—and so we both enjoyed ourselves in common! Soon my brothers and sisters heard of it. I was called a sly deceitful fellow for having kept the examination secret—but said they, "We might have known there was [something?] up on account of your having dressed so carefully." Of course I soon saw my benefactor Dr. Graves, received from him congratulations and he from me 10 guineas, which I had no trouble now in getting from my mother. Of course everyone knew in process of time and I had a good time.

Well then here I am a full-fledged Doctor with my fortune in a tin case! for I had none other! The next thing is—how to obtain a living. I might have become assistant to some medico, but this I did not like—I might have gone into practice on my own account, but being young I did not like this either. I wanted to see a little of the world, so I determined to enter HM service, but the Navy only seemed open, and so I had to choose this. Under this impression I spoke to Bransby Cooper, and he said, "Well, if you wish to enter the service, I will give you a letter to my friend the Medical Director General (I forget his name)[2] at Somerset House—and mind when you see him tell him all about what you have seen of the use of chloride of zinc in Guy's Hospital—he is full of chloride of zinc!" Well I took the letter—soon the gentleman appeared—tall—spare—wiry—active with a military uprightness. He spoke very kindly, had a small chat and said he would let me know in a few days, so he bowed me out. Now it so happened that I called on Mr. Barclay at the HB House,[3] who in the course of con-

---

[1]JSH was admitted as a Member of the Royal College of Surgeons in March 1848 (*Guy's Hospital Reports*, 2nd series, 6 [1848]: 197).
[2]Sir William Burnett (1779-1861) was at that time director-general of the medical department of the Royal Navy at Somerset House, London.
[3]Archibald Barclay (d. 1855), secretary to the Governor and Committee of the Hudson's Bay Company from 1843 to 1855. For further details see *The Letters of John McLoughlin . . . Second Series 1839-44*, ed. E. E. Rich (Toronto: Champlain Society, 1943), pp. 386-87.

versation asked me, "What do you intend doing now?"—so told him about going into the Navy, merely to spend two or three years and at the same time see the world. He thought me wrong—the expense of outfit being great and once in the Navy, it means for ever. "Besides, you may be sent to an unhealthy [?] station and in fact see nothing but water. If you want to spend a year or two at sea, I will give you a letter to Mr. Richard Green the great shipowner,[1] recommending him to give you a passenger ship going to the East Indies—this will suit your plans much better." So I thanked him, took the letter, saw Dickey Green, a tall thin dark gentleman, with a peculiar voice but kind and gentle manner—his look rickety, but awfully proud and fond of his frigate-built ships, as he well might be. In the end he said, "You can have the *Malacca*,[2] she is a small vessel, I am sorry I have not anything better to offer you"—so I thanked him and accepted the *Malacca*.

Having done so of course I immediately wrote Sir [William Burnett] at Somerset House, who told me then, that he was just about sending for me for examination and to give me an appointment to a man-o'-war going to the coast of Africa!

So I escaped Africa—yellow fever and so forth and perhaps death. The *Malacca* was a ship of about a thousand tons—[Augustus] Consitt, Commander and Caldecott second mate. I joined her at Gravesend. Mrs. Consitt was there and we had a few passengers,[3] among whom was a very handsome half-caste, a lady well educated and of excellent deportment—a brother was with her but occupied the steerage. They were returning to Bombay. There was also a Captain St. John[4]—and another who had married a clergyman's daughter—an Engineer also of the Indian Navy and a Colonel—also a few others. Captain C[onsitt]

[1]Richard Green (1803-63) helped to establish the firm of Green, Wigrams and Green, which built East Indiamen and ships for the voyage to Australia, and also the HBC vessel *Beaver* (see W. Kaye Lamb, "The Advent of the *Beaver*," *BCHQ* 2 [1938]:167). He was a benefactor of many institutions in East London and established a Sailors' Home in Poplar.
[2]A ship of 492 tons, built at London in 1842 for the London to Bombay voyage.
[3]See the advertisement in the London *Times*, 13 May 1848, in which the *Malacca* is said to be sailing from Gravesend on 25 May, having "very superior accommodation for passengers, and will carry an experienced surgeon" (see Plate 9). She actually sailed "for the Cape" on 26 May (London *Times*, 27 May 1848).
[4]Probably Frederick Arthur St. John of the 60th King's Royal Rifle Corps, the 1st Battalion of which was serving in Bombay in 1847. He was promoted from ensign to lieutenant on 5 March 1847 and became a captain on 23 March 1855 (*Hart's Army List*, 1847, 1856).

was nice and so was his wife, and at starting everyone seemed to be on the best terms—and as soon as warmer latitudes were reached there was dancing and other amusements every evening—I could not dance anyhow, and so lost a good deal of position. Clouds soon appeared—St. John and lady took the upper seat—and then the other Captain and lady took umbrage, the half-caste was neglected—and likewise the Naval Engineer and his belongings—so I had to listen to the complaining of the neglected and I felt for the clergyman's poor daughter, for her husband paid but little heed to her. There was no open row excepting with the Naval Engineer, who had a wife and her two sisters all Irish, but nice with sweet soft Irish voices. The voyage was really nothing more than ordinary—the table extraordinarily good and the human beings —well, human beings cooped up. Phillip a cadet, took to firing at Cape pigeons, and as he knew nothing about handling a musket, it went off accidentally on the poop, but altho the shot went everywhere and all the passengers were about, none were injured, but the Captain soon disarmed the novice—who rather superciliously remarked—Such accidents happened to the best of sportsmen! Of course there was some fun "crossing the line" but it did not amount to much, the ship was too respectable for this. Anyhow when we reached Bombay—each passenger went his or her own way, and probably very glad to get rid of each other—perhaps did not want to see each other again. The handsome lady, I and the mate went to see afterwards. Her father, a General, had died—and a corporal of his company gave shelter to this poor woman in his "bungalow," a very very ordinary one. No one seemed to take any notice of her, she being a half-caste—this being sufficient in the East to enable the pure whites to consider her beneath them! Poor girl, I do not know her end; she was a lady every inch—better educated and mannered than most of the whites in Bombay. They were white enough to be sure—blanched with the climate.

I liked Bombay, its fine harbour and so forth, but saw very few of the upper ten. Of course went to see the caves of Elephanta[1] and so forth, in fact the second mate, I and some others hired a boat, with a nice cabin and set off one evening in good humor and jolly—a lot of greenhorns. We landed at a place called Tannalo [?],[2] saw some hills in the distance which we thought close at hand, so started for

---

[1] A small island in Bombay Harbour famous for its eighth-century A.D. rock-sculptures of the gods of Brahmanic Hinduism.

[2] Probably to be identified with Tanna, on Bombay Harbour about twenty miles by road from Bombay, marked on an 1832 Arrowsmith map of India.

them—the mate carrying a couple of pistols in case we might find a tiger hunt! Well we got into a paddy field! The further we walked the further the hills seemed away, so decided to return—the sun was getting uncommon hot and when we found the highway again, the waggons drawn by buffalo with smooth skin were on their way somewhere. The drivers laughed at us, no doubt thinking we were what in reality we were, a lot of pretty well used-up greenhorns, without a tiger. We wanted a drink of water and when a bungalow was reached asked for such, but was told Master Sahib not at home! So did not get any water. In due time we reached the boat, where two of our companions were struck down by the heat! So we poured cold water over them and poured champagne down their throat and so the middies recovered. All now wanted something to eat, so the pies and so forth were brought forth from the lockers. The chickens were covered with red ants so we took to the pies, but on cutting them open, lo and behold, they were filled with red ants too and nothing else! So we had to confine our attentions to ordinary biscuits and drink. Of course we were glad to get away, so shaped our course for Elephanta—the cave carving and excavations of which were wonderful, but which I need not describe. The next day we returned to the *Malacca* and precious glad to get there too! Whilst at Bombay, the Captain said, "We are to have a cargo for China, so if you would like to remain in Bombay—I will give you permission and your discharge." I did not wish to remain in Bombay—and would not be a doctor there to the Indians on any account. This settled it and so in due course the good ship *Malacca* started for China, the Captain after having made due enquiries determined to get there by the "Eastern passage." We had not any passengers. In due course the Straits of Sundae [Sunda][1] were reached.

Whilst in Bombay, one day the signals were hoisted—down topmasts —&c. &c. This meant the change of the monsoon was at hand—and sure enough it soon came—a howling wind—rain came down in ropes —the scuppers were not sufficient to carry off the water, the decks were flooded—the lightning was frightful—sheet—chain—forked—steel-coloured—shooting in all conceivable directions—thunder deafening —the harbour so rough as to prevent communication with the shore— ships tumbling about; some drifting into the others—in fact a frightful storm, the like of which I have never seen since—it was horrifying and lasted three days and nights. It is necessary to see this—description

[1]Sunda Strait separates Sumatra and Java.

is almost impossible, even if I were writing for this purpose. None liked it, for it was possible that we might be struck with lightning or some other ship—however, we got safely over it. At this time the *Meeanee,* a man-of-war, was being built at Bombay of teak. I do not know whether she was ever finished[1]—however she was to be the last built there. It was curious to see how very differently the natives worked compared with the English. These teak vessels lasted for ever—some were sailing out of Bombay such as the Lowgie [Logie?] family[2]—at least a hundred years old. Of course we went to see the sacred wells—tanks of large size with stone steps leading down to the water, but I did not see any crocodiles or anything else there save beggars and fakirs—of the latter the whole country seemed full—a lot of lousy dirty fellows— probably real maniacs or maniacs by design. No doubt such as these existed at the time of Jesus, for the customs of the East do not change. I saw one or two weddings there accompanied with tambourines— shawms, trumpets and so forth, instruments described in scripture— and some feast in which the whole native town was lighted up with Oriental lanterns—a very pretty sight, which has lately been imitated here at the Park. The Hindus however use oil and small coloured lamps in their residences, which give them a peculiar lascivious light.

Well we are in the Straits of Sunda. Great Heavens how many sharks are here—hundreds to be seen at once in calm weather!! a horrible sight—that is to say knowing the character of the horrible fish. Of course the sailors caught some, but merely for sport—perhaps too for their fins, which are considered edible! Well, on the good ship goes— slowly for there happened to be a spell of calm weather. After a few days we sighted several ships ahead—these proved to be the Dutch East Indiamen—bound I think for Batavia. Bye and bye the fleet lost the wind—so they furled sail and came to anchor. "Well," says Captain Consitt, "it will be our turn soon," and sure enough it happened, and he had to do exactly the same thing, but the bottom was found to be bad —rocky bottom. However after tripping a little the anchor held. An island existed a couple of miles astern. Night came on—and things proceeded as usual on board, but when daylight came—lo and behold the ship had drifted very considerably—the island being much closer and the current very strong. Presently the anchor tripped—and away

[1]*The Navy Lists* 1846-48 describe her as at "Bombay, building." From 1849 to 1856 she was stationed at Chatham; in 1857, at Sheerness.
[2]This reference remains obscure. There is a "Logie O' Buchan, Aberdeen" among the British registered vessels in the *Mercantile Navy List* of 1857.

the ship went with the current, which unfortunately swept through the narrow channel, something like the channel at Seymour Narrows.[1] This channel was full of whirlpools—the water so clear that we could easily see the rocky bottom. Caught in this stream, onward was swept the ship and as the whirlpools caught her, she swung round and round until the bowsprit in some places swept the rocky shore—it was a fearful time —the ship utterly helpless and unmanageable. Somehow or other the vessel swept on—each moment we expected her to strike, but to our relief after an hour of this anxiety she arrived at the open Straits again, and all breathed freely once more—but it had been apparently nearly an end of the *Malacca*. Soon afterwards the natives brought mango-steens—Java sparrows—other fruits and birds. The mangosteen was a little red fruit—say about the size of an ordinary tomato—and very delicious—said to be the fruit of fruits—the apple of Eden!! In due course we ran into the Eastern Sea—a sea containing a vast archipelago of islands mostly volcanic or coral—in fact a Canal de Haro on a gigantic scale[2]—the islands larger and the channels of course very very much larger, but oh it was and is I suppose a very lovely portion of the globe—the islands clothed to the water's edge and in some instances very little above the water. One morning, I heard a good deal of unusual running-about noise on deck, and on looking out of [a?] port, about four feet square, I saw close alongside a coral island —I could have jumped to it. The boats were out and the men trying to tow her away from the danger, but of course they had but little power, nevertheless the ship passed the dangerous island. It happened to be a small one, four or five acres in extent, but clothed in verdure, trees and so forth as only seen in the tropics. These islands seem to be for the most part uninhabited—of course the large ones Celebes and others possess large populations.

On another occasion, early in the morning, the look-out reported something in the distance—he supposed it to be a raft, with people waving flags of distress. The course of the ship was directed to the object and telescopes bent thereon. As we approached nearer and nearer, the supposed raft turned out to be a floating island, the flags being trees—palms swaying in the gentle breeze. This island was pretty large—possibly an acre in extent—and are said to be not uncommon

[1]In Discovery Passage, between Vancouver and Quadra Islands. At the southern end of the rapid was Ripple Rock, an extreme hazard to navigation from the time of the first maritime explorations until it was blown up on 5 April 1958.
[2]Haro Strait, between Vancouver Island and the San Juan Islands.

in these regions—supposed to be formed at the outlet of rivers and washed away by floods or other disturbances.

It was in these regions that one morning, the water being as smooth as oil, hundreds of large serpents were seen surrounding the ship—some more than ten feet in length. They were not very active, but lolling about as it were in the water. I have always fancied they had small paddle fins along their side. I wanted to catch a specimen or two, but Captain Consitt would not allow, as he considered them of a poisonous character.[1] There were hundreds of them and perhaps had come from some river or large low islands. We did not see any more of these during the remainder of the voyage. In these regions too waterspouts are common, may be seen almost daily, at least we saw them, and indeed half a dozen of them at one view. Altho the water was calm, these things would float about rapidly, and send down as it were a tail to the water, which became then turbulent, wavy and in great commotion. These waterspouts resemble large bellows, the tail spoken of above being the lower end, long and spiral. These are not pleasant customers—if one had passed over the ship, the rotatory motion common to them would have ripped her masts out—or at least done very considerable damage, even if it did not swamp the vessel, with the enormous quantity of water in them. Consitt said, "The proper way to treat these customers, is to fire cannon balls into them—but for this guns prepared would have to be kept ready on board, as the cyclones travel very quickly." We only saw the waterspouts in calm water.

It was an awful sea too for lightning—night after night we were surrounded by lightning, so rapid the flashes, that they kept the place almost constantly light. It was for the most part of "sheet character" and fortunately did us no harm, excepting at first keeping the crew in a continual state of alarm. However we got used to it and bye and bye came to Dampier's Straits.[2] Here the natives were virtually naked —savages. All they brought off were pieces of coral of the columnar

[1]Dr. R. J. F. Smith, associate professor of biology in the University of Saskatchewan, has suggested the possibility that JSH saw a swarm of palolo worms, which come to the surface to spawn and die, often on one particular night of the year, timed by the phases of the moon. These worms sometimes reach three metres in length and have little appendages along each side which a layman might describe as "small paddle fins." On the other hand, the creatures may have been sea snakes, which are very venomous (as Captain Consitt said) but have no appendages. The curator of the Zoological Reference Collection at the University of Singapore finds JSH's description inadequate for positive identification.
[2]Dampier Strait, off the northwest tip of New Guinea.

variety and immense clamp shells. They bore some resemblance to our Northern Indian tribes. None were allowed on board—as they and all the natives round this region are considered treacherous and pirates. A fine ship lay on the rocks here and had been there for many years— indeed it had become a point for observation—New Guinea was close at hand.

In one season we arrive at the Pacific Ocean and there meeting the trade wind are wafted swiftly to Formosa, and onwards to Hong Kong. The voyage had been long on account of calms, but the Captain had taken this course from Bombay to avoid beating against the wind by the Straits of Malacca.

Hong Kong at this time was a comparatively small and a very un-healthy place. The garrison looked as tho they were recovering from illness, the most of them however being from India.[1] Beautiful docks were in course of erection, and there were a few fine granite buildings belonging to the great tea and opium firms. The Chinese in hundreds were chipping away at granite blocks—but they struck one as being very inferior to European workers. Of course I saw the Hospital and the burial ground—so-called Happy Valley, which is really a bason—serving for race course, burial ground and public amusements. Here were buried those who fell in the war—and numbers who had been killed or murdered by pirates on the river. One road had been cut through the rock, but at this time there was but few of them and so the island could not be conveniently explored. At Hong Kong exists a hill—something like Mount Douglas and sailor-like we wanted to explore it, but the hotel keeper would not hear of such a thing, as he said it was infested with fevers and—tigers. He did not wish us to go there anyhow. Today this hill is covered I am told with residences of the best kind![2] China Town of course existed. The Island did not strike me as being at all a nice place—but it suited admirably for commerce. After a brief stay the *Malacca* shaped her course for Canton, passing of course the Bogue forts.[3] The channel is here very narrow indeed and how any hostile vessels could pass these seems impossible. However probably the guns and men were inferior. Ironclads did not exist then and but few steam

[1]China had ceded Hong Kong to Great Britain at the close of the Opium War of 1839-42.
[2]The reference here would seem to be to the Peak in Hong Kong. Mount Douglas lies north of Victoria, B.C., but at 739 feet it is less than half the height of the "hill" at Hong Kong (1,810 feet).
[3]Captured by the British in 1841.

men-o'-war. The Chinese say it was not a fair fight, because the soldiers
did not come up in front of the guns, but took a roundabout course
to the rear and so conquered them by unfair stratagem! Anyhow I
wonder at the British success. When we arrive at Canton River, as we
ascend the stream in a "sampan," are seen piles driven across the
stream to prevent the war vessels passing, but I am told they did pass
nevertheless.

Canton River is very wide—its banks very low, somewhat like the lower
Fraser—cultivated on both sides with paddy fields and what not. The
labourers with their hats and coats of long perhaps bamboo leaves had
a curious appearance and were said to be very convenient in wet
weather. We landed at one place which I suppose to have been a
dairy, here the cattle were fed on a sort of sugar cane—perhaps young
bamboo. The Chinese did not welcome us, so we beat a retreat. This
river was very dangerous to travellers, being troubled with very numerous pirates, and very many have been murdered by them, particularly
after nightfall. In process of time we reach Canton, and off it the
floating city. This floating city must have been a mile in length, built
on barges, and thickly occupied we were told by men and women
of not very reputable character and unsafe for foreigners to go there;
the women were dressed in handsome colours, with hair dressed according to the national custom, which may now be seen in Victoria.
Of course business took us first to the agents. The foreigners were
allowed a piece of ground outside the city. On this the English and
so forth had put up fine buildings, offices and so forth. The whole square
was beautifully clean and terribly silent and dull—at least it was when
we were there. Very very few people were moving about—and these for
the most part Chinese servants.

From this we went to the city proper—that is to say the city outside
the walls. This to say the best was a dirty place, with very narrow lanes
—so narrow that a horse and cart could scarcely move through or turn
in them. There were the usual small Oriental shops on either side of the
street. Here they sold goods to foreigners—china—silver—paintings &c.
&c. and great bargainers they were. Our agent supplied me with a
Chinaman—a guide or a guard—he showed me about—the temples and
joss-houses and so forth with their big ugly brazen figures of joss and so
forth—also a slaughter-house in the corner for sacrifice, where I tried
to look in but was prevented by a butcher with the proverbial knife.
Watch towers for alarm in case of fire were numerous. Most of the eating
houses had pig roasted whole in the shop front, but we have become
more familiar with most of these things in Victoria but they were less

known half a century gone. Bye and bye we came to the gates of the City proper—heavy iron gates in an arch in the stone wall. Of course I wanted to go through, and half succeeded, when a watchman turned out and said, "Not yet—too soon—bye and bye!" This meant that the time mentioned in the treaty[1] for opening the gates to foreigners in several mentioned cities had not yet arrived. I looked in however and could see one straight street—apparently very clean and in all respects different to the outside city. Of course there were all sorts of coloured signs and inscriptions hanging out—advertisements, which made the street look gay and this is all I know about the city. Cormorant Street today will give some idea of it.[2] Anyone may go into the city now, and all is known about it—but even it has a name for filthiness. There is a ditch by the city wall, where they told me it was a common thing to find female infants strangled and then thrown there. Once I went up with Captain and Mrs. Consitt—the latter of course had the usual curiosity. Well, the agent gave us a sort of upright palanquin and bearers, into which went Mrs. Consitt, but no sooner had they got into the streets when crowds came to look at her, poked their noses into the box; derided and no doubt made all sorts of insulting remarks. English or white women had seldom if ever been seen there, and of course, it is contrary to custom for Chinese women to appear in public. After being jostled very considerably and seeing precious little she and we were very glad to get out of these unsavory slums. We must have been an independent lot, for we cared no more about the Chinese than so many inferior animals, and such is the case when Englishmen visit Oriental countries—no wonder they are feared and disliked!

We called at a town on an island, called Bamboo Town—because the houses were built of bamboo and on stilts to keep them off the low marshy ground. This was even dirtier than Canton. The place was full of short-legged long-bodied pigs—ducks and chickens—so remained there a very short time indeed. It was curious tho to see how the Chinamen managed and instructed the ducks, chickens and so forth; they appeared quite obedient to orders. Anyhow this visit to China took away all my preconceived ideas of "Cathay"—there was nothing enticing to me, tho perhaps those engaged in money making might find it otherwise, for there was an immense business done in opium—tea and

[1]The Treaty of Nanking, 1842, which opened the ports of Canton, Shanghai, Amoy, Foochow, and Ningpo to British trade .
[2]Still one of the principal streets in the Chinese quarter of Victoria, named after H.M.S. *Cormorant.*

so forth—some of the ivory I saw. Of course there were lots of gentlemen Chinese with long nails, long pipes and so forth, very urbane and very polite and so let no one judge of [*sic*: *for* by ?] the Chinese seen in Victoria or imagine them to represent the respectable class of China. The upper class there are really cultivated people. As to the city, all native Oriental cities seem to be alike—dirty with narrow streets. It was queer to see the Chinese eating or shovelling into their mouths their grub with chopsticks—and drinking tea without either milk or sugar—and equally queer to see men with tables, writing and ready to write letters for anyone requiring them—a generation of scribes. Of course they wrote with a sort of paint brush—love, business or any other epistles! Some of our men had dysentery—an American medico told me the best way of treating dysentery was Epsom-salts and small doses of antimony—I have often found it successful since!

Anyhow we could not get a return cargo in China, so had to go more or less seeking and so left this very disappointing part of China. On our seeking voyage we called at Singapore.[1] Most assuredly this was by far the nicest place I had yet seen. There was lots of cultivation—groves of oranges, nutmegs and so forth—the streets were clean and so was the market. This contained all manner of things—lovely birds among the rest. Of course the population was Orientally cosmopolitan—Chinese and goodness knows who else. The Europeans for the most part "lived out of town" and so I saw very little of it or them. Of course it was under European government and so had the usual characteristics of cleanliness and order. Not being able to get a cargo here, we shaped our course for Columbo Ceylon, stopping however at one of the settlements in the Straits of Malacca for a few days. In this region of country—the grub was either turtle! or fat pork—turtle all over the [blank in MS: place?] cooked in every conceivable manner, until the whole ship and crew stank abominably of turtle! I have no particular wish to eat these famous dishes any more—it was an experience. Ceylon I saw very little of—of course lots of boating traders came off and wished to sell rubies and all sorts of precious stones, but as we knew them all to be manufactured, they did not sell us many— but there are always fools on board ship and we were no exception to the rule. These traders always have some tempting pretty things—for travellers to buy and take home for presents!! Anyhow what little I did

[1]Singapore Island, opposite the southern tip of the Malay Peninsula, was ceded to the British by the Sultan of Johore in 1824.

see of Ceylon struck me very pleasantly, and I have no doubt it is one of the nicest of Oriental places—tho I believed it to be inferior to Singapore. No cargo at Ceylon, so off we go to Bombay, and beat up against the monsoon. Bombay is at length reached. One day on going to the esplanade I was amused by seeing the native laundry-men beating the clothes against the stone wall sides of the well. Presently a pair of trowsers went swish swish swish againt the wall and then I saw my own name on them. The reason of their coming home without buttons was explained!

Bombay was of course just the same—the usual bearers and ox carts —and women carrying and balancing things gracefully on their head. If a man wanted another he seemed to beckon him to go away—they seem to do everything the reverse of what Europeans do.

Ship has undertaken a cargo of cotton! There are thousands of bales of cotton lying in the sun baking—almost red hot. They have been pressed until solid as wood—and rats—big fellows—in abundance! Hitherto I had had a cabin about ten feet square, with a very large port and plenty light. When passengers were on board the table was pretty luxurious—at least as far as luxury in these days meant. Every passenger was allowed a bottle of claret for breakfast—plenty wines &c. at dinner. Green's ships were looked on as floating palaces.

Well the ship is laden—cotton everywhere. All our cabins, now below, are built of cotton bales and not large cabins at this. The heat from these roasting hot bales is insufferable—weevils and other insects abound —so thick that on going down the scuttle the insects seem to be pressed up in clouds—in myriads. Rats galore—of course one tried to sleep or slept with simply a sheet over him and this more to keep the venomous musquitoes, which were very numerous, off. Musquito nettings seemed stifling. During the night the rats would scamper in droves from one end of the ship to the other. In their course the regiment of rats would scamper over my body and their sharp claws seem to penetrate the sheet and go into my skin: they seemed to come at regular intervals too. In the day-time they would pop out their heads through the air holes, so I amused myself by giving their brain a rap. Cockroaches— great big fellows too—flew or crawled about—and some of the crew complained of them eating their toe-nails and some said the rats did it too. When lamps were lighted, whew how the light attracted the flies —how many were scorched or burned to death! Altogether it was a good time for the rats, weevils, musquitoes, cockroaches &c., but a very poor one for your humble servant.

The voyage home was monotonous; everything had become stale.

There were three or four military passengers and one lady, whose name I forget. The males were supercilious—so I had nothing to do with them; but one was a sick officer invalided—he never spoke to me about his illness—however when near the British Channel, he ate a good dinner of pork—had a fit—was bled and died within half an hour. Bleeding in epilepsy either kills or cures. Near the Isle of Wight his brother came on board to make enquiries as to his death, but really I could tell him nothing.

With regard to the lady, she took quite a fancy to my blue eyes! and occasionally asked me to let her look at them. She was harmless—I suppose having been long in India blue eyes had seldom come before her. Anyhow I had nice blue eyes and a darker circle around the iris —I had black hair nevertheless. The lady after arriving home sent me a beautiful dressing case, which I have still, but I never saw her more.

A month after, I was aboard the *Norman Morrison* [*Morison*]. Holland was first officer.[1] One day he said to me, "Were you on board the *Malacca?*" "Oh yes." "Well did a lady send a dressing case?" "Yes." "She was my cousin and told me all about you and your eyes." He gave me her history and the reasons for her coming to England, but I have forgotten the most of it—nothing very unusual about it.

On the voyage home we called at St. Helena—and I scrambled up the ladders to the heights—Heaven knows how many hundred steps. I would not like to do it now, but those who had to go up and down seemed to think very little about it. There was a very nice market— plenty fruits and so forth. Napoleon's tomb must not be forgotten—but we did not remain longer than necessary. A few months before there had been a tidal wave which had smashed a good many craft and heaped them up. There is no real harbour here, but as the wind always blows in one direction, the leeward side is as good as a harbour and it has some anchorage. Anyhow at length after eighteen months' journey we reach home,[2] all pretty well tired of everybody and everything. I had seen the world—of water—there did not appear to be much else. If anyone wishes to see countries, they must not think to do this by ship! Of course I was paid off—and I told Mr. Green of the death. "Oh," he said, "that's nothing new. These people kill themselves nearly in India and many die on their way home or soon after. If you like I will give you a bigger ship next time."

[1]For the *Norman Morison* and first officer Holland, see below, p. 76n2.
[2]See London *Times*, 15 September 1849: "The Malacca, from Bombay, has arrived in the East Indian Docks. . . ."

Of course I went home. A couple of years ago when walking in Victoria, I met and was introduced to Captain [blank in MS: J. L. Dunn] of the Hudson's Bay ship [blank in MS: *Titania*] "Oh," said he, "you are Dr. Helmcken. Did you sail with my son- [*sic: for* father?] in-law Adams in the *Malacca*?"[1] "Yes I did." "Well, Adams, who became Captain and is now retired, lives at Blackheath and he told me when I left, that if I should happen to meet a young fellow named Helmcken, to give him some fatherly advice and in fact to do anything good for him. Are you the young fellow?" "Yes—I *was* the young fellow, but now I am older even than you. Is Adams a young fellow too still—he was as young as I 40 years ago?" "Why no—he is an old man too and has sons and daughters as old as he was 40 years ago!"

Well, in due course I arrive at home; of course this was like most homecomings—Mother and the rest glad to see me once more and hear the yarns of my experiences—goodness knows these were few enough after eighteen months spent.

Of course I saw very soon Dr. & Mrs. Graves, Fotherby and my old friends. Doctor asked me what I intended to do now—so I told him I meant to go into practice somewhere close bye—and he did not object nor make any recommendations.

Going into practice then meant a house, a small druggist shop, selling little things, medicines or what not over the counter. Giving advice to anyone who needed it—supplying the medicines and compounding them myself. Get a stray patient or two if possible, and so by degrees come to better things and the carriage I had promised myself. Of course it would have been slow and uphill work, success depending some on accident, as I had very few friends and no money to help me along—my practice at first would no doubt have been among the poor and so my income precious small.

Of course I soon saw Mr. Barclay at the Hudson's Bay House, to thank him for my ship &c. and give an account of myself. He like-

---

[1]Writing to Mrs. Consitt from Fort Rupert in 1850, JSH asked: "Is that paragon of sailors and inimitable chief officer Mr. Adams still treading the same planks? ...I hope he is now a Commander extraordinary..." (HC). The tea clipper *Titania*, purchased by the HBC, made five return voyages, London to British Columbia, 1886-91. Her captain, James Lawrence ("Dandy") Dunn, was accidentally killed on the night of 15 October 1890 when he stepped off the badly lighted and dangerous CPR wharf at New Westminster on his way back to his ship. For further details see L. R. W. Beavis (second mate under Dunn, 1888-90), "*Titania*, Queen of the Clippers," *The Beaver* (June 1938): 15-17; and *Colonist*, 16-19 October and 4 December 1890.

wise wanted to know, what next? I told him the same as Dr. Graves. "Well," he replied, "the Hudson's Bay Co are sending out emigrants to Vancouver's Island, their colony and of course will want a Surgeon." He told me his nephew was at [Fort] Vancouver (Dr. Barclay) but had resigned,[1] and one was wanted to fill his place; the engagement to be for five years at £100 per annum—a free passage home at the end of the term. He gave me a prospectus, which unhappily I have lost— and never seen one since.[2] "Where on earth is Vancouver Island?" says I. "If it be in Hudson's Bay, depend on it I do not go." "Oh," says he, "it is in the Pacific—here it is on the map and my nephew writes me it has a climate like that of England." He said, "If you should change in mind within the next week or so let me know, for I can get you the appointment." He was kind to me and indeed of kind disposition.

By this time I was not the same docile boy that had been—and so was not so governable. I had become a wanderer and wanted to see things. Mother did not like this and looked on me as a boy still! She scolded me a little and so in a pet I went to Mr. Barclay and accepted his offered appointment! He gave it to me there and then[3]—said, "As you will have plenty time to spare you will be Private Secretary to the Governor (Governor Blanshard)[4] and attend to the patients besides. Of course, if there be any private practice, you can embrace it, for you are the Colonial Surgeon, and there is no other. Tell me what instruments

[1]Forbes Barclay (1812-73) retired to Oregon City from the HBC service in 1850. For further biographical details see *The Letters of John McLoughlin ... Third Series 1844-46*, ed. E. E. Rich (Toronto: Champlain Society, 1944), p. 43n1.
[2]As soon as the grant of Vancouver Island to the HBC had been officially confirmed, the Company issued a set of regulations for the granting of land and published them in the London *Times*, with a note that applications should be addressed to A. Barclay, Esq., secretary to the HBC. A copy of these "Resolutions of the Hudson's Bay Company: Colonization of Vancouver Island" will be found in the "Report of the Provincial Archives Department for 1913," B.C., *Sessional Papers*, 13th Parl., 2d sess., 1914, pp. V73-74, and also in Alexander Begg, C.C., *History of British Columbia from its Earliest Discovery to the Present Time* (Toronto: W. Briggs, 1894), pp. 186-88. For a full discussion see Leonard Wrinch, "Land Policy of the Colony of Vancouver Island 1849-1866" (M.A. Thesis, University of British Columbia, 1932).
[3]JSH's agreement with the HBC as "surgeon and clerk" for a term of five years at a salary of £100 per annum, dated 12 October 1849, is in the Helmcken Collection.
[4]Richard Blanshard (1817-94) had received his commission as governor of Vancouver Island on 16 July 1849. For further details see Willard E. Ireland, "The Appointment of Governor Blanshard," *BCHQ* 8 (1944):213-26; and W. Kaye Lamb, "The Governorship of Richard Blanshard," *BCHQ* 14 (1950):1-40.

& things you want for the voyage, for the Company will provide them."
I was a little green, and so afterwards made out a very very small list,
whereas I ought to have asked for a tolerably good outfit of all kinds
of necessary instruments and medicines; but I knew nothing about
going to a wild country—where nothing could be had without twelve
months' notice. However, I had a good many instruments of my own[1]
so no one suffered on this account, either on board or ashore.

In conclusion said he, "I dabble in philology and I shall be pleased,
if you send me anything you may learn about the Indian languages.
Good day—you will be off soon, so get ready, the ship sails next week!"

This ship was the *Norman Morison*. Captain Wishart, Commander,
Holland first officer, and I had to board her at Gravesend.[2] Arriving
there somewhere about October 1849—I found the emigration commissioners and so forth, inspecting everything, which they pronounced
all right and certified accordingly. A good deal of fuss was made about
this first voyage to a new colony and some grandees were on board
drinking wine and speaking good wishes &c. &c. They went and the
pilot remained on board. I had bought [brought?] lots of seed and
canaries[3]—flower seeds particularly which I bought in Fenchurch Street.

---

[1]Several cases of surgical instruments, as well as the doctor's medicine chest and a
number of his medical books, are still to be seen in Helmcken House.

[2]The ship *Norman Morison*, 564 tons, was built at Moulmein in Burma in 1846.
She sailed from Gravesend on 21 October 1849 according to the London *Times*,
22 October 1849, although the copy of her log in PABC gives the date as 18 October. David Durham Wishart commanded the *Norman Morison* on all three of
her voyages from London to Vancouver Island, 1849-53. In 1854 he was master
of the *Princess Royal* bringing a party of coal miners from England to Nanaimo
(Barrie H. E. Goult, "First and Last Days of the *Princess Royal*," BCHQ 3
[1939]: 15-24), but in 1856 he relinquished this command to Captain J. F.
Trivett, partly, as he told Kenneth McKenzie of Craigflower Farm, because of
his "aversion to that vile man J. Douglas" (Wishart to McKenzie, 19 August
1856, Wishart Correspondence, McKenzie Collection, PABC). A legacy enabled
him to enjoy a holiday at home in England before taking command, according
to the company's promise, of another HBC ship—preferably one not sailing to
Vancouver Island (ibid.). He sailed for a number of years to Hudson's Bay
(H.M.S. Cotter to Barrie H. E. Goult, 14 February 1939, MS, PABC). George
Holland joined the HBC service as a seaman in 1835 and came to the Columbia
River in the *Beaver* in 1836. Subsequently he was schoolmaster at Fort Vancouver,
postmaster at Fort Langley, and from 1846 to 1848 postmaster at Fort Victoria.
He then asked permission to retire, as the climate did not agree with him. On his
return to London in 1848 he qualified as a master mariner and in 1849 was
appointed chief mate of the *Norman Morison*. In 1851 the HBC accepted his
resignation on the ground that he could not agree with Captain Wishart (cf. p. 80,
below) and refused to re-appoint him (see the memorandum from the Hydro-
graphic Department, Admiralty, London, 27 February 1853, MS, PABC).

[3]The district of Spitalfields was noted for its trade in singing birds.

Had I grasped the situation, I should have taken a larger assortment of these and other articles.

The ship sails. Eighty emigrants on board—chiefly men, but two or three women and all in the prime of life—no children. Some of the men are living now (1892) such as George Richardson and Rowland.[1] The weather in the Channel was dirty, the wind foul, so we came to anchor in the days [*sic*: *for* Downs],[2] among a great many other vessels. However after a day or two, the weather being fine we sailed again, beating our way down channel, in company with a lot of others. Here we very nearly came to grief: an Indiaman with soldiers aboard, on the opposite tack, tried to cross our bow instead of our stern! Wishart was a good sailor and so was the pilot—the same may be said of those in the other ship. They both altered their helm, so instead of our being struck amidship we came together broadside on. There was a smashing of gingerbread—and small spars on both sides. I recollect buttoning up my coat to make a spring, for it would have been easy to jump into the other vessel, but fortunately both vessels sheered off—sails put to rights and off we went again, not much the worse— neither do I think the other vessel was much the worse either. It was a queer experience, and by no means a pleasant one—for a little more mismanagement, and one at all events would have gone to pot. The *Morison* was built of teak and a very strong vessel and by no means a bad sailor—ten knots could be got out of her with a decent breeze. Off the Bay of Biscay we had the usual fate of a beastly gale and weather, for a couple of days and thereafter soon found fine weather and fine climate.

Just here one of the immigrants had an eruption of small pox. On reporting this to the Captain, the sufferer was brought on deck and slung in a hammock forward. Of course this created no little alarm. Some vaccine had been supplied the ship—the old fashion, matter between small plates of glass. This I used at once, but think it was only success-

[1]Richardson was proprietor first of the Victoria Hotel and then of the Windsor Hotel until his retirement c. 1902. He died in 1922 at the age of ninety-six (*Victoria Times*, 19 June 1922). Matthias Rowland, "an enthusiastic agriculturist," left the HBC service to develop a large farm in the area now called Strawberry Vale and later kept the Burnside Hotel. He died at the age of seventy-three in 1903 (ibid., 26 January 1903).

[2]The roadstead opposite the North Downs, between the coast of Kent and the Goodwin Sands. Here ships could ride out a storm before proceeding down the English Channel. According to her log, the *Norman Morison* was "At the Downs" 22-24 October 1849. See Plate 1.

ful in one instance and this a man—most of them had been vaccinated or had had small pox. Of course the holds were well ventilated and kept clean; but soon others went down until there were nearly twenty all told. Everyone was slung in a hammock on deck—every attention paid them—and everyone being in the same box, helped each other. The Captain had been through the same thing before, so he managed the whole thing. Medicines were but little used—fresh air, diet and cleanliness were the means employed. Out of the number only one died, and he had the confluent variety. The number in the ship was about one hundred and twenty, but not more than twenty took the small pox. By the time the ship neared Cape Horn, the whole epidemic had been wiped out. No more could take it. There was no great scare on board—people did not lose their senses. Fortunately the weather was splendid and warm, so there was not only no danger but the greatest benefit from slinging them all on deck or under the topgallant forecastle[1]. The dead man was buried at sea—the Captain reading the funeral service.

At Cape Horn in the winter season! The weather was beastly—foul wind—fearful gales—hailstorms—a few hours only of daylight! Such seas—beastly chopping irregular ones—I had seen the huge rollers off the Cape of Good Hope, but these chopping seas were ten times worse and more dangerous. We ran as far south as we dared, but did not see any ice floating or bergs. Then we ran back again to about where we started from and so for many days, but then the wind changed and the ship was put about. The seas came in opposite direction to that of the wind, so that they seemed as tho they would sweep over us from stem to stern—but the good ship rose to them and then we were in a valley. This went on for some hours and was far less dangerous than if they had come astern—the wind not being strong. We had precious poor grub off Cape Horn—could cook but little. I tell you pea soup and pork were relished there and so was porridge—these being the chief articles of diet, with an occasional hard-boiled dumpling. Everything was miserable indeed. Once round the Cape, which we did not sight, and into the Pacific, there was soon a very pleasant change, and with a fair wind, soon ran into warm weather.

In the Pacific a schoolmaster who was coming out to teach Gaelic

---

[1]A notebook containing JSH's medical record of the voyage is in the Helmcken Collection.

to Captain Grant's settlement at Sooke died of cancer.[1] He was a very quiet worthy old Highlander—always ailing of course. When dying he gave me his fishing rod, with which he had hoped to catch salmon in the rivers of Sooke. I kept this rod for years—my boys destroyed it. Poor Dominie—peace be with you.

On the voyage the immigrants complained of their grub, and used to pitch the tinned "Soup and Bouilli" overboard.[2] The very same that we found so good in the cabin! The Captain used to enquire into all their complaints and pacify the grumblers, but really they had nothing to complain of.

Fights among themselves happened occasionally, but the Captain "let them fight it out." Rowland was the chief boxer and our butcher too. Altogether the people were orderly and well behaved and gave very little trouble. They managed to spend their time somehow or other, but there was but little jollity among them or in the cabin either. I suppose the women did not set dancing and so forth going, and I suppose had never been accustomed to anything of the kind or even music. I do not remember anything very remarkable happening between Cape Horn and Cape Flattery—pretty good—too good—weather all the way. Off Flattery and in the Straits we had calms for days—washed out of the Straits once or twice by calms, so we had a pretty good look at the coasts of the country destined to be my home. Truly they were forbidding altho grand—nothing but mountains on both sides wooded to the top—they appeared weird and gloomy and possibly are the same to this day. Scarcely a foot of level land could anywhere be seen and we used to ask each other, "How can any of this be cultivated?" "Where is it possible to make any farms at all?" "Doctor you have brought your pigs to a pretty market indeed!" Nevertheless it was land and we were glad to see it after five months of water.

During these weary months, I had amused myself by making bird-cages of strips of bamboo, and other trifles—but it was a monotonous time.

---

[1]Captain Walter Colquhoun Grant of the Scots Greys (1822-61) arrived at Fort Victoria in 1849 as surveyor of Vancouver Island for the HBC, and with the eight men who had preceded him in the *Harpooner* earlier that year he established a farm and sawmill at Sooke, some twenty miles west of Fort Victoria. For further details see Willard E. Ireland, "Captain Walter Colquhoun Grant: Vancouver Island's First Independent Settler," *BCHQ* 17 (1953): 87-125. The schoolmaster Alexander McFarlane died of cancer on 21 January 1850, and his death was recorded in the report concerning the health of the Company's servants on the voyage out which was made by JSH to Chief Factor James Douglas on 28 March 1850 (ibid., p. 111).

[2]Stewed or boiled meat, the ancestor of bully beef.

Wishart was not a social man—he had been soured somehow or other—
but nevertheless he was kind and good to all and a thorough seaman.
Books we got tired of—the daily routine had to be gone through, and
this was better for all, than having nothing to do like the doctor. All
the most of us had to do was to speculate how long it wanted to the
bell—for breakfast, lunch, dinner and supper! Strict discipline was
kept on board—Wishart never relaxed this—he was a commander. Holland was not much of a sailor or anything else,—he and the Captain
being so different did not get on well together. Wishart took charge
of the ship and no matter how bad the weather, he would remain on
deck night and day and was always ready at a moment's notice.

Of course some natives squatting in canoes came around the ship
and possibly had fish for sale. These natives were a [lot of?] dirty
greasy nasty-smelling creatures—very dark with black hair. Everyone
had on a blanket—or in some cases less—we greenhorns could hardly
distinguish the men from the women. They did not speak one word that
we could understand, and none were allowed to come on board, indeed
none of them seemed desirous of doing so. Their canoes were then as
they are today and the Captain admired their model and so forth. Of
course they could not give us any news. *Waik cumtax* means *don't
understand*. It is said that a son or relation of Sir Robert Peel was an
officer on board one of HM Ships coming here.[1] When the officers
heard the words *waik cumtax*, they twitted Peel, saying the Indians said
they did not want any (in)cumtax![2] At length Esquimalt Harbour
was [?] reached and the ship came to an anchor opposite to where
the dry-dock now stands, [on 24 March 1850].

I need not write much about this, having related the story in a
Xmas number of the *Colonist* newspaper,[3] but a few pages more will
make a consecutive narrative.

As soon as convenient Captain Wishart went to the Fort and took
me with him. I thought the bastions at a distance were dovecotes.

---

[1]Lieutenant William Peel, son of Sir Robert, visited Fort Victoria in H.M.S.
America, Captain the Hon. John Gordon, in the summer of 1845 (see Margaret
A. Ormsby, *British Columbia: a History* [Toronto: Macmillan, 1958], p. 87).
[2]In 1842, during his second term as prime minister, Peel had re-imposed the income tax lifted in 1816.
[3]See "A Reminiscence of 1850," *Colonist*, Holiday Number, December 1887, reprinted in Appendix 2. Some extracts from this article have already appeared
under the title "A Day in Fort Victoria," in *British Columbia: A Centennial
Anthology*, ed. R. E. Watters (Toronto: McClelland and Stewart, 1958), pp.
381-88.

There was nothing else to be seen save land, water, canoes and Indians. It did not seem very inspiriting—it looked like York Factory—about as solitary, for when I was at York Factory was a busy time—for them. I fell into the charge of Dr. Benson whilst Wishart saw Mr. Douglas,[1] the end of his confab being, that the ship and crew were to be considered in quarantine, until everyone had washed and scrubbed all their belongings and themselves. I saw Mr. Douglas—he did not impress me very favourably, being of very grave disposition with an air of dignity—cold and unimpassioned. A dark-complexioned man—with rather scanty hair, but not too scanty—muscular—broad-shouldered—with powerful legs a little bowed—common to strong men; in fact he was a splendid specimen of a man. His clothes were rather shabby and seedy-looking—but I suppose he had plenty an outfit in the vessel. In fact everyone's clothes looked seedy—when compared with the Captain's and mine, for we had of course dressed respectably for the occasion, but altho the clothes were not fashionable, the wearers looked strong healthy active and clean—save Benson who looked a sloven, with a pair of sea-boots on—part of his trowsers being within them. Mr. Douglas was coldly affable—but he improved vastly on acquaintance afterwards.

The Fort has been described, but at the windows stood a number of young ladies, hidden behind the curtains, looking at the late important arrivals, for visitors were scarce here, but we were not introduced. Anyhow before going away, the room of Mr. Douglas, partly an office and partly domestic, stood open, and there I saw Cecilia his eldest daughter[2] flitting about, active as a little squirrel, and one of the prettiest objects I had ever seen: rather short but with a very pretty graceful figure—of dark complexion and lovely black eyes—petite and nice. She assisted her father in clerical work, correspondence and so forth—in fact a private secretary. I was more or less captivated. Afterwards I heard her singing in the Church,[3] and she had a beautiful voice tho uneducated.

---

[1]Chief Factor James Douglas, later Sir James Douglas, K.C.B., (1803-77) had established Fort Victoria in 1843. He was in charge there from 1849, when the HBC moved its headquarters from Fort Vancouver, until 1858, when he was appointed governor of the gold colony of British Columbia on condition that he sever his connection with the HBC.

[2]Born at Fort Vancouver in 1834. Four other children had preceded her, but all of them died in infancy (see the Douglas family tree in PABC).

[3]Construction of the Victoria District Church, later called Christ Church, began in 1853, but it was not until 31 August 1856 that the building was opened for divine service (see "The Journal of Arthur Thomas Bushby 1858-1859," ed. Dorothy Blakey Smith, *BCHQ* 21 [1957-58]: 117n35). JSH may therefore be referring to the earlier services held in the mess room of the fort, where the young

Pianos at this time were unknown in Victoria and I question very much whether one existed in British Columbia—Washington—or Oregon—the latter to me doubtful anyhow. Probably no musical instrument existed in Victoria save the howl and barking of dogs, and the discordant music of Indians from the tomtoms.

Mrs. Finlayson[1] was introduced to me by Benson at her residence, a room in her husband's office, which stood very near to where my office now stands. Having a "styin" [styan] on her eye or something else, she would not at first come forward, being bashful and at the same time but recently married. The visit was a short one.

Finlayson looked rather pallid, but was quiet and very agreeable, rubbing his hands slowly together.[2] I talked about the Fort yard being so wet—round poles existed to walk on between the different stores—altho there was a waggon road through the centre of the Fort, in a line with Fort Street. "Ah," said Finlayson, "when the Revd. Mr. Staines came,[3] a few months ago, it was much worse, and when Mrs. Staines landed we put down what we could for her to walk on. She wanted to know where the streets were? Whether this was the place they were destined for? Everything cannot be done in a day and now you have brought us more men I hope things will go on more quickly." Finlayson had built the Fort. J. W. McKay[4] was his second—a very active young fellow—

---

ladies led the hymns, for there was "no instrument and no organized choir" ("Bishop Cridge Recalls Memories of the Past," *Colonist*, 22 December 1907, p. 29).

[1]Sarah, second daughter of John Work, was married to Roderick Finlayson on 14 December 1849 (Fort Victoria marriage register, copy, PABC). She died in Victoria on 24 January 1906 (*Colonist*, 26 January 1906).

[2]Roderick Finlayson (1818-92), one of the party who built Fort Victoria in 1843, was placed in charge there on the death of Charles Ross in 1844. For further details see the biography in *McLoughlin Letters ... Second Series*, pp. 388-89. Extracts from Finlayson's autobiography (Victoria, 1891[?]) were published with explanatory comments by JSH in a series of six articles in the *Colonist*, 18 October to 6 December 1903, the last four being headed "Historical Reminiscences."

[3]Robert John Staines (1820-54), appointed chaplain and schoolmaster to the HBC in 1848, arrived at Fort Victoria with his wife, Emma Frances Tahourdin, on 17 March 1849. For further details see G. Hollis Slater, "Rev. Robert John Staines: Pioneer Priest, Pedagogue, and Political Agitator," *BCHQ* 14 (1950): 187-240.

[4]Joseph William McKay or Mackay (1829-1900) was born at Rupert House, Hudson Bay and came to Fort Vancouver in 1844. In 1852 he opened up the coal fields at Nanaimo for the HBC and the following year supervised the building of the Nanaimo Bastion, which still stands. For further details see Walbran, *British Columbia Coast Names*; and Patricia M. Johnson, *A Short History of Nanaimo* (Nanaimo: City of Nanaimo Centennial Committee, 1958), pp. 9-11.

full of vigor and intelligence, whose parents resided at Red River or someway thereabout—Fort Garry probably.

Nevin had charge of the fleet and what not!¹ A good-natured active man, but too fond of grog and women. Sangster a short man—active but slow in speech, was or had been Captain of the *Cadboro*² and was now pilot when required. He had been daily at Beacon Hill, with his telescope looking for the *Norman Morison*. At this time it was the custom of HB Ships to fire two guns after rounding Rocky Point, to give notice of arrival and I suppose the want of a pilot. At all events we followed the usual practice.

The most of the men in the Fort were either French Canadians or Kanakas—an Iroquois or two—the former were very jolly contented fellows.

There was I think a hut outside the Fort near Church Hill, occupied by one of the Company's people, but this was the only residence near the Fort. There were however some farm buildings on Fort Street. The country round about Victoria looked like a park with oak trees interspersed. Church Hill was covered with oak trees—and cut oak timber also lay about—it being intended to use them to build a ship, schooner or scows.

Anyhow the visit came to an end and we had to go back to Esquimault.

Now I do not remember whether it was at Esquimault or Victoria— but pretty certain it was Esquimault. One night while I was in bed and

¹See below, p. 125. Charles A. Nevin was first officer on the *Una* 1851-52 and on the *Recovery* 1852-53. He then apparently left the HBC service, although he is listed among the clerks of the Western Department in 1853-54 (HBC Archives, B. 239/g and 226/g series).

²James Sangster was captain of the *Cadboro* 1848-54 and also pilot and harbour master at Victoria. On 6 October 1852 he was appointed collector of customs for Vancouver Island and on 5 May 1857 postmaster at Victoria (Vancouver Island, Legislative Council, *Minutes Commencing August 30th 1851 and Terminating...February 6th 1861*, ed. E. O. S. Scholefield, Archives Memoir no. 2 [Victoria: King's Printer, 1918], pp. 17, 30). He appears to have committed suicide at his house near Esquimalt Lagoon in 1858 (cf. p. 126 below; Walbran, *British Columbia Coast Names*; and the note by Ed. Huggins on the letter from Sangster to P. S. Ogden and James Douglas, 10 May 1848, concerning the wreck of the *Vancouver*, MS, PABC). The brigantine *Cadboro* was built at Rye, Sussex, in 1824 and arrived at Fort Vancouver in 1827. She was the first vessel to enter the Fraser River (1827) and to enter the harbour of Victoria (1842). For further details see Walbran, *British Columbia Coast Names*; and *Lewis & Dryden's Marine History of the Pacific Northwest*, ed. E. W. Wright (Portland, Ore.: Lewis & Dryden Printing Co., 1895), p. 13.

asleep, the Captain woke me, and said, "Governor Blanshard has come on board from the HMS *Driver* to see you."[1] Well, I suppose I grumbled, and the Governor sent word not to bother, as there would be plenty opportunities later. I did not see him. The fact is I should have got up with alacrity, but I supposed I was tired or lazy. Having a sort of hazy idea that I was to be his assistant should have made me at once meet him and show off my best qualities, if I had any. However, Blanshard and I never became friends—he evidently did not care for me.

It was pretty monotonous in quarantine. The men and women were set to work to scrub their things—the washing and drying was done near where the Hudson's Bay store and Maple Bank[2] now are. The ship had to be painted—scrubbed &c.

During this period the Captain and I used to walk about [what is?] now called Langford Plains and thereabouts. We gave it the name of Greenwich and Blackheath. It was an awfully pretty place, covered with grass and wild flowers, and red-winged starling flitted about in the willows—how much land we travelled over there is uncertain, but Wishart had good ideas of locality and we always found our way back —pretty tired sometimes, for there were no trails in the bush then—but the bush and forest have much grown up there since. The sawmill existed at Rowe's [Rowe] Stream[3] and George McKenzie had charge

---

[1]Blanshard had reached Panama from England late in November 1849 and had been picked up by H.M.S. *Driver*, Captain Charles R. Johnson, which landed him at Fort Victoria in March 1850 (Ireland, "Richard Blanshard," p. 223).

[2]A private house on HBC property close to the Indian reserve on Esquimalt Harbour, off the present Admirals Road. In 1892 it was the residence of Captain A. E. McCallum.

[3]Rowe Stream, marked on Admiralty charts as flowing into Esquimalt Harbour, was called Millstream at least as early as 1903 (*Colonist*, 6 December 1903) and retains the name today. Here in 1848 the HBC established a sawmill about a quarter of a mile upstream from the present Parsons Bridge (W. Kaye Lamb, "Early Lumbering on Vancouver Island: Part I 1844-1855," *BCHQ* 2 (1938): 39). This mill was erected by John Fenton, a millwright and miller sent from Fort Vancouver (see *John McLoughlin's Business Correspondence 1847-48*, ed. William R. Sampson [Seattle: University of Washington Press, 1973], p. 94n148). On 24 April 1849 Fenton joined the gold rush to California and was succeeded the following year by William Richard Parson (later spelled Parsons), a miller who had arrived with JSH on the *Norman Morison* and who was landed along with the machinery for a grist mill and ten men at Esquimalt Harbour on 27 March 1850 (see the Fort Victoria Journal; copies of the relevant entries, 1847-1850, are in PABC). The grist mill was erected downstream from the sawmill, and both were in operation until much of the installation was destroyed in a freshet in 1854-55 (Lamb, "Early Lumbering," pp. 39-40).

and is still living.[1] He had a remarkably handsome half-breed wife, laughing good-natured and industrious.

The piece of land which my son James now holds took my fancy and I determined to get it somehow or other. At this time a few acres of land seemed to me a big piece—so utterly ignorant was I of land perhaps on account of having been brought up in London. I only applied for twenty acres! Well £20 was a good sum to me in those days, besides the restrictions placed on the sale of land were rather onerous— that is to say, no one could have land excepting he imported people to work it or on it! Importing people from England then was not impossible, but came very near the impossible.[2] At this time the Captain

[1]George McKenzie was a millwright by trade (see the entry concerning his son Donald, 27 April 1851, in the Fort Victoria register of baptisms, copy, PABC) and was presumably in charge of the sawmill between the departure of Fenton and the arrival of W. R. Parson. His obituary (*Colonist*, 31 October 1893) claims that he "built British Columbia's first sawmill"; James Deans, "Settlement of Vancouver Island" (typescript, PABC) also says that "George McKenzie erected the [HBC saw and grist] mill." But his name is not mentioned in the Fort Victoria Journal, and the entry for 24 April 1849 reads: "Mr. Fenton who built the sawmill leaves today for the California mines."

[2]JSH's memory of this transaction is somewhat confused. The "rather onerous" restrictions on the sale of land never applied to property less than one hundred acres, and by the end of 1852 even these had been officially relaxed (see Wrinch, "Land Policy," p. 39); also, in 1892 James Douglas Helmcken did not own the first piece of property for which JSH made application. On 28 April 1851 Douglas wrote to Archibald Barclay: "Dr. Helmcken lately applied to me for the purchase of 20 acres of land on the Fur Trade Reserve, which I informed him could not be sold without the Committee's instructions, and he has now addressed you, on that subject, in the enclosed note. The land he wants is on Lot 37 and may be sold without prejudice to the Reserve. It is a plain of about 4 acres in extent, entirely surrounded by thick woods—except on the Canal side of the Canal of Camosin [i.e. Victoria Harbour?] on which it is situated and is used neither for tillage nor as pasture land, being inaccessible to the cattle" (Fort Victoria, Correspondence Outward to HBC on affairs of Vancouver Island Colony, May 16, 1850—November 6, 1855, PABC). So far it has not proved possible to identify this piece of land, and apparently JSH did not complete the purchase, for Douglas wrote again on 4 December 1851: "In reference to the land applied for by Dr. Helmcken I shall act according to your instructions, although he has not spoken to me on the subject lately and it is rather doubtful whether he is now disposed to make the purchase" (ibid.). The Abstract of the Victoria Land Register (in Vancouver Island, Lands and Works Department, Land Sales Annual Reports, 1853-60, PABC) shows that JSH purchased Lot 9, Section VIII, Esquimalt District, 53 acres, on 15 December 1851. He completed the purchase of Section VIII, 137 acres net, on 22 June 1857 and on 1 August 1856 he purchased the adjoining Section XXVII, 14 acres net (see ibid., Land Sales to March 31, 1860). These two sections he leased for farming purposes to James Stewart, who had come out in 1853 with Kenneth McKenzie to Craigflower and who now built a house on the property, which he called Seaview Farm. The date was 1862, according to James Stewart's obituary (*Colonist*,

and I believed Esquimault to be destined to become a very important place, but neither of us thought anything of Victoria and yet neither of us thought of applying for land in Constance Cove. Anyhow it had been reserved for the Puget Sound Company.[1]

Whilst the people then are getting ready to get out of quarantine, I will say a few words about my voyage to Hudson's Bay.[2]

About the first week in June, probably 1846 or 47,[3] I appeared on board the good ship *Prince Rupert* bound for York Factory, Hudson's Bay—she made an annual trip—the Captain,[4] officers and men were all old hands—the ship built special for the service, as lined outside with thick planking and her bows were about *six feet thick*—but I never measured this.

---

24 June 1892). The only document relevant to this lease which has been traced is a tax receipt (in the possession of Mrs. Lillian Culling, granddaughter of James Stewart) for Lots 8, 27, and 92, Esquimalt, 20 June 1906, in favour of the "Est[ate] of Jas Stewart." Records in the Land Registry Office in Victoria show that JSH received a certificate of indefeasible title to Sections VIII and XXVII on 22 January 1875, and that he conveyed the property to his son James in two parts: Section VIII on 7 February 1891, subject to a lease which would expire on 6 February 1893; and Section XXVII on 31 December 1894. In 1911 James Douglas Helmcken sold some eighty acres on the waterfront to the Island Investment Company, which subdivided the property as "View Royal" and put the lots on the market in September 1912 (see *Colonist*, 29 September 1912). The area is still known as View Royal today.

[1]The Puget's Sound Agricultural Company was a subsidiary of the HBC, established in 1839 to carry on large-scale farming operations at Fort Nisqually and in the Cowlitz Valley. It operated also on Vancouver Island after the transfer of the HBC headquarters from Fort Vancouver to Fort Victoria in 1849 (Ormsby, *British Columbia*, pp. 76, 102).

[2]See above, pp. 54-55. It is interesting to compare JSH's account with that given by R. M. Ballantyne, who as a HBC clerk sailed in 1841 on the *Prince Rupert's* first voyage to Hudson Bay under the same captain (see *Hudson's Bay; or, Everyday Life in the Wilds of North America* [Edinburgh: Blackwood, 1848]).

[3]The *Prince Rupert* sailed from Gravesend on 7 June 1847 (London *Times*, 8 June 1847).

[4]David Herd made his first voyage as ship master in 1839 with the fifth *Prince Rupert* and his last with the second *Prince of Wales* in 1863. The secretary of the HBC wrote of him in 1864: "He has made 32 successful voyages to Hudson's Bay, in 26 of which he was in command of ships. During that long period he has had no casualty worth speaking of, nor was there ever a claim made on the Underwriters for losses sustained by vessel and cargo. His success has been perhaps unexampled in any service..." (Oliver Warner, "Voyaging to York Factory," *The Beaver* [Winter 1957]: 21 [York Factory issue]). In the third edition of his *Hudson's Bay* (1857), Ballantyne described Captain Herd as "a thin, middle-sized, offhand man, thoroughly acquainted with his profession; good-humoured and gruff by turns; and he always spoke with the air of an oracle" (p. 7).

The great people of the Hudson's Bay Company came on board—did their business—had wine with the Captain: among the visitors were Sir George [i.e. John] Richardson and some others, because some men and supplies were going out in this vessel on a search after the lost Sir John Franklin.[1] The *Prince Albert* was to sail at the same time for Moose Factory[2]—the Surgeon—King alias Splenus Colli—his brother having been named at Guy's,[3] Longus Colli, on account of the great length of his neck.

The Captains, Mates and Surgeon were invited to dine ashore—but I forget the name of the Hotel—with the great officials. The dinner was, rely on it, sumptuous, and a turbot was placed before me for distribution. I knew nothing about turbot but a gentleman on my right kindly guided me in the carving! Of course I had seen plenty turbot but what to do with this one was another matter—I was very green, but if the fish had been placed before me for my own use, I guess I should have known pretty well how to cut it for my own satisfaction or that of any ordinary person! However, the dinner over, we go on board in good humour: the old pilot is there and next day we get under weigh—no hurry about anything. We reach the Dogger Bank[4]—put down a long iron bar with a dozen or two hooks and bait attached. The weather being calm, the hooks lie below and in the morning we haul on board two cod fish, one of which is lousy, covered with a sort of small shrimps, the other is not much to boast of but edible.

[1]Sir John Richardson (1787-1865) had accompanied Franklin as surgeon and naturalist on the polar expedition of 1819 and on a second expedition to the mouth of the Mackenzie River in 1825. In the spring of 1847 he was placed in charge of an expedition in search of Franklin, who had been missing since 1845, and Richardson superintended the making of over 17,000 pounds of pemmican and the building of four boats. The boats, the stores, and twenty men were sent out in the *Prince Rupert* and the *Westminster* to York Factory; Richardson followed his party in 1848. He returned to England in 1849, leaving the final stages of the Franklin search to his assistant, Dr. John Rae (see below, p. 99) and soon afterwards published his *Arctic Searching Expedition: A Journal of a Boat Voyage through Rupert's Land and the Arctic Sea, in Search of the Discovery Ships under the Command of Sir John Franklin* (London: Longmans, 1851).
[2]Launched along with the sixth *Prince Rupert* at the Blackwall Yard of Wigrams and Green in 1841 (Cameron, "Ships of Three Centuries," p. 13). She sailed on 6 June followed by the *Prince Rupert* on the 7th and the *Westminster* on the 9th (London *Times* 7, 8, and 10 June 1847). See Plate 10.
[3]There are two students named King in the Guy's Hospital lists contemporary with JSH: "Mr. C. King," who received his L.S.A. in May 1847 and was a-warded a dressership in October 1847; and "Mr. George Henry King," who received his M.R.C.S. in November 1847.
[4]The fishing ground in the central North Sea, between England and Denmark.

In due course we arrive at the coast of Caithness—John o'Groat's-House. There a Caithness pilot came on board—such a specimen—no one understood his English and as to his clothing, this seemed to have been made up of detached pieces, sewn together. He was an active fellow tho, but looked very poor.

This coast was wild and looked uninhabited. However, we soon came in sight of the Orkney Islands—a lot of rolling rounded hills, without trees, but green and looked nice and picturesque, for the weather happened to be very fine. At length we anchored in Stromness Harbour and the *Albert* came in also.[1] We had come here in the usual course of things, to pick up some new servants of the Company for Hudson's Bay—I forget how many, but every one had to be examined by me, because no one would be engaged excepting he was in at least physical good health, and I found out, mentally too. These men had been collected from the various islands, and I only rejected one man whom I considered consumptive, much to the disgust of the procurer, who had brought him a good distance. The men anyhow were fine men, and altho not over-intelligent, were quite as good as the generality of secluded people—they did not know too much and had been accustomed to obedience.

Of course we went ashore, the town was a fishing village and had but little to boast of architecturally or otherwise—but astonished me a little. Over the small shops were the names of the occupants, but there only appeared to be four or five names amongst which Flett appeared to be the most frequent. Butchers were called "fleshers," and Oh—the meat exhibited—why even the sides of beef, of which there were not many, were not the size of those of ordinary calves and the sheep not larger than good sized dogs, but the meat was awfully good tho very dark. Of shops none were remarkable to me—that is to say for magnificence or greatness, they were all mean. Of course the arrival of the ships made a sort of holiday, and so everyone was astir, but Oh—the number of "Naturals" as they called the semi-idiotic people! They were met with everywhere, at least they were numerous enough to be remarkable.

Of course we wandered about for a day or two—the roads were dry

---

[1]On 17 June 1847 (*Letters of Letitia Hargrave*, ed. Margaret Arnett MacLeod [Toronto: Champlain Society, 1941], p. 225). For Stromness and its long connection with the HBC, see J. Storer Clouston, "Orkney and the Hudson's Bay Company," *The Beaver* (December 1936): 4-8; (March 1937): 38-43, 62; (September 1937): 37-39.

and very good; the fields fenced with stone, loose; in fact the whole country was stone, with a few inches of soil now and again on the surface, in some places this was cultivated, and then the mustard seemed to smother the crops chiefly I think of oats, but insignificant as to acreage; the remainder was pasture—fed by rain. Not a tree to be seen anywhere! We were told to go to Kirkwall—and there we would see some fine trees, the only ones in the island, but I did not get there. Mr. Clouston the clergyman,[1] told me they had had to cart earth from anywhere to make a garden, but even then trees would not flourish. On our wanderings we used to see fine healthy robust damsels coming to town bare-footed, but as soon as they came to the brook on the border of the town, they washed their feet and put on hose and boots! This seemed to be a matter of economy as well as choice. I knew very little of Sir Walter Scott then, had I known more it would have been more interesting,[2] but we came across a big stone building of four walls— like a big barn. We went in invited or otherwise. The walls were as rough within as without, but places had been left in the walls—like stones removed which served for shelves and small cupboards. Of furniture there was but little, the woodwork above and roof inside were dark and black from smoke, for they had a fire of peat on the floor, which was natural ground, but a big chimney also existed. At one end of this building the cows were kept, and at the other end the in-habitants lived, with intermediate places, perhaps for sheep or lambs, but I did not see either horses or pigs; anyhow all lived under the same roof and all seemed equally and perfectly content and happy. The place was nevertheless tidy and the good folk hospitable—indeed the people generally were.

The ship laid in geese, chickens and so forth. Geese cost six pence each, eggs a few pence a dozen—everything appeared to be very cheap.

Here I saw the Revd. Mr. Clouston, a venerable simple-minded man of benevolent aspect, who had spiritual charge about here—his son was

---

[1]Presumably the Rev. Charles Clouston, who married the elder daughter of Ed-ward Clouston of Stromness and lived at Sandwich Manse, five or six miles from Stromness (*Letters of Letitia Hargrave*, pp. 226, 227).

[2]*The Pirate* (1821) is set for the most part in seventeenth-century Shetland and is based on the notes which Scott himself took on his holiday in the Orkney and Shetland Islands in 1814, immediately after the anonymous publication of *Waverley*. He is said to have taken as his models for Brenda and Minna (the fair daughters of the udaller Magnus Troil) the sisters of Dr. John Rae (*Letters of Letitia Hargrave*, p. xxxiii; and *John Rae's Correspondence with the Hudson's Bay Company on Arctic Exploration 1844-45*, ed. E. E. Rich [London: Hud-son's Bay Record Society, 1953], p. xiv).

in the HBCo's service and some years afterwards I saw him, a tall active fellow, in Victoria. He had led the brigade across from Fort York, and had on the capote and red sash. He bought land now called [Garbally?]. Poor fellow he died of consumption—I fancy at Sandwich Islands.[1]

I saw Dr. Hamilton the medico,[2] a tall quiet well-built man—who had a big open sail-boat with which he used to visit patients in the neighbouring islands and of course was a good sailor. I had to leave one of our men with him for axillary abscess, as no one wished to have helpless people aboard. He introduced me to Mrs. Ray [Rae], a venerable old lady—very nice and quiet—her son Dr. Rae was in the HB service, of whom more bye and bye.[3] Hamilton's son came into the HB service and is now up country—Babine Lake or somewhere there[4] —Hamilton Moffat [Moffatt] of the Indian Department is related to this family also.[5]

[1]Robert Clouston was the son of Edward Clouston of Stromness (*Letters of Letitia Hargrave*, p. 226n2) and consequently the brother-in-law, not the son, of the Rev. Charles Clouston. He entered the HBC service in 1838 and replaced William Mactavish as accountant at York Factory in 1848. His wife Jessy (daughter of Donald Ross of Norway House) died of tuberculosis in 1849, and he went on furlough because of the same disease. He was later agent for the HBC at Honolulu, and he died on 14 August 1858 on his way from Hawaii to San Francisco (ibid., passim; and *Victoria Gazette*, 17 September 1858). The Victoria District Official Map, 1858, shows that Robert Clouston owned Section V, 110 acres, on Selkirk Water, and the name which JSH could not remember was probably Garbally, since Richard Woods of Garbally House is listed in the Victoria District Assessment Roll for 1863-64 as the owner of Section V, 53 acres. The present Garbally Road perpetuates the name.

[2]Dr. John Macaulay Hamilton married Marion, a sister of Dr. John Rae (*Rae's Arctic Correspondence*, p. xiv), and the couple later joined her brothers Richard and Thomas in Hamilton, Upper Canada (*Letters of Letitia Hargrave*, p. xxxiv).

[3]Margaret Glen Rae was the widow of John Rae, whom Edward Clouston had succeeded as the company's agent in Stromness c. 1836. Three of her sons, William Glen, Richard, and Dr. John entered the HBC service (*Letters of Letitia Hargrave*, p. xxxiii). For Dr. Rae, see below, p. 99.

[4]Gavin Hamilton (1835-1909) arrived in Victoria on the *Norman Morison* on 16 January 1853 and served in the New Caledonia district, where he established trading posts among the Babines. He retired from the HBC in the 1870's and erected a saw and grist mill on the Cariboo Road, which burned down in 1879 (*Colonist*, 26 August 1879). He afterwards made his headquarters at Lac La Hache. For further details see A. G. Morice, *History of the Northern Interior of British Columbia* (Toronto: W. Briggs, 1904), p. 337; and the obituary in the *Colonist*, 31 July 1909.

[5]According to the obituary in the *Colonist*, 14 April 1894, Hamilton Moffatt (1832-94) was "the nephew of the late Dr. John Rae" and was presumably therefore the son of Janet Rae (see *Rae's Arctic Correspondence*, p. xiv). He came to this coast in 1850, served at Fort Rupert and in New Caledonia, and retired

The Orkneymen were proud of a patent slip for hauling up and on damaged vessels—I suppose a small affair now. A "mail," a horse and cart perhaps, went once a week to Kirkwall, but I think steamboats existed not—everything seemed rather primitive.

King and I determined to have a dinner at the Hotel—a Scotch dinner ordered. So the landlady gave us cock-a-leekie soup and a goose stuffed with raisins and some other dishes besides. Well we would have some buttermilk; the landlady thought it not to be fresh enough but for all this I drank some, possibly for the first time in my life and I think the last. Well we had not finished dinner very long, when we went out for a walk and thought of having eaten too freely—first loosened one button and then another until with open waistcoat and loosened trowsers I managed to breathe a little more freely—but gracious goodness I had become protuberant—swollen with flatulence and so round that I might have been rolled about like a football! Well I am living still but no more buttermilk or geese stuffed with raisins for me.

Curiously enough the people here did not consider themselves Scotch or Scotsmen, at least the landlady said so, but of what independent country they were, I have yet to discover.[1]

Of course everybody knew Captain Herd, Mate Reid and Captain Royal, the commodore[2]—they were quite at home here.

How many fishing boats they had here I do not know, but I was told they gathered seaweed—for procuring iodine?

At length we get away and shape our course for Hudson's Straits —weather fine—tho sometimes foggy and it feels cold.

One morning, when in my bunk, I heard a grating dull heavy grate alongside my ear apparently, and could not make it out—so I called the Steward. "We are in the ice, Sir," and sure enough when I got on deck, there was thick ice floating round about us and now and

---

from the HBC service in 1872. The next year he joined the Department of Indian Affairs at Victoria and served there until a few months before his death. For further details see Walbran, *British Columbia Coast Names*.

[1]From 865 to 1498 the Orkneys belonged to Norway. J. Storer Clouston quotes from one "Murdoch Mackenzie's account written in 1750" as follows: "The language is English in the Scotch dialect, with more of the Norwegian than any other accent, these islands having formerly been a province of Norway, of which they still retain some of the customs and a little of the language, which they call *Noren*, much the same with what is presently spoken in Iceland and the Faroe Islands" ("Orkney," p. 8).

[2]Presumably the Thomas Royal of the *Mercantile Navy List*, 1857. He was the captain of the *Prince Albert* (*Letters of Letitia Hargrave*, p. 225n3).

again scraping the ship's side! "Shall have lots of it this time," says
Captain Herd—this was at the entrance to the Straits. We carried this
ice all the way to Hudson's Bay—passed Mansfield Island, where the
greatest jam seemed to be. Icebergs all around, innumerable—some
seemed to loom as high as St. Paul's Cathedral! Anyhow they were
taller and larger than any block of building in Victoria, and of all
kinds of architecture. Some looked beautiful blue in the caverns—
waterfalls about them common—there were hundreds of them in sight!
The ice was in motion—the floe ice eight or ten feet thick—the sheets
from an acre or more in size to much smaller and of all shapes—it
looked impenetrable. However, lanes opened among the ice and the
ship directed through them—then this lane would close and we had to
wait until another opened to let the ship proceed—of course the most
promising lanes were chosen, and here the Captain would sometimes
amuse himself by playing billiards with sheets of ice of comparatively
small size. "Now see me make a cannon"—so the ship's bows struck
the ice and it bounded off to strike another, to the joy of the skipper.
Any ordinary vessel would have had her bows stove, but the *Rupert*
—she did not care for pieces of ice eight or ten feet thick, provided
they were not large but movable. Sometimes we had to anchor the ship
to an ice floe and take in sail—of course the anchors are only a sort
of hooks to the ice made for the purpose, but we tried never to anchor
near a berg, for these fellows have the nasty habit of toppling over occasionally or breaking in halves and so forth. Altho everything seemed
silent yet the grating of the ice and apparently breaking of icebergs
or toppling over kept up occasional loud roaring sounds—not so loud
as deep. The wind generally was fair, so the wind was in one direction,
the ice flowing in another towards the ocean we had left. How many
days it took us to get from the mouth of the Straits to Hudson's Bay,
I do not remember.[1] Of course among the ice it felt cold—big great-
coats were comfortable anyhow—the water smooth of course. The
coasts were hilly but awfully barren, weird and brown—desolation.
Esquimaux occasionally came about the ship—in their skin-covered
canoes. They seemed small, greasy and covered with sealskin coats,
some of which coats had long tails—of course of hair seals. They
wanted tobacco or iron or anything else—and were said to be good-

---

[1] Cf. James Hargrave's comment to Dugald Mactavish Senior, 9 September 1847:
"... a very tedious voyage of about nine weeks from Stromness during four of
which we were detained among the ice in Hudson's Straits" (*Letters of Letitia
Hargrave*, appendix, p. 291).

natured but great thieves. They had but little to sell, save seal skins or dresses and the skins of white rabbits, the fur of which was very very long, but were said to be valueless as no one had discovered how to fix the fur so as to prevent it coming out so very easily. I bought some rabbit skins and a sealskin dress—one with a long tail, for something very trifling, tho I recollect not what.

Another ship had sailed with us, with supplies and men for Sir John A. [*sic*] Franklin's search—she carried boats and all sorts of para-phernalia.[1] She had only been sheathed with planking, but managed to get through all right. One day we in the Straits were apparently within a mile of each other becalmed. So Ross a new clerk[2] and a couple of others determined to walk across the ice to the ship. They did not reach her—for after they had gone half a mile or so the ice began to open—so the Captain fired a gun to bring them back. They had trouble enough to get back too—having to leap from ice to ice, and go round about to do it—for of course the ice was in motion. They got aboard at length entirely used up and the Captain blamed himself for allowing the fools to go on so hazardous a frolic. Had anyone tumbled into the water we could not have helped them. Bye the bye I had a musket on board—bought to shoot bear and whales and rhi-noceros and all this sort of thing, so the Captain asked me to bring it up and fire it off. I did it, but really I knew no more about handling a musket than an elephant and the Captain found this out too! Anyhow as we only saw one white bear, and this a long way off, my gun did not come into use either here or on shore. What on earth induced me to buy a musket, I know not, but it was a nice light one, purchased in Leadenhall Street. I saw too but very few seals, but I noticed round holes of some depth in the sheet ice, and at the bottom of the holes was always some dirt. Well I collected it and put it in a bottle and when I showed my curiosity at Hudson's Bay, they said, "It is only the excrement of the seal!"

Now the time we went through all this ice must have been the end of June and beginning of July—the Captain was not surprised but thought the ice rather heavier than usual but still thought it nothing extraordinary. I may here state that on our return in September, the ice

---

[1]The *Westminster* (see Richardson, *Arctic Searching Expedition*, p. 45; and *Letters of Letitia Hargrave*, p. 225).

[2]David Hume Ross, said to be "a discarded middy, grandnephew of the historian Hume," who was sent home the next year and "got tipsy on the schooner going down the river" (*Letters of Letitia Hargrave*, pp. cvi, 234, and 239).

had all disappeared, save that one evening, the look-out reported, "Fog bank ahead, Sir." We went up to see—"You damned fool, don't you know that is no fog bank but an iceberg—port the helm or we shall be on to it." The weather was otherwise clear and fine, sunshine—and the Captain said. "These icebergs in such weather are always sur-rounded by a dense mist." The ship cleared it at a pretty good dis-tance.

We had on board a new clerk for the service named Ross. He was a little puffed up and talked big about "Edinburgh the modern Athens" —a spoiled man for some reason or other. The Steward said to me one day, "Doctor, as soon as I open a tin of jam or jelly, the remainder always disappears. If this goes on I shall have no jelly for return home, because a tin ought to last three days!" "Well, Steward, have you any suspicion?" "I do not like to accuse anyone, but I thought you might help me to find out." So we lay our heads together and decided that I should put some tartar emetic into the remains of the next tin. This was accordingly done and a pretty good dose too. On the same or at all events following day, I was very suddenly called to see Ross, who had been rapidly taken ill—vomiting, purging, collapse and so forth —he might have been tied into knots, so limp was he. "Well Ross what is the matter?" "Oh, I am dying with this cholera.— No, I have not eaten or drunk anything unusual." I said, "It looks like poison, but there is no one else ill. Steward, what became of the jam poisoned for the rats?" "All gone, Sir!" "My God—I am poisoned then, for I ate some of that jam—I am dying—there is no clergyman on board—no one to take my confession!" "Oh, damn the confession—let's see what can be done"—so we put him through [it?] and after a day or so he was well again, but my word, I thought he had had a great deal too much tartar emetic, for the fellow had eaten the half tin of jam! Rely on it he was limp and ghastly indeed, and looked like, and I feared him to be, actually dying—so who just then felt the worse I know not. Ross did not remain long in the service. I heard subsequently that he was or became a "morphine fiend," tho how this could happen is a puzzle, anyhow he proved useless.

Chief Factor Hargrave and Mrs. Hargrave[1] and nurse were passengers

[1]James Hargrave (1798-1865) was sent to York Factory in 1827. For further de-tails see *The Hargrave Correspondence 1821-1843*, ed. G. P. de T. Glazebrook (Toronto: Champlain Society, 1938), introduction. Letitia Hargrave (1813-54) was the sister of William and Dugald Mactavish of the HBC and married James Hargrave in 1840. For further details see MacLeod's introduction to her letters.

also—so the Captain and the above and I had a rubber of whist every night, when possible. I knew nothing about whist, but they broke me in, and account was kept of the games with the debt and so forth! At the end of the journey, I had only four shillings to pay! Not much for learning—Hargrave was a good player, and helped me along.

In due course we arrive at "five fathom hole," a few miles below the river, for this is shallow at this season of the year, tho a torrent earlier. We had been in soundings long before we saw land, for the land hereabouts for very very many miles is about on a level with the sea. A tall beacon had been erected and this is what the Captain had to look for. The land apparently had nothing on it, save stunted pine—Hargrave said it was a mere morass extending hundreds of miles.

A small schooner came down to take the passengers away and I went with them and after various bumpings over cobbles and boulders we at length arrive at the Fort.[1]

Now altho Hargrave, the Chief Factor and in charge of the Fort and district, had been so very familiar and affable on board, no sooner did he set foot ashore than he became dignified cold and distant! Like an admiral, who may be pleasant and urbane ashore, but the moment his foot touches the deck, he is the admiral—discipline prevails, and he may or may not be a tyrant. Hargrave was nevertheless kind in his way, but at this time there happened to be several officers collected at York Factory and the brigade had come in from Red River—i.e. Winnipeg; so he had to go into harness at once.

I did not see much of the brigade—the big heavy boats were there and some birch bark canoes. The men were half-breeds, Indians with some Canadians, and the most these had to do apparently was gambling. Anyhow there was nothing to me very interesting about them, and so after had their "regale" and got the outfits packed for the interior and Norway House, they went off, but I suppose I did not see them go, at all events I have no recollection thereof, but I did want to go as far as Norway House, but the negative came to pass, it being doubtful whether I would be back in time for the ship sailing.[2] The Factory was surrounded with palisades—none of the large posts as at this coast, but

---

[1]For detailed information see the York Factory issue of *The Beaver* (Winter 1957).
[2]Norway House was near the north end of Lake Winnipeg, over three hundred miles from York Factory.

flimsy things and if I remember right, one above the other. The interior
was like other forts tho this was on a larger scale—mess room, warehouses and so forth. Here I saw McTavish [Mactavish], the accountant, who was the brother of Mrs. Hargrave and also of Dugald Mactavish (our Victoria Chief).[1] Mactavish was "sandy"—pleasant but
not talkative—a thinking man. When I went to Ottawa, I met Dugald
Mactavish at Montreal[2]—he had just received a telegram from his
brother, who had arrived in New York. Dugald pressed me to go with
him there, and as I had a couple of days to spare I went. Poor Mactavish was near his end, of consumption. He left and died as soon as
he reached Scotland. Dugald put up at the Brevoort House—paid all
my expenses of the trip—this House is very aristocratic.

   There were of course other officers, from various places and belonging to the Fort itself, but I do not remember their names, but one
was from Churchill, who was not liked because he was considered a
sneak, going about taking notes and an eaves-dropper. He had a son
affected with snow blindness, the first I had seen. Dr. Smiley [Smellie]
was the medico[3]—he seemed to have to attend to other duties not at all
connected with his profession, which he did not like—possibly serving
out rations or attending to some store. He asked me to stay and allow
him to go home for a holiday, but as I had to be back at the Hospital
and assuredly did not like the Factory and surroundings, I politely
declined. He was a good fellow too but seemed out of place. He showed
me the furs &c. and I wanted to buy some martens, Hargrave said the

[1]William Mactavish (d. 1870) entered the HBC service in 1832, along with his
brother Dugald. He came to Rupert's Land in 1833, was governor of Assiniboia
1858-70 and of Rupert's Land 1864-70. At the time of the Riel Rebellion in
1869 he was seriously ill with tuberculosis, and Riel therefore found it easier
to seize authority. After the rebellion had been suppressed Mactavish left the
colony and died on his way home to Scotland. For further information see
Dufferin-Carnarvon Correspondence, 1874-1878, ed. C. W. deKiewiet and F. H.
Underhill (Toronto: Champlain Society, 1955), biographical notes; and Norah
Story, *The Oxford Companion to Canadian History and Literature* (Toronto:
Oxford, 1967). His younger brother Dugald (1817-71) came to Moose Factory
in 1833 and in 1839 was transferred to the Columbia Department. He served at
Victoria from 1858 to 1865. For further details see the article by William R.
Sampson in *DCB* 10.
[2]In 1870, during the Confederation negotiations in Ottawa, the delegates made
a trip to Montreal to see Prince Arthur invested as Knight Grand Cross of the
Order of St. Michael and St. George (see below, p. 261).
[3]William Smellie, M.D., the son of a Freechurch minister in Orkney (*Letters of
Letitia Hargrave,* pp. 207, 248).

rule was, that anyone purchasing would have to pay the highest ruling price in London for the kind of fur. Of course the young men were full of fun—but of course this seemed to be their festival.

The first time I dined at the mess, Hargrave at the head and Mactavish at the foot of the table, Hargrave descanted on the beauties and benefits of "white fish" of which some small ones were on the table —caught I suspect in the river. However, ducks came on—and asked whether I would take duck or goose—duck—so a whole one was put on my plate! Not [a ?] very large one to be sure, but I did not know how to begin eating it, but before I had begun my neighbour sent for another! "Oh," said he, "if you were here in the winter, you would see us eat two or three geese each!"—they kept these stored in ice. Then came cranberry tarts—cranberries are plentiful and each tart being about two feet long and 8 inches or so broad—of course this had to be cut into pieces. There was Madeira wine—and it was said that Madeira was sent from England to be stored away for seasoning and then returned to England again, for the HBCo magnates.

No musquitoes—"Oh," said my neighbour, "if you had arrived a couple of weeks earlier, you would not have sat so quietly in your open cane-bottom chair—these pests are awful here in their season."

They had a powder magazine built of solid masonry—imported from England—but the ground hereabouts a couple of feet from the surface is always winter and summer frozen solid, so if a man is to be buried, they have to blast out a grave!

Hargrave shewed me a shed covered with glass, in which they tried to grow radishes, turnips and vegetables—some grew to the size of marbles, but as a rule the young plants were destroyed by flies. Nothing in the shape of vegetables can be cultivated here.

I saw the dog kennels and outside big seals almost as large as men— this to feed the dogs of whom a Highlander was in charge, but the stench from seals and dogs was not pleasant and so I soon quit—and thus know nothing about the HBC stables—for dogs are the only animals used in winter season.

For hundreds of miles the country round about the Fort is but one vast morass—in summer dangerous—this morass seemed covered with small stunted pine, and lots of blueberries and others grew amongst the moss—of course I did not penetrate far into it. The only land to walk on was a narrow bank along the river front! And a small quantity leading to and about the dog kennels—it was and is a miserable place —apparently worthless, and yet along the bank, grew wonderfully fine black currants—and a shrub covered with beautiful red edible berries

—strawberries grew too but were out of season now. Burke the botanist,[1] an eccentric fellow, had come from the interior and having been spilt into the river, had lost everything. He had trowsers too long and coat too short, the best the Company's store, not much stocked, could supply, but which made him very grotesque—this did not matter here. Of natives there were but few. A woman went away to gather sticks, returning with the sticks and a baby which she had passed in her travels, into the bargain. She had only been gone a few hours.

The people about the Fort seemed happy and healthy enough—but were longing for winter! because then the swamp was frozen and covered with snow and they could drive their sledges for hundreds of miles on a level!

Mrs. Hargrave was one of those nice ladies, one occasionally meets with, kind and affable.[2] Altho not handsome she had a decidedly nice face—and a very pleasing expression with a very good figure—her house was a few yards from the Fort proper—small but of course nice and nicely kept. A daughter, small and bright, named Tash, and I think a baby born on the *Rupert* there also.[3]

Anyhow Mrs. Hargrave made things pleasant for me, for I had nothing

[1]Joseph Burke had come to York Factory in the summer of 1843 with a commission to collect plants and animals in North America for the Earl of Derby and the Royal Botanical Gardens then under the direction of Sir William Hooker. He spent three weeks at York Factory, wintered in Saskatchewan, and crossed the mountains to the Columbia in the spring of 1844 (see *McLoughlin Letters . . . Third Series,* p. 59n3; and *Letters of Letitia Hargrave,* p. 161n., which adds that according to the HBC Archives no published account of Burke's North American journey has been found). Letitia herself wrote to her mother, 14 September 1843, that he was "evidently not a literary character—I don't think he will publish his travels" (ibid., p. 176).

[2]Mrs. Hargrave set down her impressions of JSH in letters to her family. The Hargraves had come to Stromness by steamer from Edinburgh (James Hargrave to Dugald Mactavish Senior, 5 April 1847, *Letters of Letitia Hargrave,* appendix, p. 290), and as soon as the *Prince Rupert* anchored Letitia "immediately sent on board for the medico, as I did not like to trust myself with an Orkney Doctor. The ship man is called Helmkill at least it sounds so. He is young but seems rather 'cute & tho' a prodigiously little man seems like a gent[lema]n. . . . It seems that our Dr., Mr. Helmside, is a German educated in Eng[lan]d. Both he & the Albert's surgeon are rather queer looking & evidently very young. The other's name is King. They are very agreeable in their own way" (ibid., pp. 225, 229).

[3]Letitia Lockhart Hargrave (1844-80), called Tash, was indeed aboard the *Prince Rupert* in 1847 with JSH; but her younger sister Mary Jane was not born till 10 July 1848, and she, like the three other Hargrave children, was born at York Factory (see Letitia to her mother, Mrs. Mactavish, 22 August 1848, *Letters of Letitia Hargrave;* and *Hargrave Correspondence,* p. xviii).

to do but loaf in this constricted place—there was but little to interest me anyhow—and no "lions" to be seen—no neighbours within hundreds of miles.

Whilst there, however, Dr. Rae arrived.[1] He was an active powerful broad-shouldered man, of medium height—dark and bronzed—full of energy and as active as a squirrel and good-humoured and natured. He had been on an exploring expedition, possibly in relation to Sir J. Franklin. All he had was a couple of large heavy boats and a few men, with what may be termed a very scanty outfit—a typical Hudson's Bay Co exploring party—where everyone had more or less to shift for himself and make the best of circumstances—always of a natural kind of course. He had been away a couple of years goodness knows where —Boothia Felix and round about to the best of my recollection and had made some geographical discoveries, but I think nothing of importance about Sir John Franklin. In the winter season, they built snow huts and if lucky enough, they had seal oil for lamplight or blubber to make a sort of fire, but he said in the snow houses it was not very cold, in fact they managed to live comfortably—probably in the Arctic sense of comfortable. On the voyage home he asked me to copy his journal and I commenced it, but unfortunately I was attacked with inflammation of the eyes and so could not go on. Anyhow his narrative was published and since that he has become a great man.

The men for the exploring party arrived too, but somehow on the voyage from London, some men on board had been attacked with scurvy, —supposed to have arisen from the men having been too long at sea on a previous voyage to hot countries and having had but little rest since. Well the Fort supplied them with black currants, cranberries and other indigenous berries and they soon recovered. Burke the botanist came in very useful here.

---

[1]On 6 September 1847 (see his own *Narrative of an Expedition to the Shores of the Arctic Sea, in 1846 and 1847* [London: T. & W. Boone, 1850], p. 197). John Rae (1813-93) was born in the Orkney Islands and after taking medical training at Edinburgh joined the HBC in 1833. He served at Moose Factory 1834-43 and in 1846 was sent to complete the survey of the northern coast, in the course of which he proved that Boothia was a peninsula. Late in 1847 the Admiralty asked the HBC to allow Dr. Rae to serve as second in command of Sir John Richardson's party going in search of Franklin, preparations for which were already under way. The two leaders left England (where Rae was on leave) on 25 March 1848 and overtook Richardson's men, who were under the command of John Bell, in June. Richardson returned to England in 1849, leaving Rae to complete the task assigned. For further details see Rich's introduction to *Rae's Arctic Correspondence*.

Meat of course did not exist—save frozen venison or dried meat from the interior—I ate some of the venison, but it seemed to me tasteless, altho very short and tender.

Mr. Bell from McKenzie's [Mackenzie's] River was here—and he took charge or had to take charge of the expedition.[1] Bell had been at Mackenzie's River a very long time and was a very silent man—I am told that most people living in solitude are not talkative—they know and talk about their surroundings, but outside of these they know nothing save from books and observation. Many I have found well read and well informed on various subjects, but their library being as a rule small, the whole of it is digested and as it were becomes part of themselves. As to what was going on in Europe they learned nothing until often a couple of years after they learned of notable events, somehow or other!

[Volume III]

How many months night and how many daylight, I forget, but he said altho the night was long, they could travel about more or less on account of the bright starlight—aurora and the "light of the snow." During this season they had but little to do, and spent time in reading and what not—possibly trapping too. Of course all their provisions had to be obtained on the ground and preserved for the winter—but I forget the kind of provisions.

Bell had a perfect contempt for the outfit of the expedition which he had to lead to Mackenzie River. They had brought boats, pemmican and heaven knows what else—how on earth were these to be transported? He pronounced the boats useless—more suitable ones could have been built in the country—the most of the outfit being an incumbrance and I believe the pemmican turned out useless—in fact the Government have been imposed on—possibly a job.[2] The men were fine fellows. What the result I know not, but compare this with Dr. Rae's expedition. Anyhow the expeditions are very dangerous and I suppose necessary to have stores of provisions and so forth—but these expeditions will become more simplified.

The ship took some time to unload, and to get the furs on, but the

---

[1]John Bell (c. 1799-1868) was sent by the HBC to the Mackenzie District in 1824 and there carried on various explorations. In 1846-47 he was on leave and on his return was attached to Richardson's expedition. In 1851, at his own request, he was transferred from the Mackenzie District to Athabaska. For further details see *Minutes of Council, Northern Department of Rupert's Land, 1821-1831*, ed. R. Harvey Fleming (Toronto: Champlain Society for Hudson's Bay Record Society, 1940), p. 427.

[2]See above, p. 87n1.

whole time we were at York Factory, the Captain was in a fidget to get away lest he should be caught in the ice going home—that is to say new ice. This freezing-in had not been very frequent or infrequent—but these ships always had a double allowance of everything, thus providing against such accidents and detentions—the ships at this time were uncommonly well fitted out—the HBCo being a pretty profitable concern.

At length we sail—I had a buffalo robe and the seal[?]skin dresses before mentioned—no 'curios' of any moment to be had—in fact the whole interest of the country seems to depend on ice! Why Pizarro or some of the buccaneers should have gone to Hudson's Bay for plunder seems non-understandable—yet they went! For passengers we had two or three military officers from Red River—one dying of consumption—the remainder I know nothing about. Wemys [Wemyss] Simpson, son of Sir George—and a Mr. Campbell—a Chief Trader from Athabasca.[1] Of the former there is nothing to be said, save that six months ago, he called on me in Victoria, now a very old man. Our boatswain we had lost on the voyage out. He fell into the sea near Mansfield Island. The breeze happened to be fresh; the water clear, and as he was encumbered with heavy boots and clothing, he sank and was no more seen—the water of course was very cold.

There was nothing of any importance going home, save the iceberg before mentioned. Of course the pilot picked us up in the Channel and gave us some news—the soldiers left in the pilot boat.

Campbell went with us as far as Gravesend[2]—where he went ashore in full tog—such as had been worn half a century earlier—possibly the clothes he had taken out with him! A sort of frock coat, the collar reaching about up to his ears and the skirts coming down below the knees. He had a yellow waistcoat coming low down, and trowsers very tight about the legs—of course—shirt with a big collar up and a sort of "stock" or neckerchief. Well he got to London all right, but there he

[1]Wemyss McKenzie Simpson (1825-94) was the son of Geddes McKenzie Simpson and Frances Simpson and brother to Lady Simpson. He was thus Sir George's cousin and brother-in-law, not his son. For further details see *Letters of Letitia Hargrave*, p. 205n2. Robert Campbell (1808-94) was sent to the Mackenzie District in 1834 and remained there until Fort Selkirk was wiped out by Indians in 1852. It was not until 1856 that he was placed in charge of the District of Athabaska. For further details see Clifford Wilson, *Campbell of the Yukon* (Toronto: Macmillan, 1970).

[2]The *Prince Rupert* arrived there on 29 October, 1847 (London *Times*, 30 October 1847: "Arrived ... the Prince Rupert, from Columbia River [*sic*]").

was stared at and then the hoodlum boys followed him, making their usual remarks—so being too much annoyed he soon found a cab and was driven to the George and Vulture in Lombard Street, the common rendezvous of old Hudson's Bay men. He took home as curiosities some alabaster pipes, shaped exactly like the ordinary clay—also some hazel nuts from Athabasca! I never saw him again, but heard of him years after from Captain Dodd of the *Beaver*,[1] he having had some communication from him on the coast up north. I believe the Indians in his district had destroyed some of the HBCo property.

I took my seal skins and the buffalo robes home—thinking they might be valued as curiosities! but my folks say, "How dreadfully fishy they smell—we can't have them in the room," so they were consigned to the cellar and I suppose rotted there! If they had been sables the course would have been different.

It was time to go to the Hospital, in fact the session had commenced (October) [1 October 1847] and Cock said I was the picture of rugged rude health—to me the weather felt very warm. The ship went into dock—to be there until wanted the following June! Captain Royal I think being "ship's husband."

Before leaving Hudson's Bay, Hargrave told me, that if I wanted to return to Hudson's Bay in the service, he would write recommending me to the Governor and Committee, but assuredly I never felt like going to Hudson's Bay any more! However, the voyage there did me a great deal of good—I had become robust and had a few sovereigns to boot, but it was an awful waste of important time.

I was advised to apply at Somerset House, for the allowance of the Surgeon bringing home invalids and soldiers, but was told that there was no allowance made for this—the HBCo would pay me! What a

---

[1]Charles Dodd (1808-60) came to Fort Vancouver in 1836 as second officer in the *Beaver*. In 1842 he was chief mate of the *Cowlitz,* in which Simpson visited Fort Stikine, and Simpson placed him in charge of the fort (Simpson to John McLoughlin, 27 April 1842, *McLoughlin Letters . . . Second Series,* p. 344). He succeeded Captain W. H. McNeill as captain of the *Beaver* in 1844 (McLoughlin to the Governor and Committee, 20 November 1844, *McLoughlin Letters . . . Third Series* p. 31) and remained as her captain until March 1851, when he retired, only to rejoin the company the next year and to take command of the *Beaver* again (*London Correspondence Inward from Eden Colville 1849-1852,* ed. E. E. Rich [London: Hudson's Bay Record Society, 1956], p. 190). Dodd held this post for the next four years (Derek Pethick, *S.S. Beaver* . . . [Vancouver: Mitchell Press, 1970], p. 67), presumably until in 1856-57 a new set of boilers was installed. After the refit John Swanson took command (ibid., p. 70). For further details concerning Dodd see Walbran, *British Columbia Coast Names.*

trouble I had to find the (medical) Department—and as when found, I went in rather suddenly—one young fellow slipped a pewter pot into a cupboard, and the other stowed away pipes &c. After they discovered me to be a young medico, they invited me to have a share of the beer &c. I guess this does not go on now; the young fellows were medicos of some shape or other or related thereto and really seemed to have nothing to do. They said, "If you want to push your pay, and it can only be a small sum, here are the papers, a regular sheave to be filled in, but take my advice and don't bother yourself about the matter— it is not worth the trouble!—for you will not get anything."

Having left the immigrants by the *Norman Morison* washing clothes &c. it may be as well to trace them further. They were all located in the Fort, in one or more of the large block buildings.[1] Very little preparation had been made for their reception, excepting that bunks had been fitted up for sleeping places, as tho they were still on board ship—in fact this for the most part was the fashion of housing the HBCo's employees—the officers had Bachelors' Hall or residences in the Fort. The married immigrants were housed in the same way (there were only three or four married ones) but soon they had divisions—curtains and so forth—everything was in the rough. They had to cook their own food —supplied with this and wood—in fact had to help themselves. As soon as they tumbled into conditions they appeared tolerably satisfied and were set to work on the farms or doing any labour that might be required. It was not very long however before some of them began to desert—the gold fever had attracted them and they wanted to get to California either by Puget Sound or some sloop or craft sailing thence or from our own port, for even at this time sloops and so forth were beginning to come from San Francisco for piles to build wharves with— and sawmills were in project or process of erection on Puget Sound. Some of these immigrants are here still, such as George Richardson— Rowland—and some others. Of course many have died; others went to the States or returned to the old country. However I was only here a month at this time—the future will disclose itself as I proceed.

The district of Victoria was at this time like a large park—patches of forest and open glades; these all had names—such as Minnie's [Minie's] Prairie and Punchbowl—the latter around Harris Pond and

[1]For the fort and its buildings see JSH's article, "A Reminiscence of 1850," and cf. the descriptions in Deans, "Settlement of Vancouver Island" and James Robert Anderson, "Notes and Comments on Early Days and Events in British Columbia" (typescript, PABC, p. 151). See also Plates 11 and 12.

the former a little further, the grand prairie is now Tolmie's, & so forth.[1]
A large portion of what is now Victoria City was then cultivated fields
and so was a portion of James Bay—i.e. Dutnall's farm,[2] where the
upper portion of Menzies and streets about exist now. A barn was on
Fort Street covered with large slices of cedar bark, indeed all the
roofs of all the buildings were covered with this, and a capital roof
too, save that it became mossy and so liable to catch fire. A dairy with
sixty cows occupied what is now Pemberton's—the North Dairy existed, outside of these there was but little. No thrashing machines or
agricultural implements of today, but an extraordinary thick pole with
long wooden spikes, made to rotate somehow or other, occupied the
place of a thrasher—this was a grotesque invention of Finlayson's—I
never saw it at work—but it stood as a monument even then of bygone
days. All around James Bay roses, red currant, natalia mock orange and
spirea grew in abundance—very little wind reached in from the sea
because forests of pine between the harbour and sea intercepted it—in
fact forest surrounded the whole space, even coming as close as Cormorant Street. Thus the climate was delicious, the cold sea breezes
having no access. Mr. Douglas would not allow the forest sheltering to
be cut down, as he thought if removed the harbour of Victoria would
not be sufficiently sheltered. We often wish now that the protecting
forests stood there still. Wishart and I used to travel over these grounds
and enjoyed it—he had a bump of locality. Sometimes we would meet
an Indian or two, of whom I was timid, but they never bothered us in
any way. Benson was too lazy to walk much. In these plains bands of
horses, cayuses, existed and so did cattle of the Spanish variety, with
horns goodness knows how long and pointed—these were much more

---

[1]According to the Land Sales Annual Reports, "Frédèrique Miniè" bought
Town Lot 361 in July 1853. On 31 March 1853 the Legislative Council chose
"a site near Minie's Plain" for a public school, the forerunner of the present
Central Junior and Senior High School on the same site. According to Anderson's
"Notes and Comments," p. 155, the road leading from the fort eastward past the
garden and stables went round the head of the swamp then at Fort and View
streets, "thence past the springs at Spring Ridge, across the stream which drained
quite an extent of flat country and what was afterwards known as Harris' pond,
across country to the North Dairy farm." This farm was situated on the HBC
reserve, Section XXXII, east of Swan Lake. Dr. W. F. Tolmie's estate,
"Cloverdale," is commemorated in the present road of that name.
[2]John Dutnall (1812?-85) was in charge of the HBC farm established by Chief
Factor James Douglas between the fort and Ogden Point. It was later called Beck-
ley Farm (*Colonist*, 15 February 1862 [obituary of Dutnall's wife]). For further
details see Dutnall's obituary in the *Colonist*, 1 September 1885.

dangerous than the natives,[1] but fortunately we were never molested, so soon we became accustomed and roamed about to Cedar Hill,[2] Mount Tolmie &c., without any fear whatever! and altho it was only the end of March or thereabouts the weather was lovely and some shrubs in full bloom. Of course we were lost occasionally in the woods, but altho lost we knew pretty well where we were, and so managed to get home again without mishap. On Beacon Hill, stood a pole with a cask on top, and another beacon closer to the beach, these were guides to the harbour, hence the name Beacon Hill. The cask was riddled with bullets, it being a target at which some practised for fun. Most of the old HBC Company's old servants could use the musket well —the HBCo musket, but rifles or double-barrelled guns were scarce, and a sort of treasure of some of the officers.

I have described the Fort &c. in Christmas numbers of the *Colonist*,[3] so need not go over this again, likewise the Indian village and the Fort band, i.e. the dogs—their praying and howling at meal times, to the sound of the bell. The same may be said of the mess room—meals—the folk seen there—the parson and his residence; the stores and the furs— the abundance of sea otter and what not—sealskins were not "all the go" then; Benson and his eccentricities—possibly many of the faces may come in again.

At length I am off to Fort Rupert and must have arrived there in May—the weather lovely. I have described my voyage to this place in the *Colonist* and my life there,[4] so nothing need be said on this subject

[1]Presumably these had come originally from the herd purchased in 1841 from the governor of California (see *James Douglas in California,* ed. Dorothy Blakey Smith [Vancouver: The Library Press, 1965], p. xviii). According to H. H. Bancroft, *History of British Columbia,* Works, vol. 32 (San Francisco: The History Company, 1887), p. 106, "wild and unmanageable" cattle, chiefly of Mexican origin, were brought from Nisqually to Fort Victoria when the HBC headquarters were moved from the Columbia in 1849. The "Wild Spanish or California Cattle" at Fort Vancouver "were as Wild as deer and could not be approached so that when we Wanted to kill any for Beef We had to hunt them as deer ..." (John McLoughlin to Archibald McKinlay, 30 November 1847, *McLoughlin's Business Correspondence,* p. 75).
[2]Later called Mount Douglas.
[3]"A Reminiscence of 1850," and "In the Early Fifties," *Colonist,* Supplement, 1 January 1889, reprinted in Appendix 2.
[4]On Beaver Harbour, on the northeast coast of Vancouver Island, established in the summer of 1849 under the direction of Captain W. H. McNeill, to protect the coal deposits recently discovered there and also in some measure to take the place of Fort McLoughlin (abandoned in 1843) as a trading post. In 1852, when the development of the Nanaimo coal field began, the Fort Rupert workings were abandoned, but the HBC maintained a trading station there until 1885,

further, than that with regard to the murder I knew little or nothing
about the circumstances, for altho living in the Fort, each one did
his own business and one knew little or nothing of what the others were
doing. Bancroft tells lies—Muir assisted him and led him into this and
that fellow Duncan maliciously copied Bancroft, altho he must have
known better, but at this time I had become an opponent of Duncan's
on account of his agitation of the Indians about the land question.[1]

---

when the property was sold to Robert Hunt (see below, p. 109). The officers'
quarters were destroyed by fire in 1889 (*Colonist*, 6 June 1889). For further
details see Patricia M. Johnson, "Fort Rupert," *The Beaver* (Spring 1972): 4-15.
JSH was certainly there by 28 May, when under the title of "Superannuated
Rhubarb" he was made an Honorary Member of the "Independent Order of
Antediluvian Eccentrics," at a Grand Conclave held at "their Hall Transitory
on board the U.S.S. *Mass[achusetts]*." The certificate in the Helmcken Collection is dated at "Fort Rupert, Beaver Cove, Vancouver Island" and signed by
"Amputating Sawbones," "Indurated Adobe," "Hard Knocks," and "Petrified
Crawfish," among others. For JSH's recollections see "Fort Rupert in 1850,"
Colonist, 1 January 1890, reprinted in Appendix 2.
[1]The confused and controversial story of "the Fort Rupert affair" in 1850 has
been admirably dealt with by W. Kaye Lamb, in "Richard Blanshard," pp. 11-
17, 29-31. Briefly, in 1849 a party of Scottish miners under John Muir had arrived
at Fort Rupert to work the coal deposit. Trouble arose between them and George
Blenkinsop (left in charge by the departure of Captain McNeill in April 1850 for
the gold mines on Queen Charlotte Island), and Blanshard appointed JSH as a
magistrate to deal with the situation. But further trouble arose when three deserters from the *Norman Morison* were murdered by the Nahwitti Indians, and in
October 1850 Blanshard himself had to go up in H.M.S *Daedalus* to settle matters.
   Bancroft told the story in his *History of British Columbia*, pp. 273-75. He based
his account, highly critical of the HBC and the government, on a narrative by
John Muir's son Michael, dictated in 1878 and giving only the point of view of
the malcontents. William Duncan (1832-1918) had come to this coast in 1857
and had founded in 1862 the model Indian community of Metlakatla. In 1886
his dispute with Bishop Ridley and his original sponsors, the Church Missionary
Society, led to a confrontation with the government of British Columbia in the
matter of the Indian title to the land proposed for the Metlakatla reserve.
The difficulty proving insoluble, Duncan proposed to move the whole community
into American territory in Alaska. For a full-length study of William Duncan,
see Jean Usher, *William Duncan of Metlakatla* (Ottawa: National Museum
of Man, 1974). Henry S. Wellcome published *The Story of Metlakatla* (London
and New York: Saxon & Co., 1887) in order "to place the story of the indubi-
table wrongs of the Metlakatlans before the American people and enlist public
sympathy." In an appendix, Wellcome printed various documents, including a
series of letters from the *Colonist*, October and November 1886, entitled "Correspondence on the Church and State Coercion and the Indian Land Rights."
The series contains a letter from JSH, 2 November 1886, commenting on what
he calls "the Metlakatla 'fizgig,'" and Wellcome adds: "The name of Dr. Helmcken is not new in British Columbia history; his name will long be remembered
in connection with the subjoining case of high-minded justice. Bancroft in des-

Even if Blenkinsop[1] had offered rewards for the arrest of the deserters, he would have done no more than followed the practice of the naval ships here—a practice here to this day. These were of great importance at Fort Rupert at the time, for if more had deserted the place would have been without defenders against the three thousand Indians outside. As to Blenkinsop offering a reward for the deserters "dead or alive"— this bears the lie on the face of it. As a matter of fact the murder seems to have had no connection with Blenkinsop or the reward for deserters inasmuch as the Indians were foreign to Rupert altogether. Bancroft however, an American, had the American proclivities to speak evil of the British, if he could only find an excuse, even a supposed one, to suit this purpose.

I find also that more recent history shows, that allow the Ruperts were not cannibals, in the catch-em-cook-em-and-eat-em style, that still in their medicine orgies and infernal practices—they did make use of dead bodies—did not eat them—but I am told, tore the flesh off with their teeth, and threw it out. I am still not aware and doubt very much, whether they killed anyone at the time I was at the Fort for this purpose or for sacrifice.[2]

---

canting on the treatment of the Aborigines under the combined rule of the Hudson's Bay Company and Colonial Government writes: ..." And then follows the passage from Bancroft's account, cited above, and Wellcome comments further: "Who now will question, the propriety of Dr. Helmcken's sitting in judgment upon the rights of the Natives?" It is natural enough that JSH should blame "that fellow Duncan" rather than Duncan's defender Wellcome for this "malicious attack" upon him.

[1] George Blenkinsop (1822-1904) came to this coast as steward in the *Cowlitz* (*McLoughlin Letters ... Second Series*, pp. 35, 45n1) and was made assistant to Charles Dodd at Fort Stikine in 1842, Simpson stating that though Blenkinsop was "merely a common sailor, [he] was of regular habits and possessed a good education" (*Narrative of a Journey Round the World* ... [London: H. Colborn, 1847], 2:183). Bancroft casts "dark reproach" on Blenkinsop for his part in the Fort Rupert affair (*History of British Columbia*, pp. 194, 272-73), and JSH countered these accusations directly in "Fort Rupert in 1850." Blenkinsop wrote from Beaver Harbour on 21 April 1890 to thank JSH for coming to his defence (HC). For further details of his career see Walbran, *British Columbia Coast Names*.

[2] On the topic of cannibalism, "the touchiest in northwest coast ethnography," see Warren L. Cook, *Flood Tide of Empire: Spain and the Pacific Northwest 1543-1819* (New Haven: Yale University Press, 1973), p. 190n107, where the earlier sources rejected by Franz Boas are set down; and cf. Erna Gunther, *Indian Life on the Northwest Coast of North America: As seen by the Early Explorers and Fur Traders during the last Decades of the Eighteenth Century* (Chicago: University of Chicago Press, 1972), p. 60; and pp. 325-26 below.

Anyhow I was summoned to return to Victoria about Xmas 1850 and left Rupert with a mixture of regret and pleasure.[1] Mrs. McNeil [McNeill] had died just before in her confinement, attended by Indian women, from haemorrhage after twins had been born. These twins are still living.[2] Mrs. McNeill was a very large handsome Kigani [Kaigani] woman, with all the dignity and carriage of a chieftainess, which she was. I left one Kanaka ill—he had had pneumonia—he said he would die if I left, and die he did soon after. Blenkinsop said if a Kanaka take it into his mind to die, he will die sure. Otherwise there were but few remaining at Rupert—Blenkinsop and Moffatt were the chiefs. Beardmore had gone[3]—found his way to Australia—and years afterwards he sent for his daughter, who had been baptized at the time of Governor Blanshard's visit in the *Driver*. She was in Victoria, called the Princess and lived a sort of abandoned life—curiously enough I never saw her,

[1]JSH was summoned to Victoria in December 1850 because Governor Blanshard was ill. Dr. Benson had been transferred to Fort Vancouver to replace Dr. Barclay, and in November Dr. W. F. Tolmie had been called in, but he had returned to Fort Nisqually a few weeks afterwards (see the entries for 19 November and 12 December 1850, in Victor J. Farrar, "The Nisqually Journal," *Washington Historical Quarterly* 12 [1921]: 146, 220, cited by Lamb, "Richard Blanshard," p. 25n82. Beardmore (see note 3 below) wrote to JSH from Fort Victoria: "This canoe goes to fetch you. I remain to take care of the Governor till I can turn him into a Doctor's hand as in the place of Pharisees[?] he would die alone. The Priest wants to poison him but Charley would not let him . . ." (HC).

[2]Wife of Captain W. H. McNeill. For details concerning him see the article by George R. Newell in *DCB* 10 and pp. 105n4, 106n1 above. One of the twins, Rebecca, married Thomas Elwyn in 1879 (*Colonist,* 5 October 1879). He died in 1888 (ibid., 12 September 1888), and in 1891 she married J. H. Baker (ibid., 31 January 1891). The other, Harriet, married John Jane of Savona in 1889 (ibid., 15 October 1889). He died in 1907 (ibid., 12 July 1907), and she subsequently married John David Jones. She died a widow in Victoria in 1934 (Victoria *Times*, 22 February 1934).

[3]Charles Beardmore was second in command to Blenkinsop at Fort Rupert in the absence of Captain McNeill. Although JSH shared Beardmore's quarters and referred to him as "my chum" and "a good-hearted, racy individual," Beardmore caused considerable trouble by giving JSH "a totally false report" after he had been asked to investigate the murder. About a month later he gave Magistrate Helmcken what he now said was a true report, excusing himself first because he had not been on oath previously, and second because he had wished to tell the true story personally to Chief Factor Douglas (see "Fort Rupert in 1850"; and JSH's Fort Rupert diary cited in Lamb, "Richard Blanshard," pp. 14-15).

at all events did not recognise her. I think she refused to go to her father. Hunt was left at Rupert and he is there still!![1]

Of my voyage down in a canoe some account too will be found in the Christmas number of the *Colonist* of about four years ago.[2]

Anyhow I returned to Victoria—Benson had been sent to Vancouver (Columbia River) the post I ought to have had. I suppose Mr. Douglas preferred Benson's absence—he was a radical—a grumbler—had become attached to Governor Blanshard, and shared with him the mutual grumbles about the HBCo. These people were in too much of a hurry, and thought a colony could be formed in a day. Doubtless the Governor and the parson and everyone else had to put up with many inconveniences, and only think of the civilized life they had left, but they did not adapt themselves to a rough and ready country—if they had they might have been much more comfortable and happy. They wanted a great deal more than could be supplied them from the limited means at disposal—they wanted the luxuries of a civilized and populous country. Besides no one even then would tolerate the airs of superiority they chose on all occasion to put on. Everyone was about on an equal footing—even the men of the HBCo felt the coming times—of more equality. Anyhow Benson was a sterling, honest, kind-hearted upright man, always ready to do good, but somehow did not fit in. Possibly he could not serve two masters, Blanshard and the HBCo in the shape of Mr. Douglas—in fact this divided authority led to "parties" and was the source of very much bad feeling and trouble afterwards.

Anyhow I suppose I was very much the same as I have always been and possibly am still—friendly with everyone—with plenty of good feeling and common honesty—but curiously enough never had any intimate friend—and intimacy—no one to rush to to pour out your heart and receive his in exchange. Altho I was never reserved—perhaps too outspoken and passionate, going off like a flash of gunpowder—still I was more or less self-contained and lived within myself—but never brooded over troubles—in fact hardly knew that they existed—and yet I was not selfish—perhaps had too many friends and not one in par-

---

[1]Robert Hunt (1828-93) remained in the service of the HBC until the company closed the post at Fort Rupert. According to the records in the Land Office, the property was transferred to him by the HBC on 15 December 1885; he obtained a certificate of purchase on 9 November 1887; and he received his crown grant on 21 March 1888. He remained at Fort Rupert until his death on 25 March 1893 (*Colonist*, 2 April 1893).

[2]See "In the Early Fifties."

ticular. Well I am old now, and my passionate character has toned down! Have I always been a frivolous butterfly? Always flying from sweet to sweet—always in action—never idle—a sort of perpetual motion, without design or without thinking of what it might like to [*sic: for* lead to?]. A man without any plans but adapting himself to anything that came along. Ah—at the time I was young, active, vigorous—but certainly not vigorous. I never had muscular strength, in fact was weakly until I arrived in this country.

With all this I was bashful and reserved to new people—almost distant. Formality I hated and would absent myself from formal affairs whether dinner parties or any set affair—they were not what I had been used to in my poor days and the feelings incident to these poor days never left me—altho now I considered myself at least equal to the best —a rough and ready altho gentle sort of fellow—would not be and hated to be patronized. No doubt this feeling made me keep at a distance— and kept people from coming too close. Altho friendly with everybody, I was intimate with few—and this intimacy only on account of a personal liking for some qualities. Antecedents of people were to me as nothing—the only question was what are they now! I did not take generally long to find out the good or bad qualities, for population being scant, their coming in and going out were known to everybody!—and for the most part no one had knockers to the doors. When the door was ajar anyone walked in, but if not open one's knuckles or a stick gave the signal of a visitor and as the residences at first were very small, it did not require much of a knock to let the inmate know someone was outside seeking a parlay. Of course there were conventionalities in all this.

Anyhow here I am in Victoria once more—very little changed during my six months' absence—the faces the same—scarcely anything more than the Fort yet, but Yates' house was in process of building and this is my office now[1]—some of the men had left for outposts. Victoria

---

[1]JSH is in error here. The house which James Yates was building outside the fort (cf. p. 112 below) was never the doctor's office (cf. his own statement, p. 126 below). In another undated MS (catalogued as "Reminiscences," [HC]) JSH says that his surgery, originally a room off Bachelors' Hall in one of the large buildings within the stockade, "was removed to a log building in the Fort: first occupied by Mr. Yates—then by the post office and master—then by the harbour master." Cf. Deans, "Settlement of Vancouver Island," p. 6: "On the right entering by the front or south gate, was a Cottage, in which was the post office, it was kept by an officer of the Company, a Captain Sangster." JSH continues: "This was put into something very orderly for the period, and lasted until two or three years ago when it was pulled down and a stable erected in lieu thereof!"

was like many other places in the country since—save that it seemed out of the world and had no communication with it—this was its chief peculiarity. No doubt places have since sprung up, but none that have been so solitary—so free from intercourse. This however did not last long, for Olympia had come into existence, the capital of Washington Territory, and Port Townsend and Whiby by [*sic*: *for* Whidbey] Island soon had a few people and sawmills soon came to the fore. Bye and bye Port Angelos [Angeles] came into notice. Victor Smith wanted it to be the port of entry to the Territory,[1] but for some reason or other, Port Townsend was chosen. Bye the bye a curious accident occurred at Port Angeles. Some dam or jam in the river gave way; the torrent came down and swept the houses away: there were not very many and of course only comparatively small and flimsily built, but had they been more substantial, they would have gone nevertheless.[2]

Soon schooners arrived—chiefly those going to the Sound for piles—they wanted some supplies here, and brought some also, such as flour —and spirits. The latter were sold to the men so that drunkenness was not infrequent. On one occasion the men were all intoxicated. Mr. Douglas gave orders to search for the liquor: after much trouble a barrelful was found hidden under the floor of the men's house. The men would defend it, so we all had to go, the parson with a long sword

---

Emily Carr, born in 1871, whose family were all patients of JSH, describes his office in *The Book of Small* (London: Oxford University Press, 1942), p. 201 as "a tiny two-room cottage on the lower end of Fort Street [which bisected the old Fort property] near Wharf Street. It sat in a hummocky field; you walked along two planks and came to three steps and the door." Up to 1895 the directories list JSH's office at 8-12 Fort Street or as "Helmcken Alley, from Fort." From 1897 on, the Pacific Transfer Company is listed at 14 Fort Street, and it appears reasonable to assume therefore that c. 1896 the firm erected a stable on the site of JSH's office.

[1]After his appointment as a special agent of the U.S. Treasury Department in 1861, Victor Smith recommended the transfer of the customs house from Port Townsend to Port Angeles, and this was accomplished by an act of Congress on 18 June 1862. He was then appointed collector of customs and moved from Port Townsend to Port Angeles in the autumn of 1862. For further details see G. M. Lauridsen and A. A. Smith, *The Story of Port Angeles, Clallum County, Washington* ... (Seattle: Lowman and Hanford, 1937); and John McCallum and Lorraine Walcox Ross, *Port Angeles U.S.A.* (Seattle: Wood and Reber, 1961), chap. 4, "Victory for Victor."

[2]Victor Smith built the new customs house and the collector's home at the mouth of Valley Creek. On 16 December 1863 they were swept away along with many other buildings when a log jam broke on the creek above; two men lost their lives (see *Colonist*, 21 December 1863, quoted in Lauridsen and Smith, *Port Angeles*, p. 25; and the eye-witness account of Smith's son Norman, in McCallum and Ross, *Port Angeles U.S.A.*, pp. 21-22).

which had belonged to one of his celebrated ancestors, who had been hung for something against the state. The men were all forced to our end of the room, whilst we got out the whisky. Staines stood with his sword stretched out across the room—and called "Pass this who dare!" One or two men soon came up drunken—"Pass this if you dare!" So the men jeered and said, "We don't want to pass it," and went back to their fellows! The barrel was out—taken into the Fort Yard and Mr. Douglas said, "Knock the head out Mr. Finlayson"; and in the head went—the grog ran down the gutter in a stream—the men rushed out, threw themselves on the ground to drink it as it ran or collected in holes—some on their knees scooped it up with hands, others lay down and sipped it from the earth! Finlayson said, "What is to be done now?" So I rushed in, got some tartar emetic and sprinkled the whisky on the ground.— Ere long all the drinkers began to vomit and lay about the ground limp and worse than seasick!

Men too began to come from San Francisco and the Sound—ragged —boots minus soles—unshaven, tattered, dirty and forlorn—miserable-looking beggars—but active. These people would get an outfit and then looked like gentlemen, which many of them were and what is more were rich, that is to say most of them had leathern bags filled with gold dust —of which they were not miserly.

The HBCo had large stores and so as time proceeded men used to come from the other side to buy goods, spirits and so forth, for at this time, there were no customs dues—Free Trade pure and simple. Many wanted medicine, which I sold them as far as my store allowed, and some were ailing and so patients began to come in. In fact Victoria was soon the headquarters for all the surrounding country—and people soon began to multiply on the American side, because the Government gave 640 acres of land to every bona fide settler! This was so different to our five dollar per acre business, that some of our own immigrants deserted, attracted by this liberal treatment. Of course this attracted immigrants from the East and Oregon and California, because at this time, California was considered unfit for agricultural purposes—the sandhills and so forth supposed to be unfruitful and unfit for cultivation!!! Of course few or none settled here—but business grew apace.

Yates got permission to leave the service and build outside: got some waterfront and lots on Wharf Street.[1] Captain Reid had lost his ship, so

[1] James Yates (1819-1900) came out in the *Harpooner* in 1849 as a ship's carpenter, but after eighteen months he terminated his agreement with the HBC and went

he had to shift for himself and he took land adjoining Yates and his wife and daughters carried on a small haberdashery business—and by degrees others took to living outside also, so Victoria became a village —and assuredly a pretty prosperous one.

Yates had come out as ship carpenter:—to build a schooner or something for the HBCo—he was a powerful cantankerous being—a dark-coloured Scotsman. Mrs. Yates was a nice active agreeable pleasant little woman with auburn hair. One child was born inside the Fort pickets, and as on this day, two children happened to be born, Mr. Douglas to celebrate this extraordinary occurrence had wine on the mess table and toasted the two babies, as glorious additions to the population—small things in these days were comparatively great ones—and by the same token small grievances of little moment, were considered tremendous obstacles to progress and &c. &c.

Captain Reid was mate of the *Rupert* on my journey to Hudson's Bay!

Imagine then Victoria slowly forging ahead in this way for seven or eight years—more little buildings of various sorts, residences and what not. The Hudson's Bay Co did not pay their men in money, but they had accounts in the store; so their money did not circulate—so this led to an agitation against the truck system. The HBCo ought to import coin to pay their men—then everyone would have a chance. This question soon settled itself—not by the HBCo importing money, but by gold dust and coin coming in from the U. States!

There were other conditions that made Victoria grow. Fresh immigrants from England. In 1851 the *Tory* came with the Skinners, Langfords and their people—Captain Cooper likewise as also the Parkers and others.[1] The Langfords occupied new Bachelors' Hall, where the Five

---

into business for himself as a wine and liquor merchant and a dealer in real estate. For further details see R. E. Gosnell, *A History of British Columbia* (n.p., Lewis Publishing Co., 1906), pp. 328-29.

[1]The *Tory* arrived on 14 May 1851 (see Macdonald, *A Pioneer 1851*, p. 6; and the entry for 21 May 1851 in Farrar, "The Nisqually Journal," *WHQ* 13 (1922):135. She brought Captain Cooper (for further details see the article by Margaret A. Ormsby in *DCB* 10), but the Skinners, the Langfords, and the Parkers did not arrive until 16 January 1853 on the *Norman Morison*. For Thomas James Skinner, who came out as bailiff of the PSAC farm at Constance Cove, see Walbran, *British Columbia Coast Names*; and the obituary in the *Colonist*, 2 June 1889. For Langford, who came out as bailiff of the PSAC farm at Colwood, see Sydney G. Pettit, "The Trials and Tribulations of Edward Edwards Langford," *BCHQ* 17 (1953): 5-40. John Parker (1828-1917), a master farrier and blacksmith, came out under contract to the HBC but left the company at the time of the gold rush and ran a stage on the Harrison-Lillooet route (*Colonist*, 22 October

Sisters block now stands[1]—the bakery was there also. The Skinners occupied a house on Yates Street at the corner and one of their children was born there. They occupied these buildings until they had built residences, the Langfords at Colwood, the Skinners near what is now the Naval Hospital. Of course these took time to build and their men helped to put up the houses and do farm work. They all belonged to the Puget Sound Company and were all gentlemen and ladies, people who had seen better days.

In the following year the *Norman Morison* returned and in her were the McKenzies and number of Scotsmen and women, the best specimens of Scottish men and women to be found.[2] Several are still living. J. D. Pemberton and B. W. Pears [Pearse] had arrived also[3]— but Captain Grant preceded both and had some employment given him by Mr. Douglas in the shape of surveying—he ran a base line from about Loch-end to Mount Douglas, and had some other surveys to do about Sooke, where he had located. He had of course to make a re-

---

1861). By 1862 he was farming at Rocky Point, Metchosin (ibid., 2 April 1862), and by 1874 he was established as a butcher in Victoria. He died on 22 July 1917 (Victoria *Times*, 23 July 1917). The article by his great-granddaughter Kathleen Goodall, "The Rocky Point Parkers," (ibid., 16 May 1942, magazine, p. 6), supplies more information but appears to be inaccurate in some details.

[2]The Five Sisters' Block, built in 1891 from the design of Thos. C. Sorby and W. Ridgway Wilson (*Colonist*, 28 January 1891 and 1 January 1892), was at the corner of Fort and Government streets, on the site of the log building which housed the HBC bakery (Edgar Fawcett, *Some Reminiscences of Old Victoria*, [Toronto: W. Briggs, 1912], p. 172). According to the centenary edition of the Victoria *Times*, 13 March 1943, it was named for the five daughters of James Douglas. No evidence is offered in this article; but the notice calling for tenders (*Colonist*, 4 February 1891) makes the cheque accompanying each bid payable to Dennis R. Harris, who had married Martha Douglas in 1878. The building was gutted by fire in 1910 (ibid., 28 October 1910).

[2]On 16 January 1853. Kenneth McKenzie (1811-74) and his party of seventy-three people came out at the same time as the Langfords and the Skinners, on the *Norman Morison*'s third and last voyage to Victoria. McKenzie was bailiff of the PSAC farm at Craigflower, and the house he built on the shore of Portage Inlet is now an historic site, restored as far as possible to what it was when the McKenzie family made it a social centre for naval officers and officials of the colonial service. For further details see the article by William R. Sampson in *DCB* 10.

[3]Joseph Despard Pemberton (1821-95) was appointed in 1851 as colonial surveyor and engineer for the HBC in Vancouver Island. For further details see Harriet Susan Sampson, "My Father, Joseph Despard Pemberton," *BCHQ* 8 (1944): 111-25. Benjamin William Pearse (1832-1902), a civil engineer, came to Fort Victoria in 1851 as assistant colonial surveyor and engineer. For further details see "The Journal of Arthur Thomas Bushby," biographical appendix (hereafter cited as "Bushby Appendix"); and the obituary in the *Colonist*, 18 June 1902.

port—and of course had to make a copy of this—so he would occupy an hour and then get Benson to copy for an hour and then someone else, but they managed to get through it in process of time; of course the manuscript in various hands—this for the Honble HBCo's eyes!! Captain Stamp came a few years afterwards,[1] but Brotchie had preceded the lot in the ship *Albion*, which the Americans had seized because she had cut spars at Dungeness without leave or license.[2] Pelly laid [*sic*] for Brotchie—for the treaty had hardly been signed long.[3]

Of course these arrivals brought other wayfarers, mechanics and others. There had been a rush to California which still continued, and so many disappointed found their way to Victoria and Puget Sound.

Add to this the almost constant presence of a man-of-war or two at Esquimault. These were of course sailing vessels—two or three deckers—each deck having massive guns on each side in rows—forty-ton guns being considered enormous, and were so, being moved without machinery. The crew was very numerous—in fact ships then consisted of hosts of cannon and hosts of men, whereas now they are armoured, have very few guns, fewer men, but of course engineers, stokers and so forth. The ships now and then bear no resemblance—the men used to fight then—but now it seems to be a matter of fighting with rifled guns at long range—more a matter of science than of brute courage. The officers and men now are different. One of these large vessels under sail was a beautiful sight. The officers too were a different class: generally well off and connected with the landed gentry of England— they had been accustomed to firearms and so were good sportsmen and thus enjoyed themselves. They were quite at home here and had the run of the place—horses and what not—and having now the Langfords, Skinners, McKenzies and the HBCo's people to call on, times with

[1]Edward Stamp (1814-72), master mariner, first visited the Pacific Northwest coast in 1857 and came back to purchase spars and ship-timber for London firms. For further details see the article by W. Kaye Lamb in *DCB* 10.

[2]Captain William Brotchie (1799-1859) of the HBC's naval department was engaged from 1849 to 1855 in cutting spars on Vancouver Island in what was to prove the vain hope of selling them to the Admiralty. For further details see Walbran, *British Columbia Coast Names*; and Lamb, "Early Lumbering," pp. 33-38.

[3]Sir John Henry Pelly, Bart., governor of the HBC 1822-52. The Oregon Boundary Treaty had been signed in 1846; and Dungeness, on the southern shore of the Straits of Juan de Fuca, was consequently in American territory.

them were pleasant.[1] They too did not wish to put anyone to trouble, but would eat and enjoy ordinary fare, cigars and tobacco—in fact they were welcome everywhere and behaved themselves like what they were—gentlemen. No harm came from them to the ladies, but in process of time, the boys were spoiled, because the youngsters associated much with them, and thus the officers having nothing to do apparently, these youngsters thought this a fine thing, and so neglected or did not take to work. In fact the place was small and so the various changes in everybody could be noted—and so it was that before long rude simplicity gave way before the rising desire to do things properly, put on airs and graces, live more expensively and make a little splurge. Interiors of houses looked after by ladies, now became nicely furnished and ornamented, for women can do and understand making rooms pretty with comparatively little outlay and by using trifles to the best advantage. Gardens and flowers were cultivated about the houses and in fact the country became like and as civilized as any respectable village in England, with the few, very few, upper ten leading—and of course the usual jealousy arose as to who was to be the leader— they were no longer satisfied to be on an equality—and so "what we were in England or Scotland" was burnished and made the most of!!!

During all this time there was a perpetual grumble that the Hudson's Bay Co did not send out immigrants enough—the country would not grow at this rate of progress. The grumblers did not heed that the length and expense of travel and unwillingness to come to an unknown country were great drawbacks—they wanted to see the country made populous all at once. The Company were abused because they did not send out more ships and send with quick despatch all the little orders of the settlers—in fact it was asserted that the Company would not make room for these orders as they trespassed upon their monopoly. No one however was willing to subscribe to get more settlers or more ships —the Company had to do and must do it all, according to their charter of colonization, they would be repaid in the end by the Government, when they took repossession of the Island. True, the Company

---

[1]Cf. the comment of R. C. Mayne (lieutenant in H.M.S. *Plumper* in 1857) in his *Four Years in Vancouver Island and British Columbia*, p. 31: "No ceremony was known in those pleasant times. All the half-dozen houses that made up the town were open to us. In fine weather, riding parties of the gentlemen and ladies of the place were formed (cf. p. 129 below), and we returned generally to a high tea, or tea-dinner, **at** Mr. Douglas's or Mr. Work's, winding up the pleasant evening with dance and song."

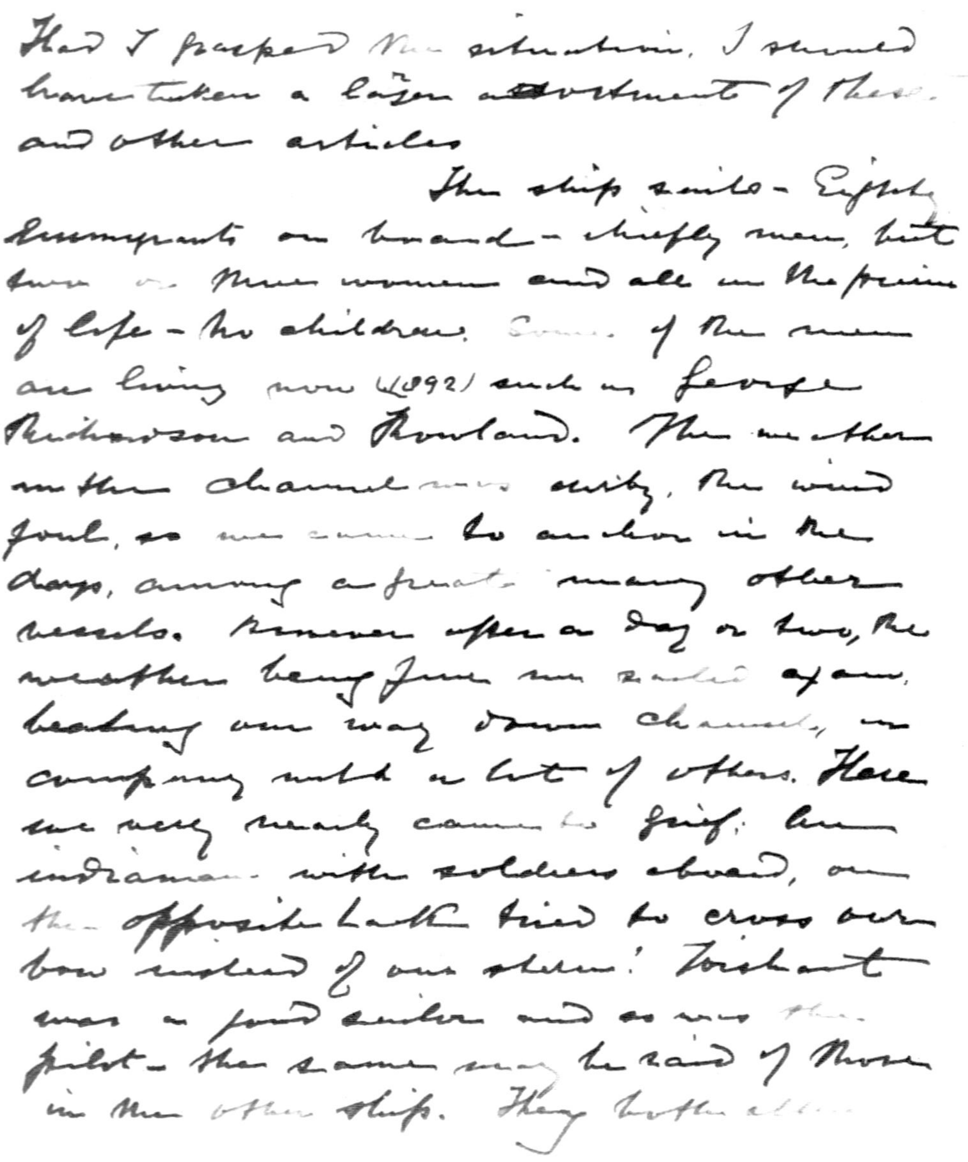

Had I foreseen the situation, I should
have taken a larger assortment of these
and other articles

        The ship sails — Eighty
emigrants on board — chiefly men, but
two or three women and all in the prime
of life — no children. Some of the men
are living now (1892) such as George
Richardson and Rowland. The weather
in the channel was sultry, the wind
foul, so we came to anchor in the
days, among a great many other
vessels. However after a day or two, the
weather being fine we sailed again,
beating our way down channel, in
company with a lot of others. Here
we very nearly came to grief; an
Indiaman with soldiers aboard, on
the opposite tack tried to cross our
bow instead of our stern! Tushart
was a good sailor and so was the
pilot — the same may be said of those
in the other ship. They both all...

Plate 1. The page of manuscript recording the sailing of the *Norman Morison* in 1849 (see p. 77).

Plate 2. Whitechapel and environs, 1843. Arrows indicate Helmcken's home in Great Alie Street, Dr. Graves's residence in Trinity Square, and Guy's Hospital.

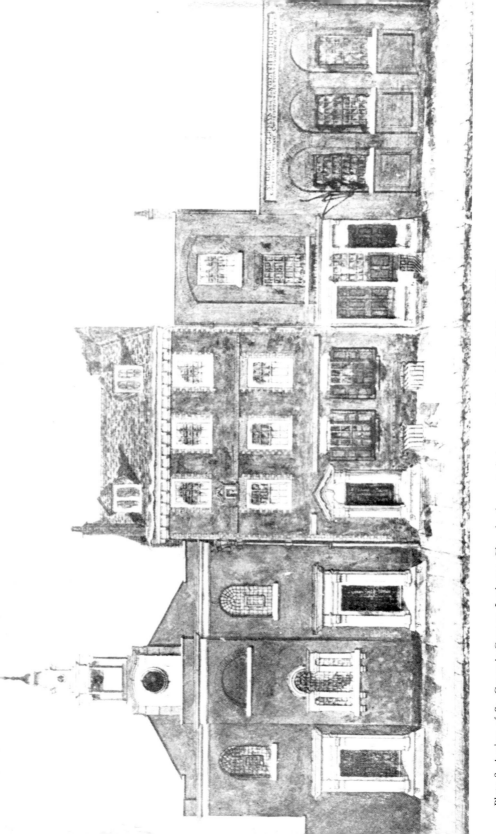

Plate 3. A view of St. George's German Lutheran Church, the pastor's house, and the school building, in 1821.

Plate 4. The sugar refinery of Messrs. Charles and John Frederick Bowman in 1851 (from a lithograph by Vincent Brooks).

Plate 5. Mrs. Claus Helmcken (Catherine Mittler), J. S. Helmcken's mother (from a daguerrotype by E. Fehrenbach, London).

Plate 6. The silver medal awarded to Helmcken at the end of his first session (see p. 44).

Plate 7. The operating theatre of Old St. Thomas's Hospital, adjacent to Guy's. Constructed in 1821 and recently restored, this is the only early nineteenth-century operating theatre which has survived.

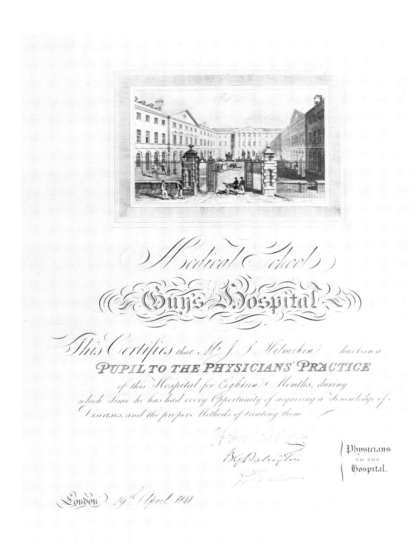

Plate 8. One of Helmcken's medical certificates, showing the quadrangle at Guy's.

Plate 9. Advertisement for the sailing of the *Malacca*, London *Times*, 13 May 1848 (see p. 62).

Plate 10. The Hudson's Bay Company ships *Prince Albert* and *Prince Rupert* sailing from Gravesend on the annual supply voyage, 8 June 1845 (*Illustrated London News*, 21 June 1845).

Plate 11. Interior of Fort Victoria, c. 1851 (from a painting by Lieut. Matthew Fairfax Moresby, R.N., son of Rear-Admiral Moresby).

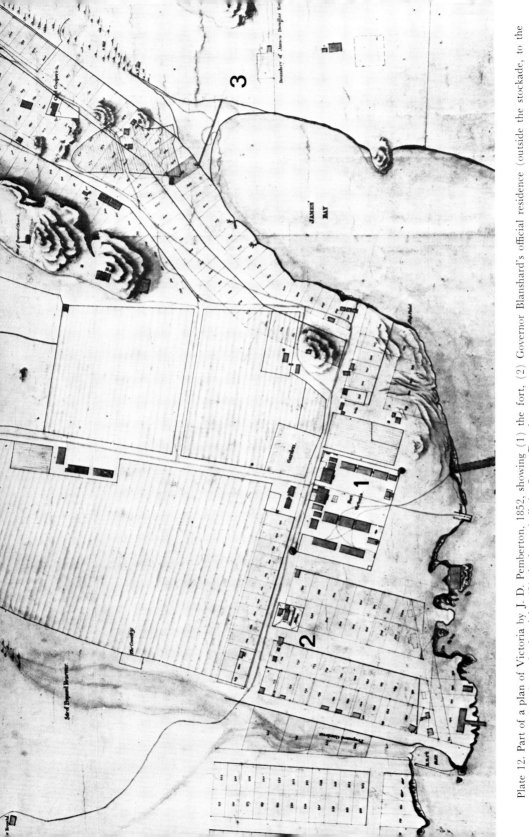

Plate 12. Part of a plan of Victoria by J. D. Pemberton, 1852, showing (1) the fort, (2) Governor Blanshard's official residence (outside the stockade, to the left of the picture) and, on the far right, (3) the house built by James Douglas.

Plate 13. *Upper left.* James Douglas, chief factor at Fort Victoria and later governor of Vancouver Island and of British Columbia.

Plate 14. *Upper right.* Amelia (Connolly) Douglas, wife of James Douglas.

Plate 15. *Lower left.* Cecilia (Douglas) Helmcken, who married J. S. Helmcken in 1852 and died in 1865.

Plate 16. *Below.* The Helmcken children, c. 1870. Seated: James Douglas; standing: Harry Dallas, Catherine Amelia (Amy), Edith Louisa (Dolly) (from a photograph by Frederick Dally).

Plate 17. *Lower right.* J. S. Helmcken, c. 1860.

Plate 18. Songhees Indian Village on Victoria Harbour, c. 1868 (from a photograph by Frederick Dally).

Plate 19. The first Legislative Assembly of Vancouver Island. Back row, left to right: J. W. McKay, J. D. Pemberton, Joseph Porter (clerk); front row, left to right: Thomas Skinner, J. S. Helmcken (speaker), James Yates. Absent are John Muir, member for Sooke, and Dr. John F. Kennedy, member for Nanaimo.

Plate 20. The House of Assembly, soon after its completion in 1859, showing the balustraded platforms, later removed, on the roofs of the wings (from a photograph by F. G. Claudet).

Plate 21. The first Legislative Council of British Columbia outside the Legislative Hall at New Westminster, January 1865. Left to right: Henry Holbrook, George A. Walkem, W. O. Hamley, Chartres Brew, H. M. Ball, A. N. Birch, C. W. Franks, Peter O'Reilly, Walter Moberly, J. A. R. Homer, Charles Good, clerk (in shadow), H. P. P. Crease. Helmcken's fellow members in the 1867 Council were Walkem, Hamley, Brew, Ball, Birch, O'Reilly, and Crease; in the 1868 Council, Walkem, Hamley, Ball, O'Reilly, and Crease.

Plate 22. Cartoon in sugar, by Andrew W. Piper, a Victoria confectioner, showing three delegates to the Yale Convention: John Gustavus Norris, Amor De Cosmos, and Mifflin Wistar Gibbs (see p. 247).

Plate 23. J. S. Helmcken, c. 1892, when he began to write his reminiscences (from a photograph by Hall and Lowe).

Plate 24. "The Old Doctor" in the garden behind his house, c. 1917. The later additions to the original log dwelling of 1852 may be seen on the right.

did not send out shiploads of immigrants after the three or four doses, and indeed they had no encouragement to do so, as the bailiffs of the farms at Esquimault became very expensive and wanted to conduct farms as they had done in England—the men would not work as they had done at home and some of them ran away and more would if they could. Sheep and cattle were imported from Nesqually [Nisqually], but Langford was unfortunate—winter lasted long—the ground covered with snow—no pasture or food for sheep and so very many of them died—the cattle could do better—in fact none of these people knew about a new country and were unwilling and took good care not to rough it. McKenzie was pushing—established a small sawmill at Craig-flower, and also a bakery and made bread and biscuit for HM ships, but somehow or other none of these paid, and all the farms were a fearful expense, indeed clearing land is an expensive job, and the whole gave great dissatisfaction to the HBCo. The bailiffs always want-ing more and more as they were to have a share of the profits—the latter chagrined because the bailiffs did not make any. How many thousands of pounds were expended in this way I forget. The truth is the whole was a mistake as far as the Company was concerned, but those ladies and gentlemen did much good to the Colony in the shape of keeping it at a high standard of civilization, tho not at their own expense. Rough and ready folk on their own account did well and those did best who kept sober and were thrifty and hardworking, for everything could be sold that was raised and more too. Indeed from the very commencement of the settlement until now the Colony has never supplied itself with ordinary necessaries.

The scheme of colonization was a blunder—a theory—the sales of land were to pay for everything and the price was five dollars per acre, with the demand that every purchaser should send out a number of men to cultivate the purchase!¹ The Governor's salary was to be the rental of a tract of land! Reserves were to be made for the Church of England and I think for schools,² and in some instances were made. There was a heavy royalty on coal too. As no land or very little was sold save to

---

¹JSH is in error here. See above, p. 85n2. Those who purchased less than one hundred acres were exempt.
²The proposals made by the HBC for the implementation of its grant of Vancou-ver Island contained a plan for the maintenance of a minister of religion, whereby a portion of land equal to one-eighth the quantity of land sold was to be set aside, half for the support of the minister himself, and "the remaining half to be available for roads, site for church and churchyard, schools and other public purposes" (Begg, *History of British Columbia*, p. 187).

the Puget Sound Company and a few others, there wasn't any income, so the Company had to bear expenses. Pemberton used to ask us to buy land just for the money, but no one at first wanted land, and money amongst us was lacking—we were all poor! There were no duties on goods and so there was no colonial income. Again on the American continent in Washington Territory, settlers were given 640 acres for nothing—the contrast was glaring and some of our people took advantage of it, but it was a very rough life and they had to bear the cost of public necessities, which we had not. I doubt very much whether we should have had many more settlers, even if the Company had followed suit—our country being a pretty rough one with comparatively little open land. In time settlers sent for their relatives and friends and Victoria became a village with thirty or forty houses—small of course.

No doubt Governor Blanshard urged and perhaps originated a good deal of this grumbling—and he was ably backed by the parson Staines, Yates, Cooper, Dr. Benson—the Langfords, Skinners & others. Langford was in some way a connection of Blanshard's—the latter hated the HBCo for some reason or other—he was in fact a disappointed man. He soon found that altho Governor, Mr. Douglas had all the power and all the men—in fact Blanshard was troubled with tic douloureux of a bad kind—he had been in malarious countries—smoked a great deal and had to take morphine for his attacks and so being in bad health was a pessimist and blamed the conditions of things, when in fact the drawback was in his own health. Blanshard however was a gentleman—very agreeable to his friends—of rather military carriage and military moustache —but a barrister if not by profession at least by grace of the Temple.[1] Under different conditions he would have been a very different man. As it was, the divided authority led to much ill feeling and doubtless was the cause of much of the early dissatisfaction. Blanshard thought Douglas plotted in order to displace him and be Governor himself and so threw difficulties and unpleasantness in his way. There may be some truth in this, for possibly the Company found Blanshard for various reasons unsuitable—indeed it is said that the Company always intended Douglas to be Governor and he would have been had not some political parties at home objected to this,[2] thinking the Company would be

[1]He was called to the bar at Lincoln's Inn on 22 November 1844 (Ireland, "Governor Blanshard," p. 220).

[2]Cf. J. H. Pelly to James Douglas, 3 August 1849: "It was proposed to appoint you Governor pro tempore of the Island, but you will see by the Public press, from the jealousy of some parties, and interested motives of others, how next to impos-

autocratic, and the settlers at their mercy—an objection certainly true in theory, but an impossibility in practice under the peculiar condition of the people and the country, for everyone was free—and able to go to the other side.

Thus Victoria grew from nothing to a decent village—but the agricultural settlement, outside the Puget Sound and HBCo's farms, was small. At this time, everyone believed that Esquimault would be the site of the future city. Victoria served very well the purposes of the HBCo and the village, but *when* the big ships arrived and commerce became great, which everyone imagined would be, then Esquimault must necessarily be the place. No doubt, had the HBCo built Victoria Fort at Esquimault, the city would have been there—fixed fast and immovable, but Mr. Douglas chose Victoria harbour, as much on account of the small prairies about it as anything else—it was certainly very fit for a Hudson's Bay Co's post—and at the time was a lovely place. I have heard Mr. Douglas expatiate on the beauties and flowers, and how much he was enamoured by his first explorations of Victoria District and Beacon Hill.[1]

It is about time to return to my personal history. On my return from Fort Rupert, affairs had altered a little; the same faces for the most part remained save Benson's, but there was grumbling about food—the big prices for everything—the Governor grumbled at this, and like others because they could not get everything they wanted—as they could in England or Scotland. Really there was no real want—beef and mutton were scarce, but there was plenty of other wild food—fish, flesh or fowl. Yates' house was in the ascendant—Mr. Douglas' residence habitable[2] and the Governor's at the corner of Yates Street likewise—the latter was only a four-room building on about four lots; faced with planed shingles. It was comfortable but not commodious, in the present

---

sible it would have been to give you the situation" (Fort Victoria, Correspondence Inward from HBC, London, 1849-1859, PABC).

[1]Douglas had first explored the area in 1842, when the company was planning to move its headquarters from Fort Vancouver on the Columbia River. He wrote to James Hargrave, 5 February 1843: ". . . the place itself appears a perfect 'Eden,' in the midst of the dreary wilderness of the North West coast and . . . one might be pardoned for supposing it had dropped from the clouds into its present position" (*Hargrave Correspondence*, p. 420).

[2]On the shore of James Bay, on a site now occupied by the Provincial Museum and Archives complex erected in 1967. It was said to be "nearly completed" in the summer of 1851 (Rear-Admiral Fairfax Moresby to the secretary of the Admiralty, 7 July 1851, PRO Transcripts, HBC—CO, 1822-1852, vol. 725, p. 209, [transcript, p. 338], PABC).

sense of this term. The Governor was better—so I had but little to do
with him just then, and indeed never had much, for he did not take
a fancy to me and so I did not court him. I was not like Benson, not
given to grumble and complaints of the Hudson's Bay Co. I had soon
fallen in love with Cecilia, in fact had probably been before I arrived the
second time at Victoria, so I spent much of my time courting—
particularly whilst the Douglases remained in the Fort, which was for
some time after, in fact James Douglas was born here [1 June 1851].
Miss Cameron, Mr. Douglas' niece, had arrived and was domiciled there
and played propriety.[1] The courtship was a very simple affair—generally
in the evening, when we had chocolate and singing and what not—
early hours kept. Mrs. Douglas at this time was a very active woman,
energetic and industrious but awfully jealous. She was very kind to
outsiders and visited them when ill, and in fact nursed them more or
less, and I remember she remained for a long time with Mrs. Yates, when
her child was born on Yates Street, making her kneel down at the
bedside, which Mrs. Yates considered did her a great deal of good.
Mrs. Douglas liked Mrs. Yates, who indeed was a very pleasant auburn-
haired body of considerable activity—orderly and very neat and cleanly
—the opposite of her husband.

The young Douglases were very shy and very pretty—Mrs. Dallas
and Mrs. Bushby particularly so,[2] but were small and looked after by
their mother with sharpness. She and Mrs. Staines did not chum at all
—there being too much uppishness about the latter, she being the great
woman—the great complaining—and the great schoolmistress and I
may here state, that she really was the best schoolmistress ever seen even
since in Victoria—she kept the girls in order—took them out—saw
they were properly and neatly dressed—carried themselves properly and
paid much attention to deportment and was really good to the girls,
altho the latter did not like the change and her strictness. The school
and residence of the parson and Mrs. Staines was a very large portion
of Bachelors' Hall building—the ladies slept upstairs over our heads,
and the little mischiefs used to play pranks, occasionally pouring

---

[1]Cecilia Eliza Cowan Cameron was the daughter of Douglas's sister Cecilia and her
first husband, one Captain Cowan, and the step-daughter of David Cameron,
the first chief justice of the Supreme Court of Vancouver Island in 1853. She
arrived "fresh from school" on the *Tory* in 1851 (Macdonald, *A Pioneer 1851*,
p. 5).
[2]Jane Douglas (1839-1909) married Alexander Grant Dallas on 9 March 1858;
Agnes (1841-1928) married Arthur Thomas Bushby on 8 May 1862 (Christ
Church marriage register).

water upon us through cracks or holes in the flooring, for our ceiling was not ceiled. By the same token our proceedings may have annoyed them too for occasionally Bachelors' Hall was pretty noisy.

Anyhow all I had to do at this time was to attend the sick of the Company, and also to strangers who came from the other side for treatment, I really being the only surgeon for many hundred miles. They likewise used to buy various drugs, for which I had to account, but our stock was not very large then, and patent medicines existed not, save Turlington's Balsam and Juniper Peppermint. I might have made money out of these sick, but they really looked so poor, and no doubt often were, that I neglected to do so, but in process of time, I became a celebrity and had lots of patients "from the other side."

I had to supply the Hudson's Bay posts throughout the country with the medicines they required. Dozens of bottles of Turlington's Balsam and Essence of Peppermint—grosses of "purges" of jalap and calomel —dozens of emetics of ipecacuanha and tartar emetic and other simples, but bottles and corks were scarce, so that the parcels could not be said to be neat, besides they all had to be put up in small quantities for distribution to subsidiary posts—pills by the thousand, and so forth. At this time I had the power to order anything I wanted in the shape of drugs &c. from England, so ere a year or two had elapsed I had a good store, lots of bottles, corks and ordinary instruments. In those days the Company never made any complaints about this—a considerable quantity of these medicines went to poor Americans and others without charge. The treatment in the interior was simple—an emetic as soon as a man fell ill, followed by a purge—then the man was well or had to get well by simples, the Trader or Factor being the doctor there.[1] Turlington's Balsam, i.e. Tr Benzoin Co. was used for all cuts and wounds—for coughs, colds and so forth. No one died—it was

[1]Cf. "Fort Rupert in 1850," p. 325 below. Turlington's Balsam (or Drops), a mixture covered by British patent No. 596, granted to Robert Turlington in 1744, was said by him to contain more than twenty-seven ingredients and to cure a great number of diseases. When in 1822 it was analyzed by the Philadelphia College of Pharmacy it was found to contain tincture of benzoin, balsam of Peru, myrhh and angelica root, and ammonia. In 1838 John McLean called it "the universal panacea" (*Notes of a Twenty-five Years' Service in the Hudson's Bay Company Territory*, ed. W. S. Wallace, [Toronto: Champlain Society, 1932], p. 215); its use is recorded in the journals of Samuel Hearne and Alexander Mackenzie; and Dr. John Rae took half-a-dozen bottles at one shilling and ninepence each among the supplies for his expedition in search of Franklin. See Frank Ridley, "An Early Patent Medicine of the Canadian North," *Canadian Geographical Journal* 23 (July 1966) : 25-27.

always said they had to come to Victoria to be able to die. Altho these folk lived chiefly on dried salmon and game with very little flour they were a very robust healthy lot. Beef, mutton or pork did not come to their share, but old Tod at Kamloops had the credit of eating the horses[1]—this being one of the places where horses for breeding and so forth were kept, for goods for the interior were always carried on horseback—there only being trails—no waggons or waggon roads. The brigades used to come to Langley or Hope on the Fraser year after year—and it was considered a hard job to get through the mountains either at Hope or Yale—they did it nevertheless—but the horses had often very sore backs—mules were unknown. The simple medicines by degrees underwent a change—a greater variety were required and greater quantity and in process of time, numerous patent medicines were ordered, for newspapers and periodicals and advertisements in some shape or other found their way up country. The Indians used a good deal of the medicines, and altho I offered to send pounds of Tr Benzoin &c., the posts said it was of no use, for the Indians had no faith in the medicines excepting in the ancient and traditional bottles! Thus Mustang Liniment for the horse's back—Cherry Pectoral and heaven knows what, became added to the "requisitions for medicines," which I always endeavoured to supply as soon as possible. Altho such things did not occupy the whole of my time, still I was by no means unemployed— there was always something useful to be done.

As the Langfords, Skinners and so forth arrived with Miss Cameron followed by the McKenzies soon after my advent from Fort Rupert and the establishment of their farms and others belonging to the HBCo I had soon enough to do, and now had to learn to ride and travel in small canoes, for the farms were distant and trails only existed and these none of the best and very circuitous. Why, it was a ten-mile ride by land to Langford's, except indeed I chose to send the horse over to the Indian village and start from there. There were a good many men employed at each of these farms, and as many of them had wives and the consequences, I had a good deal of riding sometimes at night to do, and in fact led a very active existence. I was green too—and conscientious and what is worse, always anxious. As to riding—well,

[1]John Tod (c. 1793-1882) was placed in charge of the Thompson River district, with headquarters at Fort Kamloops, after the murder of Chief Factor Samuel Black. For further details see the biography in *Minutes of Council, Northern Department of Rupert's Land*, p. 459; and Gilbert Malcolm Sproat, "John Tod: Career of a Scotch Boy," ed. Madge Wolfenden, *BCHQ* 18 (1954): 133-238.

I had scarcely been on a horse's back before I came here! Some men were out hunting—greenhorns walking Indian file along a trail at Mount Douglas, when some careless one's musket went off—and peppered the one in front with shot—no cartridges then—his buttocks looked like a plum pudding—as I could not ride the man was brought in. Dr. Kennedy and I picked out the duck shot[1]—at least as many as we could. Of course I determined to ride, and Macdonald made me a pad to break me in Indian fashion. After a while a [I] took to a Spanish saddle—i.e. only a wooden tree, without any covering, save the parchment. I rode this always after—having a poncho in winter—and capital things these are. The men had a blue or red blanket with a slit in the centre to put the head through, so this blanket covered the man, musket, powderhorn and everything else. I soon was able to ride well enough, but never could be said to be a good rider. A horse cost twenty dollars and my best mare from [Fort] Vancouver cost me forty dollars—a high figure—I believe it was bought with iquas [hiaqua][2], which were then valuable and currency in the interior—the iquas were found on the west coast of V.I. in deep water. Soon I had a band of horses running loose—but when the Fraser River excitement broke out, they all disappeared—stolen—sent away to the Fraser for pack horses! Riding was rather troublesome by the circuitous route to Langford's—the route went to Hillside, thence towards Tolmie's and from there there was a path through the woods to the bridge across the Gorge—from there to the plain country about where the Naval Cemetery now stands. To avoid all this I would often go across to the Indian village and walk to Langford's and back again in moccasins, or take a canoe with an Indian—go up the Arm—carry the canoe across the isthmus there and so on to Rosebank, then called the Doctor's Landing because I believe Dr. McLoughlin had landed there to ex-

---

[1]John Frederick Kennedy (1805-59) was stationed at Fort Simpson from 1832 on, but he was on furlough 1852-53. For further details see the biography in *The Letters of John McLoughlin ... First Series, 1825-38*, ed. E. E. Rich ([London]: Hudson's Bay Record Society, 1941), p. 346.
[2]Cf. Paul Kane, *Wanderings of an Artist* ... (London: Longman, Brown, Green, Longman and Roberts, 1859), pp. 238-39, quoted in Don Taxay, *Money of the American Indians* (New York: Nummus Press, 1970), p. 90. "His property consists principally of slaves and ioquas [hiaqua], a small shell found at Cape Flattery, and only there, in great abundance. These shells are used as money, and a great traffic is carried on among all the tribes by means of them. They are obtained at the bottom of the sea, at considerable depth . . . ." The Chinook traders of the Columbia Valley called the shells Hiaqua, spelled hykwa in C. M. Tate's Chinook dictionary and defined as "shell money (large size)."

plore.[1] The first time I went over in a canoe—I walked from the portage to the beach—the Indians made signals which I did not understand—but soon did, for when I arrived at the canoe my leggings were one mass of fleas! I had traversed a deserted lodge. Always avoid deserted lodges, if you do not wish to be eaten by fleas. The Indians put me on a boulder in the harbour and wiped the fleas off into the salt water—but they did not catch them all! Langford's too was an awful place for fleas, that is to say—if one went near the pig styes! I and many others have often walked from Langford's to town at night after a dance or small social—these socials were not uncommon, but I did not often accept. We had a sort of feeling, that they were living beyond their means—i.e. the Puget Sound Co had to pay—yet the socials were not expensive, altho there was always wine and brandy. The naval officers used to frequent Colwood and no wonder!

Having all this work to do Mr. Douglas got permission from the Puget Sound Co to pay me £100 per annum for my services. I now had £200 per annum, rations and house free. So having become engaged, it was determined that we should be married in the spring of /53 but not before I could prove myself to be a single man of good character &c., which Mr. Douglas insisted on! These in due course came out from my mother and Dr. Graves and proved satisfactory.[2] Before this, William Newton

[1]There appears to be some confusion here. An 1854 HBC map marks a "Landing Place" on Esquimalt Harbour, not far from the mouth of Rowe Stream, the later Millstream. The association with Dr. John McLoughlin seems rather doubtful. He visited Vancouver Island only once, in 1839, when he spent a day or so inspecting, not *exploring*, "the plain on the south end of Vancouver's Island" which Captain McNeill had recommended as the site of the future Fort Victoria (see W. Kaye Lamb, "The Founding of Fort Victoria," *BCHQ* 6 [1943]: 77). The property later known as "Rosebank" comprised the neighbouring section XCVI, Esquimalt District, and it was purchased in 1859 by James Douglas (see "Return of Lands . . . for the District of Esquimalt," in Vancouver Island, House of Assembly, *Minutes of Proceedings of a Select Committee . . . [on] Crown Lands . . .* [Victoria: Harries and Co., 1864]). By 1863 a house had been erected there, for Dr. John Ash's daughter was born on 31 July 1863 "at Rosebank, Esquimalt" (*Colonist*, 4 August 1863). In his will, Douglas left the property "upon Trust for my daughters Agnes [Bushby] and Jane [Dallas] as Tenants in common," and their title was confirmed by a Supreme Court order, 21 May 1885 (copy, PABC). By about 1908 the property was the summer residence of Harry Dallas Helmcken, and at his funeral in 1912 "a few wild flowers from his country home 'Rosebank' were placed on the coffin" (*Colonist*, 28 July 1912). The property is now owned by the Department of National Defence, which has replaced the wild roses that are said to have given the estate its name by gravel fill and an oil dock.
[2]These testimonials are preserved in the Helmcken Collection.

followed me at Colwood—to know whether I had any intentions about Mrs. Langford's sister (afterwards Mrs. Dr. Benson[1]). I told him I was already engaged—that silenced the matter. At this period "Billy" Newton—who afterwards married old Tod's daughter—Williams—who married Mrs. Dodd's daughter—were added to the frequenters of Bachelors' Hall.[2] Newton was a nice agreeable young fellow—a stripling—Langford's factotum and almost relative. Williams had been a ship man and indeed was still with Dodd—he had been in Australia, and being pinched had made a living by singing in public. He was a strong handsome good-hearted chap. Both of them could sing well, and so in the evening there was always or often singing going on particularly on Saturday nights, much to the annoyance of the parson and his wife, but not so to the girl boarders. Bachelors' Hall was the rendezvous of all visitors— i.e. if they were socially admissible! so sometimes there was a good number, including Captain Grant—the captains or mates of HB ships when in harbour—and HMS officers and middies. Of course sometimes they were a little boisterous, but never much so, because the parson was on one side and Mr. Douglas only fifty feet away, in the house on the opposite side of now Fort Street! We had Nevin and Sangster too. Nevin liked whisky too much, so Benson, Grant and some others put him on to a blanket—each one taking a corner—up and down went Nevin, until he promised not to get drunk again. Tossing cannot be pleasant, particularly when the blanket is not held taut enough. It did not do Nevin any good and so he soon quitted—looked after the "Navy" i.e. Hudson's Bay Co's barges, supplies and so forth—and went to the Sandwich Islands where I think he died.

Sangster had charge of the *Cadboro* and was pilot in general. He it was who used to sit on Beacon Hill, spy glass in hand, looking for any of the Company's ships rounding Rocky Point or any other expected vessel. He liked whisky also. After Yates left the house in the

---

[1]Benson married Miss Ellen Phillips on 19 December 1860 (*Colonist*, 21 December 1860).

[2]William Henry Newton came from England on the *Tory* in 1851 as "agricultural assistant" to E. E. Langford of Colwood Farm but soon transferred to the HBC service. He married Emmeline Jane Tod on 30 September 1856 (Christ Church marriage register). For further details see "Bushby Appendix." Robert Williams came out as first mate in the *Tory* in 1851 (Macdonald, *A Pioneer 1851*, p. 4). He married Elizabeth Ann (Nancy) Dodd on 23 December 1860 (*Colonist*, 29 December 1860). He was in charge of the HBC post at Quesnel, 1869-74 and was then transferred to Victoria as factor in charge of the depot. In 1877 he was drowned while on a tour of inspection of the company's northern posts (ibid., 27 June 1877).

Fort Yard—Sangster became Postmaster, Harbour Master &c. &c. and occupied Yates' house, which is now my office. The little window in it is one that Sangster had put in—a sort of wicket, to open and shut, because he did not want people to go into the house, to ask him for letters—or anything else. He handed letters through the window. The truth is he was often very shaky after drinking—but he was an exceedingly good-hearted quiet unobtrusive man, whom all liked. After a while he too left the service, took land on the Lagoon, built a small house and gardened. There he committed suicide. Sangster's Plains are named after him—he resided there or near there in the bottom.

At this time too, the officers of the Fort had formed a company to put up a sawmill at the Lagoon.[1] Wishart brought it out, but having bought it in England, where it had been used for cutting hardwood for ships with a small gang of saws, it was not very suitable and moreover, no one knew how to put it up properly and unfortunately one of [the] cast iron uprights got broken. McKay took charge of the mill and its erection for a time and then Parker had it, but it was a failure. If it had been suitable and worked well, we should have made more money, for lumber sold at this time at forty dollars per thousand feet. I sold out to Mr. Finlayson for £100—the price of my shares, wanting the money for my marriage. A few weeks after, the mill was burned down![2] Finlayson used afterwards to twit me about the luck of getting married—he never forgot it. He—Pemberton—McKay—Wishart and

[1] JSH's recollections of this venture "on the north shore of the lagoon at Albert Head" do not coincide precisely with the account based on records in the HBC archives given by W. Kaye Lamb in "Early Lumbering," pp. 42-43. The Vancouver's Island Steam Saw Mill Company was organized at a meeting in Victoria on 28 December 1851, a year before JSH's marriage, with a capital of £2,000 in £100 shares. The original list of shareholders, all of them connected with the HBC, has survived, and it does not contain the name of JSH. "Dr. Helmcken attended the first meeting and was expected to subscribe, but failed to do so" (ibid., p. 43). However, his name does appear among the "Managing Committee" in an undated prospectus of the "Vancouver's Island Steam Sawing [sic] Mill Company" now in the Provincial Archives. The chairman was James Douglas, the vice-chairman, Roderick Finlayson, and the other members of the managing committee were Charles Dodd, W. F. Tolmie, Capt. James Sangster, and J. W. McKay, all of whom became shareholders in the company organized in 1851. Attached to this prospectus is a portion of an Admiralty chart showing the site for a mill on Cordova Bay—the same site as that originally chosen by the Vancouver's Island Steam Saw Mill Company and rejected in favour of Albert Head (ibid., p. 44).

[2] JSH implies that the mill burned down a few weeks after his marriage (on 27 December 1852). Actually the fire occurred on 29 August 1859 (*Victoria Gazette*, 3 September 1859).

the rest lost their money—they never attempted to put up another. Lumber mills were now running on the Sound. Why the mill was not erected in Esquimault Harbour, was that there seemed to be lots of trees about the Lagoon. The water-mill at Rowe Stream under McKenzie was running and I have known rough lumber to be sold there at sixty dollars per thousand feet!

Of course I had to build a house.[1] Mr. Douglas gave me a piece of land, an acre, wanted me to live on it, because being close together there would be mutual aid in case of trouble—for in these days trouble might at any time come from Indians and so forth—besides there were no servants save Indians—and they never remained long and would not live in houses. I ought not to have built there, for it was away from my work and office, and so soon found it very inconvenient. My house and office ought to have been together near the Fort—as well for commerce as profit, but this was found out by experience. A doctor's office and his house ought to be together, for it adds materially to his comfort, convenience and profit, saves no end of time and labour, besides other advantages. Of course for the time being it pleased Cecilia —she was near her mother and relatives—no small comfort to her during my absence.

The piece of land was of course very rough and cost a good deal of time and money to clear it—this being done by Indians, chiefly from the north.

To build a house now is a very easy matter—but a very different matter then. How we studied over the design, i.e. interior divisions of the building 30x25!! Then to get it done—for there were no contractors, everything had to be done piecemeal. There being no lumber, it had to be built with logs squared on two sides and six inches thick. The sills and uprights were very heavy and morticed—the supports of the floor likewise—the logs had to be let into grooves in the uprights.

Well the timber had to be taken from the forest—squared there and brought down by water. All this had to be contracted for by French Canadians, then when brought to the beach—I had [to] beg oxen of the Company to haul it to the site. Then other Canadians took the job of putting the building up as far as the logs were concerned—and then shingling—the Indians at this time made shingles—all split. All this was

---

[1]The original log dwelling with its later additions still stands, next to the Provincial Museum and Archives complex, and has been preserved as far as possible as it was in JSH's day. The mansion of Governor Douglas, completed in 1851 (see above, p. 119) beside which JSH built his house, was pulled down in 1906.

very heavy, very expensive and very slow work, for the men were by no means in a hurry. Among the names I find Maurice—Peltier—Dubois —all dead now. They chiefly took their pay in blankets and provisions and other iktas—the balance in coin.

Well the shell is up—now to get it finished—lumber very scarce and a favor to get any at forty dollars per thousand in the rough—so it all had to be planed and grooved &c. by hand! Much of it was cut by Kanakas in a saw-pit—so it was not very regular in thickness. I wrote to Blenkinsop at Fort Rupert for plank—he sent me some and also at my wish some of yellow cedar, with these latter the doors, windows and skirting boards were made.

It so happened that Gideon Halcro [Halcrow] a crofter—a mechanic of all work was here—he could do carpentering, plastering and everything connected with a house,[1] so I got him to go on with the work, but oh, the grumbling about the irregular wood—so much planing down—besides the flooring was 8 or ten inches wide—no narrow plank then. Fortunately I had bought the two lots next mine—a house stood on it, put there by the man [blank in MS] who built Mr. Douglas' house—at least who finished the inside. Here Halcrow worked and I think lived—but oh, how slowly—for I wanted the house to be finished by the springtime.

Then to get lime—this came from Langford's and McKenzie's—who burned lime occasionally for their own use—after time and trouble I got this and Indians split cedar laths—a work pretty new to them—so the laths were too thin and too springy. The expense and annoyance of all this was very great, in fact the house cost more than treble of a good house now.

Indians dug a couple of wells and lined one with boulders! The boulders left very little well—they were so large and heavy—I now wonder how the Indians handled these stones and built the well without a severe accident.

A well was an important thing then! Most of the water in the summer time had to be drawn in carts from a spring at a place now called Spring Ridge.

---

[1]Gideon Halcrow had arrived aboard the *Norman Morison* on 12 June 1852. He was later the contractor for one of the Parliament Buildings ("The Birdcages") erected by Douglas in 1859 (B. W. Pearse, acting colonial surveyor, to colonial secretary, 31 July 1860, Vancouver Island, Lands and Works' Department Correspondence, Colonial Correspondence, PABC) and died in 1870 (*Colonist*, 12 January 1870).

Of course whilst all this was going on I was "courting"—but never outside—save on Saturdays, when lots of horses were driven into the Fort, and the clerks, ladies, Mr. Douglas and others would form a party and ride to the country round about. Everyone kept his own horse then—one or more. Altho we all started together—we certainly returned in small parties—having gone helter-skelter everywhere.

Mrs. Douglas never went—she was awfully particular at home and did not like to lose her daughters and in consequence did not like me over much. Miss Cameron played propriety—she helped us along—but then she was not much over twenty years of age. Some of the younger daughters used to come in occasionally but as a rule there was no company—Mr. Douglas did not keep any—none to keep. How is it that the courting business does not become very monotonous? To look back in our old age, this courting seems very absurd—but nevertheless it is instinctive and will forever go on—with modification.

It so happened that at this time a Cowitchin? [Cowichan] Indian committed a murder and as usual it was determined that he must be had, but the chiefs could not or would not give up the culprit. Mr., now Governor, Douglas determined to go with an expedition to seize him.[1] A man-of-war and men went with him. The marines and sailors landed—cut roads through the bush to drag the cannon—had encampments, patrols, and a regular military discipline—fires put out at night and so forth. At length they came to the desired spot, not having been molested on the journey, shewing that the Indians were either afraid, or were willing that the murderer should be seized—for Indians do not like murderers. A council is held—and on the following day, the Indians are all on the plain and the military and sailors in battle array, ready for the fray. Governor Douglas walks forward—perhaps to seize the Indians or to parley, when the Indian murderer suddenly comes forward armed and fires, but the musket, an old flint-lock, misses fire—on this the Indian is seized—tried by court martial and hung. The Governor had a very narrow escape it is believed. Douglas was a cold brave man, he had entered an Indian lodge before to seize the murderer of Mr. Black—they had followed this Indian for years—more or less.

---

[1] On 5 November 1852 a HBC shepherd was murdered by a Cowichan brave and the son of a Nanaimo chief. Early in January 1853 Douglas led a force of 130 marines and seamen from H.M.S. *Thetis* together with the small corps of Victoria Voltigeurs (ten or eleven men) in pursuit of the murderers, who were captured and executed at Nanaimo on 17 January 1853 (see B. A. McKelvie and W. E. Ireland, "The Victoria Voltigeurs," *BCHQ* 20 [1956]: 225-31).

They found him in a lodge and Douglas walked in and seized him—the other Indians did not interfere.[1] There was something grand and majestic about Douglas—in the first place, he was broad and powerful and had a wooden hard face when necessary, which said very plainly, "I am not afraid but *noli me tangere.*" When in this state he had the shape of a horseshoe on his forehead unmistakably—and we all knew then to be cautious, for there was something wrong, something to be put to rights, whether with the officers or others.

A short time before he went on the aforesaid expedition, Mr. Douglas spoke to me—saying, "I am going on this expedition—it is dangerous and what may happen to me is uncertain. I have made my will and so forth. You design to be married at Easter, but it would please me were you to marry before I go, then I would go feeling that if anything happened to me my daughter would be in safe hands and Mrs. Douglas would have some one to look to as well as my children"—and so forth. Of course I immediately consented and so my marriage was fixed to come off hurriedly and unexpectedly early. A true account of my wedding I have given in a Christmas number of the *Colonist*—a marriage in high life.[2] Joe Pemberton was my best man and Charley Griffin my Jehu.[3] Charley was a splendid fellow—a rushing active spirited lithesome and blithesome fellow—a Canadian, at home with a canoe and horses—a sort of typical Canadian young man—with a French dash in him. Skinners and so forth arrived after my wedding.

My house not being finished it was arranged that we should live in

---

[1]Samuel Black was murdered by an Indian at Kamloops in 1841, but it was John Tod, not James Douglas, who was involved in the pursuit and death of his murderer (see above, p. 122n1). JSH may be thinking of the notorious incident at Fort St. James in 1828, when Douglas confronted an Indian who for five years had been sought by the HBC for the murder of two HBC men at Fort George. For a number of conflicting reports of this encounter see Douglas's own report to the HBC (*McLoughlin Letters ... Third Series,* p. 311); Sproat, "John Tod," pp. 164-66; Morice, *History of the Northern Interior,* pp. 138-40; Victoria *Standard,* 25 February 1873; and Douglas to his daughter Martha, 25 February 1873 (James Douglas, Letters to Martha Douglas, 30 October 1871—27 May 1874, PABC).

[2]The marriage took place in the mess room of the fort on 27 December 1852, by the Rev. R. J. Staines (Fort Victoria marriage register). For a detailed description see "In the Early Fifties."

[3]Charles John Griffin, HBC clerk, who on 13 December 1853 established the company sheep farm on San Juan Island (E. O. S. Scholefield and F. W. Howay, *British Columbia from the Earliest Times to the Present* [Vancouver: S. J. Clarke Publishing Co., 1914], 2:301) and was in charge there at the time of the San Juan dispute in 1859. He died in Ottawa in 1874 (*Colonist,* 18 August 1874).

Government House—i.e. Governor Blanshard's house formerly.[1] So we lived there for some months, had two rooms and a kitchen, with mighty little furniture—but quite enough for two. I had Dick my Indian for a servant, and cook—he married—and then we had *Ju*[?] Dick and his wife, but the latter would not stop in the house, so after a while both lived in their lodge at night at the Indian village. Of course the most of the work had to be done by self and wife, but the Indians were very useful for chopping wood, carrying water and doing odd jobs. I think Dick was paid two blankets and a shirt per month and Indian provisions occasionally. He was really a good boy and is living still—a sheep farmer. Of course there was not much to be done—our wants were but few—and ordinary fare supplied by the HBCo. Golledge at this time was the Governor's Private Secretary[2]—and found a sleeping place in the house somewhere.

The night of my marriage or the night after, a [I] was called up— Lord [blank in MS: Fitzwilliam] and his companion came—he was bilious and wanted a black draught and so forth—I told him to go to the devil and Dr. Kennedy, who was here at this time—Lord Fitzwilliam thought this a good joke! These touring young lords used to come occasionally—armed with letters from the Honble Hudson's Bay Co. As a rule they were pretty nice, but sometimes supercilious. Fitzwilliam was the one who called me out of bed—and he turned out very unfriendly to the Company—but I am not positive about he being the identical man.[3]

---

[1]At the southwest corner of Government and Yates Streets, outside the fort. See Plate 12. For the Indian village see Plate 18.

[2]Richard Golledge came to Fort Victoria in 1851 aboard the *Tory* as apprentice clerk. He "wrote a beautiful hand" (Macdonald, *A Pioneer 1851,* p. 4) and became private secretary to Chief Factor Douglas, a position which he retained after Douglas became governor and held until 1859. He remained in the government service until 1864, when he was suspended from his office of acting gold commissioner and justice of the peace during the gold excitement at Leech River on the ground that he had "for a long time been addicted to drunken and dissolute habits of life" (A. E. Kennedy to Edward Cardwell, 30 November 1864, Vancouver Island, Governor Kennedy, Despatches to London, 25 March 1864 —19 November 1866); and cf. Vancouver Island, Executive Council, Minutes, 23 and 29 November 1864, PABC. He lived for years among the Songhees Indians and died destitute on 5 September 1887 at the age of fifty-five (*Colonist,* 7 September 1887).

[3]Charles Wentworth Fitzwilliam, the uncle of Lord Milton, had spent the winter of 1852-53 in Oregon and Vancouver Island and, according to his own statement, came to Fort Victoria in March 1853 (see Great Britain, Parliament, House of Commons, Select Committee on the Hudson's Bay Company, *Report,* 1857, [P.P. 197], p. 114). Ormsby, *British Columbia,* p. 125, accepts this identifi-

The snow was very deep at this time and partly for this and modest reasons my wife would not go out, but after a few days we went to see Mrs. Douglas, who scolded us for neglecting her—and she was really angry—the snow offered no excuse. Anyhow we made it all right. Of course Mrs. Douglas at this time was anxious, the Governor being at Cowichan. No telephones then, and Douglas' house seemed a good distance off. Dr. Kennedy was here but he refused to occupy my position for a time. Captain "Billy" Mitchell was about the first who came to see us.[1] He was in the service and commanded the [blank in MS] a regular rough jolly good-natured laughing sailor, who disdained umbrellas—never wore a greatcoat, altho his red face was blue with cold —and whose waistcoat was always on the fly and no underclothing of any consequence. He had plenty tales and was fond of repeating "Bartlemy [?] Fair" and the Zoo show—this is the golden eagle &c.—or this is Adam in the lion's den, you may know Adam, by his green inexpressible &c. &c.[2] He had but little to do and in process of time became a sort of pensioner—i.e. called to do anything on emergency. He became great friends afterwards with Mrs. Blinkhorn, Captain Ella having been his mate.[3] He died at their house of dysentery, Mrs. Blink-

---

cation and adds that Fitzwilliam felt he had been uncivilly treated by the officials at Fort Victoria in general. He indeed proved to be, as JSH says, a hostile witness against the company.

[1]Captain William Mitchell (1802-76) came to this coast in 1837 and served continuously in HBC vessels (Walbran, *British Columbia Coast Names*). In the summer of 1851 he was in command of the *Una*, which took a HBC mining party to the Queen Charlotte Islands in search of gold, but she was wrecked in a gale near Cape Flattery on Christmas Eve that year (Douglas to A. Barclay, 3 January 1852, Fort Victoria, Correspondence Outward to HBC, 1850-55, PABC). On the Cowichan expedition of 1853 (see above, p. 129) he commanded the *Recovery* (see John Moresby, *Two Admirals* [London: John Murray, 1909], p. 128). When the *Beaver's* charter by the Navy ended in 1870 Mitchell had charge of her until she was sold in 1874 (*Colonist*, 2 September 1874). He died at Mrs. Ella's home on 13 January 1876 (ibid., 14 January 1876).

[2]A wild beast show formed part of the celebrated Bartholomew Fair held annually in London from the twelfth to the middle of the nineteenth century. JSH is obviously thinking of some sort of recitation like "The Humours of Barthelmy Fair," *The Universal Songster or Museum of Mirth* (London: Routledge, n.d.), 1:118-19. In this piece, verses describing "all the fun of the fair 0" alternate with prose passages, marked *Spoken,* in which the showman urges the crowd to "valk up" and see "the wonderful beastes and beastesses," "the vonderful and surprizing Hottentot Wenus," and "the vonderful sun eagle."

[3]Mrs. Thomas Blinkhorn (formerly Ann Beeton) came aboard the *Tory* in 1851 with her husband, an independent settler, and her niece Martha Cheney, who afterwards married Henry Ella. For further details see "The Diary of Martha Cheney Ella, 1853-1856," ed. J. K. Nesbitt, *BCHQ* 13 (1949): 91-112, 257-70.

horn nursing him faithfully like a baby. His assumed hardihood cost him his life. We remained at "Government House" a few months, and then had to remove to my residence, still standing. It was habitable—roughly finished, plastered &c., but inner doors were wanting, so to supply these, grey cotton curtains were hung across. The furniture did not amount to much, but we were soon better supplied, as I received some from England—the horsehair chairs remain—the Windsor chairs came from the HBCo store.

Halcrow still went plodding along, but another man took his place whose name I forget, but was employed by the Governor at the same time at his house. Any[how] my first-born came along, before the doors had been hung. We had only three rooms and a kitchen altogether. Of course the boy-baby was a wonder, a light-haired blue-eyed fair little fellow. When he was about a month or two old we found him dead in the bed one morning.[1] The anguish felt at this is indescribable. The poor little fellow was buried in the garden where the holly now grows— close by our bedroom window. An oval of white daisies were planted around with a daisy cross in the centre. I had daisies—the first was brought to Victoria by Captain Mouat[2] from California in a little garden pot and I paid one dollar for it—a red one, double. The single daisies were imported from Scotland by Douglas in seed—and the shamrock by Mr. Work[3]—the thistle was an accidental coming—but no one supposed that the daisies or the thistles would have become the troublesome critters they now are. I recollect the first one that grew in my garden accidentally—it was looked on with great favor—probably came in the grass or other seed from the old country.

---

[1]According to "The Diary of Robert Melrose," ed. W. Kaye Lamb, *BCHQ* 7 (1943):132, this child was born on 29 October 1853. He was baptized Claude Douglas on 11 December 1853 (Fort Victoria register of baptisms), and the Fort Victoria register of burials (copy, PABC) records this name on 19 January 1854. The inscription on the family tomb in Pioneer Square reads: "Douglas Claude, died Jan. 17, 1854, aged 3 months."

[2]William Alexander Mouat (1821-71) came to Fort Vancouver as second mate of the HBC bark *Vancouver* in 1845 and in 1850 was master of the *Mary Dare*. For further details see the article by Dorothy Blakey Smith in *DCB* 10.

[3]John Work (c. 1792-1861) came to the Columbia District in 1823 and was in charge of Fort Simpson 1836-52. He then settled in Victoria as a member of the Board of Management for the Western Department and became one of the largest landowners on Vancouver Island. For further details see Henry Drummond Dee, "An Irishman in the Fur Trade: The Life and Journals of John Work," *BCHQ* 7 (1943): 229-70.

At this time I was a great gardener—worked hard—up at 5 or 6 o'clock digging &c. Indians cleared out the stumps and so forth— grew our own vegetables &c. &c. In process of time the land was got into some sort of shape—and I planted with sods the grass plot as it now stands. Looking back the whole seems to me ridiculous and an awful waste of time—if I had spent the same time with patients or other pursuit it would have been better. Doctors should not have such hobbies. I wanted 'black' currants and the Californians sent me red—with black labelled on the small bushes. We could get anything we ordered from California—the labels on the consignment were all right, but when grown they proved to be quite different.

The Governor had a gardener, an old Englishman named Thomas[1] —a pretty rough sort of gardener, but knew more in his own opinion than anyone else, but the Company's men from Kent were decent gardeners too and "Tom" Flewin had charge of the Company [garden?] which extended from Government to Douglas, bounded by Fort and Broughton Street.[2] Thomas said the best of all flowers was the cauliflower! Anyhow Governor Douglas' garden was laid out by the aforesaid Thomas—and remains very much the same to this day. The Governor received many presents of roses and other bushes from his admirers— sometimes a sprat to catch a salmon, but he also imported bulbs and other roots, which used to come by ship in "Wardean [Wardian] cases"—that is to say, glass cases into which neither air nor water entered.

So you see I am now in my house, pretty comfortable—very active and always at work either at home or abroad—have my horse or horses, for Cecilia was a good rider and used to go sometimes with me. We had our Indian servants but Cecilia used to do most of the work—Chinamen existed not yet. The town grew and more people appeared at the Company's farms—so I had plenty to do, and soon found it inconvenient

[1]Presumably George Thomas (1835?-1910), a native of Surrey, England. He arrived aboard the *Tory* in 1851 as a labourer with the HBC and is said to have left the fort in 1863 for a farm in North Saanich. For further details see the obituary in the *Colonist*, 18 January 1910; and Victor E. Virgin, *History of North and South Saanich Pioneers and District* (Saanichton: Saanich Pioneer Society, [1959]), pp. 40-41.

[2]Thomas Flewin (1843?-1901), a native of Kent, arrived aboard the *Norman Morison* on 16 January 1853. For further details see the obituary in the *Colonist*, 4 June 1901; and for the garden, see Plate 12.

to have my house and office away from each other. Bailey opened the Uplands Farm—he was followed by old Leigh.[1]

I have mentioned Governor Blanshard—Well he left in [blank in MS: September 1851] under the plea of ill-health, disappointment and possibly uselessness, but probably his action in the Fort Rupert murders and the hasty report he made had something to do with his resignation. I am not aware that he was ever employed in the government service afterwards. He is still living and is said to be a rich man. Of course in his time things had no shape, but he was Governor and wanted to act as such, but the power all lay in the hands of the Company at home and here—he did not like to put it mildly, the Hudson's Bay Co in general and Douglas in particular, and so these two never pulled together—in fact it was generally believed and probably truly, that the Company wished Douglas to be Governor and so he himself wished to be, and thus the Company have everything in their own hands. To add to the difficulty Blanshard took sides with Langford, Skinner and so forth, who of course were or became averse to the Company likewise, but really I never see that under the condition of things and their agreement, they had much to justly complain of. They had spent a great deal of money belonging to the Puget Sound Company, lived well, were comfortably housed and had no prospect of making money. Nevertheless they wanted more money and supplies, which at length the Company refused. In the end their agreement expired—and a settlement come to—but there was really nothing coming to any of them.

Blanshard was really and truly a gentleman—with a military moustache and fine features—but he was out of place—it could not be otherwise seeing that he took part and became querulous about the Company. They thought they knew their business about colonization and Blanshard held a contrary opinion. Douglas and Blanshard were seldom brought into actual collision, save when Blanshard summoned him to

[1]Uplands Farm (c. 1,112 acres) was surveyed by B. W. Pearse in 1856 (see the *Minutes . . . of the Select Committee . . . [on] Crown Lands,* 2 December 1863). "Bailey" is probably to be identified with the "Bayley Bailiff and family" in the passenger list of the *Tory,* 1851, as well as with the Charles Alfred Bayley who is said to have founded the first hotel in Victoria about 1854 (*Colonist,* 14 June 1883). It would seem that C. A. Bayley was in charge of the Uplands Farm from 1856 or earlier until 1859, for the *Colonist,* 24 June 1859, reported that he had "again become the host of Bayley's Hotel." According to Fawcett, *Some Reminiscences,* p. 54, William Leigh was in charge of Uplands Farm in 1859, but he entered the service of the City of Victoria soon after its incorporation in 1862 and served as town clerk from 1864 until his death on 1 May 1884 (*Colonist,* 3 May 1884).

appear before him, because he had signed the ship's register on change of captains, which the Company had always done. At the time it was a small thing in its way, but gave Blanshard an opportunity of showing his authority, much to the delight of Yates, Langford, Skinner and that ilk. Douglas was dignified but attended. Oh, once the men became riotous —drunk probably—there were no police—but Blanshard I think got some special constables and I saw him walking his verandah with sword at his side, vowing that he would have peace and be very severe on those who broke it. I am not aware that anyone was brought before him. At this time the Government Street bastion was supposed to be the prison, but it was tenantless—and had no officer. The first man I saw in this was a half-Kanaka, half-Canadian or perhaps half-coloured man. He was fed there three meals a day and in the morning was turned out and told what to do—I think to improve Fort Street. No one looked after him and he returned to his meals and prison sleeping room regularly![1]

Douglas of course was appointed Governor and all were summoned to hear the Commission read—naval officers were there too. I absented myself for some nasty reason or other and went to see a patient at Colwood. On returning Mr. Douglas was Governor and *Vice-Admiral* &c. &c. and there was a great deal in the Commission about flotsam and jetsam— infiefs and outfiefs I was told—but no one knew what they meant and cared not either. Who swore him in I know not.

I suppose too I was not present when Mr. Douglas made the treaty with the Indians in 1850 to surrender their lands. It must have been just before or just after I went to Rupert, still I have a glimmering of having seen them collecting.[2]

Douglas is now Governor, but he has plenty disagreeables before him —the seeds of discontent sown do not subside, but grow and as he is the agent of the HBCo—the Puget Sound Co and goodness knows what, he cannot please everyone. Imagine now Douglas Governor—the settlers more or less dissatisfied and with little reason—the few people are di-

---

[1] In a memorandum dated 5 August 1895 (HC), answering questions concerning the date of his service with the B.C. government and the number of years in that service, JSH said that "during 1851 a man (William Kingston, colored)" was imprisoned in the lower floor of the bastion. "Here then originated the 'prison' and I being surgeon had to look after his health." The prisoner was let out to make a sidewalk on Fort Street by placing small rocks side by side. "Here then," adds JSH, "is the origin of the chain gang but without chains or keepers."

[2] In the spring of 1850 Douglas concluded agreements with the Indians of Victoria, Metchosin, and Sooke. For further details see Wilson Duff, "The Fort Victoria Treaties," *BC Studies* 3 (Fall 1969) : 3-57.

vided into parties for or against the Company and Governor,—politics are discussed—whisky drank—tobacco smoked. They must have something to do and so air their grievances real or supposed, and are more or less encouraged in this by wayfarers and curiously enough by several of the HBCo's officers here also. They held a double allegiance—to themselves as colonists and to the HBCo as masters—but they did not feel that the two need clash. In fact at this time many of the officers of the Company as well in Victoria as elsewhere were thoroughly averse to the Company taking or having taken the colonization of the island on their shoulders. They thought it brooded [*sic: for* boded] ill for their dividends, for some supposed that the expense would fall on the Fur Trade when it really had nothing to do directly with fur trade or wintering partners, save making use of the latter in furtherance of the scheme and assisting in the supplies, accounts &c. of both Colony and Company. There is no doubt that the Company's officers in Victoria wished the Colony well—and further that they had determined to become colonists for the benefit of their belongings and further there is no doubt that both Governor Douglas and the HBCo desired that all their old retired or retiring officers and servants should settle in Vancouver Island.

Anyhow there was dissatisfaction—because the Colony did not grow fast enough! They argued that if the Govt (HM) had undertaken the colonization, then in this case there would have been civil and military officers and service, and all the paraphernalia of a Crown Colony and so much money spent, in fact the whole thing seemed to turn upon the point that these few villagers wanted to make money somehow and quickly too. (Is it not the same now as in the early days in this respect?) Had HM Govt done this the expense would have been charged to the Colony, to be repaid when the Colony wanted an independent form of government—and indeed it happened under the HBCo regime when the Government resumed possession, but as the Legislature had not sanctioned the expenditure, HM Govt did not force the claim, thanks to Sir James.[1] Governor Blanshard I think wrote a despatch wanting a

---

[1]The exclusive trade privileges of the HBC were revoked in 1859, but the settling of the accounts proved so complicated that it was not until 1867 that Vancouver Island was re-conveyed to the Crown. Douglas did well for the colony, for example, in the matter of the Parliament Buildings erected in 1859. He paid for them through the sale of the land around the fort, which the HBC insisted was fur trade land, not government land at all, as Douglas claimed. But the company allowed the sale to proceed on the understanding that they would eventually be reimbursed by the Crown. For a long time the British Government refused to pay; finally the matter went to arbitration and the HBC won its case. See *Papers in Connection with*

company of soldiers to protect the settlers from the Indians![1] They never came, the Colony had to depend upon perhaps a better arm—HM Ships. It seems absurd that this small community should have required all the paraphernalia of a large community—really they had very few and small disputes to settle—and easily settled by a little sense. If they had looked to the simple government of new communities in the U. States, they might have gained a good lesson, but being all unused to rough settlement and all being from the old country almost direct, they wanted things to be the same as in the old country—but had they been asked to pay for these luxuries—Whew! not a bit of it—they wanted everything but not to pay for their wants. It is true that there was at first [for a ?] few years a feeling of insecurity about Indians, but this wore off—our Indians were never very troublesome, but the dread was of the northern tribes—but when these came our population had increased—still they were not to be despised—but they were a long distance from their own country and knew the effect of British gunboats—marines and so forth, which were occasionally paraded for them to see.

It is possible had the Colony here began like an American one— there would have been more self-reliance and it would have had a perpetual effect on the succeeding population—not to require the Government to do everything for them and not them for their Government, but I doubt whether such a community would have existed— or if it managed to exist long in this isolated spot—it would have thrown in its lot with the Americans, for at this time HM Govt cared little about the Colonies and indeed some few years later told us and Canada we might do as we pleased in this respect and almost in as plain language! Today it is not a little different!

One often hears the discipline of the HBCo mysteriously spoken of by ignorant people. The truth is the Company was a commercial and not a military body. The only discipline was that of an ordinary factory, each man had his own work to do and did it—and the bell for meal time rang three times a day for meal times and additionally for service on Sundays. The same bell collected the officers &c. to meals or religious services—marriages and so forth all held in the same room—

Crown Lands in British Columbia and the Title of the Hudson's Bay Company (**Victoria**: Government Printing Office, 1881).

[1]See Blanshard to Earl Grey, 18 September 1850, *Vancouver Island, Despatches, Governor Blanshard to the Secretary of State, 26th December, 1849 to 30th August, 1851* (New Westminster: Government Printing Office, n.d.).

the mess room! All this was a mere matter of organization—call it discipline if the name pleases better. The clerks and accountant went to the office (Finlayson's)—others went to the shop—McKay to the Indian trading one—and different ones to the fur and other stores— hours from 6 in the morning to 6 in the evening in summer, less in the winter. The men went to the fields to look after the farms—horses or barns—the dairy people resided at the dairies—everything went on like clock work—and a pretty easy clock too. All that was asked was do your work. Governor Douglas or rather Chief Factor would oc- casionally ask—"How is this, that or [the] other thing getting on?" of the individual in charge, and give instructions or directions, per- haps scold a little if they did not suit his desires or opinions. This keeping the thread of everything was a ruling principle of his whole subsequent life—perhaps carried to excess—he took too much heed of details—got pertinaciously through an immense amount of work.

After the day's work of the officers and employees were over, they could do virtually as they pleased and spend the evenings as they liked, sometimes invited to take tea with the ladies in the Governor Chief Factor's house.

There would [be?] a few special demands. No one was allowed to trade on his own account—or to trade in any way in opposition to the Company—this even referred to the Captains of the Company's ships from England. Anyone doing this was dismissed as happened in a well- known instance.[1] Next, each had to be ready to depart to any other post or travel at a very short notice and in travelling no one was allowed to carry more than one hundred pounds, excepting indeed on the coast, where water carriage could be had. I have seen one or two officers who had to go to the interior at 24 hours' notice! and much less was required to start with mails or anything else to Nisqually or Fort Vancouver—these latter having to be done by canoes. This matter of being liable to be sent away of course had the effect in many in- stances of keeping people on their good behaviour,—and promotion too depended on zeal and good behaviour with intelligence. At mess table

---

[1]This reference remains obscure. JSH may possibly have had in mind Captain James Cooper, who as master of the HBC's *Columbia* in 1848 violated regulations by trading on his own account at Honolulu, and in 1852 fell foul of Douglas by taking to San Francisco, in his own schooner *Alice*, cranberries which he had got from the Indians on the Fraser in defiance of the company's monopoly. But in the first instance, Cooper seems to have left the service voluntarily to become an independent settler on Vancouver Island; in the second, he was no longer in the HBC service (see Margaret A. Ormsby's article on Cooper in *DCB* 10).

each one talked freely and much more freely among each other of course. Mr. Douglas usually sat at the head of the mess table and Mr. Finlayson at the foot—and nothing frivolous was spoken there. Mr. Douglas was not humorous—never joked—always staid and decorous and often had some subject to talk about which often he had picked up in a review or newspaper, but personal experiences were not much talked about, excepting when the Chief Factors and Chief Traders happened to collect in Victoria or strangers asked questions. I suppose all such experiences were or had been an oft-told tale and therefore stale and insipid, but it is a pity some Boswell or other had not reduced them to writing.

As to military organization there was not any and no attempt made at Victoria to teach anyone—at Fort Rupert there was a little difference, the green ones were instructed in the use of the musket, but some of the English labourers having been poachers knew all this beforehand; the others soon learned—and could if required defend the pickets. I know nothing about the Interior, but expect it to have been much the same. At the outposts of course they had to be very wary—and equally so on the coast, but South the Indians had become accustomed to the whites. If anything untoward happened at the Fort—a cannon was fired, thus warning any outside to get in as soon and carefully as possible—but I have no recollection of having heard such a gun fired.

No doubt when the Fort was first erected under Finlayson and before my time affairs were not so humdrum—indeed the pickets showed many signs of having been penetrated by bullets.

It was usual to fire a salute from the bastion, whenever the *Beaver* or any Chief Factor or Trader made his appearance from abroad— these were always treated with great shew—as much to impress the Indians of the importance of these individuals as anything else. Salutes were also fired on the Queen's birthday.

On one occasion a year or so after my arrival—a salute had to be fired from the common carronades in the [bastion?]. Fish and some others went off in high glee to do it—they knew little about cannon, and had not fired many times, when poor Fish's hand went off with the rammer. Poor fellow he died of ensuing mortification, altho I amputated his arm twice.[1]

---

[1] Charles Fish arrived with JSH on the *Norman Morison* in 1850. He "had his arm blown off, which caused his death, on the occasion of a salute being fired from the southwest bastion of the Fort in honor of the arrival of the Tory, in 1851" (Anderson, "Notes and Comments," p. 171). He was buried on 26 July 1851 in

On another occasion Spelde had a like accident befall him from a similar cause—a good portion of his hand was saved, but remained ever after very much crippled—he only had the index finger and thumb left. Tolmie helped me at this,[1] but McKay as a rule was my surgical assistant, but there was but little of surgery—the Indians being their own surgeons—except on one occasion when a tree fell and crushed a leg. We attended him in the Fort, but he died after his thigh had been amputated—I forget what ship of war was here then—the assistant medico assisting—for which the Senior gave me a scolding. Spelde afterwards married and became the grave-digger in the old cemetery.[2] On another occasion an Indian had killed a cow—the slayer became known—and so of course he had to be punished to prevent such outrages in future. He would not come to the Fort and the Chiefs could not or would not give him up to justice. Douglas must have this man brought to book and an expedition of two boats is sent off to seize the culprit, who was in the Indian village opposite—no bridge then[3]— apparently a nice place to land, walk up and seize the fellow. The boats were manned with the newly arrived—and the men were armed with clumsy American army regulation muskets. McKay had charge of one boat—I of another—and I do not think there was a third. I had three men—McKay more. He made of [*sic: for* for] the beach, but when the boat neared the shore, instead of the men jumping into the water and trying to rush ashore, the Indians rushed into the water

---

Victoria's first cemetery at the corner of Douglas and Johnson Streets (ibid.; and Fort Victoria burial register).

[1] William Fraser Tolmie (1812-86) was superintendent of the sheep farm at Nisqually in 1843 and chief factor there in 1855. For further details see S. F. Tolmie, "My Father: William Fraser Tolmie," *BCHQ* 1 (1937): 227-40. W. F. Tolmie's diaries, 1830-43, have been published under the title *William Fraser Tolmie, Physician and Fur Trader* (Vancouver: Mitchell Press, 1963).

[2] John H. Spelde, a native of Holland, died at the age of forty-six on 20 June 1874. The obituary in the *Colonist*, 21 June 1874, adds that "all interments in the old cemetery, numbering some 2,000, took place under Spelde's eye." Since the Ross Bay cemetery had been opened in 1872, "the old cemetery" has reference to the Quadra Street cemetery, now Pioneer Square, which had been laid out in 1855 and to which the bodies in the original graveyard at Douglas and Johnson Streets had been removed. For further details see "The Journal of Arthur Thomas Bushby," p. 142n111.

[3] The first bridge across Victoria Harbour was a wooden structure built in 1854-55 by "the hands attached to the Surveying department" (Douglas to A. Barclay, 26 August and 20 December 1854, Fort Victoria, Correspondence Outward to HBC, 1850-55). This was demolished in 1862, since other bridges at Rock Bay and Point Ellice had been built in 1861 (*Colonist*, 14 May 1862).

to the boat and took the muskets from the men after a little tussle.
I fared a little different—standing in the bow of the boat, a double-
barrelled fowling piece in hand. I told the men to give way, but the
shores were lined with Indians—some blackened—all yelling—having
muskets, axes, knives and what not, but the nastiest things were their
long poles (herring fishing pole) with sharp spears at the end—pointed
towards *our* stomachs—which the men could not stand. I had to turn
on my heel to keep my face to the enemy—and on looking round for
the cause of this rotatory motion—I found two of my men in the bottom
of the boat and the third pulling frantically with one oar. What happened I never knew, but I found my boat, men and myself back at the
Fort, the other boat having preceded me. All I had lost was my hat—a
tattered soft one. Douglas was not pleased and looked grim, but said
nothing to me anyhow. He had given orders to take care and not kill
anyone but only to seize the culprit. This fellow lay behind a log, we
afterwards learned, with a musket—he did not intend to be taken and
doubtless he had many of these wild fellows on his side.

After this I walked along Wharf Street alongside Mr. Douglas—and
the bullets were whistling from across the water. I had become a little
excited and annoyed at this bravado on the part of the Indians. I proposed to go back again and have a fight at all hazards—but Douglas said,
"Never mind—patience and it will come all right"—so we walked
along there with slow deliberate step—as much as to say—we are not
afraid! I do not pretend to be a fighting man, but I can understand now,
how in actual warfare men get excited and prudence and fear thrown
to the winds. Very little was said about the matter—no one had covered
himself with glory, no killed, no wounded—the trophies remained with the
natives!

On the following morning a deputation from the village appeared
before Mr. Douglas and a pow wow had—the end being the Indians
were to pay the value of the cow, and to bring back the trophies. In
the afternoon they brought the payment and the trophies and then
said, "Of what use are these guns? The locks are rusted and they
won't go off"—which was true, and the greenhorns had loaded them
improperly too—powder last, ball first—and some had two balls! They
surrendered my hat into the bargain, but I have lost this curiosity. I
relate this story merely to show up the erroneous idea of the standard
military discipline of the Fort—there was nothing of the kind. It shows
too how quarrels were settled Indian fashion by payment of damages.
This Indian idea of law—and indeed it is their law—of payment applies
even to persons killed, as shown too by their offer to pay for the murdered

men at Newittie [Nahwitti]. This Indian law was often acted on at Fort Rupert and suited very well—none other would—or could—have been put in force. Douglas perhaps might have landed and seized the Indian here or at Nahwitti—but I do not believe even he would have tried. I had had a good deal of experience of rows at Fort Rupert—but then we always managed to be within the pickets as soon as possible. Nahwitti and Victoria were the only two serious matters in which I was brought face to face with warlike Indians and in looking back I rather wonder at my temerity and foolishness. I would not like to do it now at all events—but now I am old, and this makes a very considerable difference. I must say, however, that no Indian has ever done me any injury but on the contrary at Fort Rupert the Chiefs sometimes warned me not to go in a particular direction as danger lurked there—perhaps from foreign or excited Indians. Thieves and liars they were assuredly —but as far as I know they never clandestinely abetted our destruction, indeed the contrary was the case.

I have given my personal life so far—rather mixed up to be sure, but now pass a few years—going on in much the same style—physick—gardening and so forth with additional children. I imagine too the village gradually growing, politics and grumbling flourishing—and looking back one hardly knows what for—save for some little excitement, for the colonists were well-to-do—but mind the California gold discoveries and the people coming from there had excited and more or less unhinged the minds of the whole of us—we wanted Victoria to grow as fast as California and blamed the HBCo because it did not. It is true the land laws were bad—but this really had little to do with the matter, as shown by subsequent experiences in this line. The land was all wooded and those who wanted land as a rule merely wanted it for speculation, and they did not wish the HBCo to have all the speculation, for it now began to be believed that Vancouver Island had a grand destiny in the near future—it has always been in the near future!—What is the near future to a country that will last to eternity! Anyhow the very simple old village life was passing or had passed away—the Langfords, Yates and others, including of course the gold excitement, causing or assisting at the burial. Things were now pretty lively in the small community—but the liveliness was in small things—yet appeared great to some and laughable to others, and so the time was not dull, being enlivened by discussions on the events of the day—and little events were abundant of talk and pastime—sometimes of little quarrels, which did not kill anyone, but which kept on burning metaphorically —the blaze greater or smaller but always more or less present.

The parson Staines was an excitable politician and a very dissatisfied man, and of course belonged to the dissatisfied, altho he did not mix with them at Yates' spirit house. Anyhow the malcontents determined to send home a delegate to lay their grievances at the foot of the throne, and poor Staines consented to be the man—perhaps his vanity and visions of glory assisting his desire—his love of his profession not being great enough to counteract the worldliness.

In [blank in MS: February 1854] he determined to start by [blank in MS] from Victoria, but he, for some reason or other, procrastinated and shortly afterwards sailed in a ship from Sooke. When this ship reached the mouth of the Straits, she was overtaken by a storm lasting for a few days—men were washed overboard—the ship on her beam ends and poor Staines died clinging to the mast! His body washed away.[1]

When intelligence of this came there was a general pity—he was praised or blamed—a martyr or a fool as the case may be, but all nevertheless regretted his end. Of Mrs. Staines I need not speak—anyone can imagine tho not realize feelings and condition.

Of course she had to go home,[2] but whether the malcontents subscribed anything for her I do not know. Victoria lost a most excellent schoolmistress, as shown by her work, but her pupils were by no means in love with her strictness. She had her grievances too and aired them.

I complained once quietly that the young ladies had poured through the crevices of the floor above, dirty water on my bed, so that I had been obliged to make a canopy over it with cedar mats. "Thank the Hudson's Bay Co for it," said she, and bringing me a milk pan full of holes from rust or what not, said, "These are the only utensils in use by the scholars and no wonder their water may leak through the floor. I have asked Mr. Douglas for the usual toilette services for the children, but can't get them from him. You had better speak to him about it."

---

[1]See Slater, "Rev. Robert John Staines," p. 224. According to Annie Deans (letter to her brother and sister, 29 February 1854, Annie Deans Correspondence, PABC), Staines intended to leave the colony by "a ship from the Coal Mines to take him to California." The vessel was delayed, and he finally sailed in the *Duchess of San Lorenzo* on 22 February from Victoria. This ship "foundered at sea off Classet . . . everyone of the unfortunate persons on board perished with her, except one man, who was picked up at sea some days afterwards clinging to a part of the rigging . . . he did not long survive his deliverance" (Douglas to Barclay, 6 April 1854, Fort Victoria, Correspondence Outward to HBC, 1850-55). Neither Douglas nor Annie Deans (in a further letter dated 10 September 1854 reporting the catastrophe) identifies the "one man" with Staines.
[2]She sailed for England aboard the *Princess Royal* on 16 January 1855.

Staines was fond of giving suppers—salads—the lettuces grew outside the Fort pickets. He discovered that someone stole his vegetables, so he kept watch on the gallery and early one morning he was repaid by finding a French Canadian, named Minie stealing the coveted food. He coughed—Minie looked up—"Good morning Minie—You had better take the whole whilst you are about it!" Minie politely raised his hat and said, "Thank you Sir I will" and went on filling his bag! Staines wanted to prosecute—but the question arose—Did not Staines give him liberty to take them? Of course there were no law courts then.

On another occasion Mrs. Staines gave a salad supper—no uncommon occurrence, and on these occasions, some of the lady visitors occasionally slept the night in the house. During the night, people would meet—one going down the passage—the other coming up with a modicum of lighted candle—and the watchman tapped to learn whether anything serious was amiss.

In the morning they appeared a little the worse at breakfast and began comparing notes. It could not have been the salad, for that was voted lovely. At last Mrs. Staines said, "Mrs. Blinkhorn where did you get the oil for the salad?" "Out of the old salad oil bottle the same as usual." "Oh," said Mrs. Staines, "I forgot to tell you I had a fresh bottle, and had filled the one you used with castor oil—it is a mercy we were not all killed!" A few years after this, Mrs. Blinkhorn, who was a good old soul—almost toothless but beloved by all, was thrown out of a carriage at the corner of Fort and Government Street. The concussion drove out the last tooth she had—a great loss. So all the townspeople hunted about for some time to find Mrs. Blinkhorn's lost tooth, but did not find it and so came to the conclusion that it had broken a window in the corner shop and shattered into fragments and so could not be discovered. The gravel thrown up by the horses had broken the window.

When Mrs. B. reached her 80th year, she must needs have a celebration of the event, and numerous were the visitors—and presents. Poor woman, she was attacked with dysentery immediately after and died after a week or two.[1] There was no one more liked or respected in Victoria than this ever-industrious kind-hearted old lady—one of the olden time. Captain Cooper, formerly in the HBCo's service, which he left or which left him,[2] came out in the *Tory* (I think). A fine-looking

---

[1]The party "Honoring an Octogenarian" was held at the residence of her niece, Mrs. Ella, on 11 August 1884; she died on 29 August (*Colonist*, 13 and 30 August 1884).

[2]Cf. p. 139n1 above.

florid stout able man, but of an irascible grumbling disposition. He bought land at Metchosin and at Esquimault—next Stuart's [Stewart's] and built a house there;[1] built also a sloop for trading purposes, but subsequently he located in Victoria about the junction of Douglas and Humboldt, here he established a store and sold spirits, wine, beer and tobacco. For some reason or other he did not prosper and we find him next in England (wife and family I think remaining here) where he appears before a Parliamentary Committee to enquire into the affairs of the HBCo—their lease of British Columbia being about to expire.[2] To this Committee he rehearsed the grievances, but also complained that the Company did not make roads—in fact no good one had been made to his farm twenty miles distant! He had not at this time even paid for the land and so his money would not have assisted to build it anyhow. Road-making through the forest was a very expensive matter. He complained of the want of a judiciary, particularly of Mr. Cameron,[3] who he said (partially true) was not a lawyer and knew nothing about law, because he always had to consult books before giving a verdict! He was asked whether this was peculiar to the judge at Victoria—and whether judges did not do exactly the same thing in England. He testified against the Company and gave them no credit at all.

Mr. Cameron was at this time "all the Law Courts" and altho not a lawyer dealt out justice and did very well for the early stage of the community—but of course became unsuitable as time and expansion went hand in hand. He was the husband of Governor Douglas' sister and Miss Cameron was the offspring of a former husband.[4] Cooper, when he returned, brought with him a "silver service" for me, which I still retain with pleasant memories. A number of people, whose names are preserved in the address in my library, subscribed for this and commissioned him to purchase it. The most of the subscribers belong to

---

[1]The Esquimalt District Official Map, 1858, shows that Cooper owned Section III, adjoining Section XXVII, which was owned by JSH and leased to James Stewart c. 1862 (see above, p. 85n2).

[2]British Columbia as such did not exist until the proclamation of the gold colony in August 1858, but in 1857 a select committee of the House of Commons was appointed to investigate the whole of the HBC's operations in North America. The company had exclusive trading rights in the territory west of the Rocky Mountains until 30 May 1859 (Ormsby, *British Columbia*, p. 98).

[3]David Cameron (1804-72) was appointed judge of the Court of Common Pleas in September 1853 and judge of the Supreme Court of Civil Justice on 2 December that year. For further details see the article by William R. Sampson in *DCB* 10.

[4]See note on Miss Cameron, p. 120 above.

Craigflower and Colwood farms, with whom I was rather a favorite, on account chiefly of professional service rendered. I certainly felt proud of the recognition altho generally speaking I had an inveterate dislike to receiving presents.[1]

Cooper remained here some time after this and had children born to him. Mrs. Cooper was a very handsome Englishwoman and her children became handsome also. Cooper was a Member of Council instituted by Governor Blanshard before leaving. Cooper subsequently drifted for some reason or other to the United States—he ought to have been prosperous here (V.I.), but for some reason or other was not.

Revd. Mr. Cridge succeeded Staines.[2] The first time I saw Mr. & Mrs. Cridge was in the HBCo's store. They were young people and Mrs. Cridge a nice amiable pretty-looking and slim young lady, but had had no children then.

Probably the Church on the Hill, called Christ Church, had been built about the time of his arrival, as also the Parsonage, which stood at the junction of Humboldt and McClure Street—the site in fact of the earlier pigstyes, noted for being well shingled and well built, in fact when I arrived here, the pigs were said to be far better housed than the human family—better fed and happier whilst living. This, however, is not true—but the pigs were well off. This early church caught fire and was burned to the ground and the fire was a fine sight.[3] I was at West-

---

[1]The Helmcken Collection contains two lists of subscribers for this testimonial: one, headed by James Cooper, includes the names of prominent people in the town; the other, headed by Kenneth McKenzie, the names of people on the Craigflower Farm. Some $200 was collected for this "tea and coffee service," and McKenzie commissioned Captain Wishart to buy it in London. The captain's wife chose the set, but unfortunately the money collected was not enough to cover the coffee pot, so Wishart sent out in the box a "Book of Patterns" with the price of the 'Heraldic' marked, so that "the inhabitants or Helmcken himself" could complete the set. It was inscribed "in the latest fashion": the full inscription on the principal piece, initials only on the others (Wishart to McKenzie, 19 August 1856, Wishart Correspondence, McKenzie Collection, PABC). The inscription, according to the subscription lists (HC), was to read: "Presented to J. S. Helmcken Esqre Surgeon by the Colonists of Vancouver Island as a Testimonial of their Esteem and Regard, which he has won by his unvaried attention and kindness to all classes, requiring the aid of his profession. A.D. 1857." The silver plate was presented to JSH aboard the *Princess Royal* now under the command of Captain J. F. Trivett on 17 February 1857 ("The Diary of Robert Melrose," p. 292).

[2]Edward Cridge (1817-1913) replaced the Rev. R. J. Staines as chaplain to the HBC, arriving at Fort Victoria on 1 April 1855. For further details see "Bushby Appendix."

[3]On 1 October 1869 (*Colonist*, 2 October 1869). The cornerstone of a new cathedral was laid on 20 May 1872, and the building was consecrated before the

minster—and when returning the Captain of the boat, Swainson [Swanson] I think,[1] and the whole of us said, "There is something strange about Victoria," but none of us knew of the strangeness until on landing, we heard of the destruction of Christ Church. No telegraph in those days—but came soon after.[2]

The present wooden Cathedral was erected in its place, designed by Sir Joseph Trutch and built by subscription. Leigh of the HBCo and then Clerk of the Corporation of the City managed to erect the tower.

The first Christ Church had been built by the HBCo. Indeed to the best of my recollection the HB prospectus designed that lands should be set aside for the Church of England—and assuredly once there was a "church reserve"—I think in Victoria district. With the change of government policy it was sold.[3]

Just before Governor Blanshard left, a petition had been presented to him signed by even some of the HBCo officers, containing a résumé of the grievances they laboured under and of others of a more or less visionary character that would or might occur, were the Colony left solely at the mercy of the HBCo.[4]

This document comprises more than all of the real or fanciful

---

end of the year (ibid., 21 May and 6 December 1872). This wooden building was replaced by the present stone cathedral erected in 1929 on an adjacent site. The old landmark was finally razed in 1933 (ibid., 10 December 1933), and the site is now occupied by the Law Courts.

[1]John Swanson (1827-72), master mariner, came to this coast in 1842 and was in command of a number of HBC vessels, including the *Enterprise*, 1868-70. For further details see Walbran, *British Columbia Coast Names*.

[2]Actually Victoria had been linked to the mainland by telegraph, via the San Juan Islands, on 24 April 1866. See the headline in the *Colonist*, 25 April 1866: "The line open. Communication with the East."

[3]The reference here is not entirely clear. The HBC prospectus did set aside land for religious purposes (see above, p. 117n2), and a "clergy reserve" and a "church reserve" were both made. The whole of the clergy reserve, some 2,100 acres (see Plate 12) "in Victoria District, outside the boundaries of the City of Victoria [was] sold by the Land Office, sanctioned by the Secretary of State, . . . on October 8th 1855" (see Vancouver Island, House of Assembly, *Report of the Committee on Crown Lands* [Victoria, 1864], pp. 8-9). The church reserve (on which the Victoria District Church was opened in 1856) is so designated on the Victoria District Official Map of 1858 (Section LXXXVIII, 23 acres). Early in 1859 the HBC, ignoring the official map, sold privately some portions of the church reserve (J. D. Pemberton to W. A. G. Young, colonial secretary, 1 May 1861, in *Papers in Connection with Crown Lands . . . and the Title of the Hudson's Bay Company*, pp. 26-27) ; the remainder of this reserve was in 1862 "conveyed by the HBC to Trustees for Church purposes" (Edward Cardwell to A. E. Kennedy, 14 August 1865, cited in Wrinch, "Land Policy," appendix C).

[4]This petition is printed in Scholefield and Howay, *British Columbia*, 1: 524-26.

grievances and in my opinion, if not actually penned by Blanshard, was instigated by him—the grievances had been commonly talked about —new ones occasionally arose which could be traced to the Governor's coterie and their conversations.

Governor Blanshard, in accord with the instructions contained in his Commission, appointed a "Council"—a Legislative? Council—Mr. Douglas—Captain Cooper—(old) John Tod.[1] The constitution of this Council was right in itself, but its powers were unknown or not definite anyhow—perhaps it was more for consultation than legislation—and I am not aware that it did anything during the remaining days of Governor Blanshard.

When Mr. Douglas became Governor Mr. Finlayson and Mr. Work were added to the number and subsequently Donald Fraser and in course of time others.

Mr. Douglas soon found that money was wanted for ordinary improvements and payment of ordinary officers, and with this end in view designed a "license" on houses selling spirits and so forth. This would affect the HBCo—Cooper—Yates and one or two other houses. The cost of the license $500.00 (five hundred dollars) per annum.

The Council were summoned and the plan submitted [29 March 1853], but the opposition was great and the Governor had to combat the idea that the HBCo had to pay and provide the ways and means for everything. He held that the colonists had to pay for what they wanted in the shape of local improvements. This doctrine was rather a surprise, as the general belief was that the Company should pay all costs of whatever kind, to be repaid them at some future time by HM Govt—the colonists to have no charge placed on them at all!! Again the license would affect Cooper and the HBCo—and this of course was special. The Council consumed a couple of hours in the morning discussing the matter; no reporters, no newspapers existed—closed doors. They adjourned to dinner and dined at the mess table. In the afternoon the business was resumed. Tod gave in, but Cooper remained obdurate, so as things became tedious or unpleasant, the Governor ordered Madeira, pipes and tobacco to be brought in. Now these things are very consoling and insidious in effect so Captain Cooper, who liked a glass of good wine (and in those days the wine was of the very best) took more than one, and then altho the room was smoky, he began to see more

---

[1]On 27 August 1851. For information concerning the various members of the council and its proceedings, see Vancouver Island, Legislative Council, *Minutes.*

clearly the subject was not without some reason and so his determination weakened a little—a glass or two more—"Pass the decanter, gentlemen"—the wine is good and generous (the Governor took but little himself, and was always very abstemious, but could smoke a great deal gently and deliberately) so Cooper took some more, and from being disagreeable became amiable and at length subsided, saying he would not consent—consented. There was a little more wine and friendship after this and then the first Council adjourned—having passed the first law— the "Licence Law."

As soon as this was known, there was no little excitement among the politicians at Yates', and Cooper came in for a good [many ?] rancorous remarks—the excitement spread outside and Captain [blank in MS] ran about the village shouting "No taxation without representation— beware of the first take—the rights of the colonists have been trampled in the dust—down with the HBCo—down with tyranny or there will soon be more taxes—down with the Governor"—and down he (the Captain) went sprawling.[1] Of course this was a source of amusement to some, the contrary to others; but for all this the various parties took out the license and paid the money—I think the whole amounted to four hundred pounds or so.[2]

Now this looks all plain straightforward sailing, but in those days everything done by the Governor or Council had to be sent home for the approval of HM Govt—every account &c. The home authorities were very particular and paid great attention to these things and likewise to the complaints of colonists. No doubt this license law was sent in due course and the intimation of the necessity of its enactment—perhaps also some account of the opposition encountered. I am not aware that the law was either disallowed or assented to, but in [blank in MS: 1856] the Governor received instructions to call a Legislative Assembly,[3] because HM Govt doubted whether a colony founded by Englishmen (not a Crown Colony) could be governed save by laws enacted

[1]There is another version of this incident in JSH's article, "In the Early Fifties." Here the incident precedes, instead of follows, the actual passing of the tax; and instead of saying that "Captain [blank in MS] ran about the village" JSH writes "... one man excited ran about shouting 'Beware of the first tax....' "
[2]The fees were £100 for a wholesale licence and £120 for a retail licence (Vancouver Island, Legislative Council, *Minutes*, 29 March 1853).
[3]See H. Labouchere to Governor Douglas, 28 February 1856, Vancouver Island, House of Assembly, *Minutes ... August 12th, 1856 to September 25th, 1858*, ed. E. O. S. Scholefield, Archives Memoir no. 3 (Victoria: King's Printer, 1918), pp. 5-7.

by themselves, that is through their representatives. I suppose as much as to say the colonists had inherent rights which they carried with them to their new place of abode; for they were still British. It is most probable that these instructions were given in order that revenue might be raised by the people voluntarily taxing themselves and not by emanations from the irresponsible Legislative Council. Of the calling together of this Assembly, I have told in the Xmas number of the *Colonist* and so need not repeat it.[1]

The Legislative Council continued to exist; some new members added, but their names are not remembered.

I have no doubt the Legislative Assembly had almost the ordinary power of the House of Commons, still there was no charter or anything else defining its powers—indeed there is none for the House of Commons, only "precedents"—we had no precedents.

Altho probably the House had the power, still this could be controlled more or less by the Council and indeed on account of the HBCo holding the Island for colonization purposes, the power was very much cramped indeed, unless the House could have got rid of the rights of the Hudson's Bay Co by purchase—or at all events pay all the colonial officers, which however was never thought of. The House therefore had the power but not the means of borrowing, for they had no security in the shape of land or anything else to offer. They might have made demands on the HBCo and indeed were almost recommended to do so, but the House did not deem it advisable to recommend or sanction this procedure as it would have made the Colony liable by consent, and would have had to pay some day with possible interest when HM Govt repossessed the Island.

The Assembly took umbrage at the Council altering a tax bill—I think an improved license law, and so told them that they had no right to do so, that tax bills rested entirely with the House. The Council denied this exclusive power and maintained they were part of the Legislature and shared all power with the House. This led to some declarations on both sides, but they fell to the ground, the House not being learned enough to maintain their position: indeed as I said before

---

[1]The *Colonist*, 1 January 1891, "The First Legislature," reprinted in Appendix 2 below. The first House of Assembly in British territory west of the Great Lakes met in the mess room of Fort Victoria on 12 August 1856. For its proceedings during the next two years, see the *Minutes*. JSH was elected for Esquimalt and Victoria District on 2 July 1856, according to "The Diary of Robert Melrose," and he was re-elected in 1860 and 1863. See also Plate 19.

neither had any defined authority and so I suppose had to make rights by force or argument as the Commons had done.

The Council was the more learned body as it contained at this time Donald Fraser assisted by Cameron and outsiders, and so it was that with their assistance and amendments a Franchise Registration Bill was ultimately framed and passed[1] and so the first House of Assembly came to an end—its last work being its most if not the only important work accomplished. During their time the questions of land and so forth were discussed with as much gusto and difference of opinion as now. So the first House made the second and left the stock-in-trade, machinery and so forth for plays to be acted after on the same boards. The Legislative Assembly lasted from 1855 [*sic: for* 1856] to 1859 when it naturally expired—in fact it dissolved itself by the Franchise Bill. At first this Assembly gave but little trouble to me—I often lighted fire and got things ready, and on one occasion Amor De Cosmos made his appearance[2]—my first acquaintance with him—he was loud about the invaluable geographical position of V.I. Towards the end the House gave me very much work, in fact I did nearly all the work and correspondence, drawing up bills, addresses, remonstrances and so forth—the Members had to criticize! I could do them better now—but was green then. However before the House came to an end we had been practically broken in to ordinary parliamentary practice. In addition to this work I attended to my practice, garden &c. A couple more children had been born[3] and it was a very busy time indeed with me night and day—but being young it did me little harm—probably brightened me by education. At this time I seemed to smoke cigars perpetually—and as I could ride now, company was cigars only.

One day I rode to Langford's. At this time there was a fence across

---

[1] An Act to amend the law relating to the Representation of Vancouver Island and its dependencies was passed by the House of Assembly and the Legislative Council on 3 November 1859.

[2] Amor De Cosmos (1825-97), born William Alexander Smith in Nova Scotia, had a successful career as a photographer in California (where he changed his name by due process of law) before coming to Victoria in 1858 and founding the *British Colonist*. He was not elected to the Legislative Assembly of Vancouver Island until 1863. For further details see Walter N. Sage, "Amor De Cosmos, Journalist and Politician," *BCHQ* 8 (1944): 189-212; and H. Robert McKendrick, "Amor De Cosmos and Confederation," in *British Columbia & Confederation*, ed. W. George Shelton (Victoria: University of Victoria, 1967), pp. 67-96.

[3] Catherine Amelia, born 19 March 1855, and Margaret Jane, baptized 9 March 1858. The inscription on the Helmcken family tomb records that the latter died on 11 March 1858 aged eighteen months (see below, p. 212).

the "portage," enclosing thus the peninsula. On a board over the gate McCauley [Macaulay]¹ had put up this inscription: "All drivellers who drivel this way, man woman or child—please shut the gate" (!)

On another my horse had eaten some goose grass, and in returning from the Langfords my horse suddenly went down and spilt me—my cigars and et ceteras flying about the trail.

After a few minutes the horse got up, and I started again when a similar result ensued. After a while whilst walking beside the horse I met Macaulay—"Oh," said he, "[he ?] has the grips!" "Well Macaulay, take him to your stable" and he did. I met him a day or two after. "What about my horse, Macaulay?" "Oh—he is all right, I got an old shoe—roasted it and covered his mouth and nose with it—this cured him. Ah, a fine remedy is an old shoe roasted!" Admiral [blank in MS: Fairfax Moresby]² gave a picnic to Victorians in Sailor Bay —Macaulay gave the water and helped generally—the Admiral gave him a glass of wine and thanked him for his assistance; so Macaulay made a speech, beginning—"Sir, you are the *finest* Admiral I ever did see—You are the *first* Admiral I ever did see"—and here he broke down and swallowed his dose. Picnics were not uncommon then. Macaulay was a Highlander or a crofter, a most trustworthy man; spoke peculiar English: long and spare: he had charge at this time of the sheep farm at Macaulay's Point. It joined Skinner's farm. He was a witness in court one day and was very "cautious"—more deaf than usual—and it was amusing to see him put his hand to his ears— he couldn't hear a bit! Poor fellow he was put in charge of a powder barge in Esquimault. At night she sprang a leak, went down and Macaulay with her. Macaulay's daughter, a handsome girl, married William McNeill,³ son of Captain McNeill—so determined to have a proper and grand wedding. This consisted in having a fiddle or two, a fife or two and some other primitive musical instrument. The minstrels went first—the married couple followed—and behind these the "best men and women" with some few invited friends—they perambulated the city which then consisted (McNeill said) of thirty-

¹Donald Macaulay was in charge of the PSAC farm called Viewfield, including the point which still bears his name, 1850-60. He was drowned in Esquimalt Harbour in 1868 (*Colonist*, 21 September 1868). For further details see Walbran, *British Columbia Coast Names*.

²Presumably Rear-Admiral Fairfax Moresby, who was commander-in-chief, Pacific Station, 1850-53.

³William McNeill married Mary Macaulay on 3 June 1853 (Fort Victoria marriage register).

six houses outside the pickets. Whenever a wedding took place we all went to it and joined in the celebration. I was dancing once with Mrs. Parker on Johnson Street—presently my partner went down—a plank or two had given way and there she was like a flower in a garden pot—but unhurt! Scotch reels and suchlike dances were the order of the day then and were danced with a vim and activity worthy of the legs of young people.

Now then comes a conglomeration and sort of confusion which must be comprehended in order to understand the growth of Victoria and subsequent history.

About 1857 Governor Douglas at the mess table shewed us a few grains of scale gold—not more than a drachm—which had been sent him from the North Thompson. This was the first gold I saw and probably the first that arrived here. The Governor attached great importance to it and thought it meant a great change and busy time. He spoke of Victoria rising to be a great city—and of its value, but curiously enough this conversation did not make much impression, as some of [them ?] thought it was a sort of advertisement to sell "town lots."

A few weeks after this Mr. Douglas showed us a soda-water bottle half full of scaly gold, which had been collected I think by the Indians in the North Thompson. The Legislature existed at this period, but took no heed of these discoveries. One Sunday morning we were astonished to find a steamer entering the harbour from San Francisco —[blank in MS: the *Commodore*].[1] There was a regular colony of coloured men on board, who had come to settle in Vancouver Island, because at this time adverse feeling ran high against them in the States. They landed and some kneeling down prayed and asked for blessings [on those ?] who lived in a land of freedom under the red white and blue.

Somehow or other the gold discoveries were magnified by steamboat companies in San Francisco and we were startled by shiploads of miners coming to seek their fortunes in the gold fields. When told that we knew little or nothing about such fields, they would not believe, thinking we wanted to keep the whole for the Hudson's Bay Co! Of course there was not any accommodation for them, but they built tents of grey cotton: hundreds of these tents dotted the land from

[1]The *Commodore* arrived on the morning of Sunday, 25 April 1858 (Ormsby, *British Columbia*, p. 139).

Government Street almost as far as Spring Ridge—but they were peaceable law-abiding people. Here then was a city of wayfarers: sprung up like mushrooms. The HBCo and local shops did a rushing business. New stores were hurried up by American and other traders—wharves were built—Wells Fargo Express established and the [blank in MS: *Victoria Gazette?*] established, but De Cosmos' paper the *British Colonist* had preceded it.[1] Thus altho everyone had previously supposed that Esquimault would be the business centre—and so did many merchants who came now—still here the city was, no doubt occasioned by the fact that the miners landed here from steamboats that came into Victoria harbour and came here no doubt because the HBCo and a town and supplies already existed here. There was nothing more wanted and the site seemed invaluable and uncommonly well suited by grade and openness for a city—so much better in this respect than San Francisco and her sandhills. The town of course thus grew and grew and as the steamers to other places started from here—small they were—they fixed the place too.

Everyone wanted to get to Frazer's River—but the water being high there at this time of the year, no gold could be had and curiously enough all thought the gold to be in the Fraser, and that as soon as the annual freshet was over, they would collect no end of gold from its bed. Soon steamers came from San Francisco, to trade between Victoria and the Fraser. On Wharf Street and hereabout, the miners were building boats, sawing wood and so forth—the whole was an ant-hill. The boats were built exactly of the shape of coffins and in these frail craft very many started for the Fraser. Some got there—some were lost and doubtless some caught by the Indians, the inmates murdered. No one can have any just or correct idea of the number who perished—they were never heard of more and of course in the main were unknown to other miners—these in turn scattering through the country only had their attention, time and industry occupied by the excitement and madness of looking for gold.

Some influential merchants from San Francisco, bought land at Esquimault and endeavoured to establish a town there, but failed most completely—nevertheless they said, "Bye and bye you'll see"—"The com-

[1]JSH appears to be confused here. The *Colonist*, first published on 11 December 1858, had been preceded, not followed, by the *Victoria Gazette*, first published on 25 June 1858 by James W. Towne & Company of California and edited by Henry C. Williston and Columbus Bartlett. The *Gazette* ceased publication on 26 November 1859 (see below, p. 163), leaving the field to De Cosmos and his *Colonist*.

mercial town must be there"—"If you can only get the steamers from San Francisco and those going to the Fraser to make Esquimault their rendezvous, the thing would be done"—but they could not get the steamers to do so, altho some on account of their large size had to land their people at Esquimault. This led to the establishment of the wharf there.[1]

Others said, "The City will not be at Esquimault"—for, said they, "Whoever heard of a naval station and a commercial city existing in conjunction?"

Of course the naval station was not then what it is now, but the buildings had been erected there for to provide for any casualties that might occur in consequence of the Russian War. The unfortunate Petropoloski [Petropavlosk] expedition filled these buildings with wounded and sick in former days.[2] Among the sailors there was but one feeling, that the whole attack had been a mistake—they had to land on the face of a wooded hill—when sharpshooters picked them off—and they said, "The officers urged us on, but did not advance themselves." Inside the harbour was a man-of-war or two moored and other batteries erected. A German named Smith, who afterwards had a farm and made coal discoveries at Saanich North,[3] lived I think at Petropavlosk and gave the Admiral (Price I think) every information about the place, fortifications &c., said they ought to have landed at a place he told him, where a road led to the rear of the fortifications. Be this as it may, there can be no doubt whatever that the British received a tremendous defeat there, but whether on account of mismanagement

---

[1]See *Colonist*, 21 August 1873: "The old wharf at Esquimalt, built by Mr. Selleck [i.e., William Selleck of the firm of Williams and Selleck, Steam Boat Hotel] in 1858 . . . yielded to the ravages of the marine worm . . . yesterday morning, and crashed into the harbor."

[2]England and Russia had gone to war on 27 March 1854, and early in 1855 Rear-Admiral H. W. Bruce, commander-in-chief, Pacific Station, 1854-57, asked Governor Douglas to construct a naval hospital near Victoria for possible casualties of the Kamchatka expedition. Douglas erected three buildings at Esquimalt. Actually no casualties from the Crimean War were accommodated there, but these buildings were the nucleus of the naval base at Esquimalt, which became the headquarters of the North Pacific Squadron in 1865. See Madge Wolfenden, "Esquimalt Dockyard's First Buildings," *BCHQ* 10 (1942): 235-39; and for an assessment of the disastrous Petropavlosk expedition see Barry M. Gough, *The Royal Navy and the Northwest Coast of North America 1810-1914* (Vancouver: University of British Columbia Press, 1971), pp. 114-22.

[3]It may be noted that the 1861 assessment roll for North Saanich lists one John Smith as the owner of Sections 16, 17, and 18, 2E, 257 acres.

I think is open to grave question. The Admiral subsequently shot himself.[1]

In the above sketch I have related how Victoria became located to be the chief commercial city instead of Esquimault—the thing was not intentional but accidental—HBCo had virtually but little to do with the matter save the establishments here.

[Volume IV]

Singularly enough before the actual excitement a ship appeared in the harbour, she anchored off Lang's ship-yard, the real entrance to the Harbour. The Captain was a very nice fellow, but I do not know what he declared to be his business. However, he ingratiated himself with us all and was very sociable and American. One night I went home, when lo and behold the Captain was there with a nice fire—he had taken the eggs and found the grog and was brewing punch for us when we came home! We thought this rather cool but he was a nice fellow. He remained some time, and gave little dinners on board—dined at the mess and so forth, sang a song at night and became quite at home. At length one day—he said, "I can stand this no longer—where is the gold about here?—I have come purposely on this account." We were all not a little astonished and told him plainly we knew nothing about gold mines or mountains of gold, but he did not believe, and considered we and the Hudson's Bay Co were keeping it a secret! He had boxes on board to pack the gold in. At length disgusted he determined to go North and load a cargo of ice for San Francisco.

When I was in New York in /70[2] he left his card for me at the Brevoort House, but I had left for Ottawa—he wanted to make things pleasant for me, but I did not know this until after I returned to Victoria, where the card had been forwarded.

At this time too there was a fine-looking man in Victoria who was also agreeable. He gave us to understand that he was an actor and was studying for the profession. He gave us one or two exhibitions of his histrionic powers—a King somebody, and did the acting very well. What became of him is beyond my ken, but I do not wish him to be considered a spy—altho he might have been, or anything else.

It is quite possible that a part of this excitement arose from the dis-

---

[1]Admiral David Price, who had succeeded Fairfax Moresby as commander-in-chief, Pacific Station, in 1853, shot himself on 30 August 1854 (Gough, *The Royal Navy*, p. 117).

[2]See above, p. 96. During a lull in the Confederation negotiations JSH made a trip from Montreal to New York and then returned to Ottawa.

covery of gold in Queen Charlotte's Islands.[1] Doubtless gold was there, but parties who went out failed to get it. Several ships went there with expeditions, but the vein had been exhausted or it dipped under the sea which was here deep. As soon as the prospectors made a blast the Indians rushed for the rock, but threw it away in disgust. A quantity of the rock was brought to Victoria containing gold and it was valued by Finlayson and bought by specific gravity. A good deal was pitched into the harbour as worthless, but a good while after was recovered and found to contain gold also. I saw the gold from Q C Island—large junks, which seemed as tho composed of small pieces hammered and molded together. There were not very many ounces in all, but really I cannot say how much there was—I might exaggerate.

I need hardly say that this rise of Victoria and the gold excitement upset us all. We scarcely knew what to make of it or how to use it to advantage. To see people mad about town lots was a new experience, and many sold their lots for small profit, but this did not last long, there being not many for sale and we ourselves soon took up with the mania and valued our lots at the raging price—not so much then as now however.

The HBCo sold the town lots at one hundred dollars per lot—the newcomers laughed at this—HBCo were too old-fashioned and could make more money by selling in a different manner, but this did not alter the regulation.[2] There was an immense demand for lots, but the survey of the town had not been completed, so the would-be purchasers had to wait until more lots had been marked off, but to make amends every applicant's name was taken down, so that each might take his lot when on the market in rotation. I think the number to each was restricted. When the time came there was a string of people from the Fort gates to the Land Office (i.e. mess room house) anxious and trying to be

---

[1]Gold was discovered in the Queen Charlotte Islands in 1850. For further details see Great Britain, Parliament, House of Commons, ... *Correspondence Relative to the Discovery of Gold at Queen Charlotte's Island,* 1853 (P.P. 788 and 788-I).
[2]Cf. Douglas to Lytton, 13 October 1858: "The Hudson's Bay Company have always sold suburban lots, consisting of 5 acres of land, at the rate of £25 each lot; and Town Lots measuring 120 x 60 feet, at first sold for £10-8-4 have now risen to £20-16-8 a lot ... any number of Town lots may now be bought at the original price of £20-16-8. There was a time last summer when private sales of small parcels of land in good situations were made at the rate of £100 an acre, but that unhealthy inflation was temporary, and met with no countenance from Government ..." (Vancouver Island, Governor Douglas, Despatches to London, Dec. 15, 1855—June 6, 1859, PABC).

first in, altho this would not have made any difference.[1] Then there was lots of grumbling and disappointments because everyone could not get what he considered the best lots and argued that preference had been shown beforehand,[2] but the rush was soon over and the lots changed hands at big figures and so on and so on—a speculative mania, based on the gold fields.

Esquimault had been cut up into five-acre lots[3] and many speculated in these lots and a few more houses went up, but this town made no progress at all—and is very much the same today as it was left then.

In addition to all this, food and goods from San Francisco were rushed in, at this time there being virtually Free Trade in Vancouver Island—the supplies were enormous. Flour once fell short and the merchants wanted to corner the whole, but the HBCo would not join and at the command of Chief Factor i.e. Governor Douglas the HBCo went on selling at the usual rates, but only in comparatively small quantities to individuals, for which they received much praise from the consumers.

Affairs were not a little mixed. Douglas was Governor and Vice-Admiral in Vancouver Island—the HBCo had an exclusive lease of the Mainland for trading purposes. In spite of this the miners of course would go there—they saw nothing but gold. They could not be prevented—no one thought of preventing them, so Governor Douglas took the bull by the horns and acted as quasi-Governor of the Mainland too, and made certain regulations, amongst which was that all goods

---

[1] In June 1858 the Land Office, by order of the governor, issued a "Public Notice" regarding town lots in Victoria: "Pending completion of the plans, purchasers may on and after the 21st instant pay for any number of Lots not exceeding Six (60ft x 120ft) at this Office, taking a simple receipt for the payments naming an Agent at Victoria who will be empowered to select from the unsold Lots when the plans are complete, in the order in which they have paid." There is a copy of this public notice in PRO Transcripts, HBC-CO, 1856-58, vol. 727, pp. 208-9 (transcript, p. 243). Wrinch, "Land Policy," pp. 172-73, calls this a "Land Proclamation" and points out its significance as the earliest form of pre-emption.

[2] Captain Langford, for instance, complained to the Duke of Newcastle on 10 March 1860 that in the summer of 1858 he had made "personal (that being the usual) application at the Land Office to purchase a certain tract of land [near Colwood Farm] and was informed by the Colonial Surveyor Mr. Pemberton that the land was already disposed of to Mr. Dallas": this statement, Langford declared, was untrue. See Great Britain, Parliament, House of Commons, ... *Correspondence between Mr. Langford and the Colonial Department, relative to alleged Abuses in the Government of Vancouver Island*, 1863 (P.P. 507).

[3] In 1857. See Douglas to W. G. Smith, secretary of the HBC, 7 October 1857, acknowledging the receipt of the HBC's approval of "the purchase of the lot of land, in Esquimalt District, for re-sale in 5-acre lots" (Fort Victoria, Correspondence Outward to HBC on affairs of V.I. Colony, Dec. 11 1855—March 3, 1859, July 8, 1859, PABC).

and ships going to the Fraser should enter and clear at Victoria—in addition to this, tonnage dues were imposed and a duty imposed on some things.[1] One of HM Ships [the *Satellite*] was stationed at the mouth of Fraser River to enforce these regulations as also to preserve peace and be protective, for there was a dread lest these newcomers should be troublesome or even annex the country as far as they could, to the United States. There were a large number of Americans among the new arrivals, but also many Englishmen, some of whom had become American citizens, some from choice others from necessity—the number of Cornish men was large.

New towns were projected and rising in the U.S. viz. Whatcom[2] and others, and no little vim was used in pushing these forwards, to become the commercial city to supply B. Columbia. A large number of houses went up and there was great activity in the American sense; they determined to build a road to Fort Hope,[3] to send in supplies this way, and in a short time, the road was reported open and a mule train running—but it soon turned out that the mule train only went a few miles and then returned every night somewhat altered—the road of course had not been made—but the boom went on a little longer. To counteract this—to keep the trade in British territory, the regulations about ships and goods had been made—much to the chagrin of the Americans. The regulations worked and Victoria held the supremacy.

Intelligence of all this reached England. Officials were sent to the Colony—Cary, Attorney General—Judge Begbie—O'Reilly—Brew—Ball —and several others and later appeared Colonel Moody and the Engineers.[4]

---

[1]On 8 May 1858 Douglas as governor of Vancouver Island issued a proclamation which "threatened the confiscation of any goods imported without a licence from the Hudson's Bay Company and a sufferance from the customs officer at Victoria. . . . in August, a tariff of 10 per cent *ad valorem* . . . was substituted for the original licence obtained" from the HBC (Ormsby, *British Columbia*, p. 152).
[2]The modern Bellingham.
[3]Built in 1848 at the junction of the Fraser and Coquihalla Rivers, some ninety miles from New Westminster.
[4]Of the men listed here only Cary, Begbie, Brew, and Moody were officially appointed by the secretary of state for the colonies. The others all received appointments from Governor Douglas but came out to the gold colony in the first instance purely "on spec." George Hunter Cary (1832?-66) served as attorney-general 1858-64. Matthew Baillie Begbie (1819-94) was appointed judge of the Crown Colony of British Columbia in September 1858. For a full account of his career see the four articles by Sydney G. Pettit in *BCHQ* 11 (1947): 1-14, 113-48, 187-210, 273-94. Chartres Brew (1815-70) was sent out as inspector of police, to establish a force for the maintenance of law and order among the miners. For further de-

Governor Douglas had a townsite laid out at Langley—the lots were sold at auction[1] and realized 400 or 500 [dollars] per lot and some improvements were made, but after the arrival of Colonel Moody, he considered the site bad for military and other reasons and in course of time New Westminster was chosen, laid out by Colonel Moody and Engineers. This occasioned confusion, but was settled by allowing those who had bought at Langley to use the scrip in purchasing at New Westminster. These bickerings delaying the town on the river favored Victoria. There was a sort of quarrel about the name, Queensboro was proposed—doubts whether it should not be Queenboro or Queenburgh—this was sent home and Downing Street settled the matter by giving the name New Westminster. Langley's name was to have been Derby.[2]

I had some lots on Government Street where Hibbens' book store now stands. I sold one to Captain Stamp for one thousand dollars and thought I had done well—I sold its neighbour to a German named Smith [John Schmidt] for a like sum, and [Samuel] Nesbitt the baker one on Broad Street.[3]

At this time all payments were made in gold—American coin—and I remember carrying the gold home in a handkerchief! and when I got it there hardly knew how to keep it safely! Gold pieces were plenti-

---

tails see Margaret A. Ormsby, "Some Irish Figures in Colonial Days," *BCHQ* 14 (1950): 61-82. Richard Clement Moody (1813-87) was placed in command of the detachment of Royal Engineers sent out in 1858 and was also appointed chief commissioner of lands and works in British Columbia. For further details see Madge Wolfenden, "Pathfinders and Road Builders: Richard Clement Moody, R. E.," *Journal of the Department of Public Works* (April 1938): 3-4. Peter O'Reilly (1825-1905) was appointed by Douglas as magistrate at Hope on 19 April 1859 (*Victoria Gazette*, 26 April 1859). For further details see Ormsby, "Some Irish Figures." Henry Maynard Ball (1825-97) was appointed magistrate at Lytton on 8 June 1859 (see Colonial Secretary to Ball, 8 June 1859, British Columbia, Colonial Secretary, Correspondence Outward, PABC). For further details see the obituaries in the *Colonist,* 9 October 1897 and the Ashcroft *B.C. Mining Journal,* 16 October 1897.

[1] In Victoria, on 25 November 1858 (*Victoria Gazette*, 27 November 1858). For further details see Robert E. Cail, *Land, Man, and the Law: The Disposal of Crown Lands in British Columbia, 1871-1913* (Vancouver: University of British Columbia Press, 1974), p. 7.

[2] For further details concerning the site of the capital of British Columbia, including a discussion of the "sort of quarrel about the name," see Dorothy Blakey Smith, "The First Capital of British Columbia: Langley or New Westminster," *BCHQ* 21 (1957-58): 15-50.

[3] These transactions are confirmed by the assessment roll for Victoria Town, 30 September 1861.

ful in town and there was no further trouble about currency or paying people in money instead of truck.

I need not say we all lost our head—we were too green to make much money—somehow we could not comprehend and did not believe the change in Victoria to be permanent—others thought differently and speculated largely, buying at high figures. Legislation become irksome and it was hard to get people together—they had better work to do. I had plenty patients among the tents, but charged them nothing. American doctors came up with the miners, some very queer fellows, but I had no communication with them. Dr. [blank in MS: George Johnston] had established himself at the corner of Government and Yates Street doing well[1]—and soon Langley's store appeared.[2] Among the miners were many gentlemen and to these were soon added many from England. Soon there came a reaction. The miners when the river fell did not find their notions realized—the lower the Fraser fell the less gold there appeared to be instead of more—the gold was washed from bars and it was chiefly fine and so there was a very great exodus, many of the miners going as fast as they had come or as quickly as they could find means to get away. Many however tried to trace the source of the gold and so penetrated to the interior of the country—a wild almost trackless wilderness, but it is not for me to give the history of this—my writing being only personal recollections.

The failure of the mines and exodus of so many miners, produced great depression in Victoria, and Whatcom collapsed. Many merchants left for San Francisco again, and the stores of goods were sent back to San Francisco. San Francisco before this had been trembling for her supremacy—real estate had fallen to a very low figure, there had been a sort of panic there, but now they brightened up and soon the old prosperity arrived.

The value of real estate fell in Victoria—I was offered part of my property back for less than I sold it for, but declined to buy and the

[1]Presumably George Johnston, who came in the *Tory* in 1851 as "surgeon and clerk." In JSH's MS notes on the medical profession in British Columbia (HC), he says that Johnston succeeded him as the HBC surgeon at Fort Rupert and that when the mines closed there Dr. Johnston settled in Victoria, where he held considerable property in the vicinity of Government and Yates streets (a statement confirmed by the assessment rolls of 1861 and 1864). JSH adds that Dr. Johnston returned to his native England and died there; it may be noted that his residence in the 1861 assessment roll is given as "Birmingham."
[2]The firm of Langley & Co., druggists, was established in 1858 by Alfred John Langley (1820-96) in partnership with his brother James.

same happened to others—everyone was depressed and gloomy, the reaction had come with a vengeance. Many of those who had speculated
could not pay their assessments or due bills and were virtually ruined—
everything looked blue and remained so. The American paper in time
closed its doors and the owners returned to San Francisco, where
they did well.[1]

Victoria however had grown, had become a town, with a large number of active live people in it—people who had been all over the world
and experienced its uprisings and downfallings, so there were many
hopeful still and like Mark Tapley could smile amidst misfortunes.[2]
There was still a good deal of business doing, and as Free Trade existed
here a great smuggling business with the States ensued and many made
a great deal of money—a sort of compensating balance. Free Trade
had this good effect then, but people were asking, "How is it that no
one settles? How is it there is no agricultural production—is there no
back country to support Victoria?" The truth is the Island was too
large and had it been more rocky and barren, Free Trade would not
have been disputed, but it had a good deal of land, and people began
to think this ought to be cultivated and they soon found that the competition with the plains of the States would not allow of cultivation
here at a profit; the cost [of] labour and time expended in clearing
wooded land being excessive.

At this time the streets of Victoria were in a virgin state and during
the winter, Wharf Street was almost impassable: the drays sinking up to
the hubs and often had to be dug out, in fact there was a great want of
passable roads everywhere, but there was no money to put them in order,
the useless Legislature would not levy taxes or grant any money, there
was no charter for a city, so Governor Douglas had to do the best he
could and certainly did a great deal, but with a great deal of grumbling
too—the idea still prevailed that the HBCo ought to do everything. Mr.
Dallas was now here.[3]

---

[1]The *Victoria Gazette* ceased publication on 26 November 1859. See above, p.
155n1.

[2]A character in Dickens's *Martin Chuzzlewit*, noted for his indomitable good humour.

[3]Alexander Grant Dallas (1816-82) was elected a director of the HBC in 1856
and the following year was sent to Victoria to assist Chief Factor Douglas in the
business administration of the company and more particularly to straighten out
the affairs of the PSAC. When in 1858 Douglas was made governor of British
Columbia and severed his connection with the HBC, Dallas was appointed the
representative of the HBC for the Western Department. For further details see
"Bushby Appendix."

An excitement now arose—the San Juan difficulty occurred, the Americans claimed the island and so did Governor Douglas for the British. There was fear lest the Americans should make a filibustering expedition and appropriate San Juan if not Vancouver Island too, in fact the rowdy element there threatened to do so, but the Americans in Victoria frowned on this.

Of the history of this San Juan difficulty anyone may see who chooses to consult the books, but on the American side many misrepresentations were made. Dallas went in the *Beaver* and certainly not in a man-o'-war.[1] At this time some American frontier men had settled in San Juan. I subsequently knew very well Paul K. Hubbs,[2] he was one of the men so common in frontier life—a rowdy—ignorant hoodlum—who thought an American ought to be boastful and a bully—and he acted as such. He married Flora Ross—treated her badly—so she left or was divorced from him—and became the efficient superintendent of the woman's part of the Lunatic Asylum as well in Victoria as subsequently in New Westminster.[3] The last I heard of P. K. Hubbs occurred a couple of years ago, when he wrote me requesting a certificate that he had disease of the heart as he was applying for "a pension from the U.S. Govern-

---

[1]The San Juan affair has been fully documented (from sources going far beyond "the books" available to JSH in 1892) in Hunter Miller, *San Juan Archipelago: Study of the Joint Occupation of San Juan Island* (Bellow Falls, Vt.: Windham Press, 1943), and James O. McCabe, *The San Juan Water Boundary Question*, Canadian Studies in History and Government, no. 5 (Toronto: University of Toronto Press, 1964). See McCabe, p. 50, for the statement of General William Selby Harney that Dallas had come to San Juan in a British warship for the purpose of seizing an American citizen and transporting him by force to Vancouver Island to be tried by British law—a statement which, Miller points out (pp. 63-64), Harney repeated on at least five other occasions. It was manifestly false, for Dallas had actually gone in the HBC vessel *Beaver*, as JSH says. See also p. 166n1.

[2]Paul Kinsey Hubbs was the U.S. deputy collector of customs on San Juan Island from c. 1856 (*Victoria Gazette*, 4 August 1859). He died on 17 November 1874, aged seventy-five (*Colonist*, 25 November 1874).

[3]She married Hubbs on 6 December 1859 (Christ Church marriage register). Flora Ross (1842-97) was the youngest daughter of Chief Factor Charles Ross, who had been placed in charge of Fort Victoria on its completion in 1843. She had resumed her maiden name by 1870, when she became matron at the Victoria jail, where mental patients were cared for until 1872. In that year the Royal Hospital (built in 1859 on the Indian reserve across the harbour) was converted into a lunatic asylum, and Mrs. Ross continued as matron when in 1878 the patients were moved to New Westminster. She died on 2 November 1897 after twenty-seven years of faithful service (see the tribute in "Report of the Medical Superintendent of the Provincial Asylum for the Insane . . . 1897," B.C., *Sessional Papers*, 7th Parl., 4th sess., 1898, p. 836).

ment." Of course I refused to do this excepting he came to Victoria to be examined. This he never did.

Of course there was tremendous excitement in Victoria, where the population now had completely changed, being now composed of Americans—of adopted ones in whole or in part—Jews in large numbers, but it must be said in fairness, that they did not complicate matters, but were on the side of law and order—of course with some exceptions. To add to the ill feeling [blank in MS: John Nugent] came from San Francisco in what capacity I do not remember, and on his return published a very scurrilous letter against Governor Douglas. The Americans here took this up—declared the letter a veritable libel and were (many) incensed against this American libeller and braggart.[1]

Things were precious lively in Victoria—any items of news anxiously looked for or awaited, but altho San Juan happened to be only twenty miles away comparatively little could be heard of a reliable nature, anyhow a collision was fully expected. The Americans sent all the warships in the neighbourhood—and had their military, but the number of English ships and men here at the time, would have made short work of the whole—indeed it seems as tho the overpowering strength of HM Ships and men, was the reason of putting this off at all events.

I know there would have been a collision and the island would have been captured had Governor Douglas had his own way—but altho he was Vice-Admiral—the commanders of HM Ships were dubious and wanted plain orders. Fortunately or unfortunately the British Admiral just then arrived[2]—so he superseded the authority of Governor Douglas

[1]See Robie L. Reid, "John Nugent: The Impertinent Envoy," *BCHQ* 8 (1944): 53-76. When Governor Isaac Stevens of Washington State protested against the "impositions" (such as mining licences) placed by Governor Douglas on American citizens going to the Fraser River mines, the U.S. government sent a special agent to investigate. They chose John Nugent, "an Irishman with an inveterate and rabid hatred of England" (Thomas Rowlandson of Victoria to Lytton, 6 September 1858, quoted ibid., p. 61). After completing his tour of the mining region Nugent published (as a paid advertisement in the *Victoria Gazette*, 16 November 1858) a "Farewell Address to the Citizens of the United States in Vancouver Island and British Columbia." The *Gazette*, whose proprietors were Americans, (see above, p. 155n1) took strong editorial exception to this address. De Cosmos, a persistent critic of Douglas, agreed that Nugent "had told some truths" about the administration but thought the attack unjustified; the San Francisco *Evening Bulletin* said that Nugent had "gratuitously offered insults to the local government" and called the sentiments expressed "ungenerous, undignified, illiberal and malicious" (Reid, "Nugent," p. 67).

[2]Rear-Admiral Robert Lambert Baynes had succeeded Admiral Bruce as commander-in-chief, Pacific Station, on 8 July 1857 (Gough, *The Royal Navy*, p. 249).

and would not embroil the nations in war on any account—there should be no bloodshed about this matter as far as he was concerned —he would await instructions. Governor Douglas was no little chagrined at this, and subsequently told me if he had had his own way the affair would have been quickly settled, the island occupied by the British and the diplomacy would have settled the matter—he thought possession of great importance. Anyhow things could not remain in this condition, both nations would hear and had heard ere this—(no telegraph existed but I think the overland express did)—and soon General [Winfield] Scott appeared on the part of the U.S. in these waters, but did not come to Victoria. He like our Admiral was averse to war—so the end was that the island was to be occupied by military camps of both nations until the rightful possession of the island should be decided.

Not six months ago, I read a lecture by Major Haller at Seattle reviewing very fairly the whole circumstances and he concluded that General Harney wanted a row, in order that the U.S. might be occupied and engaged in war with England, and so give the Southern States an advantage and enable them to gain their independence![1] This may or may not be so, anyhow a few years after, the Civil War in America occurred.

There is no doubt there was a great deal of American bluster and questionable manners as well as bullying on the part of Harney and the Americans in this matter. One hardly understands how it has come about that the Americans, brave and bold as they are, should always resort to bullying. The U.S. will be a very aggressive nation some day.

Anyhow this affair led to a Commission being appointed to survey the

---

[1]Granville O. Haller, captain and brevet major, commanded I Company, Fourth Infantry, and Port Townsend, in 1859 during the San Juan crisis provoked by General Harney, who on 27 July landed a detachment of sixty men on San Juan Island on the pretext of protecting the American settlers from the HBC and the British authorities. He had no orders to do so. PABC has a copy of a pamphlet containing an address which Haller delivered in Tacoma on 16 January 1896, under the title *San Juan and Secession.* Here he discusses "Possible Relation to the War of the Rebellion—Did General Harney Try to Make Trouble with the English to Aid the Conspiracy? . . ." On p. 16 of this pamphlet he says that twenty years ago he had published a similar article in the Port Townsend *Argus;* and the Bancroft Library has a typewritten MS by him entitled "The San Juan Imbroglio," dated 1889 (Keith Murray, *The Pig War,* Pacific Northwest Historical Pamphlet no. 6 [Tacoma: Washington State Historical Society, 1968], bibliography). Thus it seems quite possible that Major Haller could have delivered a lecture in similar vein "not six months" before JSH wrote his reminiscences in 1892.

boundary of B. Columbia, which included of course the islands.[1] Admiral Prevost was at the head of this Commission, but rightly or wrongly he was here considered a veritable old woman, unfit to cope with the American side.[2] Sufficient leaked out to show that Governor Douglas—i.e. the civil officers on V.I. and Prevost did not pull together.

One would have thought it a very easy matter to have settled where the centre of the Gulf of Georgia was at the 49 parallel—but the question arose where was the centre at the time the treaty was made. Did or did they not (i.e. the Treaty makers) know that the islands at this point overlapping Vancouver Island, were formerly considered the coast of V.I.? Did they know that any islands existed at all even the Canal de Haro and the Haro group of islands? There was no mention of them in the Treaty anyhow, and it seemed as tho, when the makers said a line should be run from the centre of the Gulf of Georgia to the Strait of Juan de Fuca, they imagined it to be all clear water!

It is useless going into this matter, suffice it to say, that the whole affair was referred to the Emperor of Germany, who decided the present boundary[3]—he had only to choose between the Canal de Haro and the Rosario Strait! There were and are other channels through this cluster of islands. No one doubts but what the Germans came to a right conclusion from the evidence laid before them, but here again it is said the Americans sent in their documents in better shape, more elegantly and more modernly put up than the English. Anyhow the affair was settled for the time adverse to England and I cannot help thinking to the great detriment and disadvantage of Canada, should any war at any time ensue. On the other hand no one knows what shape war and battles may assume in the future.

Leaving out the occasion of the collision and so forth, I may just as well here state, that the American officials sent to define the boun-

---

[1]JSH is in error here. The North West Boundary Commission, whose function was to determine (under the Oregon Boundary Treaty of 1846) "that part of the line which runs through 'the channel which separates the continent from Vancouver's Island,'" was appointed in 1856, before the San Juan affair of 1859, not as a result of it. See Marcus Baker, *Survey of the Northwestern Boundary of the United States, 1857-1861*, U.S. Geological Survey, Bulletin no. 174 (Washington, D.C.: Government Printing Office, 1900), p. 73.

[2]Captain (later Admiral) James Charles Prevost (1810-91) was on the Pacific Station 1852-60 and in 1856 was in command of H.M.S. *Satellite*. For further details see "Bushby Appendix."

[3]On 21 October 1872.

dary, as also those occupying San Juan, were considered very nice sociable gentlemanly fellows, and as far as San Juan is concerned they were as brothers.

It seems singular, that what Benton described as "the derelict of all nations"[1]—namely Vancouver Island, should have become so important a place now—the corner-stone—the key-stone, of the Dominion of Canada! What may take place in the next half or whole century?

I may as well here state a few words about "land laws." At the foundation of the Colony the money obtained from the disposal of land was apparently by the projectors deemed sufficient to pay the expense of colonization. They seem to have had the English ideas of the value of the soil—when in truth the soil, markets &c. bore no resemblance. The land in England was valuable because money had been spent on it—to clear, drain, improve and make it fit for cultivation and production. Here the case was exactly the opposite—land covered with a dense forest, very difficult to clear—had it been open prairie it could have been sold and settled, but naturally people shirked woods and Indians.

Five dollars per acre was the government price of land—and even then it was on condition that a certain number of settlers should be imported to cultivate it! I paid five dollars per acre for all the land I bought at Esquimault, rocks as well. The Puget Sound Co did the same —the HBCo held land for about ten miles around Victoria as their right without payment—a sort of possessory claim of the Fur Trade branch.

It was soon found that very little money came in from the sale of land. Those who bought did not do so from speculative purposes, but because they wanted land to live on in their old age or to leave farms for their children. No one supposed land to be or likely to become of great value and five dollars was thought exorbitant, particularly when in Washington Territory people could get 640 for nothing or for one dollar per acre in Oregon or even California under the United States land law. This cheapness of land there was supposed to be the reason

---

[1]See Senator Thomas Hart Benton (1782-1858), *Speech of Mr. Benton, of Missouri, on the Oregon Question* ... (Washington: Printed at the office of Blair and Rives, 1856): "Forty years ago it was written by Humboldt, that the banks of the Columbia presented the only situation on the northwest coast of America fit for the residence of a civilized people. Experience has confirmed the truth of this wise remark. All the rest of the coast, from the Straits of Fuca out to New Archangel ... remains a vacant waste, abandoned since the quarrel of Nootka Sound, and become the derelict of nations. The Columbia only invites a possessor; and for that possession, sagacious British diplomacy has been long weaving its web."

why people did not buy and settle here—truly there were not many anywhere to settle at first—added to which a great part of Oregon was in
plane country—where it was only necessary to tickle the unencumber-
ed land, to make the ears of corn laugh. Of course there was a great
deal of truth in this.

Anyhow money did not come in to pay expenses, and often the Government was hard up for cash—the Land Office was the seller and Pemberton used almost [to?] beg of some of us to buy, but refusal was
general—no one would give five dollars for rocks that were incapable
of producing anything.

All this was referred home and the Land Office afterwards was given
permission to sell the land and throw the rocks without payment into
the bargain and subsequently swamps went in the same way.[1] In this
way the rocks and swamps were thrown in and I bought section C under
this arrangement.[2] It was a derelict piece of land, which no one would
look at—and indeed which I knew very little about—but the money
was wanted—and the HBCo I presume wanted to show a decent report
to HM Govt. This derelict piece of land I have still—and an awful
piece it is. A hundred dollars per acre will not make the land plough-
able.

The Esquimault land I bought for my children—for them to have
something to live on when they came or grew up.[3]

No one nowadays seems to understand the conditions of the early
days—land was worthless and could not be sold and indeed remained
so until the gold discoveries and even then there was but little demand—
the country seemed so forbidding. Had anyone foreseen the rise of Victoria and the future value of proximate lands, he might have bought
the whole country had he the money. The worst of it was—none of us
had any money! So we could not indulge much in this even at the
time of excitement—save perhaps Pemberton and Pearse who chose
Victoria for their investment and Yates the Arm. Finlayson and Work

---

[1]According to the evidence of B. W. Pearse before the Select Committee on Crown
Lands, 2 December 1863, rocks and swamps "were never charged for up to the
year 1855, by instructions from the Company." These instructions were, he says,
"under great pressure of business revoked in 1858" (*Minutes*, p. 20).

[2]In Esquimalt District, running into the head of Portage Inlet. The report of the
land sales to 31 March 1860 (Land Sales Annual Reports 1853-60) indicates that
JSH bought Section C in July 1858 and that the acreage was 147.75 gross, 52 net.

[3]By 1861 JSH was the owner of Sections VIII, XXVII, XCI, XCII, XCIII, and
C in Esquimalt District, comprising 616 35/100 acres in all (Vancouver Island,
Government Gazette, 14 October 1861).

had had their land long before, and indeed had cleared and cultivated some and built a residence too—at all events the latter must have been about the same time. Where Finlayson's house now stands was then a thick forest. Douglas' was not so bad, being partially open with oaks growing. My piece had some fine old pine stumps—and heaven knows what it cost to remove them, I do not. Dynamite was unknown then, so the roots had all to be cut out and the stumps rolled somewhere and burned, but heavens what a job to burn them! The stumps of Douglas pine[1] never seemed to rot—I have seen them pretty solid after twenty years!

The local officers had to be paid from the proceeds of land—at least they were supposed to be, but the HBCo used their own people as much as possible for this purpose by way of assistance and they received nothing for it. When the excitement arose other officers of course had to be appointed—I was Coroner for instance.[2] At this time HM Govt sent out people to fill places, such as Brew—Hamley—Franks[3]—all good men, in addition they gave recommendations to others coming here. In addition there were lots of young men attracted by the gold, of these many were gentlemen—old army or navy officers and the usual crowd attracted to diggings. Many of them went there and failed, others were more or less successful, some worked on the roads and so forth. Pooley cleared garden patches for Bushby at West-

---

[1]One of the former names for the tree now called the Douglas fir (Pseudotsuga Menziesii). See the prospectus of the Vancouver's Island Steam Sawing Mill Company (PABC): "The Timbers which the Company proposes chiefly to work upon, and which are abundant in the neighbourhood, are I. (*Pinus Douglasii*) The Douglas Pine. . . ." *Pinus Douglasii* is one of the eighteen names applied to the Douglas fir which are listed by Vladimir J. Krajina, "A Summary of the Nomenclature of Douglas-Fir, Pseudotsuga Menziesii," *Madrono* 13 (October 1956): 266-67.

[2]JSH was acting as coroner as early as 21 October 1857, when he signed the notice offering £50 reward for the apprehension of Richard Jones, charged with killing an Indian (Vancouver Island, Governor Douglas, Correspondence Outward, 1850-1859, PABC, p. 225). He resigned the office the following year (*Victoria Gazette*, 7 July 1858).

[3]Wymond Thomas Ogilvy Hamley (1818-1907) was appointed by the Queen on 21 September 1858 as collector of customs for British Columbia (British Columbia *Blue Book,* 1860) and arrived aboard the *Thames City* with the main body of the Royal Engineers in 1859 (*Victoria Gazette*, 16 April 1859). For further details see the obituary in the *Colonist*, 16 January 1907. Charles William Franks did not arrive in Victoria until 1864 (ibid., 23 August 1864). He served on the Legislative Council of British Columbia as treasurer 1864-66 and returned to England soon after the union of the colonies (ibid., 2 February 1867).

minster and many of the now prosperous citizens began in a very small way, such as Rithet—Turner and others.[1]

Cameron did all the duties of Judge—and altho perhaps it was not all technical law, still people said he gave justice. He had a pretty good notion of his own capabilities; rather obstinate but not given to loss of temper: perfectly upright and honest. He came here I think from Demerara, but of his history previously I know little or nothing. Of course he would not suit when legal professionals arrived—but he was nevertheless appointed to Chief Justice, more I suppose to give him jurisdiction than anything else. Cary would have none of him. Ring and Pearkes were here at this time.[2] Ring was rather eccentric—a good artist and would drive about with an equerry behind with the traditional yellow leather waistband! To him is attributed the saying in the House, that he had listened to the diarrhea of words of a certain honorable gentleman.

Pearkes on the other hand was a little active fellow, troubled with a skin disease. I think he held the office of Attorney or Solicitor General subsequently. Mrs. Cameron and her daughter were here also and for some time occupied or lived with Governor Douglas, her brother. She bore a great resemblance to him—a tall stout—dignified—rather muscular (with a little fat) lady, with the West Indian manners—very polite

[1]Arthur Thomas Bushby (1835-75) had been appointed registrar-general of deeds for British Columbia in August 1861 and had a house in New Westminster. For further details see the article by Dorothy Blakey Smith in *DCB* 10. Charles Edward Pooley (1845-1912) came to B.C. in 1862. After an unsuccessful attempt at mining in the Cariboo, he came down to New Westminster and "cut cordwood at $1.50 a cord: laid out gardens and dug drains" (see his election speech in the *Colonist*, 16 July 1882). He was later registrar of the Supreme Court (British Columbia, *Government Gazette*, 1 March 1870) and sat in the Legislative Assembly as member for Esquimalt from 1882 to 1906. For further details see the biography in Scholefield and Howay, *British Columbia*, 4:90-93. Robert Paterson Rithet (1844-1919), importer and commission merchant, was the founder of the firm of Welch, Rithet & Co., and later president of R. P. Rithet & Co. Ltd. For further details see the biography, ibid., pp. 1134-36. John Henry Turner (1833-1923), an Englishman, came to Victoria in 1862 after a business career in the Maritimes. He was premier of the province of British Columbia 1895-98 and agent-general in London 1901-16. For further details see the obituary in the *Colonist*, 11 December 1923.

[2]David Babington Ring (1804-75), a native of Ireland, was called to the bar in England in 1841 and came to Victoria in 1858. For further details see the obituary in the London *Law Times*, 13 March 1875. George Pearkes (1826-71) came to British Columbia in 1858 and in August of that year was appointed crown solicitor and attorney for Vancouver Island (*Victoria Gazette*, 28 August 1858). For further details see "Bushby Appendix."

and nice, but she differed from her brother in that she liked a joke and laughed rather pleasantly. Cameron was her second husband—the first named Cowan had gone to the States; she followed him but could not find any traces altho she travelled much through different states in difficulty and distress—no tidings came to her of him. She always spoke in the most heartfelt manner of the American people, who had been very kind and hospitable, assisting her in every possible way—she liked them. Miss Cameron—properly Miss Cowan—married W. A. G. Young—who had a position with Captain Prevost and had part in the negotiations about the San Juan affair: at last becoming Colonial Secretary.[1]

Mrs. Cameron died at Esquimault, where a house had been built, called Belmont, I think after some estate in Demerara.[2] Being at Esquimault, the naval doctor attended her, so I know or knew very little of the disease—like all the Douglases she died pretty suddenly. Cameron too died there[3]—found dead in fact—he lived a sort of anchorite and virtually alone. Edith, his daughter by Mrs. Cameron, married Doughty who had fallen in love with her when here in one of HM Ships[4]—such matches were not uncommon then as seen in two of Langford's daughters and one of Skinner's[5]—sometimes however the sailors after leaving here forgot their engagements.

[1]William Alexander George Young, R.N. (1827-85), was appointed "secretary to the Commission for determining the Northwest Boundary" in 1856 (Douglas to Edward Cardwell, 28 May 1869, Vancouver Island, Governor Douglas, Correspondence Outward, 1867-70, private letter book, PABC) and arrived in H.M.S. *Satellite* on 13 June 1857. He married Cecilia, the step-daughter of Judge Cameron, on 20 March 1858 (Christ Church marriage register). Early in 1859 he was appointed colonial secretary for British Columbia and acting colonial secretary for Vancouver Island, and he remained as colonial secretary after the union of the colonies, 1866-69. For further details see "Bushby Appendix."

[2]On 26 November 1859, at Belmont, the Cameron estate in Esquimalt District (*Colonist*, 29 November 1859).

[3]On 14 May 1872 (*Colonist*, 15 May 1872).

[4]Henry Montagu Doughty (1841-1916), a midshipman in the Royal Navy who served in H.M.S. *Satellite* (on this station 1857-60), married Edith Rebecca Cameron on 21 August 1860 (Christ Church marriage register) and took her back to England. For further information see *Burke's Landed Gentry*.

[5]Captain Langford's eldest daughter, Louisa Ellen, married Commander John James Stephen Josling (who had been lieutenant in H.M.S. *Thetis* on this station 1851-53) in London in 1857 (Walbran, *British Columbia Coast Names*). The third Langford daughter, Emma, married John Augustus Bull, master of H.M.S. *Plumper*, on 7 February 1860 (Christ Church marriage register). The Skinner family left Constance Cove Farm for Cowichan in 1864 (*Colonist*, 31 May 1864), and in September 1865 Annie Louise was married there to John Bremner, assistant paymaster at the Naval Dockyard, Esquimalt (Walbran, *British Columbia Coast Names*).

It is about time to come to the second "parliament," which lasted from 1860 to 1863. Whatever may be said of the irregularity of calling together the first parliament (which I hold to have been a true parliament) nothing in this respect can be said against the second, for it was called into existence and election by the Act of the Legislature, assented to by HM Government.[1]

The second Legislature differed very much from the first for in it were Cary—Waddington—Franklin—Crease—Tolmie—Southgate—myself and Cooper for Esquimault. Cooper had to resign and then came in Burnaby, John Coles, Foster—also with some others.[2] Undoubtedly the members were above the average and all men of experience and travel and certainly for the most part honourable. Many others would have been candidates, but a clause existed in the Act debarring those who had taken the oath of allegiance to any foreign country—this being aimed at those who had been whitewashed in the U.S. of which there were many here—in fact it is even now doubtful how far Franklin, Southgate and Waddington had gone in this respect.[3] Many had to take the oath in San Francisco for business purposes and not with any idea of renouncing England. California at this time was in a very disturbed condition, tho it had been vastly improved by the Vigilance Committee, who had executed a few of the "roughs and toughs." Anyhow there was

[1]See above, p. 152n1.

[2]The members of the second Legislative Assembly, 1860-63, were as follows: for Victoria Town, G. H. Cary and Selim Franklin; for Victoria District, H. P. P. Crease (who resigned in October 1861 and was succeeded by J. W. Trutch), Dr. W. F. Tolmie, and Alfred Waddington (who resigned in October 1861 and was succeeded by Dr. James Trimble); for Esquimalt Town, G. T. Gordon (who resigned in January 1862 and was succeeded by T. Harris, who resigned in September 1862 and was succeeded by William Cocker); for Esquimalt District, J. S. Helmcken and James Cooper (who resigned in October 1860 and was succeeded by Robert Burnaby); for Lake District, George Foster Foster; for Sooke District, W. J. Macdonald; for Saanich, John Coles; and for Saltspring Island, J. J. Southgate.

[3]Under the Franchise Act of 1859 a voter was disqualified if he had "taken the oath of allegiance to, or become the citizen or subject of a foreign state or nation, unless three months previously to the time at which he may claim to be registered in the lists of voters, he shall have taken the oath of allegiance to Her Majesty. . . ." For Selim Franklin see "Bushby Appendix," and for the difficulties he encountered in taking his seat in the Legislative Assembly see David Rome, "First Canadian Jew in a Legislative Assembly," in *The First Two Years: A Record of the Jewish Pioneers on Canada's Pacific Coast 1858-1860* (Montreal: A. M. Caiserman, 1942), pp. 56-63. For Joseph James Southgate see Walbran, *British Columbia Coast Names*; and for Alfred Waddington, see the article by W. Kaye Lamb in *DCB* 10.

a dread at this time in V.I. lest the whitewashed should legislate for the Colony—vague ideas existed that they might annex it in principle to the U. States, altho now we know there was no very great danger—some anyhow, as we may see bye and bye.

I was chosen Speaker of this Assembly—had a Clerk—and Serjeant-at-Arms—and a new building, the present Legislative Hall, but it was not so sumptuously fitted up as now.[1]

The election whereby these Members were chosen was a very exciting and excitable one.[2] Governor Douglas had been appointed to a second term, the best that could have been done under the circumstances, but he had to resign his position with the HBCo which later led to complications—he could not longer make use of the Company for colonial purpose as he had hitherto done, feeling that the welfare of both were identical and hanging one on the other. Mr. Dallas on the other hand considered Douglas to be using the Company unfairly, and at this time Dallas was the HBCo Commissioner in Victoria, and as such had to do the best he could for the Company. Dallas was a very shrewd active business man, but by no means a liberal one—make profit whilst the opportunity offers.

At the election of course the government by the Hudson's Bay Co was denounced and must be got rid of—Governor Douglas came in for a good share of abuse and criticism, but he had many friends now that he was attacked. The *Colonist* under De Cosmos had been from its very commencement hostile, vituperative and abusive of and to the Governor, the Government and everything in general. He seemed altogether too violent—but it pleased the dissatisfied and made them more so; but many Americans cried shame—in our country it would not be long allowed! As for the candidates, they had a wide field—everything had to be done—established—commenced—new land regulations—education and what not—new franchise act. Some talked of joining partnership with the Mainland and protection to industries. Others were for Free Trade now and forever—Union would destroy Free Trade and thus

---

[1]The legislature sat in this building, erected in 1859, until 1898, when the stone Parliament Buildings still in use today were opened. In order to permit construction to begin in 1893, the old hall had to be moved to the rear of the grounds, and after it had been abandoned by the legislature in 1898 it was fitted up for the use of the Department of Mines, which occupied it until 1957, when fire destroyed this last survivor of "The Birdcages" of 1859. See Plate 20.

[2]It took place in January 1860, the exact date varying with the district.

ruin Victoria and so the Island. The addresses at this time give the history of the day, for some were voluminous.[1]

I had to work for my election too—it did not matter whether morning noon or night. I courted Mr. Rowland's vote and assistance—he could influence half a dozen ignorant people. I waited half the night to get it—sang as many songs as I could and smoked like a volcano but kept sober—I never drank much! At last he promised me and kept his word—I had done much for him previously before—Justice of the Peace McKenzie worked in a whole-souled manner for "the cause," with his men, some of whom were kicking over the traces. Skinner and Langford were a bit doubtful—the fact is Captain Cooper altho not running against me was a candidate and so was Burnaby.[2] Cooper, Skinner, Langford went hand in hand in abuse of the HBCo—but not against me—yet Cooper had to be put in. The day arrived—the voting open—so one could see which way the wind blew. In the afternoon many held back; whisky became not a rare thing—people from town harassed them and so did our side. De Cosmos came down too and was told by Burnaby he was only fit to be a boot-black, which riled him very considerably. Some voted the wrong way, both sides said so: so the grog perhaps influenced them or something else, anyhow I and Cooper were elected, and there was not a fight. After the election Mrs. McKenzie gave us a jolly good dinner—i.e. self and Burnaby and friends. The men regaled themselves in the kitchen and after a while came in to congratulate us—Burnaby sang some comic songs—in fact there was a feast of reason and a flow of soul till midnight. The McKenzies were whole-souled people and felt the victory as much or more than the candidates, for not much love existed between them and the Langfords, Skinners and Coopers, but they were not enemies. Cooper resigned afterwards and Burnaby was elected. Why Cooper resigned I do not recollect.[3] It was a hard-fought battle and we learned the new dodge of hosts [?] from Victoria interfering with district elections—with voice, carriages and spirit.

---

[1] For examples of these appeals to the voter, see the files of the *Colonist*, 15 December 1859 to 7 January 1860.

[2] Robert Burnaby (1828-78) came to Victoria in 1858 and founded the firm of Henderson and Burnaby, commission merchants. For further details see the article by Madge Wolfenden in *DCB* 10. Burnaby did not himself run in the January 1860 election but in a by-election necessitated by the resignation of James Cooper in October 1860.

[3] In 1858 Cooper had been appointed by Lytton as harbour master at Esquimalt, "chiefly for the purposes of British Columbia," and had continued to reside on

Now about Victoria City election—a very exciting one, for Cary and De Cosmos came forward as also Franklin and probably someone else.[1] At this time and afterwards the political meetings at the old Victoria Theatre were numerous—boisterous, a bye word. Of course at this time the residents were new and numerous—a kind of government they had not been accustomed to.

Cary was a very clever lawyer, as sharp as a needle—had plenty of tongue quite as sharp too and no end of go and work in him: an excitable fellow and almost a cripple from rheumatism, which he said he had become accustomed to. He had a very good idea of his talent and importance but occasionally was not a little rash. He was an inveterate opponent of Cameron, passionate and he said felt degraded at having to appear before Cameron, whom he called an ignorant pig-headed old fool who knew nothing about law and rules and orders, of which bye and bye I do not think there were any special, but those used in England were supposed to rule—when applicable. Cary seemed to get into a row occasionally with everybody and on one occasion I had him in the old jail for a cause I do not remember—some small row I suppose. Here he was terribly despondent for the few hours there—cried and stormed to fill up the vacancies. He considered himself degraded and would not be comforted by his friends or anyone else. Then he had a row with D. B. Ring[2]—Ring considered himself a big man too and certainly was a nice sort of fellow and an artist.

Vancouver Island. On 17 March 1860 he was ordered to reside at New Westminster, the capital of British Columbia, and so was obliged to resign as member for Esquimalt District in the Legislative Assembly of Vancouver Island (see Margaret A. Ormsby in *DCB* 10).

[1] The only candidates were Cary, Franklin, and De Cosmos (see the results of the poll, *Colonist*, 10 January 1860).

[2] Cary was arrested for "furious riding" on the James Bay Bridge in 1859, but the case was dismissed (*Victoria Gazette*, 17 September 1859). In 1860 he was fined ten dollars for riding his horse on the footpath on Fort Street and had to sell his gun to pay the fine (*Colonist*, 28 January and 21 February 1860). But the only time he seems to have gone to jail was in the course of the "row with D. B. Ring." He accepted a challenge to a duel with Ring, was charged "with an intention to commit a breach of the peace," and was sentenced to twelve months' imprisonment or a bond for five hundred dollars to keep peace for a year. When he refused to post the bond, he was "politely shown into one of the 'comfortable cells' of the Victoria jail," but he was released later in the day on a writ of habeas corpus (*Victoria Gazette*, 22 October 1859). By this time the jail had been removed from the fort bastion to the police barracks completed in 1859 (ibid., 21 April 1859), the site of which is now occupied by the court house erected in 1889 in Bastion Square.

Cary made money—so he took it into his head to build a small castle—
of which he had a picture, but let him who buildeth a tower first
count the cost thereof. The cost was very great—labour very high, so
he satisfied himself in the end with a wing—the present stone portion of
Government House. This building was purchased by Mrs. Miles, and she
lived in grandeur here, but subsequently sold to the Government and
occupied at first by Governor Kennedy—wooden additions being made.[1]
I may as well state here, that Cary was afterwards attacked with iritis,
which incapacitated him for a time, but he would use his eyes when
possible—his rheumatism also troubled him much. Poor fellow in the end
he became insane, and had to be sent home, where the doctors said,
he had paralysis of the brain. He never recovered, and he was a pitiable
creature.

Mrs. Cary was a small eccentric woman—very pretty—but witty,
sarcastic and her tongue a little venomous. She had feet more or less
crippled too—was adored by Cary who considered her the sharpest and
cleverest woman perhaps ever made. Anyhow she was awfully nice to
her friends. Cary and I were very good friends—so of course I had my
full share of work at this election. We rode over the country and we
went to Saanitch [Saanich] to vote for and look after Gordon[2]—
Cary rode like a fury—in a devil of a hurry. He was fond of horse-racing
and whenever a race took place at the race course—then around Beacon Hill—Cary would be there, clad in greatcoat &c. &c. after the
English fashion and he would bet too, but he never had any horses of
his own. He liked excitement—he was all excitement himself at dinners
and so forth. Cary was undoubtedly a very brilliant lawyer—ready to face
anybody—indefatigable—but had to be paid pretty liberally—of course
not overburdened with the ordinary ideas of right or wrong—he was all
lawyer and pleader. Genius and madness in him were closely allied.

Back to the elections. The candidates appeared on the stage at the
Victoria Theatre—here Cary was in his glory—lashed De Cosmos to fury

---

[1]Elizabeth (Meeson) Miles, widow of John Miles (d. 1861), bought Cary Castle
in 1864, re-named it "Stoneleigh House," and sold it to the government in 1865
(*Colonist*, 13 July 1866). Various additions were made to render it suitable
as a residence for Governor Arthur Edward Kennedy, who had succeeded
Douglas in 1864.

[2]Captain George Tomline Gordon (1823-68) was appointed treasurer of Vancouver
Island in 1860 (*Colonist*, 21 July 1860) and sat in the Legislative Assembly as
member for Esquimalt Town from March 1860 until 24 December 1861, when he
was arrested on the charge of embezzling public funds (*Colonist*, 27 December
1861). For further details see J. A. Venn, *Alumni Cantabrigienses. Part II. From
1752 to 1900* (Cambridge: The University Press, 1922-54).

and got furious himself—what shouting—cheering, hissing and all kinds of noises there were to be sure when he made some slashing remarks which did not suit everybody! On one occasion De Cosmos appeared on this stage—performed all sorts of semi-theatrical attitudes—boasted of travelling through California, with a revolver in each boot or something of this kind—was vainglorious and egoistic to the utmost degree. The theatre was crowded—De Cosmos was drunk![1] This settled the matter, he lost at the election—it might perhaps have been otherwise had he avoided this night—he took a little too much, for I am told he always "took a little" before appearing on a public platform. At this time De Cosmos was a radical and demagogue—a good speaker—knew all the captivating sentences for the multitude—well read—a free-thinker in religion—a sort of socialist—and uncommonly egotistical—nothing was right, if he said the contrary—and nothing good done but what he had been the author thereof. One newspaper made the remark that they could not report De Cosmos' speeches in full, because they had not a sufficient number of capital I's!

The election went off all right—a few verbal rows—no fighting— but plenty smoking and drinking—champagne the usual "wine"—in fact the word "wine" meant champagne in these days, and it was very good, there being no duty and the imports direct—the same with cigars. The victors were hilarious after the vote had been made known, which all knew beforehand as it was open voting! How many people had to swear they had not taken the oath of allegiance to any other nation! They all swallowed the oath!

The House at length meets—the constitution very much the same— Cary may be considered the leader—Waddington possibly the leader of the opposition. All had work to do—the ways and means had to be provided. There was the usual talk about the HBCo; the expense of Govt—all of which has been heard often since—but not so commonly since responsible government. At this time of course more officers had been appointed. The Incorporation of the City among the first 'bills,' but this was sent back to the Assembly because it had incorporated the land and not the inhabitants! Of course the first Act was rather rudimentary. This Act did not pass until 1862 but previous to this a law had

---

[1]Cary's meeting was reported in the *Colonist,* 31 December 1859; Franklin's, on 5 January 1860; and De Cosmos's on 7 January 1860, with a comment on "his voice rendered feeble by ill health."

been passed levying a tax on real estate in the now city for local improvements.[1]

The second great measure, drawn up by Cary, I believe, and based on the Australian Act, was passed.[2]

It is however not my intention to write history, save more or less a personal one.

In these sessions also was passed the real estate tax and a general license law—dues on shipping, i.e. harbour dues.[3] Laws which had a great effect not very long afterwards.

Foster of Esquimault at this or a subsequent session,[4] moved an address to HM Govt, that the price of land should be reduced to one dollar per acre. In the end HM Govt allowed it[5]—possibly because other sources of revenue had been provided. Very few settlers were on agricultural lands—the blame being laid on the large price of land hitherto charged—in fact the want of progress and cultivation was attributed to this "illiberal policy." In my opinion a fallacy—we were too far from the sources of emigration—Washington being settled by Old Americans. The lowering of the price of land did not at once lead to much speculation, neither did it to any degree increase settlement.

---

[1]The Real Estate Tax Act was passed late in 1860.

[2]The Act to Incorporate the City of Victoria was finally passed on 2 August 1862.

[3]The Trade Licences Act and the Victoria and Esquimalt Harbour Dues Act were both passed in 1860.

[4]Major George Foster Foster (d. 1887) sat as a member of the Legislative Assembly first for Lake District and afterwards for Esquimalt Town from 1860 to 1864. For further details see "Bushby Appendix"; and for a diverting comment on his activities on "The Fever Coast," 1872-73, see James Pope-Hennessy, *Verandah: Some Episodes in the Crown Colonies, 1867-1889* (London: Allen and Unwin, [1964]), pp. 127-31.

[5]On 21 March 1860 Major Foster Foster "moved an address to the Home Government through His Excellency praying that the price of land be reduced," and on 23 March the members signed a petition to the Queen asking for a reduction from one pound per acre to four shillings and twopence (see *Colonist*, 20-24 March 1860). Douglas forwarded the petition with a strong recommendation in its favour, pointing out that "population is the great want of this Colony" and that something must be done to make Vancouver Island attractive in view of "the allurements held out by the Donation Act and the General Pre-emption law" of the contiguous U.S. territories (Douglas to Newcastle, 28 March 1860, Vancouver Island, Governor Douglas, Despatches to London, 8 June 1859—28 December 1861, PABC). The Colonial Office agreed (see Newcastle to Douglas, 28 June 1860; and C. C. Lewis to Douglas, 16 July 1860, Great Britain, Colonial Office, Despatches to Vancouver Island, 21 July 1849—10 January 1867, PABC). The lower price appeared in the Land Proclamation of 19 February 1861, which set forth the regulations for pre-emption. The relevant despatches are cited in Wrinch, "Land Policy," p. 181; the proclamation is printed in the *Colonist*, 7 March 1861.

Free Trade in Vancouver Island still continued—but customs dues had been imposed on the Mainland then called B. Columbia.[1] Whilst Douglas remained Governor this acted very well—but much ill feeling arose against V.I., as it was thought the Governor favored Victoria— the truth is Governor Douglas could scarcely do otherwise—he had to administer a Colony with two different fiscal systems.

I have nothing very unusual to relate about "this House," save that it contained a good number of talented people and was a first-rate House in this respect. Of course some members went out and others came in, among the latter J. W. Trutch—Dr. Trimble[2] and Burnaby. The sessions were fruitful of good measures and some bad, just made to suit temporary purposes, perhaps some particular individual or law suit —one to prevent Americans seizing Americans here for debts contracted in foreign countries—this on account chiefly of San Francisco worrying Americans for debts of Americans contracted previous to their leaving San Francisco or such foreign country.

Altho the House was good, political dissatisfaction remained outside —De Cosmos and others kept up a perpetual agitation for responsible government—meetings at the Victoria [Theatre?] took place, and as the time of the Hudson's Bay Co had expired, it became more virulent.

There was another important reason. The gold did not exactly come up to expectations and so the trade of Victoria had diminished greatly —the times were bad and things looked blue—real estate had gone down down down, bringing some down with it. The Americans put on cutters to prevent smuggling—for under Free Trade this had become a very large and important business—not only to the State of Washington, but also to B. Columbia—Free Trade did not mean fair trade. The people chiefly advantaged were commission merchants—they were all right anyhow—but with the decay of business and excessive imports previously, many consigned goods were sold at a good sacrifice, particu-

[1]See above, p. 160n1, the B.C. Proclamation of 2 June 1859, and The Customs Amendment Act, 1860.
[2]Joseph William Trutch (1826-1904) succeeded H. P. P. Crease as member for Victoria District in October 1861, when Crease was appointed attorney-general of British Columbia. For further details see Hollis R. Lynch, "Sir Joseph William Trutch: A British American Pioneer on the Pacific Coast," *Pacific Historical Review* 30 (1961): 243-55; and G. Smedley Andrews, *Sir Joseph William Trutch* ... (Victoria: British Columbia Lands Service, in cooperation with the Corporation of Land Surveyors of the Province of British Columbia, 1972). Dr. James Trimble (1818-85) succeeded Waddington as member for Victoria Town in 1861. For further details see the obituary in the *Colonist*, 3 January 1885.

larly European goods—but the agents nevertheless received their commission. At this time the farmers from the other side brought their produce, and as the buyers were few they could on occasions club together and buy at their own price; on the other hand those who brought produce wanted goods and so the one was exchanged for the other. In this way the farmers of V.I. who however were really few and had but comparatively little to sell, were left in the background—and complained that the people in town would not buy their produce, which in reality was true in the main. On the other hand the merchants complained, that the natives would not fulfil their orders punctually —and put them to great inconvenience, particularly in supplying ships at a short notice. Anyhow the farmers soon had a dislike to Free Trade, and when the real estate tax came into use, they disliked it still more— as the Americans did not pay any tax, save perhaps some small dues on boats under seven tons. No one seemed inclined to farm—and those who did grumbled. The truth seems to be that V. Island was too large to have an emporium like Singapore or Hong Kong—Vancouver Island had land—so the settlers and townspeople came into opposition—and soon their representatives would overcome those of the trading communities.

Before this too a royalty had been charged on coal, but the HBCo had wiped out this regulation.[1] Of course the mines or their holders were Free Traders. They exported coal and brought back esculents and goods in their ships—they did not encourage in any way agriculture.

---

[1]In their colonization proposals the HBC had fixed a royalty of two shillings and sixpence a ton (Begg, *History of British Columbia*, p. 187). This was still in force in 1857, though in the year 1855-56 no royalty had been paid because no coal had been exported and none used. But Governor Douglas did not approve. In his message to the House of Assembly, 8 June 1857, he said: "Whenever the coal is sold the proprietors will be called upon to pay the royalties; though I hold, as an incontrovertible maxim, that the taxation of native produce is, in all cases, ruinous in its effect on commercial enterprise and directly opposed to every sound principle of political economy" (Vancouver Island, House of Assembly, ... *Correspondence Book August 12th 1856 to July 6th, 1859,* Archives Memoir no. 4, ed. E. O. S. Scholefield [Victoria: King's Printer, 1918], pp. 28-29). By 1864 Douglas's view had apparently prevailed, for on 29 April 1864 the minutes of the Legislative Council of Vancouver Island recorded that "it is inexpedient, at present, to enforce Royalties upon Coal Minerals or Timber, because it is the policy of the Colony to foster these industries which are yet in their infancy and the yield from which is so small as not to justify the imposition; and because such an imposition might interfere with the principles of free trade hitherto maintained by the Colony successfully." Presumably the original HBC royalty was finally wiped out when the Company re-conveyed Vancouver Island to the Crown in 1867.

Somewhere about this time—I do not remember the year—some Americans privately got up an agitation and tried to persuade the British settlers to petition the President of the United States to use his assistance to have the Island annexed to the United States. Of course the same arguments and persuasions were used then as since, that it would be for the immediate and permanent benefit of the Island, and that all would become rich. They pointed out too the fact that HM Govt cared but little about the Colonies and was willing to let them go, they being at this time of Free Trade agitation and success, an incumbrance, an expense of defence, and liable to lead the mother country to war or in case of war the cost of defending them. These doctrines were at this time in the ascendant among the Free Traders—who considered that the Colonies only would stick to England, until they became independent like the United States.

There is no doubt that some, who would not like their names mentioned now, signed this petition and that it was duly forwarded to the President, but I never heard that it was in any way acted on. I never even saw this petition, much less signed it and indeed I only know from hearsay some who are said to have signed it, and altho I have often striven to get a sight of the copy said to exist in Victoria, I have never succeeded —I think some petition of the same kind was got up in Canada, so it seems to have been a semi-organized thing. Anyhow I have no doubt I was asked to sign it and listened to what they had to say, but as usual laughed and was non-committal.[1] Many talked more or less about annexation—and in process of [time?] when the question of Union with B. Columbia and subsequently Confederation came up, doubtless many debated whether it would not be better to be at once annexed instead of waiting until the whole of Canada had been gobbled up—for I think too before this the Americans had bought Alaska[2]—a purchase that is destined to have a vast influence on the future not only of B. Columbia but of Canada in general. In relation to this, Governor Douglas told me that the British might have bought it, in fact a Russian agent had been here and offered to sell the HBCo or the Government that coast strip of land from Portland Canal to Sitka which the Hudson's Bay Company had leased from Russia for trading purposes. I think Governor Douglas wrote

[1]For full details see "The Annexation Petition of 1869," ed. Willard E. Ireland, *BCHQ* 4 (1940): 267-87. This petition, now in the National Archives at Washington D.C., is here printed for the first time, and forty of the forty-two persons who signed it are identified. The signature of JSH, as he says, does not appear.
[2]The United States purchased Alaska from the Russians in 1867.

HM Govt on this subject—if so, however, the correspondence as far as I know was never made public.[1] After the Americans bought it they boasted of Canada being sandwiched—ready to be gobbled up— but who knows what revolution may take place in the U.S.

On one occasion Governor Douglas made a formal call on Secretary Seward at Consul [blank in MS: Allen Francis] house on Pandora Street. He was an old gentleman, kind and amiable in manner, with rather a slow careful speech. Governor Douglas told him and twitted me with being an unruly Member and so the Secretary advised me to be governed by my seniors, who knew more about matters possibly than I did. The visit was more a formal matter than anything else. Poor man, I do not recollect whether this was before or after the endeavour to

---

[1]This reference remains obscure. In his discussion of the agreement negotiated in 1839 between the HBC and the Russian American Company, E. E. Rich, *Hudson's Bay Company 1670-1870. Volume III: 1821-1870* (Toronto: McClelland and Stewart, 1960) says (p. 655): ". . . Simpson's agreement with Wrangell placed the Company in a favourable position—so favourable that Great Britain was offered the prior option on buying the Russian possessions in North America, before they were sold to the United States. . . ." Rich gives no date for this offer— made presumably not to the HBC but to the British government; and certainly no such offer was made immediately prior to the sale to the Americans (see *Certain Correspondence of the Foreign Office and the Hudson's Bay Company* [ed. Otto Klotz] [Ottawa: Government Printing Bureau, 1899], Part V, "Foreign Office Correspondence North-West Coast America—Alaska," pp. 5-7). In a subsequent passage Rich says (p. 779): "The agreement with the Russian American Company continued to afford satisfaction . . . and the agreement was renewed in 1863 for two years to 1865. The Russians then offered the outright sale of their American territories to the Company, but by that time the ownership of land was becoming less and less attractive and the lease, and finally the ownership, of Alaska, passed to the United States." Commenting on this offer to the HBC in 1865 John S. Galbraith (in *The Hudson's Bay Company as an Imperial Factor 1821-1869* [Toronto: University of Toronto Press, 1957], pp. 170-71) is of the opinion that this was not a firm offer: "Although Rutovski implied that the Russian government might consider selling the leased territory to the Hudson's Bay Company, he made no mention of a possible purchase price, nor did he provide further details to indicate that such a transfer was seriously proposed." In 1865, of course, James Douglas was no longer an officer of the HBC, having severed his connection in 1858; but he did remain as governor of Vancouver Island until March 1864. It may therefore be pertinent to quote Benjamin Platt Thomas, *Russo-American Relations, 1815-1867*, Johns Hopkins University Studies in Historical and Political Science, series 47, no. 2 (Baltimore: Johns Hopkins Press, 1930), p. 47: "It is said that in 1860, and again in 1864, the Russian Government offered Alaska to Great Britain for $5,000,000, but that each time the offer was refused." Thomas here cites "A Russian American Diplomat," *Jew Baiting in Russia and her Alleged Friendship for the United States* (Washington, 1903), pp. 27-28; he then adds: "Although this is probably untrue, it is certain that the Russian government . . . had by this time fully decided to sell." No despatch on the subject from Governor Douglas to the British government has been traced.

murder him, but he had something amiss with his jaw. Little did anyone think at this time that his son would be foully murdered.[1]

There was trouble in the air and in 1862 or thereabout, Victoria was
in a state of great excitement—the fratricidal war had broken out in
the United States [on 12 April 1861]. The Americans here were
numerous—some for the North and others for the South. Many Southerners subsequently came here, possibly fleeing from the war or from
arrest. Victoria was in a state of unrest, every item of war news was
eagerly sought and devoured; much of it however being actually false
or highly colored. The *Gazette* no longer existed—the telegraph had not
come into use here, so we had to await the arrival of steamers from
San Francisco and the Sound. How everybody rushed to get the news!
This state of excitement lasted a couple of years—the Americans
wanted gold—Garesche,[2] for Wells Fargo, sold greenbacks—at fifty or
sixty cents to the dollar—I wanted to speculate in them, but had no
money. Governor Douglas said we must remain neutral. The first news
was in favor of the South and great was the rejoicing of the Southerners—of the subsequent history it is written and may be consulted. As
a rule North and South in Victoria lived quietly—without public de-
monstration but there were some hot-headed fellows who would not be
controlled—the Confederate flag was hoisted in Langley Street after a
battle and the North cut it down and vice versa, leading to a fight or
two, a few only however taking part in it.[3] However, it was soon under-

---

[1]In the summer of 1869 William Henry Seward (1801-72), U.S. secretary of
state from 1861 to 1869, visited Alaska, whose purchase in 1867 he had instigated and completed. On his way home he visited Victoria, staying with the U.S.
Consul Allen Francis (*Colonist*, 27 August 1869). Seward had still not recovered
from the carriage accident of 5 April 1865, in which his arm was broken and his
jaw fractured on both sides, nor from the attempt at assassination made on him
only nine days later. One of his sons was severely injured in the assassination
attack, but he recovered, all three sons surviving their father (see Glyndon G. Van
Deusen, *William Henry Seward* [New York: Oxford University Press, 1967],
pp. 411, 413-15, 559; there appears to be no reference here to any son being
"foully murdered"). Allen Francis (1815?-87) was U.S. consul in Victoria 1862-
69 and 1877-84.

[2]Francis Garesche (1829-75) was the agent of Wells, Fargo & Co. as well as a bank-
er. He was lost in the wreck of the steamer *Pacific*, which had on board at the time
$500,000 in gold dust which he was taking to the mint in San Francisco
(*Colonist*, 13 November 1875).

[3]According to an editorial in the *Colonist*, 12 November 1862, a secessionist hoisted
the Confederate flag; the loyal Americans then took their own flags down in
protest; and the secessionist later hauled down his flag of his own accord—there
was no violence. The next year the secessionist (one Shaphard) hoisted the Confederate flag again, but the May Day procession of the Victoria Fire Department

stood that such must not take place in a neutral British Colony. For the two years the Americans did not abuse their asylum—it was neutral ground and safer for all to be law-abiding. Many of the Southern refugees were very nice people, and associated with the best British here— hospitality was not ostentatious, but plenty of it of a domestic nature. None seemed to be poor, tho undoubtedly they must have been in many instances. Of the many here I do not remember their names, but many of the officers who had had a hand in the San Juan affair, joined the Confederates, including I think Governor Stevens—deCourcy the English magistrate at San Juan joined I think the Southerners. On the other hand Gordon the defaulting V.I. treasurer found himself on the Northern side or vice versa.[1] They do not seem to have distinguished themselves very much—at least not in written history—but I think the pair became prisoners. Of the feeling in Victoria, of course it was divided—but there was a sort of sentiment for the underdog the South, but really as far as the principle of the war—if it had any—slavery and so forth—the British public seemed to care but little and indeed were very cautious in giving their or any opinion. The number of Americans made business more lively, and this was more to the taste of traders, than sentiment about slavery or anything else. There were also a goodly number of colored people here also but no one molested them, and they did not make themselves obnoxious. There was a sort of feeling existing at this time, that the Southerners were "gentlemen" and the Northerners, rough and ready ill-mannered boastful speculating money grubbers. Anyhow we had a couple of years of great excitement —in fact from the time of the San Juan trouble and the discovery of gold on the Fraser and previously on account of the gold in California,

---

ignored it, and "nothing occurred . . . to mar the harmony of the day" (ibid., 2 May 1863). There is a highly coloured account of "The Fight for the Standard" in D. W. Higgins, *The Mystic Spring* . . . (Toronto: W. Briggs, 1904).

[1]Major Isaac Ingall Stevens (1818-62) was the first governor of Washington Territory, 1853-57, and then a member of Congress. He was a firm opponent of secession, joined the Union forces in 1861, and was killed in action in 1862. For further details see the biography by his son, Hazard Stevens, *The Life of Isaac Ingall Stevens* . . . (Boston and New York: Houghton Mifflin, 1900). Major John Fitzroy de Courcy was appointed magistrate at San Juan at the beginning of the trouble with the Americans (*Colonist*, 29 July 1859). He left the colony for Washington D.C. in the summer of 1861 (ibid., 23 and 26 October 1861) and served in the Union forces (see the obituary in the London *Times*, quoted by the *Colonist*, 21 December 1890, "From a magistracy to a peerage"). G. T. Gordon, on the other hand, served with distinction in the Confederate army 1862-65 (Venn, *Alumni Cantabrigienses*).

Victoria seemed to be ever in a state of ebullition. Has it not continued more or less until now? Of course when this horrible internecine war ended many Americans had to remain here still—and doubtless might have continued still had business warranted their so doing. The war being over had a depressing effect on Victoria, altho in reality there had been no war on the Pacific coast.

This war caused the Govt of the U.S. to hasten the construction of the overland railway—in part as a military measure and in part to keep California in the Union.

Of course I played no part in all this, but had to go through the whole nevertheless. What with politics, physic, rows from the Fraser and other matters, it was enough to turn one's head, and indeed indirectly had an influence on subsequent legislation—an important influence too.[1]

In earlier days, on one occasion the Fourth of July was celebrated by Americans at Cadboro Bay—the Declaration of Independence read, speeches made &c. &c. No one cared a straw about this: but in a subsequent year, some Americans wishing to celebrate, went to Governor Douglas and asked permission to raise the American flag and fire a salute from big guns. Of course Governor Douglas, in his official capacity could not recognize this and gave them kindly and politely to understand this, but the Governor said to me after, "How foolish of them to sue to me an official for permission! Had they gone to Beacon Hill and had their jollification, I should not have known anything about the matter, and they might have fired as many guns as they pleased and read as many declarations as suited them—but I could not possibly give official sanction to this." However it all ended pleasantly but without the guns.

The position of things at this time it is advisable to understand for what is to follow. It must however be understood, that at this time the yield of gold had been enormous. Miners used to come to Victoria with lots of gold and exchange it for U.S. coin—this they absolutely squandered—chiefly in brothels or gin shops—so these places flourished and so did dance houses[2]—and of course business in the necessary

[1]JSH has added here, and then deleted, the following comment: "for it made Canada anxious to have B.C. in the confederacy."
[2]Defined in the journal of the Rev. J. B. Good of the Thompson River Mission at Lytton as "those vile institutions in which white men and the worst class of Indian women meet" (Columbia Mission, *Eleventh Annual Report . . . for . . . 1869* [London: Rivingtons, 1870], p. 20).

articles flourished also. Hyder [Haida] women and men came in flocks, to go away ruined forever—Indians from the North West coast met with the same fate, from which they have never and never will recover. In process of time Chinese women came and they in some measure took the business of the local Indians, Haidas, Chimpsehans [Tsimshians] and so forth and to end the matter the small pox and local demands drove them home in their own canoes, and hundreds perished on their way to their own country.[1] I may say here that nearly every Indian attacked with small pox died—whether he was taken care of in the Indian small pox hospital or not—and it was also said whether he had been vaccinated or not. I do not believe the last assertion because the Songish [Songhees] Indians kept comparatively free from the disease and many of them at various times had been successfully vaccinated by me—arm to arm.[2]

About this time too, some Americans, not being able to obtain domestic servants—(for as I said before the early settlers employed Indians with very indifferent success—the settler's wife did the work—the Indians were "helps")—sent to San Francisco for their own Chinese servants or other Chinese—white labour was out of the question. Of course they let their friends know what a good field there was here, so the Chinese heathen soon became abundant and then they monopolized the market garden and the washing trade.[3] At this time the Chinese were believed by all to be an advantage and an improvement. Previous to their advent the supply of vegetables had been scant, for Indians never took to this business, excepting in so far that they grew potatoes in small quantities.

As soon as Wiley [Wylly] published the assessment roll of the value of real estate and the tax thereon, there was a general outcry against what was said to be the extravagant valuation[4]—the people of Victoria

[1]For the smallpox epidemic of 1862, "the most terrible single calamity to befall the Indians of British Columbia," see Wilson Duff, *The Indian History of British Columbia. Volume I. The Impact of the White Man*, Anthropology in British Columbia, Memoir no. 5 (Victoria: Provincial Museum, 1964), p. 42.

[2]On 26 April 1862 the *Colonist* reported that "Dr. Helmcken [had] vaccinated over 500 natives since the disease first made its appearance here [on 18 March]."

[3]Chinese came into the colony with the Fraser River gold rush in 1858, and since mining was a seasonal occupation many found their way into other forms of work.

[4]So sharp was the criticism of the assessment roll of 1861 (see, for example, the *Colonist,* 12 April 1862) that late in 1862 the Legislative Assembly passed an Act to amend the Real Estate Tax Act, 1860. The Real Estate Tax Amendment Act, 1862, provided for the appointment of a paid assessor for Vancouver Island and

growled and so did also those outside the City. Old Mr. Work was agitated one day—"What's the matter?"—"Look at this tax on my property— too bad—too bad." "Oh," I said, "Mr. Work, you never knew before how well you were off—and now knowing how rich you are, pay the taxes, they give you a respectable name and station." "Oh I would rather not know than have to pay the taxes." The real estate tax in 1862 realized about $32,000.00[1]—tax 1 per cent per annum on valuation.

The value of gold exported (not reckoning that in private hands) by Wells Fargo and other companies in 1862, was a little over two million dollars—and from 1858 to 1862 inclusive six million dollars!!!

At the same time the imports for 1862 amounted to three and a half million dollars! a million more than the gold yield. Of these imports only a little more than half a million worth came from England.[2]

What became of all this money from the mines? It simply leaked out of the country to foreigners—made no industries save perhaps the gas company, a brewery and a sort of distillery.[3] Victoria had no end of interests in mines, most of which never paid a cent—all outlay. Merchants were reckless in sending goods to the Interior and giving credit without any substantial security whatever. They suffered for it afterwards! but assuredly Victoria goods made the mines to be worked. Of course I am now speaking of Cariboo, i.e. Williams Creek, Lightning

---

required him to post the assessment roll for each district in three places. Charles G. Wylly was appointed (ibid., 5 January 1863), and the assessment rolls were printed in the Vancouver Island *Government Gazette*, the date varying with the district, between 11 November and 27 December 1863.

[1]The figure given in the *British Columbian and Victoria Directory* of 1863 is $32,415.44.

[2]The round figures given here agree with the precise statements in the *British Columbian and Victoria Directory*, 1863: Gold exported in 1862, $2,167,183.18; gold exported in 1858-1862 inclusive, $5,373,211.48; imports in 1862, $3,679,-328.00. The directory cites the *Daily Chronicle* as authority for these figures.

[3]The Victoria Gas Company was incorporated by an act of the Legislative Assembly in 1860, and gas was first lighted in Victoria on 30 September 1862 (*Colonist*, 1 October 1862). The preface of the *First Victoria Directory*, 1860, states that the town has two breweries; later in the text Alfred W. Bunster is listed as agent of the Colonial Brewery and J. D. Carroll advertises himself as "sole agent for the Victoria Brewery." JSH's reference to "a sort of distillery" is not clear: Laumeister & Gowen are listed in the 1863 directory as "brewers" and in 1867 Messrs. Laumeister & Co. are reported as having established a distillery and grist mill on Victoria Harbour (*Colonist*, 11 April 1867). This is said to be an elaborate enterprise, expected to produce two hundred gallons of spirits in ten hours; but there may have been earlier attempts at a distillery.

Creek and so forth—the lower Fraser had failed. The population at Cariboo was not very large.[1]

In connection with this may be mentioned the bold and successful work of Governor Douglas: the construction of the road from Hope to Yale to Cariboo.[2] Before this flour and bacon had been as high as one dollar per pound at the mines—other things in proportion; the cost of transport by mules being enormous and reckoned by the pound. The opening of the road lowered this—[the] road led to great diminutions and so the tax on mules to make it was beneficial to all.[3] Trutch had the contract to build the suspension bridge and made well out of the tolls.[4]

---

[1] In the period 1859-65 the annual estimate of the number of miners is given as c. 4,000 by Paul A. Phillips, "Confederation and the Economy of British Columbia," in *British Columbia & Confederation*, p. [61]. According to Ormsby, *British Columbia*, p. 209, "the population of the mining communities of Cariboo was impossible to estimate—some figures ranged as high as 10,000 or 16,000 —but officials doubted whether the total population of British Columbia was much in excess of the Vancouver Island figure of 7,500."

[2] The Cariboo Road through the Fraser Canyon to the gold fields at Barkerville was commenced at Yale in 1862 and completed in 1865, the year after Douglas retired as governor of British Columbia. But communication between Hope and Yale continued to be by steamboat or trail until 1876, when a road between Hope and Yale was completed ("Report of the Chief Commissioner of Lands and Works . . . 1876," B.C., *Sessional Papers*, 2d Parl., 2d sess., 1877, p. 287).

[3] The proclamation of 31 January 1860 (printed in the *Colonist*, 9 February 1860) placed a tax of one pound sterling on "every pack-horse, mule, or other quadruped" leaving Port Douglas or Yale for the mines, the proceeds to be applied to the improvement of the roads. Governor Douglas instructed the gold commissioners to "use every effort to render the measure palatable" to the miners and supplied them with arguments (see, for example, Douglas to E. H. Sanders, 14 February 1860, British Columbia, Colonial Secretary, Correspondence Outward, May 1859 —July 1860, PABC). However, so great was the opposition that the tax was not enforced, and by 1860 it had been suspended (Colonial Secretary to certain petitioners at Yale, 13 March 1860, ibid.).

[4] The Alexandra suspension bridge across the Fraser near Spuzzum was completed on 1 September 1863. After the C.P.R. was built it gradually fell into disuse, and in the great flood of 1894 the portions near the shore were washed away. Settlers continued to cross the river on the naked cables until 1913 the Public Works Department had these dynamited into the river. A second bridge, built in 1926, made use of the old piers, but the present structure, completed in October 1962, is a quarter of a mile downstream from the original site (see "Report of the Chief Commissioner of Lands and Works . . . 1894," B.C., *Sessional Papers*, 7th Parl., 1st sess., 1894-95, p. 389; "Report of the Minister of Public Works . . . 1912-13," ibid., 13th Parl., 2d sess., 1914, p. S76; "Report of the Minister of Public Works . . . 1926-27," ibid., 16th Parl., 4th sess., 1927, frontispiece; and the article in the Vancouver *Province*, 29 August 1926, magazine, p. 6). Trutch had a seven-year licence to collect tolls, and these "were believed to have been quite lucrative (estimated from $10,000 to $20,000 per year)" (Andrews, *Trutch*, p. 6).

At this time too Waddington and others tried to make a road from Bute Inlet.[1] I was engaged in this and other enterprises—that failed! Of course during this period Victoria may be said to have been prosperous—and really it seemed so. Money was plentiful—with the miners —but how about the goods that were sent up country? The returns did not come in—only part—but more goods went away; the HBCo sold their goods in the same way and in the end they lost enormously as well as other merchants. Victoria had apparently got over the depression of 1860 when thousands of miners left and merchants too—but the future told a tale of the effects of imprudence and recklessness and cutthroat competition.

The cost of the Executive Govt for salaries in 1862 amounted to fifty thousand ($50,000) dollars from nothing in 1857. Of course at all events the most of this was absolutely necessary on account of the changed condition of the Colony—a regular governmental staff had now been established. Under the head of mails in the proposed expenditure for works &c. $16,000.00 are put down for 1862. This I think was paid to subsidize [a] steamer to San Francisco.[2]

Under another head may be found three thousand (3,000) dollars on account Gordon's defalcations.[3] Gordon was treasurer—an English gentleman—had his wife here also and had letters of recommendation. I walked with him once in Victoria, and many touched or took off their hats saluting him. "Do you know why these people salute? I owe every one of them money! If I did not they would not be so damned polite! The only way to gain the respect of people is to be in debt to them!" Well his roguery with government money being found out—he was jailed in the brick prison in the old Victoria jail—but he cut a hole through the brick wall and escaped.[4] Of course many said the authorities con-

[1]Waddington was convinced that the best way to the Cariboo goldfields was by way of a road from the head of Bute Inlet, and in 1862 he was granted a charter for the building of such a road. The Chilcotin massacre of 1864 put an end to this scheme.
[2]According to the colonial estimates published in the *Colonist*, 23 January 1863 and in the *British Columbian and Victoria Directory* of 1863, the expenditure for the establishment in 1862 was $47,366.60. Under "Conveyance of mails" the expenditure for 1862 is given as $16,179.92. The government voted £2,500 as a subsidy for a mail steamer running direct between San Francisco and Victoria or Esquimalt, and the contract was awarded to Holladay and Flint, who in 1861 had bought the northern interests of the Pacific Mail Company (*Colonist*, 22 January 1862; *Lewis & Dryden's Marine History of the Pacific Northwest*, p. 100).
[3]See above, p. 177n2. The figure is given as $3,155.71 by the *Colonist* and the 1863 directory.
[4]According to the *Colonist*, 19 May 1862, he had made his escape the day before "by unlocking with a false key the gate between the barracks and the kitchen."

nived at this, but I know not. He escaped to the U.S. where the next we hear of him is in the U.S. Civil War as a Captain in the army. He was a fast man—tall with beard and whiskers and polished.

It is advisable to hasten on. A new house was elected in 1863 which continued to 1866. Important as the previous one had been, this one was destined to alter the course of the history of the Island. The election of course was an exciting one—many new faces came to the front. I as usual became Member for my old place and as usual chosen Speaker. This office had now become pretty troublesome and occupied much of my time, but of course I had no longer the direction of affairs, yet Members used to consult me on various subjects. Care had also to be taken in giving decisions [on] various points of order, tho this was not carried to the ridiculous extent of Members and Houses of the present day, when it seems to occupy more of the time of the House than ordinary business. My decisions were usually acquiesced in, for at this time the Chair was looked on with respect and as one worthy of trust.

Sometimes a [I] took part in the debates in Committee—perhaps because it was more pleasant than confining myself to my room. On one of these occasions I argued about a point of order, in order that some particular thing might be carried, and was on the high road to do it, when some grey-headed old rat suggested that the point of order should be referred to Mr. Speaker! Of course it was but a few moments from the floor to the Chair—and when there I gave the decision entirely against myself! This occasioned much laughter and then cheers; so I gained much respect, the Members believing me to be honest, which I had indeed always endeavoured to be when in the Chair—friends or foes to any particular order or party, were not taken into consideration—the point of order only; our own precedents were but few, so they became the authority on all these questions.

Burnaby my former brother, had become paralysed. Poor fellow what a change—from a pleasant mirthful active honest pleasant little fellow —talented and full of business, he suddenly became a crying weeping child pitiful to behold, whenever anyone went to see him. He improved

---

It appeared however that he had "at first intended to escape through the brick wall which fronts on the Boomerang Inn, as a space 2½ feet long by 1 foot wide had been made in the brickwork with a large rasp file, but he was doubtless unable to finish the job before daylight came upon him and so chose the readier method of picking the lock of the gate." He was next seen en route to Beacon Hill, where presumably he obtained a boat to the American side of the Straits of Juan de Fuca.

a little and then was sent to England to his friends.[1] After him Dr. Ash filled his place in the House,—McKenzie as usual doing the honors with whole-souled delight. Ash was a clever well-read man with a good memory; of remarkable physique and structure—very broad shoulders and of bulldog style, very pleasant to his friends but of hasty and quarrelsome temper—hated to be contradicted—his opinion being final. Compelled to wear spectacles on account of short-sightedness, he was useless without them. I cannot say he was quarrelsome, but he could easily be made so. On one occasion Ash and De Cosmos had some dispute in a debate—they were on opposite sides and both of them looked ugly, but broke through no order. The House being over, Ash met De Cosmos outside, and near the bridge[2] an altercation took place and blows were struck. De Cosmos always carried a stick and Ash asserted this had been used on his head. I came up at this time and with the aid of others induced them to go their way, for Ash had his "monkey up" and was able to throw De Cosmos over the bridge. I induced Ash to walk with me up Bird Cage Walk—and there he found his face bleeding and his glasses broken. "Oh," I said, "here is a clean pool of water, let me wash the blood off." At this he flared up; did I want to make him a spectacle in the public street, and I thought he was about to pitch into poor weakly me. He did not, would not come into my house and walked growling to his own house on Fort Street. In the evening Governor Douglas met me, and said, "Mr. Speaker, are you aware that your authority ceases when out of the House? You had no authority to interfere, when gentlemen out of your jurisdiction wished to settle their little difficulties. You had better have let them have it out—as it is neither is satisfied." I laughed at the Governor's grim humour—he had no love for De Cosmos and vice versa—and probably would have been inwardly pleased, had Ash pitched De Cosmos into the Bay! There were a large number of the same mind, for De Cosmos had hosts of opponents as well as friends. Of course De Cosmos and everyone else did not take many liberties with Ash after this. Ash was honest and honourable almost to a fault—but let no one thwart him, either in opinion or action. Hospitable and fond of society—pleasant at table and generally liked

---

[1]Burnaby resigned his seat in 1865 and was replaced by Dr. John Ash (*Colonist,* 29 November 1865). After a visit to England he came back to Victoria, but in 1869 he retired from business because of ill-health, and he returned to England for good in 1874.

[2]A bridge over James Bay had been erected in 1859 to connect the town with the site of the proposed Parliament Buildings.

—but let anyone who played a partner with him at whist, beware of making mistaken or careless play in the opinion of Dr. Ash. One day Ash's Chinaman was insulted and mildly assaulted in front of his office by a "white man"! Ash rushed out and threatened to smash every bone in the white man's body—and the man knew he could do it too—but better counsels prevailed and Ash had him summoned to court where he was fined. He was staunch to his friends, but let foes beware.

It must be remembered that at this time the Commission of Governor Douglas had nearly expired and the right of the Hudson's Bay Co also —the latter had to be settled with in accordance with their charter in re Vancouver Island Colony, the latter would have been done much more readily and I believe equally honestly and well, had it not happened that Mr. Dallas, the son-in-law of the Governor and at the same [time?] Commissioner of the Hudson's Bay Co was resident in Victoria. Mr. Dallas believed the Governor to be acting illiberally and unjustly towards the Company and so a great deal of ill feeling existed between the two—the one of course wishing to deal honestly and fairly with HM Government, the other for the HBCo. Doubtless Governor Douglas would have gained more for the colonists and Colony but he would have offset this in another way to the Company. Dallas on the other hand was a pretty penurious man and looked after comparatively small things—the bawbees—he was a business man—shrewd—sharp, sensible and active, fond of dogs and horses—mercantile business his forte and he looked on the settlement between the HBCo and the Government from a business point of view only. On the other hand Governor Douglas was a statesman and had different ideas, both were honest under these conditions—but they appeared to be irreconcilable.[1]

There seemed to be a general feeling outside too, that the HBCo wanted to get as much out of the Government as possible, but the truth is the accounts of the Colony had been sent in yearly and the House did not consider themselves responsible for any debts, such as the lighthouse at Rocky Point and Government buildings, church &c.[2] The chief quarrel or rather dispute was about land. The Puget Sound Co held the

[1] On this point see their correspondence of 1860 in *Papers in Connection with Crown Lands . . . and the Title of the Hudson's Bay Company.*
[2] A lighthouse on Fisgard Island at the entrance to Esquimalt Harbour and another at Race Rocks were built in 1859-60 and both were operational before the end of the year (Walbran, *British Columbia Coast Names*). The Parliament Buildings ("The Birdcages") were built in 1859. The Victoria District Church was built between 1853 and 1856.

peninsula from Macaulay Point to the head of Victoria Arm and like-wise Langford's Plains, i.e. Colwood. They had paid for these and so no legitimate dispute existed about these. On the other hand the HBCo claimed the townsite of Victoria and I think ten miles round. They held these by "possessory right" by occupation previous to colonization, and further that according to the Oregon Treaty the Company had been given possessory right in the United States, which however the squatters and so forth more or less disregarded and gave much trouble. On the other hand it was claimed that the colonization charter gave the whole island for colonization purposes and did not make any exception for the possessory rights of the Company—so the townsite belonged to the city and the neighbouring lands likewise. Governor Douglas claimed certain parts for the Government, such as the site of the Post Office—the first Governor's residence at the corner of Yates and Government Street and some others and here it was that Governor Douglas and Mr. Dallas came to loggerheads. I may say here that all this occasioned much controversy and use of paper between the Government, HBCo and the local authorities, but at the settlement the HBCo paid one pound per acre for most of the land and certain portions surrendered to the Government—unsold portions of the City proper. All this could have been easier if not better arranged had it not been for the antagonism between Governor Douglas and Mr. Dallas. Undoubtedly Governor Douglas wished to do the best for the Colony, but would at the same time, not be unjust to the Company—but it was a period of excitement—of inflated values and huge ideas of the almost immediate phenomenal rise of the Colony—destined however not to be realized, for a collapse afterwards took place.

All this had an effect on the elections and Members of the House —it was a good opportunity for making political capital—and altho doubtless some were honest in believing that the Company were grasping and trying to gain what they were not entitled to, on the other hand there were a few (I know) who were dishonest and had the idea that they could get pecuniary benefit by their agitation—they were disappointed.

A Committee of the House was granted to enquire into these matters and sat day after day for weeks—collecting all sorts of evidence from so-called witnesses, who however in many instances knew little except from hearsay and considered antipathy and prejudice reason. Tolmie was put on the Committee and he attended regularly, listened to the examinations and probed the witnesses occasionally. During all this time I know neither the HBCo nor HM Government interfered in the matter

—the Committee allowed full swing and as far as the contracting parties were concerned, these shewed indifference if not contempt for the proceeding. Of course the Committee came to an end in time, but at present I forget whether they made a report or not.[1] Anyhow altho the Committee had some influence on the public and showed what their, the Committee's, ideas were, I believe their proceedings had little or no effect on the negotiations between the Government and the Hudson's Bay Co. Dallas was an important man in this and additionally the Company were powerful. In the end the Government got off pretty cheaply and the HBCo did not get any more than they were honorably entitled to—the whole negotiations were honorably conducted, but HM Govt were by no means favorable to the Company.

In this matter the Governor, Douglas, took the part of the Colony, and altho HM Govt wished and indeed did put down the expense of the lighthouse and other matters as a debt to be paid by the Colony, Governor Douglas succeeded in getting HM Govt to wipe them out and bear the expense.[2] It was plain that the local House were not parties to the expenditure—neither were they parties in the negotiations. If Governor Douglas had not been thwarted by the House and Mr. Dallas, the Governor would have done much more for the Colony and in the end HM Govt would have had to pay the piper. It so turned out that HM Govt paid—but who could be certain that this would happen![3] Anyhow

[1]On 18 September 1863 a select committee was "appointed to enquire into the present condition of the Crown Lands of the Colony, with reference to the Proposal of Her Majesty's Secretary of State for the Colonies, dated 15th June 1863, to hand over the Crown Lands to the Legislature." The committee sat until 15 June 1864 and both the minutes of its proceedings and its report were printed in 1864.

[2]For a full discussion see "Papers Relating to the Claim made by the Imperial Government for repayment of Advances made to the Colonies of British Columbia and Vancouver Island for the construction of lighthouses," B.C., *Sessional Papers*, 3d Parl., 3d sess., 1880. In the memorandum dated 9 August 1878, which gives the history from 1858, it appears that the British government advanced £7,000, half of which was to be repaid by the colony, which was also to bear the whole cost of maintenance. The account was presented in January 1864; but because of the change of governor and the later union of the colonies it was never collected. The B.C. Executive Council successfully argued in 1880 that the expense had been undertaken mainly for the protection of Imperial interests, and that the lighthouses had "undoubtedly been the means of preserving many vessels of Her Majesty's Navy from destruction" (ibid., pp. 373-74).

[3]After protracted negotiations the Hudson's Bay Company finally re-conveyed Vancouver Island to the Crown on 3 April 1867. The British government paid £57,500 "in full discharge of all the Company's claims." The document of re-conveyance is printed in Scholefield and Howay, *British Columbia*, 2:692-94.

I think I and the earlier Houses interfered a great deal too much, we would and could not do anything ourselves and placed obstacles in the way of him who would! Probably the best criterion of the drift of public opinion at this time may and will be found in the published addresses of Members or rather the candidates for seats in the House, for at this time it was usual for candidates to publish pretty long addresses, stating their position or opinions on the subjects of the time —a rule of convenience and honor more honored nowadays in the breach than observance!

At this time elections had become pretty expensive and the candidate had to bear the cost—the voting was open and the Members [got?] no pay. A system however was gradually growing up without any organization at first, when parties for fun, frolic and excitement— honest or otherwise—party of course, would club together, go out into the rural districts and have a jolly good time, gaining votes as well by persuasion as tobacco and grog and music. It is but fair to add that they usually paid their own expenses, and generally without stint too, for money was not so much thought of or so scarce with some as now— besides in a state of excitement, the evening's diversion will not always bear the morning's reflection, but this mattered little—come day go day—they went in to win—no matter which side they were on— promises were as plentiful as brambles and as troublesome. Ordinary bribery by money or goods was almost unknown. Possibly the expense of elections, honor and no emoluments for Members, was productive of better Members than now—in many instances mere ignorant and professional politicians, to whom a few hundred dollars per annum afford almost a livelihood—this may be however a libel whether in B. Columbia or Ottawa—in the latter there is more truth in it than defamation.

I may just as well allude here to a very remarkable—at least then thought remarkable—occurrence in the House. The last business on the list was a Bill to prolong for another year an Act in which private interests were concerned—to do with real estate.[1] The House was to be prorogued on the following day at 2 o'clock in the afternoon. The minority determined to oppose the progress of this Bill—De Cosmos—

---

[1]The bill to afford relief to certain owners of real estate sold under the Real Estate Tax Amendment Act, 1862, also called in the House of Assembly the Sheriff's sales bill, authorized the government to redeem certain property sold for taxes during the preceding year.

Trimble—McClure[1] and some others. Cochrane[2] on the other hand was
the promoter of the Bill.

The House met as usual at 3 o'clock [23 April 1866] and after the
usual routine business, this Bill came to the front. After a few words
from the promoter, the opposition came in, at first this was looked on
as an ordinary matter, but it soon became apparent that the speeches
were only against time[3] but as the House had still 24 hours to live, it
was believed that the opposition could not fill up this period. To adjourn therefore was virtually to kill the Bill, to talk until next day would
kill the Bill also—so both parties were in a very tight place. Of course
at various times there was the usual motion to adjourn—adjourn to a
particular period, which of course came from the opposition and so
always lost. At this time there was no "closure" and indeed not now,
so people could talk as long as they pleased. Trimble made a speech
of an hour or so, but his speech was made up of readings from various
blue-books. When called to order as being irrelevant, he simply remarked
that all he said was connected with the matter, as Mr. Speaker would
learn later on. Someone on the opposition made a short answer—of
course complaining of the unusual and unfair course of proceedings;
but finding out the intention of the opponents, the promoters and those
in favor of the extension of time determined to be silent and thus
throw the whole time to be consumed by their opponents, who being
few in number, it was supposed would sooner or later either wear themselves out or give way. After a little skirmishing De Cosmos spoke for
four hours. It was getting well on in the evening now, but none would
retire for dinner or refreshment—if one could starve the others could
too. McClure at length took up the strain and spoke and spoke and went
on speaking—hour after hour. Midnight came—on and on he went, and
something suspiciously like port wine and water—of course said to be
water—was given him by his friends occasionally. At length the dawn
appeared but McClure was still on his legs and some early wayfarers

---

[1] Leonard McClure (c. 1836-67), an Irish newspaperman, at the time was editor
of the *Colonist*. For further details see Madge Wolfenden, "Early Government
Gazettes," *BCHQ* 7 (1943): 181-83.

[2] John James Cochrane (c. 1827-67), a civil engineer, land agent, and real estate
auctioneer, came to British Columbia in 1859. He was elected member for
Saanich late in 1864 (*Colonist*, 1 November 1864) and sat till 1866. For further
details see "Bushby Appendix."

[3] Detailed accounts of this famous twenty-three-hour filibuster, in which McClure,
with some assistance from De Cosmos, talked out the bill, may be found in the
Colonist and also in D. W. Higgins, *The Passing of a Race* ... (Toronto: W.
Briggs, 1905), pp. 51-55.

dropped in to see what was the matter—and soon others from the town got wind of the matter and came in also. It must have appeared pretty ridiculous to them—everybody fagged—sleepy—worn out, for altho I had looked often to find a want of a quorum still both sides took care that this should not occur—at all events it was now evident that the want of a quorum meant the defeat of the Bill. No one of the Members of course listened to the talk, but as many as possible always retired to the private room, but kept a look out that a quorum be kept. Broad daylight now appeared—still on and on went McClure—interruptions only helped him, by giving him a few minutes' rest—he still kept the floor—and in fact he was the last man on that side who had any right to speak, for they had all had their say—the promoters would say nothing of course, so McClure held the fort, but in the morning, the promoters had to give way—there would be no time to finish and engross the Bill before the prorogation or the Governor came down and so the victory remained with McClure. The Bill was really of very little public importance and as for myself I cared little which way it went. I think if I had to go over the same thing again, I should stop the speakers, but even this would only give time, by making a wrangle as to the correctness of the Speaker's point. Anyhow it shows what a minority can do, if inclined to oppose public business. Of course McClure was used up, utterly exhausted—but still with pluck left.

What an awful time I had sitting in the Chair—stiff aching uneasy restless! How to keep myself awake I knew not, so I nodded occasionally and slept a moment or two, soon to be aroused, for this afforded even some fun. Of course I was obliged on one or two occasions to leave the Chair, but had to get permission—and then a talk would arise as to whether Mr. Speaker having left the Chair, the House had not ceased to exist for the day! Every Member was better off, because each could take his turn in Mr. Speaker's room, but even they were tired out.

McClure I think was an Irishman, possibly thirty-five years old or so, not by any means a bad fellow, in fact agreeable, and if I remember rightly at this time edited a newspaper, so he must have been tolerably well up and indeed very intelligent—and a pretty good debater, but by no means aggressively so. He had borrowed a qualification to enable him to be elected—for at this time all Members had to be possessed of a certain amount of freehold property. Of course this was known, but no "proof" existed. It took McClure some days to get his voice and strength, but some months or a few years after a [he] died of kidney disease. Why this Bill was so deadly opposed I forget, but suppose some interested in passing, others interested in opposing it.

In 1863 Governor Douglas was deservedly knighted[1] and in March 1864 his second term of office expired. At his retirement a grand banquet was given in his honor, I think at the Victoria Theatre.[2] Everybody was there, and it was a noble exposition of praise and satisfaction. Everybody knew Sir James and respected him, but great uncertainty was felt about his successor. At this banquet Sir James was presented with a casket inlaid with Cariboo gold in nuggets—the work made in Victoria.[3] Sir Matthew Begbie sat next Governor Douglas, and during the dinner Sir Matthew brought forward his everlasting pipe and smoked! This was universally considered a wilful breach of good manners, and highly disrespectful to Sir James, but I believe it to have been nothing more than a habit on the part of Sir Matthew, who at this time smoked and his guests too during dinner.

Sir James had lived down all his enemies of any consequence, retiring with honor. He was a very self-contained man—rarely giving his confidence to anyone, and to me scarcely ever, he considering me to be a "Radical"—his abhorrence. Before this we had not been on the most friendly footing, with which however politics had nothing to do, but I think arose from a dispute about some land at Constance Cove, which I believed belonged or ought to belong to me, but which was decided in favor of W. A. G. Young, who had been Colonial Secretary and had married his niece Miss Cowan. It was a mighty small affair to make a breech, but at this time the gold excitement continued, in fact had just arisen. The waggon road to Cariboo was the greatest of his works—a wonder at the time—as well in projection as the determination to carry it out to its completion. Of his bravery, courage, boldness and sagacity there is no question; he inspired respect—carried himself with dignity—natural to him, but which some supposed, put on. The Indians loved him—looked on him as a father or friend and felt certain of favor and justice at his hands; so much so that his name

---

[1]In December 1858 Douglas had been made a Companion of the Order of the Bath in recognition of his service as governor of Vancouver Island; in 1863, when he closed his term of office as governor of both Vancouver Island and British Columbia, he was made a Knight Commander of the same order.

[2]For a detailed account of the banquet in the Victoria Theatre on 10 March 1864 see the *Colonist*, 11 March 1864.

[3]The casket, whose purpose was to contain the address presented to Douglas on his retirement as governor of Vancouver Island, was later on display in a Victoria shop. A foot long, it was made of ten different kinds of wood, "heavily mounted and ornamented with Cariboo gold, resting on four massive gold dolphins." The chasing and embossing were carried out by Mr. Charles Bennett of Victoria, and the whole cost seven hundred dollars (see the *Colonist*, 19 and 20 April 1864).

and character extended from one end of the coast to the other and
to the Interior likewise. He was a man of temperate almost abstemious
habits—smoked in moderation but always on the verandah—at, but
never in, his own house. Early to bed—early to rise. A very indefatigable
worker, in fact the great fault he had was attending too much to details, a property probably inherited—arising from his HBCo's education.
Of his love for the Colony, none gainsay, trying ever to promote its
interest as well with HM Govt as the public.

Immediately after his retirement he took a trip to England,[1] as it
seems to be an understood thing that the old should not meet a new
Governor. It must be remembered that Governor Douglas had been Governor of two Colonies—that of Vancouver Island under representative
institutions and in 1859 [*sic: for* 1858] of the Mainland. In the latter
he exercised autocratic power, and laws and regulations were issued
in an autocratic manner beginning with "Whereas I Sir James Douglas
K.C.B. have been empowered &c. &c."[2] This autocratic power was
absolutely necessary on account of the gold excitement having burst
suddenly on the Mainland—and there being no material to form a
Council immediately, indeed Governor Douglas, when the excitement
first struck the country, assumed responsibility and command over it
—this step being subsequently upheld by HM Govt.

It must be remembered that at this time the HBCo had the exclusive
right by lease of trading in B. Columbia, i.e. the Mainland, which
rendered this step apparently high-handed and led to some complications with the HBCo but they had to acquiesce because it was quite
plain they were not able to manage the flood, and their lease was about
to expire.[3] Governor Douglas was determined that the trade of the
country should be had by British Columbia and the British & fortunately
at this time Free Trade virtually existed in V.I. Whatcom and other
places on the American side came into existence and with the usual
enterprise of the Americans, they tried to make the commercial centre
there and boasted they would build a road to Fort Hope and indeed
attempted to do so. In a short time they had a mule train, or pre-

---

[1]He was away for over a year, returning to Victoria in July 1865. His diary covering
the trip is in the Provincial Archives. See also W. Kaye Lamb, "Sir James Goes
Abroad," *BCHQ* 3 (1939) : 283-92.

[2]Since Douglas was not knighted until his retirement this preamble is obviously
inaccurate. The early British Columbia Proclamations follow the regulation pat-
tern.

[3]The HBC's licence of exclusive trade was due to expire on 30 May 1859, and
Douglas revoked it by his proclamation of 3 November 1858 at Fort Langley.

tended to have, going to Hope, but it turned out that the mules only went a short distance and returned in the evening a little altered in color! Of course this was intended to boom the place and for a time succeeded—business and other houses sprung up there.

To counteract this, Mr. Douglas declared the Port of Entry for the Mainland to be in Victoria and all goods destined for this region must be entered at Victoria and the duties paid thereon, for Douglas had imposed Customs dues—Port and Harbor dues likewise came into existence. One of HM Ships was stationed at the mouth of the river to prevent smuggling and to see that all vessels had a proper clearance. Licenses for a period were granted American boats (for we had not any) to carry goods and passengers up river and they were soon put on and so Whatcom rather slowly decayed and the trade centred in Victoria.[1] At this time attempts were made to make Esquimault the commercial centre, but failed, the population was in Victoria. Governor Douglas at this time laid out a townsite at Langley, to be called Derby, but soon Colonel Moody and Engineers arrived, together with necessary officers for the Mainland, such as Hamley—Brew—Begbie —some others and lots of parsons—the carrion was there! Moody objected to Langley so Westminster took its place and was to have been called Queenboro, but as a question arose as to whether it ought to be Queenboro or Queensboro, the question of name was referred home and the answer came New Westminster.[2] This alteration in the site of the City favored Victoria of course, but soon a city arose at Westminster and then, as a matter of course, there arose jealousies about Victoria being the Port of Entry and so Westminster became the established centre for the Mainland, but nevertheless Victoria kept the trade. All British goods came to free trade Victoria—and the quantity was enormous—and so did those from the States, for the navigation to and of the Fraser, at this time not generally known, was as it really was, considered dangerous. Had the town remained at Langley what would have been the result? Of course everything was prosperous in Victoria, but a drawback took place in the following year, when most of the newcomers left, not finding the Fraser full of gold. Cariboo afterwards came to the front and prosperity again arose, but in 1863 things had become bad and growing worse. Too much credit had been given and so the payments were not forthcoming. Lots of British goods were sold

[1]See above, p. 160.
[2]See above, p. 161.

very cheaply, but the commission merchants got their commission and something more. In some instances American goods were returned to San Francisco, still Victoria had risen to a city of 5,000 or 6,000, but the business was not sufficient for the whole and there was not any local production—things looked and were rather blue—very blue as compared with previous phenomenal prosperity—and Cariboo began to give out.

The tax on real estate and the direct taxes gave great dissatisfaction, as they had to be paid but once a year in a lump sum, which many thought very large and so some began to think Free Trade not so very good after all. The expense of Government had increased of course very much, but still was not excessive and no one received inordinate salaries. Political agitators arose, to do away with "Nepotism" and high salaries, and some went in for customs dues—De Cosmos in the latter and indeed in all—and it began to be thought that the whole country could be more economically administered by one government, but Free Trade stood in the way of this. In the midst of this unrest and surmises of the future and a wondering what sort of Governor would take the place of Governor Douglas, for no one supposed a new man would be so interested personally in the interest of the Colony, two new Governors came to the front: Mr. Kennedy as Governor of Vancouver Island and Mr. Seymour, Governor of British Columbia.[1]

The Government of Vancouver Island undergoes no change. It is still governed by representative institutions—but the Mainland becomes a Crown Colony, with a Council composed of a majority of officials, the minority consisting of elected representatives[2]—one then is a free government, the other virtually the contrary. Under such conditions and previous ones, there must needs be jealousies—each Government would try to do the best to promote the prosperity of its own people—there is Free Trade in Victoria and direct taxation: on the Mainland, Customs and other dues, the two countries are at variance therefore—possibly each one naturally trying to get the better of the other.

Governor Kennedy is received with acclamation—new brooms sweep

---

[1] Arthur Edward Kennedy (1810-83), governor of Vancouver Island 1864-66, and Frederick Seymour (1820-69), governor of British Columbia 1864-69. For further details see Ormsby, "Some Irish Figures"; and Margaret A. Ormsby, "Frederick Seymour, The Forgotten Governor," *BC Studies* 22 (Summer 1974): 3-25.

[2] The first Legislative Council of the mainland colony of British Columbia met at New Westminster on 21 January 1864 with a total of thirteen members, only five of whom were elected.

clean—and the first question that arises is the housing of Governor Kennedy, for Douglas resided in his own house, and there was not any "Government House," I think he was first housed in Mr. Trutch's residence[1]—he, Mrs. Kennedy and two nice daughters.[2] There was a good deal of talk about the site. Kennedy preferred the Esquimault Road as being midway between the "fleet" and the city—convenient to both or neither—others believed the Government Buildings or ground there at James Bay should be the place, but in the end Cary Castle was purchased from Mrs. Miles and this became Government House.[3] I remember opposing for some reason or other (which I forget) the erection of a Government House and other matters and a meeting took place at the Victoria Theatre.[4] When I attempted to speak there, I was met with hisses and no end of uproar, so could say but little and felt very small. Anyone on the same side met with a similar fate and it was known afterwards that Governor Kennedy and his Secretary Wakeford[5] were in one of the boxes with curtains closed. They must have been delighted, because it was hurled against me that I was only inebriated by jealousy and that the days of the Douglas regime had gone bye—never to be resumed. Of course it was a packed meeting—such were common enough, but in truth I was very foolish to have taken publicly any part in this housebuilding affair, as I ought to have known it would be set down to spite. I had no such feeling—possibly expense governed me. Anyhow it was a good thing that I was defeated—as we now had a

[1]When the House of Assembly refused to provide a residence for the governor, on the ground that this was the responsibility of the British government, Kennedy rented Fairfield House, the residence of J. W. Trutch, who was away on a private trip to Britain from September 1864 to June 1865 (Andrews, *Trutch*, p. 9).

[2]Kennedy's elder daughter, Elizabeth Henrietta, was married in London on 17 June 1867 to Lord Gilford, who had been in command of H.M.S. *Tribune* while on this station 1862-64 (*Colonist*, 19 and 20 August 1867). Georgiana, who was also in Victoria 1864-66, died unmarried.

[3]See above, p. 177.

[4]For a full account of "The Monster Meeting" see *Colonist*, 12 April 1864. JSH was "received with mingled groans, hisses and cheers," and his first attempt to speak was cut short by "tremendous cries, hisses, catcalls, etc." However, he still attempted to justify the conduct of the House of Assembly in refusing to pay for a residence for the governor, on the ground that "the Duke of Newcastle had, without consulting this colony, doubled the salaries on the Civil List."

[5]Henry Wakeford was appointed acting colonial secretary on 27 May 1864 (Vancouver Island, *Government Gazette*, 31 May 1864). He was later appointed auditor of Vancouver Island and at the request of Governor Seymour retained that office until 31 December 1866, after the union of the colonies (see Wakeford to the Governor, 19 November 1866, H. Wakeford Correspondence, Colonial Correspondence, PABC).

Government House, which came into use in after days and helped to settle the "Capital" question.

At the first meeting of the Legislature after Governor Kennedy's arrival the Estimates of course came down, and the Legislature was no little surprised to find more government officers and more salaries—no retrenchment but an increase of burdens—which would not have mattered much had the place been prosperous, but this additional expense gave advantages to political agitators—the cry, the Colony could not afford it, and I remember writing a leader or letter stating too much government &c. and that it was useless erecting a Nasmith [Nasmyth] hammer to forge needles—some much more simple contrivance would suit and be more appropriate.[1] When I saw Governor Kennedy the next day on official business, he threw this quietly at my head! Anyhow under direct taxation, trade licenses &c. &c. the way to meet the increased expenditure was not pleasant and did not meet with much favor—indeed the question of King Log and King Stork was not unfrequently quoted in private conversation.[2]

I suppose Governor Kennedy received advice to endeavour to unite the Colonies,[3] for at this time Confederation was uppermost in Canada. Governor Kennedy told me that he thought it might be thought by some to be better to remain separate in order that Vancouver Island should be able to make her own terms with the Canadian Government as he looked on it as certain, that B. Columbia would join the Canadian Confederation. I know Governor Douglas disliked the idea of Union, because he foresaw the Free Trade in this case would go by the board and he believed that Free Trade would be the means of keeping the trade in Victoria and causing her ultimately to become a large city like Hong Kong and Singapore. On the other hand the U.S. Government disliked the free trade Colony, because she dabbled so very much in smuggling and further menaced her trade and gave advantages to

---

[1] See the editorial in the Victoria *Evening Express*, 18 April 1864.

[2] In Aesop's fable of *The Frogs asking for a King*, Jupiter first sent the frogs a log of wood, which they despised; he then sent them a stork, which devoured them.

[3] On 15 June 1863 Newcastle had written to Governor Douglas: "I should have much desired, if it had been possible, that these two colonies should have formed one Government. I am aware that the prevailing feeling is at present strongly adverse to such a measure"—hence the appointment of a governor for each colony. Kennedy was asked by Cardwell (30 April 1864) to let the government have his views as soon as he had assessed the situation for himself. Cf. also p. 208n1. The relevant despatches will be found in Great Britain, Parliament, *Papers relative to the Proposed Union of British Columbia and Vancouver Island*, 1866 (Cmd. 3667, 1st series).

British goods—that is people would come here from America to buy! HM Govt likewise did not like to be troubled with complaints from the U.S. Free Trade in Vancouver Island alongside an intelligent people and civilized country, is and was a very different matter to having an isolated spot devoted to Free Trade—a free trade city, surrounded by a semi-civilized unenlightened but industrious and producing people.

Now then turn to Westminster. Here Governor Seymour reigned, but having a Council in part official and in part elective, he was not an autocrat. A Government House had been erected there at Sapperton[1] —and a Legislative Hall built by the Engineers at Sapperton likewise, which was nicknamed Noah's Ark. It was a fine building in design, substantial and sightly inside, that is to say had it been properly finished and decent means of warming it erected.[2]

Of course being a separate Colony it had all the officers and offices necessary—and the officers were undoubtedly of a superior description —for the most part educated to official duties and of the upper class and taking all in all were socially gentlemen and very nice fellows.

---

[1]In 1859-60 a house had been erected in the Royal Engineers' camp at Sapperton (a mile up the Fraser from New Westminster) to serve as a residence for Colonel Moody, officer commanding, and also as Government House during Governor Douglas's visits to the mainland colony. When the Engineers went back to England in 1863, a wing was added, and the structure then served as the Government House of British Columbia from the arrival of Governor Seymour in April 1864 until 25 May 1868, when the capital was moved to Victoria. See Plate 21.

[2]Erected by the Royal Engineers in 1859 as "a Temporary barrack to accommodate single men" (R. C. Moody to Governor Douglas, 25 July 1859, British Columbia, Lands and Works Department, Correspondence Outward, March—August, 1859, PABC), this building was afterwards used as a military chapel (ibid.; and Violet E. Sillitoe, *Early Days in British Columbia* [Vancouver: Evans & Hastings, Printers, 1922], p. 8). The first Legislative Council of the mainland colony met during 1864 in private, in a room which had formed part of the officers' quarters, vacated when the detachment was disbanded in November 1863. But at the opening of the second session of the second Legislative Council on 12 January 1865, the meetings were thrown open to the general public. Hence larger accommodation was required, and "the old Sappers' Church" (*Colonist*, 9 March 1879, quoting the *Mainland Guardian*) was taken over. The New Westminster *British Columbian*, 14 January 1865, commented on the "severe, almost naked simplicity" of the interior: "The members sit at a long table in the middle of the room. The presiding member's chair is on a raised dais at the head of the board. The main body of the hall is divided from the entrance by a partition running across the room, and from the public seats by a railing. Round the sides of the room seats were provided for the ladies." In March 1879 the old building, said to be "remarkably well put together," was raised on jacks for repairs to the underpinning, and a strong wind "toppled it over with a mighty crash" (Victoria *Standard*, 8 March 1879, quoting New Westminster *Mainland Guardian* and *Dominion Pacific Herald*).

Generally speaking all were inimical to Victoria—i.e. they wished to do their best and make Westminster occupy the commercial centre. Of course Customs dues were imposed, but the duties were made payable on the price of goods at the last port of shipment, which of course happened to be Victoria, excepting indeed they were *in transitu*. This was rather alarming, perhaps unfair, from a Victorian point of view as it gave an advantage apparently to direct shipments from abroad, notably the U.S. As a matter of fact Governor Seymour said that Victoria on a mill pond was only fit for a fishing village and would soon be reduced to such.[1] This had a dispiriting influence on many—but it encouraged smuggling from Victoria—a lucrative business. The Legislative Council of course did their best to reduce Victoria and their public utterances were to say the least irritating, causing Victorian irritating rejoinders in return. Westminster must be the seaport and should be made by artificial laws and so forth, but no means existed of improving or even surveying the River to render navigation safe—or at all events better known and less intricate.

They reckoned wrongly, for the trade still centered in Victoria, because she was on the sea side and had Esquimault to boot, further had considerable capital and supplied virtually the whole country with goods—recklessly without doubt in many instances—and without any adequate security—which pretty nearly swamped Victoria merchants in the very near future, for the debtors did not pay. There was reckless competition and lots of commission merchants. There cannot be a doubt but that Victoria—her goods, her investments in the mines at Cariboo—loans to miners and merchants, developed Cariboo and in return Victoria was the Mecca for all Cariboo miners.

This condition of things was most displeasing to Westminster, its Governor and Council and undoubtedly very much ill feeling and jealousy existed between the two. In addition Westminster (i.e. B. Columbia) found the expense of government very heavy—in fact they had the same complaint on this score as Victoria, but the former had a sort of consoling idea, that soon the tide of commerce and prosperity would run up the River, so a little inconvenience and expense must be borne, temporarily as they flattered themselves it would be. Borrowing capital abroad in these days was not so easy as now and indeed

---

[1] Cf. Ormsby, *British Columbia*, p. 223-24: "In the Royal City both the Governor and the editor of the *British Columbian* were quoted as having referred to Victoria as being located 'on a frogpond.' " In return the editor of the *Colonist* on 9 April 1867 spoke of New Westminster as "the City of Stumps."

by [*sic: for* but?] little practised as neither side had very good security to offer, so in cases of emergency money was borrowed locally from anyone who would advance it, the rate of interest being usually about ten per cent per annum. The truth is both Colonies were poor, at least they fancied themselves so—and I think just now erroneously— but at the time I agreed.

Hamley was a very strict and upright head of the Customs Department. Nothing escaped him at Westminster. On one occasion the Governor gave a Ball—the wines went from Victoria, but on arriving at Westminster, Hamley would not allow them to pass until duty had been paid! but I really do not know just now how the question was settled. The wines undoubtedly went to the ball-room (Noah's Ark I think) but suddenly intense cold set in—the wines—beer and beverages were frozen in the bottles—there were no means of warming the room, and so the people were frozen too and it was difficult to get the steam up, or be jolly under such a complication of difficulties. I forget how long the River remained frozen and closed to navigation.[1]

Thus things went on for a year or two, bickerings and jealousies increasing, but during this period business had gone from worse to worse in both places, perhaps most in Victoria: Cariboo mines did not now do so well as formerly—the miners were neither so rich, so reckless as formerly—many were poor. The merchants were in a bad state; the packers to whom huge credits had been given without adequate security could not pay, but the goods were gone, tremendous losses—so they were obliged to draw in their horns and abolish this reckless credit system— the banks too had been carried away by excitement—had losses and they too became hardened—business was bad all round and at the same time there were too many merchants to do the amount of business required either then or previously—the stores were full of imported goods without any sale. Exporters complained of want of returns, or that goods were sold at a loss. There were no manufacturers, no productions of any consequence, no settled agriculturalists to make up for the other

[1]On 28 February 1865 the members of the British Columbia Legislative Council gave a ball in their council chamber, i.e., Noah's Ark. The thermometer in the ballroom stood at 15 degrees F. despite the stoves (*Colonist*, 4 March 1865), and H. M. Ball remarked in his diary (MS, PABC), that "the supper would have been good but it was all a case of frozen chicken & jellies. Beer & soda water all froze and burst the bottles." Governor Seymour's ball was given the next evening, in the cosier confines of Government House, and Ball found this much more enjoyable. The winter of 1864-65 was the severest for many years, and the *Enterprise* was ice-bound at New Westminster for several days after the ball.

shrinkage. Smuggling had been considerably checked by agents of the U.S. Government residing in Victoria and keeping watch—but with some it was said to be made all right. The expenses of government went on continuously increasing—Kennedy was not at all particular about this. Retrenchment was demanded, some little saving made by cutting down salaries, but this made but little difference. Dissatisfaction too existed about the real estate and license taxes—the whole taxation apparently rested on the few—but they did not consider that the few reaped all the benefit—owners of farming land growled most loudly. Free Trade began to be more and more doubted—and Union with B. Columbia talked freely about—it being thought that by this means Victoria would certainly continue to be the commercial centre! jealousy, envy and rivalry more or less done away with—the expense of government diminished and made within the means of the united Colony. It was somehow understood also that HM Govt wished the amalgamation.[1]

Wakeford, Governor Kennedy's private secretary, was an unpopular man—he was considered a sneak and a spy. Kennedy was an Irishman anyhow. No one trusted Wakeford—public and private talk were carried to the Governor—public servants of all grades were suspicious of him, and so the Executive became somewhat unpopular also. I do not suppose the devil was as bad as painted, but the dissatisfaction all tended to promote the Union of the Colonies.

It must however not be supposed that the people of B. Columbia or Victoria were at this time badly off—the contrary was the case, for in 1863 the production of gold in Cariboo reached its highest point. Miners spent money lavishly—chiefly in public houses and dance houses and extravagance was general. Miners thought the gold would last for ever, so those who had made money wasted it—they said they could get more where this came from. These lucky ones were few—only a

---

[1]In his message to the Legislative Council regarding the site of the capital, 27 March 1867 (Great Britain, Parliament, House of Commons, ... *Correspondence ... on the Subject of a Site for the Capital of British Columbia*, 1868 [P.P. 483], pp. 6-7), Seymour said (p. 7) that "on his acceptance of office in this Colony, the present Governor was instructed to use all means in his power to bring about an entire Union of the two Colonies"; yet he "stoutly opposed either the federation or the legislative union of the colonies" (Ormsby, "Frederick Seymour," p. 10). When he returned to England in September 1865 for his marriage, he found that the Colonial Office, the Treasury, the Foreign Office, and the Admiralty were all "very anxious for a union of the two colonies" (Seymour to H. P. P. Crease, 1 February 1866, Correspondence Inward, 1864-1868, Crease Collection, PABC, quoted in Ormsby, *British Columbia*, pp. 217-18). And cf. p. 204n3 above.

few creeks yielded abundant[ly?]. There were a very large number of miners who had made nothing, were poor and could not pay their bills—they had lived on credit—in fact the credit system was general in Cariboo also—large credits given on the supposed ground, that various claims would pay and reimburse the packers and merchants in time— but such did not turn out to be the case. A few were lucky, by far the larger number the contrary, but of course it was hoped that the unlucky one would succeed in following years. Those who had money in many instances used it to develop new claims and lost it. Victoria people too had many shares in mines which in the end were failures; so one class seemed to live on the other. But about this time the yield of gold began to diminish—and much of that got cost more in the getting than it was worth, which did not help the suppliers much, so things began to look a little blue—coupled with the antagonism at Westminster made some doubt. In fact everything had been overdone— the suppliers too many. Altho so much gold was taken from Cariboo it all found its way out of the country to pay for imports. Miners and others did not take to agriculture or originate producing trades or enterprises—so the lands remained unoccupied and manufactures none.

Such was the condition of affairs when the new parliament (the 3rd) came into existence in 1863. It lasted to 1866. When beginning to write, I had no intention of writing history and indeed do not pretend to do so now, but only personal recollections—so dates may be a little confused occasionally.

Of course I was Speaker in this parliament also, but do not mean to say much about its business—those who wish to know may hunt it up in the newspapers of the times.

After 1863 the gold yield began to diminish and in a year or two became less—so business became bad and merchants were almost ruined—government expenses were great—taxation as ever was thought excessive—opponents too on the Mainland. To remedy matters Union of the Colonies was seriously thought of and in the end the House of Assembly 1866 [*sic: for* 1865] asked for the Union of the Colonies[1]— like the apothecary—"My poverty but not my will consents."

---

[1]The resolution of the Vancouver Island House of Assembly asking for the union of the two colonies was introduced by Amor De Cosmos, passed on 27 January 1865 by a majority of eight to four, and reported by Kennedy to Cardwell on 21 March 1865 (*Papers Relative to the Proposed Union of British Columbia and Vancouver Island*, pp. 8-11).

Of course Westminster had to follow suit, because at all events the government officials were the majority in the Council.

In due course the case was laid before HM Govt, who nothing loth but probably very pleased passed an Act amalgamating the two Colonies and so the Union of the Colonies was consummated.[1] The representative institutions of Vancouver Island ceased to exist and Vancouver Island became merged into the Crown Colony and so became part of the Crown Colony of British Columbia. The Customs dues and tariff were imposed by the same Imperial enactment on Vancouver Island so *Free Trade ceased to exist,* but I think the system had been somewhat encroached upon in V.I. previously.

This Union was not in reality brought about by the failure of Free Trade, for on the other side depression and almost bankruptcy had resulted from reckless credit given by them—and also by wildcat speculations in mines and so forth—the merchants were on their last legs; the stores however were still full of imported goods—either for sale by commission or personal property obtained possibly by credit or notes payable. There did not appear to be any sale for these goods, for credit being curtailed and the miners depressed, many miners poor, so many supplies were not required and moreover there was not sufficient gold to pay for them—Victoria backed down from her former position of risking all for the development of the mines. The fact is the primary consideration of Victoria at this time was the success of the mines— these failing, the country would go to pot. Free Trade was but a secondary consideration. People were here to make money rapidly and go away—they had not any interest in and could not patiently wait for the revival of business by Free Trade, export &c. &c. and so forth. They had come here under peculiar exciting conditions and these conditions failing—they failed too—in fact the mercantile population were far in excess of the demand at this depressed time. Of course many left—others could not. Naval supplies at this time helped many along —in fact this was the only safe business, but soon HM Govt sent out her own supplies[2]—indeed the whole condition of things was artificial, ephemeral and not able to continue—a sort of boom.

---

[1]The Act of Union (29 & 30 Vict. c. 67) was passed on 6 August 1866 and proclaimed in British Columbia and Vancouver Island on 19 November 1866.
[2]See Gough, *The Royal Navy,* p. 192: "By the close of 1863 . . . a small staff [had been brought out] from England to take charge of the store houses at Esquimalt. Stores were then transferred from Valparaiso to Esquimalt and provisions were sent directly from England to Esquimalt. . . ."

It must not be thought that this resolution of the House was brought about unanimously or suddenly—altho the depression was more or less sudden—annexation and all this sort of thing was spoken of, and many thought the solid basis of Free Trade had been lost sight of, which was true. Personally I forget what part I played,[1] but now I feel that Free Trade would not have answered, the surrounding conditions being so different to those of other places. Had V.I. been a mere rock with foreigners surrounding, the case would have been otherwise, but being a large island—capable of great development—and so having a diverse interest—Free Trade was more or less out of place—under it agriculture and manufactures could not succeed. It is quite true that Free Trade need not have been continued on every article, but this would have made more complications, more expense and still greater antagonism and hatred to and from New Westminster—a country likely to become great and prosperous, and as I said before the cost of government had become too great for the number of inhabitants to pay. Free Trade is all very well for commission agents and middlemen and the foreigner, but not for the public generally in a new country. Import dues again collects the more, more easily and by degrees, and can be made as well for the encouragement of productive enterprises as for taxation and revenue. Anyhow I think the Union altho doubtful at the time has been proved [to] be beneficial by occurrences since.

Now mark what happened. As soon as the Colonies were amalgamated Governor Seymour thought that the goods in the shops and warehouses at Victoria should pay the Customs dues, that they would have paid under the Customs dues of New Westminster! This was of course repudiated by us and in the end no dues were collected on goods already here and possibly some allowance made for goods *in transitu* —this is doubtful.[2] Anyhow a whole cargo arrived for the HBCo only a few days before the Union! Now then the merchants of Victoria had

[1]According to the report of the debate in the *Papers relative to the Proposed Union of British Columbia and Vancouver Island*, p. 9, JSH declared himself "as much in favour of free trade as ever.... He did not consider that free trade had anything whatever to do with the present depression.... His own impression was that free trade was the best policy, both hitherto and still.... His opinion was that union with British Columbia and free trade in Vancouver Island would conduce to the best interests of both Colonies and also be a very large saving in expense."

[2]The British Columbia Customs Ordinance no. 3 15 February 1865 was repealed by no. 18 of 25 March 1867, An Ordinance to amend the Duties of Customs. It had been pointed out that goods shipped from Vancouver Island to British Columbia

large stocks of goods, spirits, wines and so forth on hand—increased theoretically really in value by the amount of dues imposed—to those who could hold them for a time. Now the fact is that this very thing set the merchants on their legs again and prevented many bankruptcies —altho business did not increase immediately—some could sell out to better advantage and go away too, and thus a very considerable amount of the business depression in process of time disappeared—but the gold yield went on diminishing. It may be said that Victorians for a present benefit had killed the goose that laid the golden eggs. I think not—the goose at first was all right, but she had laid all her eggs—and the consumers in want.

[Volume V]

Of course in all hitherto written I had a hand in, but they were public matters, so it may be as well here to say a few words about private life. In the main no doubt it went on as private life usually does, neither much better nor much worse. At all events, I was very busy professionally and politically—home did not see me very much as my office was in town, in fact the same as now, and in addition patients often kept me at their residences. At this time I had the same number of children as now,[1] but when Cecilia lay confined with one of the children, my little girl Daisy took croup. She was attended by Dr. Ray of the *Satellite* but died.[2] I did not know so much of croup then as now—in fact it was for the most part a very infrequent disease here. Daisy was a little blue-eyed flaxen-haired, fair child—full of pleasant tricks, and always hid herself behind the door in order to frighten me when she heard me coming in. Poor little thing she was a pet and

---

were being charged with a greater amount of duty than goods shipped from any other country. See Great Britain, Parliament, *Further Papers Relative to the Union of British Columbia and Vancouver Island*, 1867 (Cmd. 3852, 1st series), p. 8.
[1]In 1892 JSH had four children living: Catherine Amelia (1855-1922), who had married George A. McTavish in 1877 (*Colonist*, 5 December 1877); James Douglas (1858-1919); Henry (Harry) Dallas (1859-1912); and Edith Louisa (1862-1939, who had married William Ralph Higgins in 1889 (ibid., 24 April 1889).
[2]James Douglas Helmcken was born on 2 February 1858 (Victoria *Times*, 2 April 1919); he was baptized on 25 April 1858 (Christ Church register of baptisms, copy, PABC). Daisy died on 11 March 1858 (see above, p. 152n3). Dr. Ray has not been identified. H.M.S. *Satellite* was on this station 1857-60; but in 1858 her surgeon was Henry Piers and her assistant surgeon Peter W. Wallace. Also on this station in 1858 was H.M.S. *Havannah,* and one Henry Johns Ray was serving in her, but as assistant paymaster, not as surgeon. Possibly JSH's memory supplied him with the name of "Dr. Ray" from his encounter at York Factory in 1847 with Dr. John Rae.

methinks I see her now. We buried the poor little thing in the garden and I made an oval of white daisies with a cross in the centre over the grave. The holly stands there now—my first-born was buried there also.

Of course domestics were still very scarce, at this time Jim Todd's [Tod's] mother[1] nursed Cecilia, but soon Chinese servants became common and we had one.[2] When I look back now, domestic affairs seemed to have been carried on pretty roughly and Cecilia had more work and less comfort than she ought to have had and would have were it now—but at this time I cared little for household matters, and the accommodations were small and very indifferent. Nevertheless we managed to have little dinner parties occasionally—Elliott, Walkem[3] and such like being often present: they were very jolly fellows. Occasionally an immigrant would live with us, and we had two chiefly—Shouvert a young Canadian and [blank in MS] for it was by no means unusual for people to feed young men until they could find something to do or go home again, a circumstance of frequent occurrence. A young man from Yorkshire —his father a miller of large business and well-to-do. Fotherby gave him a letter and his father some money; the latter being spent somehow or other, he took to being a pie man, and carried the usual heated tin apparatus about, selling pies in the street or to the miners at public houses, and he said he did well! He was a little wild: married a very

---

[1]Catherine Birstone, with whom John Tod had formed an alliance some time before the birth of his son James c. 1818 (see Sproat, "John Tod," pp. 231-32).
[2]Cf. the comment by Florence Goodfellow in her *Memories of Pioneer Life in British Columbia* (Wenatchee, Wash., 1945). She was the daughter of Lewis Nunn Agassiz, chief constable at Hope 1862-64 (see Agassiz to Colonial Secretary, 26 October 1863, L. N. Agassiz Correspondence, Colonial Correspondence, PABC; and F. J. Hatch, "The British Columbia Police 1858-1871" [M.A. Thesis, University of British Columbia, 1955], appendix), and she writes (p. 14): "While we were in Hope a shipload of coolies arrived from China and all the families got some for house boys. We got one bound for two years. The Chinese merchants would bring them out by the shipload and bind them out to work until they had paid their passage money. Ours was a good boy and it was not long until he was quite a help. The Chinamen, like everyone else, had come for gold, and at the end of the two years he had paid his passage and saved enough money to buy himself an outfit and he left us to seek his fortune."
[3]Andrew Charles Elliott (1829?-99), an Irish lawyer, arrived in 1859; he sat as magistrate for Lillooet in the Legislative Councils of 1865 and 1866. George Anthony Walkem (1834-1908) came in 1862; he sat in the Legislative Council 1864-70. Each of them became premier of British Columbia after Confederation. For further details see S. W. Jackman, *Portraits of the Premiers: An Informal History of British Columbia* (Sidney, B.C.: Gray's Publishing Co., 1969), pp. 43-50, 31-40.

unsuitable girl—carried on—spent his remittances wastefully—and in due season had a child—a boy. The father went up-country—to mine. A few weeks after her confinement at Mrs. Mason's house, the mother asked Mrs. Moss[1] to take care of her child for a short time, as she had to go to California. The woman never returned, but Mrs. Mason kept the child and brought him up as one of their own—he grew a fine-looking boy. The father got into trouble bye and bye—he robbed the post office, was sent to prison, this being the last I heard of him save that he died. The grandparents written to, never answered the letter, in fact had discarded their son, who it seems had been pretty wild, before his arrival—no uncommon thing—and often no doubt with great relief to the people at home—they go out. The boy became a sailor with a pious Captain—and I believe went home, where he was not acknowledged—he came back, went to China in the ship, and then unfortunately broke his leg—the ship left without him, but the boy returned to Victoria. I think he turned out rather wild afterwards but what ultimately became of him, I know not.

Now the above example is rather unusual, but it will give the key to the career of many a young fellow who attracted by the gold diggings left home, often with the delight of relations—sometimes the contrary. Those who worked here and roughed it, did well and have become great, but a very great number went to the bad, as indeed many of them probably would even if they had remained at home or gone elsewhere.

In 1865 Cecilia and Lady Douglas went to the opening of something on Church Hill—platforms had been erected, the weather turned out bad, both Lady Douglas and Cecilia took cold.[2] Very little notice was taken of this, and my wife kept about as well as she was able, but soon pneumonia resulted and in a few days the end unhappily came, after having given birth to a boy. Mrs. R. Finlayson kindly took charge of

---

[1]Mrs. Charles Moss was "a noted midwife," according to Higgins, *The Mystic Spring*, p. 405.

[2]No ceremony in 1864-65 for which platforms were erected on Church Hill has been identified. JSH may be thinking of the laying of the foundation stone of the Female Infirmary at Spring Ridge (later the Royal Jubilee Hospital) on the afternoon of 23 November 1864. "The frame of the building [had] already been erected, and the flooring of the ground floor laid" (Victoria *Evening Express*, 23 November 1864). On this "platform," as the *Colonist*, 24 November 1864, calls it, "a number of ladies and gentlemen interested in the undertaking" had gathered before the time appointed. Among these was observed Lady Douglas, a patroness of the institution; the name of her daughter, Mrs. Helmcken, does not, however, appear. The day was said to be fine; but the November weather

this poor little thing for a few days, but on returning home he died.[1]
I think he had been accidentally injured. He had a tooth when born,
and in this respect resembled his grandfather. Poor Cecilia was buried
in the churchyard and the two babies who had been lying in the garden
were buried with her.[2] She had been a good mother and wife—but
hardly used by the absence of servants. Indeed in looking back I am
almost led to the belief that under more favorable conditions she
might have lived—but who knows? Dr. Powell attended her.[3] Mrs.
Douglas and I think Mrs. Irving (Ma'am Grace)[4] nursed her well—
but I was but little at home and probably underrated the extent of
disease—for I never attended any of my own family when ill.

The House happened to be in session at this time—a pretty excited
time—and the usual resolution of condolence came from the Assembly.
Public duty had to yield to private loss and soon I had to be in the
House again, for there was no one else to preside and so business could

---

could easily have "turned out bad," as JSH says, by the time that the Rev. Mr.
Cridge had given the history of the institution, the stone had been laid by the
Mayoress, Mrs. Thomas Harris, and speeches had followed from the Mayor, a
Presbyterian minister, John Hall, and an Anglican clergyman, R. J. Dundas (Victoria *Daily Chronicle*, 24 November 1864).
[1]Cecilia died on 4 February 1865 (*Colonist*, 6 February 1865), and the child,
Cecil Roderick Helmcken, was buried on 27 February 1865 (Christ Church
burial register, copy, PABC).
[2]Cecilia was buried on 8 February 1865 in the graveyard adjoining Christ
Church. By her own request, upon her coffin were placed the two small coffins containing the remains of her first-born son and her little daughter Daisy, who had
been buried in the garden beside the Helmcken home (*Colonist*, 9 February
1865; *Daily Chronicle*, 9 February 1865). When her newborn son died soon after,
the brick vault was opened, and his coffin was also placed there (see the detailed
account presented by Richard Lewis, the undertaker, dated March 1865 [HC]).
The table-tomb, its five inscriptions still decipherable, stands today in Pioneer
Square, alongside Christ Church Cathedral. JSH died on 1 September 1920 and
his body was cremated in Vancouver (Victoria *Times*, 4 September 1920). His
ashes were placed in his wife's tomb on 18 September 1920, and an inscription
was added to those commemorating Cecilia and the three children. In 1938 the
British Columbia Historical Association placed a stone tablet to the memory of
JSH and his family at the foot of the table-tomb.
[3]Israel Wood Powell (1836-1915) began to practise in Victoria in 1862 and was
elected to the House of Assembly in 1863. For further details see B. A. McKelvie,
"Lieutenant-Colonel Israel Wood Powell, M.D., C.M.," *BCHQ* 11 (1947):
35-54.
[4]Mrs. Grace Irving, a former resident of Stromness, died in 1884, aged seventy-two,
at the home of her daughter Ann Jane, who in 1865 had renounced her Presbyterian faith to marry an Irish Roman Catholic, William McNiff (see the *Colonist*, 21 and 23 May 1884; and the register of St. Andrew's Roman Catholic
Cathedral, Victoria, microfilm, PABC). Ma'am Grace's husband has not yet been
identified.

not be done without my presence. I may say here that politics are destructive of domestic duties—particularly when combined with other active professional affairs. None but those of independent means—independent for the most part of business, should be members of any legislature. It may be supposed that I was enamoured of political life— the supposition is wrong, for I never had any love for it, and would have quit if I could without dislocating matters, but having undertaken the duties I endeavoured honestly and earnestly to fulfill them. No doubt like others, I was sometimes wound up to a pitch of excitement and then would work night and day for the object, whatever it might be—and sometimes these were very important matters for the future. No doubt I sometimes magnified them, but in looking at the results now I have no reason to be dissatisfied with my actions—sometimes of course apparently wrong, but to me then considered right. Anyhow I had the feeling then to get out of the matter as soon as possible, and more not to marry again, because I supposed a stepmother would do harm to my four children. This may have been a mistake too—but I was not cut out for a domestic man.

Anyhow I had now to do the best I could and so Ma'am Grace (Mrs. Irving) took charge of my house and the children. She was a good honest honorable woman and liked the children—and everybody liked her, for she had nursed a great many with success. Personally I wanted very little—so my little dinners or evenings came to an end—I had to live for the sake of the children—there was nothing else to me worth living for. After a year or two, Irving wanted his wife home and then Mrs. Forman[1]—at this time only Jane—took her place, and a more hardworking, clean, conscientious woman never existed. The boys at this time had to go to school—the Collegiate School, in connexion with Christ Church on the Hill. Woods was master.[2] This School was estab-

---

[1]This lady has not yet been identified.
[2]The Collegiate School for boys was founded in 1860 by the Church of England in Victoria. The exact date of opening is uncertain. It was advertised to open on 28 May, and it was operating in July (*Colonist*, 22 May and 10 July 1860); but at the holiday examination in December Bishop Hills said "we have been in operation only some three months" (ibid., 25 December 1860). The schoolroom on Church Way was destroyed by fire in 1882 (ibid., 18 June 1882), but the school was carried on in a temporary schoolroom at Christ Church parsonage (ibid., 21 July 1883) until in 1894 it was moved to new quarters in Esquimalt, where boarders as well as day boys could be accommodated (ibid., 31 July and 23 September 1894). By 1898 the directories indicate that the school was back in Victoria, where it continued to operate until 1929 (ibid., 28 June 1929). Charles

lished in connection with Christ Church. When the land was set aside by the Hudson's Bay Co around the Church, the conditions were that the land should pay a yearly stipend to the incumbent, Mr. Cridge, and anything over should be used for a school in connexion with the Church. The land was afterwards sold by George Columbia[1]—the School was discontinued, but of late it has been pretended that Corrig School is the continuation of this original School.[2] I suppose the Bishop's conscience began to trouble him about the proper use of the land viz. Christ Church reserve. Anyhow I used to find time to assist the boys with their lessons, Latin and otherwise and on Sundays made them go through their Bible lessons. My boys tell me now that I used to whip them pretty severely on account of unwillingness or slowness about their lessons.

When James was 12½ years old [1870] he was sent to Scotland with Mrs. Forman, and Harry a year later. At this time I had £800—to my credit—this is all, but I judged I could by work support them at school. I always had the idea, that the proper education of a boy was to teach him how to work for his living—but I am a little too previous, because other things took place previous to their departure, which I am about to relate but from memory only.

After I had been in the service a few years I was recommended for a Chief-Tradership in the service and got it.[3] This was owing to the favor of Chief Factor Douglas, Tolmie, Work and Finlayson. So I no longer

---

Thomas Woods (1826-95) came to Victoria in 1860 as principal of the Collegiate School and retained the post until 1868, when he became archdeacon of Columbia and rector of Holy Trinity in New Westminster.

[1]The land was sold by George Hills, bishop of Columbia, after the fire in 1882. An "Appeal in behalf of the building fund of the College School, Victoria," dated 30 June 1882 and printed in the *Colonist*, 4 August 1882, includes in the "nucleus of the Proposed Building Fund . . . the money value of Three Town Lots, forming the old site on Church Hill."

[2]Corrig School was not founded until 1886 (see the *Catalogue of Corrig School. Victoria, B.C. An English and Classical Boarding School for Boys. 1886*, PABC). In his "Card to the Public" printed in this catalogue and dated 8 June 1886, the principal, the Rev. C. J. Brent, speaks of "opening a private school in Victoria." When in 1890 J. W. Church took over as principal, the name was changed to Corrig College and the prospectus issued at the time refers to "this Boarding and Day School, the oldest Private and Select College in the Province of British Columbia." *Victoria Illustrated* (Victoria, 1891), p. 28, calls Corrig College "the oldest private select boarding college in the Province. Its past history, dating back as it does to the sixties. . . ."

[3]JSH was appointed a chief trader on 13 April 1863 (HBC Archives, Commissioned Officers' Indentures and Agreements, A.33/3/fos. 252,253).

had my salary from the HBC and Puget Sound Co (£150) but had to be satisfied with a share of the profits of the trade with which in reality I had nothing to do. The fur trade was bad at this time—so sometimes I only received a couple of hundred pounds a year or less, but one year it ran up to £600—this of course being made up of arrears, for the sales of furs sometimes took place years after they had been caught, but the "outfit" paying for the cost of such furs was charged to the year of their purchase from the Indians, so that my first annual income was small—but the arrears made it up, as soon we had (i.e. all commissioned officers) an allowance for board, the mess being done away with. This went on for four or five years, and then the HBCo became a joint stock company[1] and a number of Factors and Traders had to be got rid of under a new organization. I was one of the number to be got rid of and my interest (a winter partner) was calculated to be I think eight hundred pounds, which of course I had to take, but asked for another year's allowance, which of course was not granted and could not be. This £800 is what I had in the Bank of the HBCo when I sent my children home. Things of course looked rather blue, but the Company engaged my services as surgeon to look after their ships and servants generally.[2] So that with the salary—practice and work—I felt if I had health, that I could manage to pay the school expenses of the children—and they were sent at Mr. Grahame's[3] recommendations to Mr.

[1]For full details see the chapter entitled "International Finance Society," in Rich, *Hudson's Bay Company. . . . Vol. III.*

[2]On 26 July 1870 JSH wrote to the secretary of the HBC (draft, HC) accepting the proposals made in the company's letters of 8 February and 13 May. Only the second of these two letters appears to be in HC. In it W. G. Smith refused JSH's request for two years' leave of absence before his retirement: the "change as regards your position was considered necessary" and "was no fault of yours," but to grant leave would establish a precedent. In a further letter dated 6 October 1870 Smith assured JSH that "the arrangement entered into with you is not intended to interfere in any way with your retired interest under the Deed Poll" and promised to attend to the "Accounts for the board and education of your son at Jedburgh," charging these to JSH's account with the company. Presumably JSH's appointment as surgeon to the company in Victoria (cf. p. 220 below) was offered to him in the HBC's letter of 8 February 1870 mentioned above.

[3]James Allan Grahame (1825-1905) came to Victoria from Fort Vancouver in 1860 and was later stationed in New Caledonia. By 1874 he had become inspecting chief factor, in charge of the Western Department. For further details see the obituary in the *Colonist,* 20 June 1905. His son Harry was at school in Jedburgh with the Helmcken boys (see the prize list in the *Colonist,* 3 September 1874, "Young Vancouver at Cricket and School").

Fyfe's academy "The Nest" [blank in MS: Jedburgh] Scotland.[1] I may here state that Mr. Fyfe did his duty in every respect by the boys and I had every reason to be pleased as well with him as their progress—as also Mrs. Fyfe's maternal care. Moreover he taught them to be "abstainers" —a most valuable lesson, which they remember to this day.

I felt rather downcast at leaving the service, for altho I had a large and increasing practice, somehow or other it brought me in very little —I did not like charging miners and so forth who seemed (but were often not) poor and I felt a sort of repugnance to charge because my father-in-law happened to be Governor, at which my father-in-law laughed and gently hinted that I was a goose. Anyhow being in the Company's service I had qualms about trespassing on those in private practice, of whom there were now some practitioners, such as Dr. Johnson [Johnston?]—Trimble—and others.[2] In this manner no wonder my practice brought me in but little, particularly when it is recollected that my constituents (they were really poor) considered I ought to attend them for nothing for services rendered and probably I did so for a like cause for favors to come. This applies more to the time during which I was Member for Esquimault—the City of course was too big for this[3]—at least generally speaking. Knowing this from experience I have always recommended my children to keep out of politics if they wish to live and take their fees to enable them to do so. I kept this one thousand per annum until I fell sick now ten years ago.[4] After I

[1]Inserted in the blank is Jedburgh, written not by JSH but, presumably, by his daughter Edith Louisa Higgins, who had charge of his manuscripts after his death. Francis H. Groome, *Ordnance Gazetteer of Scotland*, new ed. (Edinburgh: T. C. and E. C. Jack, 1901), lists "the Nest Academy" as one of several private schools in Jedburgh. The headmaster in the Helmcken boys' time was George Fyfe, according to the inscription in the prize book (Sir Samuel W. Baker, *The Albert N'yanza Great Basin of the Nile*, new edition, 1870), awarded to James for Scripture and History in 1872 and now in the possession of his son Ainslie.

[2]Cf. p. 162 above. According to the *First Victoria Directory*, 1860 ("Prefatory Remarks," p. 20), there were at that time "eight or nine medical practitioners of different classes." A check of the list of names shows nine persons calling themselves either Dr. or physician and surgeon and one surgeon dentist.

[3]JSH sat in the Legislative Assembly of Vancouver Island as member for Esquimalt and Victoria District 1856-59, and for Esquimalt and Metchosin District 1860-66. He was then elected to the Legislative Council of the united colony of British Columbia for Victoria City (see below, p. 222n2) and served in that capacity until Confederation.

[4]Late in 1884 Victoria had a typhoid epidemic, and the *Colonist*, 6 January 1885, in an editorial entitled "A Ghastly Record," reported JSH as "lying desperately ill." On 27 February 1885 JSH's sister-in-law Jane Dallas wrote: "I am very pleased indeed to hear that you are now all right again and out of your sick room.

recovered and Mr. Smith came from England he handed me a letter dispensing with my services and I must say the Company was right, for it had no further use for my services.[1] Here let me say that in all my dealings with the Company I never had any just reason to complain— and I do not think anyone else had in reality, for companies have to deal on a broad principle and so sometimes hardship apparently results to some few.

In my early days the Company were gentlemen and liberal. I could "indent" for any drugs or instruments required, and no one demurred either here or at home, but after the change of the Company to a joint stock company, one had to be a little cautious—tho it never troubled me.

Now I had to supply the whole country from the Rocky Mountains with all the medicines they required, of which they sent a requisition handed to me in due course. The requirements at first were few and simple enough, consisting usually of jalap powders and emetics by the gross —purgative pills likewise—Turlington's Balsam—Essence of Peppermint —some simple ointment and a few other simple things and answer a few letters about some sick person in the Interior. This may seem an easy matter, but when one neither had bottles nor jars, it was not so easy, so I used to pack all the ointments in little tin saucepans and got bottles where I could—in fact did so until I ordered a supply from England and then all the people made indent for bottles, for they had to divide their medicines and sent them to minor posts. I had to pack them very carefully too in tow, for they all had to be carried by pack trains (horse) to the Interior and so had a good deal of rough handling. By degrees the wants of these posts for themselves and Indians increased in number and variety—arising in some measure from miners travelling over the country, so the posts had to get a greater variety until I received indents as long as my arm. Soon patent medicines were added to the number—any one that happened to be the most advertised or the rage or recommended by miners; the purges, emetics

---

Do take care of yourself now and don't be putting your nose into the nasty parts of town again until they are drained at any rate. I see by the papers that they are moving for the drainage of Victoria" (HC). But it was not until 1890 that a money by-law to enable the construction of sewers was finally passed (*Colonist,* 19 September 1890).

[1]See Thomas R. Smith, assistant commissioner, to JSH, Victoria, 6 October 1885, cancelling the "arrangement for medical attendance on officers and servants at present existing between yourself and the Company" (HC).

and pills were not so much sought after. So the Company had to import on their own account patent medicines, but soon in 1860 druggists established themselves in Victoria and in the Interior[1] and then the strain was taken off my shoulders and I had little to send—as the Company sent the patent medicines as an article of trade without any reference to me.

Moreover a regulation soon came into force that the officers must pay for their own medicines and medical attendance too if any—for as I said before, the Company had no surgeon in the end, my last agreement only referring to Victoria. The surgery in my present office supplied the whole country for years—the furniture—many of the drugs —and bottles are there still!! They are covered with a good coating of dust, reminders of the past and the present for I suppose I shall be covered with dust ere long too. What a history my office could tell if walls had memory and speech![2] I believe now that it was a good thing for me to have been discharged from the service, tho I did not think so then, and had got into the HBCo's routine, which more or less unfitted me for anything else, but it looked bad at the time and looked as tho I had come down a peg, not being an officer, for the Company's officers in those days were looked on with a sort of mysterious respect and wonder, and generally supposed to be enjoying tremendous incomes!!! Anyhow it put me more or less on my mettle, I worked harder

[1] In the "Prefatory Remarks" of the *First Victoria Directory*, 1860, there are said to be three chemists and druggists in Victoria. Among the advertisers are Curtis & Moore, Langley Brothers (C. & A.J.), and William Zellner, Druggist and Apothecary. The *British Columbian and Victoria Directory*, 1863, lists one druggist in New Westminster and two in Lillooet. The first druggist in Barkerville was apparently James P. Taylor, who advertised in the *Cariboo Sentinel* on 25 June 1866.

[2] Cf. the description by Emily Carr in *The Book of Small*, p. 201-2: "The outer room had a big table in the centre filled with bottles of all sizes and shapes. All were empty and all dusty. Round the walls of the room were shelves with more bottles, all full, and lots of musty old books. The inner office had a stove and was very higgledy-piggledy. He would allow no one to go in and tidy it up.

The Doctor sat in a round-backed wooden chair before a table; there were three kitchen chairs against the wall for invalids. He took you over to a very dirty, uncurtained window, jerked up the blind and said, 'Tongue!' Then he poked you round the middle so hard that things fell out of your pockets. He put a wooden trumpet bang down on your chest and stuck his ear to the other end. After listening and grunting he went into the bottle room, took a bottle, blew the dust off it and emptied out the dead flies. Then he went to the shelves and filled it from several other bottles, corked it, gave it to Mother and sent you home to get well on it. He stood on the step and lit a new cigar after every patient as if he was burning up your symptoms to make room for the next sick person."

and harder, for I had now something to work for either by choice or compulsion, and having lost my poor wife, affairs did not go on quite so smoothly and so I determined to quit politics as soon as I decently could, for as I said before and say again, I had no love for politics, but having entered on the sea at first almost by necessity, I had to do my duty—but when there was anything exciting or important, rely on it— the excitement spread to me and I fought—like any young excitable fool would!!!

I must now take up another thread. The two Colonies are now one, Seymour Governor, so he is the first Governor of the United Colonies— Kennedy has gone home.[1]

Of course one of the reasons for the Union of the Colonies was that Victoria should still preserve her condition of being the commercial and political centre, this having been threatened by the sister Colony; and the assertion of Seymour, that Victoria Harbor was only fit for a fishing place and that Victoria would soon be reduced to a fishing village, frightened people very considerably. Of course at this time there were only two places, Westminster and Victoria, the latter doing by far the greater portion of the trade and was the Mecca of miners. The desire now being that Victoria should maintain her position and be constituted and remain the Seat of Government i.e. the Capital, as she had been virtually heretofore. Doubtless Seymour was averse to this, and as the Legislature was now that of a Crown Colony, the members of the Government being in the majority, it became pretty plain that he could do pretty well as he pleased in this respect, but it so happened that some of the officials considered Victoria the most suitable place and would vote so, if left to follow their own convictions. It behoved Victoria then to get what influence she could to counteract what she believed to be the intentions, evil to her, of the Government.

An election took place and on this occasion I quitted Esquimault, ran for Victoria and was elected,[2] I thinking Victoria would have by this step more influence. Of course I wanted Victoria to be the head and honestly considered it the most suitable place for the Seat of Government, which at this time was of much more importance to her welfare than now, and let me say I became an enthusiast on this matter:

[1]For the departure of Governor Kennedy and his family see the *Colonist,* 24 October 1866.

[2]On 13 December 1866 JSH and Amor De Cosmos were elected for District No. 1, consisting of the City of Victoria and the Town of Esquimalt (*Colonist,* 14 December 1866).

somehow or other the work fell on my shoulders—possibly the old adage of the willing horse and urged on by my friends who held property.

At this election De Cosmos and I for Victoria, Pemberton for Victoria District—Southgate, Nanaimo—this was the whole representation of Vancouver Island. W. J. Macdonald sat as a Magistrate, but I do not recollect him. There were 13 official and nine representatives members—Robson—Smith of Kootenay—Stamp for Lilooet [Lillooet] —Walkem, Cariboo—Barnard, Yale—so in reality the Mainland has more representatives.¹ This seemed a pretty kettle of fish—if left to their own convictions, all would be well for Victoria—but a precious close shave at the best.

I worked like a madman—got up petitions to HM Govt—Donald Fraser, Dallas in England gave great and awfully valuable assistance. All the Admirals and officers who had been here were solicited for assistance and they gave it. I sent telegraphic despatches to Dallas and Fraser—they cost me a considerable sum—most of which I had to pay myself—and in due course I had the reins—for the people in England were friends and relatives—and upon the partisans in England the battle depended, for they had to bring influence on HM Government in behalf of Victoria. Donald Fraser drew up a voluminous petition to HM Govt, and got it signed by influential people—he worked well and hard and so did Dallas—our petitions not considered to be drawn up in proper shape. I presume the HBCo lent assistance quietly too.²

¹For J. D. Pemberton see above, p. 114n3. For Joseph James Southgate (d. 1894) see Walbran, *British Columbia Coast Names*. For W. J. Macdonald see above, p. 55. For John Robson see Jackman, *Premiers of British Columbia*, pp. 77-89; and Olive Fairholm, "John Robson and Confederation," in *British Columbia & Confederation*, pp. 97-123. Robert Thompson Smith left British Columbia for Utah in 1868 and was prominent in mining circles. He died there in a duel in 1880 and was buried with full Masonic honours (*Colonist*, 14, 15, and 22 September 1880). For Edward Stamp see above, p. 115; and for George A. Walkem see above, p. 213. Francis Jones Barnard (1829-89) was the founder of a pioneer express company; his son, Francis Stillman Barnard, was lieutenant-governor of British Columbia 1914-19. For further details of the elder Barnard see the obituary in the *Colonist*, 11 July 1889.
²Two memorials were presented to the British government (one dated 20 April, the second dated 26 July 1867) by "British Columbia Bondholders, and Representatives of Commercial, Banking, Landed, and other Interests in British Columbia, some of whom have resided in the Colony for several years." The honorary secretary of the first group of memorialists was Gilbert Malcolm Sproat, who in his fragmentary "History of British Columbia" (MS, PABC) gives an illuminating and often entertaining account of the efforts made by the "London Committee for Watching the Affairs of British Columbia" (consisting of Donald Fraser, A. G. Dallas and himself) to win supporters. One of those approached was

Under this condition of excitement the Legislature met at Westminster in Noah's Ark[1]—Birch the Colonial Secretary being president.[2]

---

the Earl of Lauderdale, formerly Admiral Sir Thomas Maitland, commander-
in-chief, Pacific Station, 1860-62: "When, as a 'Committee Man' I 'Looked up'
the Earl in London, he himself answered the door—spare, tallish figure—stern,
unsmiling face—threadbare morning jacket—neckerchief all awry, and very
large, old slippers—'What do you want, laddie?' said he." Among those who signed
the second memorial was Sir Edmund Head, the governor, on behalf of the Hudson's Bay Company. The *Colonist* printed both memorials, together with the
relevant correspondence between Donald Fraser and the Colonial Office, in the
issues of 15 November 1867 and 13 February 1868.

[1]The next eight pages of the manuscript are more than a little confused, for JSH
has here telescoped various discussions of the capital question which took place
during two sessions of the Legislative Council, 1867 and 1868. The actual sequence
of events was as follows. The session opened on 24 January 1867. On 30 January
JSH moved an amendment to Governor Seymour's opening speech: "That His
Excellency be informed that there exists a general feeling throughout the country
in favour of Victoria as the seat of Government." De Cosmos was the seconder,
but the motion was finally "withdrawn for the time being" (*Colonist,* 2 February
1867). On 13 February 1867 the estimates were brought in, and discussion continued until 5 March 1867 (British Columbia, Legislative Council, *Journals*).
On 29 March JSH moved, and W. J. Macdonald seconded, a resolution that the
seat of government should be at Victoria. The debate lasted from 10:00 A.M.
to 8:00 P.M., and the report in the *Colonist,* 1 April 1867, took up one and a half
pages. The arguments presented, chiefly by JSH and the solicitor-general, Thomas
L. Wood, were as indicated by JSH on p. 229 below, and the motion passed by a
vote of thirteen to eight. The final decision of course rested with the governor,
and he refused to commit himself without consulting the secretary of state for the
colonies. On 20 April and 26 July 1867 two memorials in favour of Victoria were
presented to the British government (see preceding note) and on 1 October 1867
Buckingham assured Seymour "you will be at liberty, in case you should decide
in favour of Victoria, to quote the authority of the Home Government in support
of that course" (... *Correspondence ... on the Subject of a Site for the Capital
of British Columbia,* p. 13). The next session of the Legislative Council was
convened on 21 March 1868. On 2 April 1868 George A. Walkem moved, and Edward Stamp seconded, a resolution fixing Victoria as the capital. This debate was
reported at length in the New Westminster *British Columbian,* 5 April 1868
(the *Colonist* carried only a telegraphic summary). An amendment was moved by
John Robson, seconded by F. J. Barnard, that it would be inexpedient to remove
the seat of government from New Westminster at this time. On this occasion Robson spoke for an hour and a quarter, but his amendment was lost, five to fourteen,
and Walkem's original motion was then passed, fourteen to five. Of the eight
members who had voted against Victoria at the 1867 session, Chartres Brew was
not a member of the 1868 Legislative Council; Robert T. Smith had left the
country (see above, p. 223n1); and no vote by W. H. Franklyn is recorded.

[2]Arthur Nonus Birch (1837-1914) of the Colonial Office came to British Columbia
with Governor Seymour in 1864 as colonial secretary and served until June 1867
when he returned to England. For further details see the obituary in the London
Times, 2 November 1914.

Bushby gave me a bed but otherwise V.I. representatives lived and boarded at the [blank in MS: Colonial] Hotel.[1]

Some days things went on smoothly enough, but on others there was considerable friction and I was very touchy, easily irritated—said things which could only have originated in excitement, but it was not our game to abuse; we wanted the officials to be our friends and indeed outside the House we were all friendly—would dine and sup and play cards with Birch and the officials—and they with us. Outside we were friends—politics sunk—we all knew each other—and as I said before some had a good feeling for Victoria such as Trutch—O'Reilly —Cox—Good.[2] Stamp was with us—Walkem doubtful—Smith a friend in need.

At length the Estimates came down and I determined after looking over them to have my fight on their ground—but hardly knew how until we got into them. They did seem very alarmingly high; and economy on account of Union certainly not apparent—in fact it seemed difficult to make both ends meet and the debt rolling up looked great—altho nowadays we would laugh at it and borrow more. In fact Governor Seymour said to me, "Why this alarm about the debt? The whole is very little more than one year's revenue"!! With Union there must be more officers than in any one before Union and the Customs renders even in some cases an increased number necessary. Westminster was at this time a very small place—a village, with virtually one street along the water front, with three or four good buildings. The people seemed peculiar—hated Victoria—sitting over hot stoves in stores or publics, eating crackers and drinking water or some apparently equally innocent beverage—indeed they seemed to live on these and politics—the latter being sufficiently exciting. What was Victoria—nothing! In a few years she would be wiped out—they would see that Victoria should not sponge on Westminster—Westminster was the place and the natural

---

[1]Presumably the Colonial Hotel, the most celebrated of all the early hotels in New Westminster, where ceremonial and official dinners were usually held. It was established in 1860 by Prosper and Frank Grelley. The brothers separated in 1861, Prosper going to Victoria and Frank remaining at the Colonial; in June 1867 Pons Arnaud bought a half interest (Margaret L. Macdonald, "New Westminster 1859-1871 [M.A. Thesis, University of British Columbia, 1947], p. 289). In the 1868 Victoria directory the firm advertised as Grelley & Arnaud.

[2]For W. G. Cox see below, pp. 233-35. Charles Good came to Victoria in 1859; he became a clerk in the colonial secretary's office and private secretary to Governor Douglas. In 1861, after an elopement that scandalized Victoria, he married the governor's daughter. For further details see "Bushby Appendix," under "Douglas, Alice."

seaport of the Mainland. As to the Capital—Had not Her Majesty declared Westminster to be this—Victoria could not and should not alter this!

Undoubtedly the Seat of Government was of much importance to them in many respects and it did not excite any surprise that they should guard it, but apparently those who had least to do and least to lose, were the loudest talkers. Of course they were not friendly with us, but this was of little consequence—we did not want their friendship but their Capital. In private houses of course it was quite different— they did not exhibit much feeling, altho no doubt it was there, but the best houses were occupied by the best persons and these generally were in some way officially connected with the Government—and in most instances the change would make but little difference to them. Of course we were very friendly with them and sought to attach them to us.

The very fact of the Legislature sitting at Westminster was a gain to them of importance, particularly as it happened at the dull season of the year, but at this time, fishing and canneries were in their infancy —there was a sawmill at Westminster and another at Burrard Inlet[1]— and but little farming or other production or industry. I pointed out to them that the Capital was of little consequence—what they wanted was settlement on the land and dyking of the low lands, in fact I proposed a resolution on the latter subject in the House, but it came to naught, the expense seeming too great and further no one knew much about it.[2] All this was of no avail in the shops or publics, a bird in hand

[1]Joshua Attwood Reynolds Homer had established the first sawmill in the lower Fraser Valley at New Westminster in 1860 (Macdonald, "New Westminster," p. 302), and operated it until the removal of the capital to Victoria. The 1868 issue of the *First Victoria Directory* lists: Homer James [*sic*] A. R. Inspector of weights &c James Bay. On the north shore of Burrard Inlet a mill run by water power was in operation by 1863 and was taken over not long after by S. P. Moody; on the south shore Captain Stamp's mill (later Hastings Mill), a steam sawmill, began to operate in June 1867 (F. W. Howay, "Early Shipping in Burrard Inlet: 1860-1870," *BCHQ* 1 [1937]: 4-15).

[2]No resolution sponsored by JSH on the subject of dyking has been traced in the *Journals* of the Legislative Council 1867-70. But see his letter in the *Colonist*, 5 October 1869, "Big Vegetables and Rich Lands": "... skilled persons assert that many of the flats can be embanked at a cost of three bits per acre," and W. H. Ladner's reply, 21 October 1869, "The Delta of the Fraser." On 31 January 1871, a committee was appointed to consider "the expediency of submitting a scheme to dyke and make suitable for agricultural purposes the delta of the Fraser." The *Colonist*, 1 February 1871, reported that JSH was opposed: "He thought if the railroad should come down the Fraser all the land would be absorbed by

was worth more than two in the bush—they wanted the Seat of Government now and not to wait for a perhaps distant future—before which event they might die or starve.

They all worked hard to get the political influence on their side—so did of course their public press—and quite right too. The excitement ran high, but it was destined to be higher still—for every now and again I got crazy apparently in the House and startled them with some resolution. Hamley used to say, "Never mind what he says, look at his eyes and you will soon see whether he means it or not. I wonder what bombshell he means to pitch into us next!" Hamley was a queer fellow; he would come to the Ark, put on a pair of slippers, take his seat, pull out *Blackwood* and read it all the time, apparently not paying any attention, but say a word about the Customs—whew—he was awake bristling—and so I used to wake him up. He and I were friendly, and when in good humour would call me to my face "Villain—rascal— blackguard—what mischief are you up to today?" One always knew when he was sulky—he would not speak—but treated us all very courteously—as gentlemen!!! Of course he was heart and soul for New Westminster, and he had considerable property there. Birch was an awfully nice fellow—lively and very gentlemanly—young and bright, probably did not care very much where the Seat of Government might be, but was diplomatic enough to laugh at the matter in private but never committed himself to any place. He used to invite some of us to little suppers and card parties; that is to say, when the House rose, altho there might have been a very acrimonious debate (?), he would tap a fellow on the shoulder, saying "Come over tonight!" No one complained of his conduct in the Chair—in fact I do not remember what rules governed or whether there were any official ones or not.

Governor Seymour invited me to his house—after dinner, in his private room, I took up the Capital question—we were alone—he suddenly left me and I left the house! W. A. G. Young afterwards told me that Seymour said, "What an excitable fellow Helmcken is—I had no idea he was of this kind—it is extraordinary that he should feel so keenly about this matter!"

We were invited to a ball, given by Seymour—he invited me to a chair by his side—but if I would, I could not say a word about the Capital,

---

the Company." In 1873 An Act to Extend the Public Works Act, 1872 and to Promote the Drainage and Dyking and Irrigation of Lands in British Columbia was passed by the legislature.

for Armstrong, of Westminster,[1] stood by all the time, and certainly did not allow an opportunity!

On another occasion Seymour took me and others out in his steam yacht.[2] I saw Douglas Island[3] and he wanted to know whether I would rent it for a rabbit warren! The island is pretty nearly under water during the freshets. However, I pitched the Capital question here too—so I must have been enthusiastic—excited—the Seat of Government on the brain —virtually insane—a monomaniac! I must have forgotten my good manners, even if I ever had any—anyhow I must at this time—aye before and after—have been a very explosive—touchy—irrepressible subject.

At length the Estimates [of 1867] have gone through the preliminary stage—the free talk business—doubtless particularly free, more so perhaps than edifying or sensible.

As usual the Estimates were made up according to Departments— and then—I had a glimmering of my path—Customs Department. We argued that the chief Customs House must be at Victoria, as all the import business was done there. This was agreed to.

Post Office—of course the chief Post Office must be at Victoria. All mails from San Francisco and the Sound were landed there—there was no other route. This was agreed to.

The Judiciary—should be at Victoria, i.e. the chief Courts of Justice. The main portion of the population was there—and in winter nearly the whole.

This was agreed to likewise!!! And so we went on *gradus ad Parnassum* —step by step—until in the end all of the chief Departments were said to be of most importance and their chief seat should be at Victoria.

In the end I and some others saw pretty plainly, that the only thing remaining was the Seat of Government—i.e. the residence of the Governor—the place of meeting of the Legislature—and one or two other matters. Having got thus far I gave notice of a Resolution that the Seat

---

[1]William James Armstrong (1826-1915), a pioneer merchant of New Westminster and a member of the municipal council. After Confederation he sat in the Legislative Assembly. For further details see the obituary in the Victoria *Colonist,* 10 December 1915.

[2]The *Leviathan.* A steam vessel of twenty-eight tons, 50.5 x 9.4 x 3.4, she was sold at auction after Seymour's death (*Colonist,* 7 September 1869). It is not known when or where she was built ("List of Vessels on the Registry Books of the Dominion . . . ," in "Annual Report of the Department of Marine and Fisheries," Canada, *Sessional Papers,* 3d Parl., 2d sess., 1875, no. 5, p. 395).

[3]In the Fraser River, at the mouth of the Pitt River.

of Government should be at Victoria—its original site.![1] The cat was out of the bag now—and made a pretty excitement. We counted the noses of our friends—and found ourselves in a pretty tight place. The Governor, if he laid any pressure on the official members, could decide the matter either way he chose, but thus far we were not aware whether he had done so or not. Even with our official friends the success of our efforts seemed very shaky. Here let me say that some of the official members were Stipendiary Magistrates, Gold Commissioners &c.—among these were Cox and [blank in MS: William Hales Franklyn] whom we named the British Lion[2]—he was all British—bristled with it all over. He had commanded ships in the East India trade. Cox was with us—the British Lion against. The debate came on at last. Noah's Ark was full of Westminster people and a few strangers. Our arguments were that they had already decided that it was necessary that all the chief Departments should be there—next the difficulty of navigating the Fraser—thirdly, the presence of HM Navy at Esquimault and last of all the general good. It is unnecessary to go over these or those on the other side, but it soon became evident that all the official members were not tied and indeed each one seemed to have free choice—but everyone knew Seymour's predilections—at least what were or had been his public utterances *before* Union. Robson was the great man on the Westminster side. Let me say here at once that the Resolution was carried!!![3]

In relation to this matter, I know that friends in England by petition and otherwise (I saw a copy of the petition the other day) urged HM Govt in our favor,[4] and I am under the impression (tho I have no authority for saying it) that HM Govt sent diplomatic despatch—private or confidential or to be read between the lines as the case may be to Governor Seymour[5]—and so the official element were left at freedom, but on the other hand, this element were very often divided

---

[1]JSH moved this resolution on 29 March 1867. See above, p. 224n1.
[2]William Hales Franklyn (1816-74) of the mercantile marine was magistrate at Nanaimo from 1860 to 1867 and took his seat on the Legislative Council on 25 February 1867. For further details see Walbran, *British Columbia Coast Names*.
[3]JSH's resolution was carried on 29 March 1867. The choice of Victoria as the site for the capital was re-affirmed on 2 April 1868, when George A. Walkem's resolution fixing the capital at Victoria was passed, after John Robson's amendment that the capital should be left at New Westminster had been soundly defeated. See above, p. 224n1.
[4]See above, p. 223n2.
[5]See Buckingham to Seymour, 1 October 1867 (... *Correspondence* ... *on the Subject of a Site for the Capital of British Columbia*, p. 13).

on various subjects—and in the main went with us, as for instance in the rehabilitation or rather in the retention of the chief Departments at Victoria, so I must come to the conclusion that the Governor left them free, and further if any pressure was brought to bear it would of course be through the President or some official intimate of the Governor.

There is a ridiculous side to most subjects—the Capital question is not an exception. Of course everyone was earnest and serious, the British Lion among the number, altho opposed to the Resolution, he was genial, near-sighted and liked a drop of the creatur[?] occasionally.[1] It so happened that Noah's Ark was cold—but this ark unlike the original had a smoking addition and a fire attached. Of course during the debate Members adjourned for a rest to the attachment. The British Lion had been at Kerr's [Ker's][2] house during the morning to be taken care of! However in the middle of the day, he made his appearance apparently all right—for his side. His turn came—he pulled out of his pocket a number of loose sheets of foolscap, so we knew we were in for a long dissertation. Cox sat on his right—O'Reilly on his left, the Lion a little shaky. Nevertheless on with his specs—the sheets in proper order are on the table. "Mr. President. When I went up the Hoogley forty years ago, the navigation was very intricate, the river full of shoals and sandbanks, a very great deal worse than Fraser River. Look at the Hoogley now—these shoals have been cleared away and ships now without any difficulty can go to Calcutta. The sandheads and shoals in the Fraser can and will be removed as trade increases and necessity demands, and then Westminster will be as easily reached as Calcutta is now." At this point the Lion put aside the sheet he had recited and looked around—Cox in the twinkling of an eye put it back again. So the Lion went on: "Mr. President, when I went up the Hoogley, forty years ago"—&c. to the end. The same turn over and the same replacement by Cox—so again "Mr. President, when I went up the

---

[1]The following incident involving W. H. Franklyn, the British Lion, belongs to the debate on 2 April 1868 and resulted in his dismissal from his post. The year before, there had been complaints that he "had been intoxicated when in attendance at the Council Chamber and had used excitable language during the debates" (British Columbia, Executive Council, Minutes, 13 May 1867, MS, PABC), and in 1868 he was dismissed with three months' salary (ibid., 16 November 1868). "Creatur" is a jocular expression for strong drink, especially whiskey; often spelled crathur after the Irish fashion.

[2]Robert Ker (1824-79), auditor-general of the united colony, was acting as treasurer during the 1868 session. For further details see the article by Dorothy Blakey Smith in *DCB* 10.

Hoogley" &c.—the same look round for admiration—the Lion had laid down his spectacles. Cox in a moment pressed the glasses out! The Lion put them on—but now could not see the Hoogley or anything else, so he wiped them with his handkerchief and put them on again—he looked puzzled that he could not read! Well, we must not laugh,—the room was full of people—and we must burst, so I proposed a recess for half an hour—contrary to rule of course.

We all adjourned to the annex—and burst! Ker was there with hot water and whisky—and at all events the Lion took some more.

The half hour expired—we all return to the chamber, as grave as Councilmen ought to be. The Lion claims to have the floor—vociferous cries of no no &c.—small uproar during which the Lion subsides—growling! What the visitors thought anyone may imagine. It turned out that his vote would not have turned the scale. Indeed I do not remember the exact vote or the individuals but they stand recorded.[1]

We Victorians determined to call on the Governor next morning. He received us cordially and enquired as to the business of our visit.—"We came, Your Excellency, to beg that you will not take any notice of the exuberance of the Lion yesterday." "What exuberance? I know nothing at all about it! You do not wish to bring it forward to me officially? Do you?" We saw it was all right and after a chat withdrew. The Governor liked his whisky too, not wisely but too well occasionally.

It will not excite surprise to learn, that the good people were exasperated and astonished at the, to them, unexpected turn of events. They had felt certain that the Governor would have directed the decision and even now many believed that the Resolution for Removal of the Seat of Government would be of none effect. We got to the Hotel safely, but had more angry looks and scowls than pleasant. After dinner Cox, Pemberton, Southgate, Stamp and I were sitting smoking in the back room—not a little bit satisfied when [blank in MS] the landlord[2] came in a little frightened, saying, "You had better not go outside! There is a crowd waiting for you and threaten to be revenged on you but particularly Cox. I am afraid they will break in soon and attack you—tho I have shut the door!"

This was a little bit unexpected, and [we] soon began taking stock

---

[1]The names are recorded in the *Journals* of the Legislative Council, 2 April 1868. They do not include the name of Franklyn, but as the vote was fourteen to five in favour of Victoria, his vote, as JSH says, would not have turned the scale.
[2]Probably either Frank Grelley or Pons Arnaud. See above, p. 225n1.

of our means of defence. Cox chose a poker and laughingly said, "This will do for a few"—others found some weapon probably very useless, but firearms no one thought of. So we awaited the attack—smoking and chatting—and tolerably brave, so after an hour or so our host informed us that the crowd were scattering, but said he, "Cox and you all had better remain, for some have gone to [blank in MS] to bribe him with a hundred dollars to thrash Cox." Now [blank in MS] was a gaunt powerful steamboat man rather renowned for his prowess and very well known. They approached him—his answer was, "You cowards why don't you do it yourselves? I am not the kind of man to do this sort of thing, but if any of you are willing to fight me for a hundred dollars or a [illegible: yard? pound?] of tobacco, I am ready, and sober, but to attack a man who has not hurt me, clandestinely, is not in my line! You may all go to ———." They went but not to the place he told them to go to.

Anyone can easily fancy the state of phrensy these people were in, but night brought them a fancied consolation: "Oh—never mind, the Governor will not allow it," and so altho we had to remain at Westminster some time after, altho of course the folk were not friendly—they did us no grievous bodily harm. For years afterwards and may be even now, I was hated—and so was and perhaps is still, Victoria altho the population has for the most part completely changed. This is of little consequence. I honestly and fairly did what I considered best, right and just. Westminster had only been in existence a few years and was only a small village—her future did not depend on the Seat of Government, but of settlement, but they would not see, that with such a river—and myriads of fish, all that was wanted, was people to cultivate the one and catch the other. I spoke to them of dyking the miles and miles of the richest land in creation, but they scorned—I had ruined them! Does it look so today? Is not Victoria better for them now than Vancouver? —the latter is a more dangerous city than Victoria ever was. I little thought when I opposed the erection of a Government House for Governor Kennedy, that my ignominious defeat then, and the purchase or lease of Cary Castle, by the Government for Kennedy, would have been of so much importance.[1] If there had not been a Governor's residence in Victoria, it is indeed very probable that the Seat of Government would not have been removed—at the time at all events. Everybody at this time thought the retention of the Seat of Government at Victoria

[1]See above, p. 203.

to be of the utmost importance—but now it may be questioned, whether it was the one thing needful. At all events it was the best for trade, being the only seaport—best for the public convenience in every respect as it contained permanently or spasmodically nearly the whole population of the country—best for the Seat of Government, because it afforded the easiest and quickest and almost only communication with the outer world and HM Ships.

Do not imagine me to be very egotistical on the above matter—I felt conscientiously right—and being a willing horse was urged and spurred by others as well in England as here, but I am of opinion that without the battle fought by our friends in England the battle here would have been most likely lost. How many telegrams (by cable) to England I sent is hardly remembered, but this much I do know, they were very expensive and the cost for the most part came out of my own pocket.

Now who was Cox?[1] his history has a moral—more than one. Cox was a tall powerful well-built man, an Irishman, good-natured—sociable and loved the fair sex—but he had for some reason or other left his wife. He was able to use his fists scientifically, and has more or less the face of a fighter—a good-humored one—yet he could use his fingers, for he seemed naturally an artist, his great forte being sketches of cocks in all sorts of postures and also bristling terrier dogs—these sketches were lovely—and wherever he lived, the plaster on the wall was enlivened by them—they cost him very little trouble. He had held the post of Magistrate and Gold Commissioner at Cariboo and Kamloops?[2] after, and on account of his office he had a seat in the Legislative Council. How he became a magistrate I do not know, but presume he had some recommendations from home, where he was well connected—but possibly had not been too well conducted or has served some purpose. He was also always cleanly clad—but curiously enough he always wore white collars and cuffs—hard and stiff—said to be made of enamelled steel—but nowadays one would say like vulcanite—these he said could be sponged clean every morning without trouble—an advantage where washerwomen were rare and expensive. In the Council he did not speak

---

[1]William George Cox (1821 or 1822-78) came to British Columbia in 1858 and in 1860 was appointed assistant gold commissioner and justice of the peace at Rock Creek. He later served in the Cariboo, 1863-67, and in Columbia and Kootenay, 1867 and 1868. For further details see the article by George R. Newell in *DCB* 10.

[2]Cox was serving as deputy collector of customs at Kamloops in 1859 (see his letters to W. Hamley, 25 July and 15 December 1859, W. G. Cox Correspondence, Colonial Correspondence, PABC).

—in fact very few officials did unless about their own official affairs—
but often made sketches of Members and passed them on—Walkem
often did the same thing—the audience believing them to be private
hints to Members! Alas they have all been lost—they only lasted for a
few minutes. We knew that Cox would vote with us on the Capital question, provided he had not to give his official vote by direction. He never
received any direction and as he found other officials ready to vote
with us, he joined them and did so, but no one could foretell the out-
come until the final vote. One would suppose that he deserved something
at the hands of Victorians, for the predilections of the Governor were
known or supposed to be known by all. The Session having come to an
end, and some interval having elapsed, Cox and one or two other Magistrates were informed that their services could no longer be required[1]—
in fact this was put down to necessary retrenchment in consequence
of bad times and the complaints of the Council, and probably it might
be so—but Cox was a marked man whether on account of his vote or
outside relations I know not. Letters came from his wife anyhow to the
Government asserting her destitution.[2]

Cox went to California—lost sight of for a time, and afterwards he
was heard of in straightened circumstances. I saw him in San Francisco—(in fact hunted him up, for he was more or less hiding from
creditors)—in a public house—he looked very much the same and did
not make any complaints, but this was only a year after his vote.

Afterwards, no doubt being distressed and pressed, he sent some beautiful sketches for sale—he wanted money—Elliott (Premier)[3] received
them but no one would buy! I went round begging for him—but was
told even by some who knew him well, drank and fed with him—
"Times are so bad, I can't afford to give"—and a hundred similar
excuses. Not one did the liberal thing—and all we collected did not
amount to a hundred dollars! This from Victoria! to whom possibly
Cox had sacrificed himself and position. The further history and end of

[1]Franklyn was one of those dismissed (see above, p. 230n1). Cox's office had been
abolished on 31 May with six months' salary as compensation (Executive Council,
Minutes, 16 November 1868), and his claim for further compensation was refused
on 16 November (Colonial Secretary to Cox, 16 November 1868, British Columbia,
Colonial Secretary, Correspondence Outward). Apparently he had some thought
of appealing to the secretary of state for the colonies, but the government refused
to supply him with copies of the relevant correspondence (Colonial Secretary to
Cox, 30 November 1868, ibid.), and he left the country.
[2]See the Sophia E. Cox Correspondence, Colonial Correspondence, PABC.
[3]A. C. Elliott served as premier from 1876 to 1878.

poor Cox—I do not remember. Peace be with him anyhow. Further comment is needless, but my advice is, never be a politician unless one has independent means. If anyone looks to the public for pecuniary support in adversity, he will, according to my experience, be treated à la Cox—a great inducement to serve the public honestly. Can anyone wonder that politicians are not always particularly honest or disinterested?

Cox governed more in Cariboo by *suaviter in modo* than the *fortiter in re* and was liked by the miners, for he did not put on much dignity— but was socially inclined—and of course fell in with a woman. Chinamen he used to swear, by ordering them to chop off a cock's head— or break a plate. "What did you do with the cock?" "It became the property of the Court and I sent him home for dinner—why it was the only chance I had of getting a chicken dinner!"

Stamp and Southgate were brothers and so were we all save De Cosmos, who never could be genial. Stamp was the youngest old boy—full of fun and it took a good deal of wine to fill him—they both were fond of tricks and good living. One night they broke loose—and soon were in fighting trim. Stamp saw Southgate at the end of the corridor, and pitched the ewer at him—Southgate returned with a basin—then they dodged each other—as soon as a face appeared, bang went something until the whole of the toilet service had gone to smithereens! They wanted to have a go at Pemberton but he had locked the door, which they threatened to burst but did not. Of course the end came—the landlord could not stand it. At the end of the month (we paid every month) Stamp was handed his account and in it were *Sherries*. Stamp called him a thief, a scoundrel—for he, Stamp, had paid for all his bottles. "Ah, you know [*sic*: for no?] comprehend—I mean the 'Sherries' you broke upstairs with Mr. Southgate." Stamp caught on—"Oh, you mean the 'Jerries'—"Oh yes, dose are de Sherries!" Stamp did not hear the end of this for some time—he was a genial lively soul—clearheaded withal—he it was who got timber limits at Vancouver and elsewhere almost for nothing—he had them anyhow altered at the recommendation of a resolution of the Council.[1]

---

[1] Early in 1865 Captain Stamp organized in England the British Columbia and Vancouver Island Spar, Lumber, and Saw Mill Company. On 15 May 1865 Governor Seymour brought before the Executive Council a memorandum of the concessions for which Stamp had applied, including a mill site on Burrard Inlet and a lease of timber land. The council recommended that "every facility be given" Captain Stamp and that the concessions be granted (Executive Council,

The Amateurs gave a performance at Westminster[1]—we and everybody went. Amongst the items was "a man with two faces under one hat"—a double-faced fellow. Well, in he comes, walks across the stage and everybody sees De Cosmos, and Robson, who sat in front of me, was delighted. The actor turned round and walked back and then—he was Robson! The difference in Robson's appearance now was rather ludicrous—he looked savage and resentful.

In a play Stamp was on the stage—ebrius in a chair. "Captain Stamp, some of your constituents wish to see you from Lillooet!" In sleepy drunken voice and visage Stamp answers—"Lillooet—where's Lillooet?" All laughed but Stamp. He had been elected for Lillooet and had not seen the place and so asked where is Lillooet! Stamp could be angry as well as jovial and of course on some subjects was rather touchy—but not often. On this occasion he was really and rightfully angry; so he went to see Governor Seymour, and laid his complaint of the officials who had acted the part. They had to apologize by letter in public and by letter and then Stamp *forgot* the matter and was as good friends as ever.

Poor Barnard had to go to a dinner, his boots, polished, stood outside the door. One of these mischievous fellows poured water into them—and when Barnard put one on—squash—he was sprinkled all over from

---

Minutes). A mill site chosen by Stamp at Brockton Point in Stanley Park was marked out on 1 June (J. B. Launders to Colonial Secretary, 3 June 1865, J. B. Launders Correspondence, Colonial Correspondence, PABC); but after going to considerable expense in preparing the ground, Stamp found that the strong currents at the point would make it difficult for ships to dock, and so on 18 July 1865 he asked permission to select a new site "about half way between the present mill site and the end of the new road" from New Westminster [i.e., the site which later became Hastings Mill, the nucleus of the City of Vancouver] (Edward Stamp to Colonial Secretary, 18 July 1865, Edward Stamp Correspondence, Colonial Correspondence, PABC). The governor endorsed the letter: "Pray carry this out. The nearer the mill is to New Westminster the better." The matter was referred to Chartres Brew, the magistrate at New Westminster, and on 11 August 1865 he gave permission for the new site (ibid.). Because of the change of site it was not until almost the end of the year that the contract between Stamp's company and the government was signed. On 30 November 1865 Stamp received the crown grant of Lot 196, G.1, New Westminster, 243.92 acres (F. W. Laing, "Colonial Farm Settlers on the Mainland of British Columbia," typescript, PABC, p. 21). According to the draft of the agreement in the Provincial Archives, he paid $245.78 or £50.13.6 for the site of the sawmill; one cent of United States current coin in gold equal to a halfpenny sterling an acre for 15,000 acres of timber land; and a dollar an acre for 1,200 acres on which to feed his cattle.
[1]The New Westminster Dramatic Club was formed late in 1866 (*Colonist*, 19 October 1866), but the particular performance described by JSH has not been identified.

head to foot. No one knew the culprit! We were generally quiet enough anyhow—engrossed with other matters, for somehow or other—a sort of gloomy responsibility settled on us for we were not at home in New Westminster. I never drank any amount of sherry—but coffee. "Why," the landlord told me, "you must drop this or you will be nervous and ill—too much coffee is as bad as too much wine." It was winter time— plenty snow—the river partly frozen, but it did not feel cold at West- minster—there was not any wind there. I wrote to Victoria and in joke asked them to send me a blade of green grass—to relieve my sight against this snowy desolation. This got into the newspaper in Victoria, and then the good people of Westminster pitched into me for abusing the country and undervaluing Westminster—"before the eyes of the whole world!" as tho one of our newspapers was much seen outside!

I went by a shop and saw a pretty cane-made set of toy furniture— bought it and wrote to my daughter to expect a pretty set of furniture by next boat. Of course she was delighted and so ordered a waggon to fetch it. The purser knew nothing of any furniture, but at length the baggage man said, "Perhaps this may be it—oh yes it is." So the wag- goner put it into the waggon, drove to the house, where they were expect- ing anxiously the arrival. They saw the waggon without any goods—and felt—well as any girl would feel—when the waggon drove up the toy set of furniture was handed out! "Oh—this is the 1st of April and Pa has made us April Fools."—It was not so—but purely accidental.

Of course we made trips to Victoria occasionally—business being put off or not ready for action. On one of these occasions, I, O'Reilly and some others left Victoria in the morning on the steamer *Otter*[1]—a very slow boat. Duncan was on board,[2] but he excited very little interest indeed then excepting among his friends, in fact no one cared about him. He was young, scrubby faced, short-haired,—as well face as head —dark—sombre colour—pretty well set and active and strong. Probably he was about to visit the Governor in relation to Indian matters—at least I have seen some public letters to the Governor of almost even date. He did not strike one as being at all remarkable, indeed not more than an ordinary person. I and friends wanted a game of whist (no gambling) to while away the tedium. The Captain offered us the pilot house—made of inch plank. We sat down inside and played. Duncan

---

[1]The HBC vessel brought out in 1853 to assist the *Beaver* in the coastal trade. For further details see Walbran, *British Columbia Coast Names*.
[2]William Duncan of Metlakatla. See above, p. 106n1.

sat down on his pack with his back against the house of inch boards. Another sat alongside him on his pack also—the latter being, I think, Revd. Sheepshanks,[1] and there was a conversation of which we could hear the drumming and vibrations—very annoying! Well, Duncan kept talking to his neighbour until dinner time, and hardly allowed his neighbour to put in a word. Well, we all went to dinner and felt and hoped that Duncan would now be got rid of. Not a bit of it,—we returned to our whist, Duncan and the other took their seats in their old position and kept on talking rapidly—he doing all the talking—until we arrived at Westminster in the evening. We wished him at—Fort Simpson!

Sheepshanks had the character of being the most voluminous eater in B. Columbia. He is said to have gone to dine at an eating house in Cariboo, and after having eaten a whole leg of mutton, asked for more and what was to come next! The landlord stared at him, for altho appetites are good in Cariboo, the parson beat all—and astonished him still more when he offered the landlord the ordinary price! Here then we had a very big talker and a very big eater in conjunction! How glad we were to reach Westminster!

On another occasion we (Members) went up in the *Enterprise*[2]— fog overtook us in the Canal de Haro—and we had to lay to, but subsequently arrived at Plumper Pass,[3] anchoring there for the night. We lay there too the next day—the fog awful, so we began enquiring about the provisions on board! There were plenty of one thing or another. On the following day—the fog continued and we and the Captain became impatient. At last the Captain said, "I think we can hit the lightship anyhow"[4] and off the steamer went. After a while Captain Swanson said,

---

[1]Rev. John Sheepshanks (1834-1912) came to New Westminster in 1859 as rector of Holy Trinity Church and remained until 1867 when he went back to England (*Colonist*, 21 February 1867). He later became bishop of Norwich, and his recollections of British Columbia, edited by D. W. Duthie, were published under the title of *A Bishop in the Rough* (London: Smith, Elder, 1909).

[2]An American vessel purchased by the HBC in 1862. For further details see Walbran, *British Columbia Coast Names*.

[3]The former local name of Active Pass, between Galiano and Mayne Islands. See Canada, Board on Geographical names, *Eighteenth Report of the Geographic Board of Canada* (Ottawa: King's Printer, 1924).

[4]Tenders were called for a lightship at the mouth of the Fraser as early as 1864 (*Colonist*, 27 June 1864), but it was not until 1866 that the "Fraser River Lightship," a wooden craft 73 x 20 x 9'6" was placed in position on South Sand Head (ibid., 4 January 1866). She had a red hull, and a ball at the light mast head, the lantern being seventy feet above high water mark ("Annual Report of the Department of Marine and Fisheries," Canada, *Sessional Papers*, 1st Parl., 5th

"We ought to be very close to the lightship now. Does anyone hear the bell?" "No."—Soon the boat was stopped, and then we heard a distant bell, but where away—it seemed all round the compass, then Swanson pushed on—the sound became clearer and clearer, but not a bit of the lightship could be seen—and then running on, the sound grew fainter —more faint—and faint—so the ship was put round with the same re-sult as before! The fog suddenly cleared up—and there was the [blank in MS: Fraser River Lightship] within a hundred yards of us. We had been going round her! We got to Westminster very late, for the fog was very thick in the river. Bells, torches and guns made sounds— so at last we got there—three days on the passage! This was not all. Captain Swanson had to get back again for Monday's trip—so on the following morning, Sunday, early—he unloaded the ship, but in the midst of this an officer came down and said this was "agin the law."[1] Swanson said he could not help it—and he wanted to get back to Victoria before the fog sprung up again—the day was now clear—and so he went on unloading and in the end sailed away!! On his return voyage he was hauled before the Magistrate (Ball I believe)[2] who fined him a nominal sum—looking on the matter as a work of necessity—for it was a matter of consequence to Westminster, that he should get to Victoria and return on Monday. The Magistrate of course told him, "Don't do so any more!" I fancy fogs were more frequent and thick then than now— but this may be fancy—I do not travel now!

Towards the end of this Session Amor De Cosmos brought up a Resolu-tion—in re Confederation, with Canada. The Union of the Provinces on the other side of the mountains was about taking place and De Cosmos wanted B. Columbia put in. No one knew much of this subject save De Cosmos and Robson and so the debate was not very lively. In the end a resolution was agreed to—amendment proposed by Pemberton—that a place should be left in the articles of Confederation allowing B. Columbia

---

sess., 1872, no. 5, pp. 258-59). In 1879 she was withdrawn from service because of dry rot and offered for sale ("British Columbia Lighthouse Division," ibid., 4th Parl., 2d sess., 1880, no. 9, p. xxvi). She was the first lightship on the Pacific coast, according to James A. Gibb, Jr., *Sentinels of the North Pacific* (Portland: Binfords & Mort, 1955), pp. 163-64.

[1]By a proclamation of 19 November 1858 English civil and criminal law was extended to the newly proclaimed colony of British Columbia. Proclamation No. 6 of 1862 (The Sunday Observance Act, 1862) specifically declared the English Sunday laws to be in force here.

[2]For H. M. Ball see above, p. 160n4. He sat in the Legislative Council in 1867 as magistrate, Cariboo, but in 1868 as magistrate, New Westminster.

to enter, when and if she found it convenient.[1] I voted for this and so did most Members—and the main reason for the vote was—the poverty of B. Columbia—poverty which had produced the Union of V. Island and B.C. was a special reason for joining the confederacy. Times were bad—the expense of government deemed almost unbearable—the public debt running up—and no apparent means of paying it! A sort of reign of pessimism existed generally, and those who had augured so well heretofore of the grand and glorious future of B. Columbia were in the dumps. Confederation was looked on as a sort of betterment—it was urged that the Canadian Government would pay all the expense of the Government of British Columbia—pay the debts likewise—in fact do everything for B. Columbia and give her a bonus into the bargain. Our action however was not altogether endorsed by Victoria—rather the contrary, and I was accused of being hasty and such indeed was the case—but the best possible was done—time given for Confederation—consideration. Somehow there was a general feeling in the Council that the Union had to be sooner or later—this was the official view—but the officers did not like it—what was to become of them! Governor Seymour thought the action a little premature at all events.

At length the Session ended [on 2 April 1867]. The Governor closed the Council with a speech—and of course said the resolutions of the Council would be placed before Her Majesty's Government and also the desire of the Council that the Seat of Government should be removed

---

[1]For a concise and authoritative summary of the story of British Columbia's entry into Confederation see Ormsby, *British Columbia*, pp. 233-51. Further details will be found in Great Britain, Parliament, House of Commons, *Papers on the Union of British Columbia with the Dominion of Canada,* 1869 (P.P. 390) and in *British Columbia & Confederation*. De Cosmos's motion was introduced on 5 March and first considered by the Legislative Council on 8 March 1867. After some debate it was withdrawn temporarily, so that a deputation consisting of Southgate, Helmcken, De Cosmos and Pemberton might request the governor to telegraph the British government, asking that provision be made in the Imperial act for the admission of British Columbia (*Colonist,* 12 and 13 March 1867). The telegram was sent on 11 March, and debate was resumed on 18 March 1867. De Cosmos wished to replace his original motion by another, advocating "immediate entrance into the North American Confederation," but the council finally gave unanimous approval to an amendment introduced by J. D. Pemberton, requesting His Excellency "to take such steps, without delay as may be deemed by him best adapted to insure the admission of British Columbia into the Confederation on fair and equitable terms" (ibid., 19 March 1867).

to Victoria.* The section of the speech in relation to this, did not at the time seem very satisfactory—either to us or anyone else, but it revived the spirits of Westminster—and so made me or us buckle on the armor again. Possibly and probably we had not been very learned or very intelligent or intellectual politicians, but I feel we made the best of the circumstances and conditions surrounding us. I further make bold to say, that at no time before or since were better men, as well official or other, ever assembled together for legislative purposes. Say what you please about the system—the official members were intelligent, honest and generally speaking honorable upright gentlemen—and they were in the main left free and untrammelled. Moreover under this system HM Govt kept a sharp eye on everything—the accounts and what not. There was mighty little room for boodling or false accounts—these were all examined in England. At the same time men were more independent because none need bore them and make them give promises of place and emolument—the great bane of so-called Responsible Government. In addition public works of magnitude could be carried on, the income not frittered away to bribe individual Members by making roads &c. to their private residences, if not to their bedrooms. In fact a continuous policy for the general good could be carried out—instead of individualism. Of course there was and must be a great outcry against this form of government, but the cry came and will come more from those who desire the emoluments of office—honest or not, than others, for say what you will, the general idea seems to be that the Government should support and maintain, what is called the people—fleece the few to bribe the many—instead of the people doing for themselves and supporting the Government! Now (1892) it is an inverted cone. All men are by nature dishonest and self-seeking! The Government *must* be the same!

At this time it was an easy matter to get up public meetings—which afterwards became so very notorious. All we had to do when at West-

---

*[J. S. H.] The petition to HM Govt by friends in England and I think drawn up by Donald Fraser is appended to this book.[1] It gives Seymour's opinions and threat. No doubt Seymour was chagrined at the result of the vote in Council—he probably supposed the Magistrates knew his opinion and would vote accordingly.

[1]See above, p. 223. No MS appendix to the "Reminiscences" has been traced.

minster, was to get up a meeting about something we wanted supported or condemned by public opinion—for Victoria was the public. So before the Session [of 1867] closed a meeting or two had been held in favor of Confederation,[1] for now many Canadians had come to mix with the British, and were dubbed North American Chinamen!

When we returned of course we were generally well received and congratulated, for having overcome the unconditional Terms of Union, but now Confederation was in the air, and it was soon found, that opinions were very various on this matter, in fact the opponents seemed to be the larger number—and they were influential people. They said, what was quite true, we are ignorant of the Terms of Confederation, and its working equally unknown. The Dominion leaders at Ottawa corresponded with their friends here to go in heart and soul for Confederation—and they did. At the same time there sprang up afresh an agitation in which many joined, that annexation to the U. States, would be much more beneficial than Confederation with Canada—this sentiment existed among the Americans of course, and they played their part—many Britishers agreed with them. The poverty of Canada—distance from British Columbia, the intermediate portion uninhabited—the difficulty of communication &c. were freely made use of; the riches of the United States and if united the population and business would flow in, all would be rich and progressive in place of stagnant and poor. Victoria and B. Columbia became a political boiling cauldron. The discussions and agitation led me to form an, or if it please better, to change my, opinion. I came to look on the Confederation as premature—it seemed like another leap in the dark—we were to be united to what we did not know, but the absence of communication governed me much—there could be no immigration from Canada, there being no means of travel. What B. Columbia wanted was population—such population must necessarily come from the East—or through the East from Europe, for Americans we had learned by long experience would not settle under the British flag—and indeed they had a better country of their own. Moreover it was known that immigrants coming across the overland railway to San Francisco, were on their journey—won over to settle in the United States and so did not get to B.C. at all. To obviate this in some measure, the *Labouchere* had been chartered ostensibly to carry the mails, but more to get people and carry merchandise, so that

---

[1]A public meeting to discuss the Confederation scheme was held in the Victoria Theatre on 18 March 1867 (*Colonist*, 19 March 1867).

Victoria might be free from the machinations in some measure of the Americans and their endeavours to swamp B.C. or rather to encourage their own country. The *Labouchere* was lost at Point Reyes on her first trip home, Captain Mouat being in command. He knew little of the coast.[1] This loss however took place some years before Confederation, but it had a very disheartening effect.

In addition to all this the Americans had by purchase acquired Alaska, and so boasted they had sandwiched B. Columbia and could eat her up at any time!!! Possibly HM Govt regrets now not having bought Alaska, but at this time HM Govt cared but little about the Colonies—they might go and do as they pleased; they were only children which when grown up would go their own way and be independent. I know Russian agents were here and offered to sell Governor Douglas the "coast belt" and perhaps the rest, but he could not do anything in the matter, tho possibly he may have sent despatches to HM Govt on the subject. It must be remembered here that Russia and England were not on the most friendly terms—that Confederation did not take place until July 1867—HM Proclamation being about this time—that is to say the Confederation of the Eastern Canada—and further that just about this time too the U.S. had virtually bought Alaska. A very nice conglomeration for B. Columbia to solve. I presume there can be scarcely any doubt about the U.S. having bought Alaska to oppose and destroy the Union of the Maritime Provinces—indeed meetings were held in the United States and a petition or petitions sent to the U.S. Government not to allow Confederation. A paper war ensued here now that the Terms of Confederation i.e. the [British] North America Act had been published, of which there had been much ignorance before, and it was these very terms that made me think B. Columbia had better pause before irretrievably committing herself. There is no doubt nevertheless that Governor Seymour had received despatches to

[1]Early in 1866 the HBC was awarded the contract for direct mail service between Victoria and San Francisco, and the paddle steamer *Labouchere*, on this coast since January 1859 (Walbran, *British Columbia Coast Names*), was taken to San Francisco to be fitted up for the accommodation of passengers. On her second voyage after the refit she was lost off Point Reyes on 14 April 1866 (*Colonist,* 27 April 1866). William Alexander Mouat (1821-71), master mariner, came to Fort Vancouver in 1845 and served in various HBC vessels on the Pacific coast until 1855, when he took command of the *Otter*, then plying between Victoria and Fort Langley. Subsequently he was master of other HBC vessels on the Fraser River run. For further details see Dorothy Blakey Smith in *DCB* 10.

favor the entry of B.C. into the confederacy,[1] and please remember the Government had full controul of and in the Legislature at this time, but let it also be remembered that the Governor always declared that the opinions of the elected members would always receive the greatest consideration as being the opinions of the multitude.

Governor Seymour having given his opinion at the close of the Session, that Westminster should be the Seat of Government according to law and justice, set me and everyone else in Victoria to work again—the work however falling chiefly on me. At this time I had the whole thing in leading strings, and so got the friends of Victoria in England, to renew their efforts—as all seemed now to depend on them. They renewed their efforts with a will—approached HM Govt, and got up a petition stating the whole case. This petition was drawn by Donald Fraser and Mr. Dallas and set forth the reasons why the Seat of Government should be at Victoria.[2] There is a copy of this amongst my papers. The petition we sent to England was not considered ship-shape and so this one was drawn up and sent, but not to displace ours. In the end HM Govt declared the Seat of Government to be at Victoria.[3]

Previous to this Governor Kennedy in a conversation said, he thought the Union had been a little premature, because if Confederation had to be, in this case it would have been better for Vancouver Island to have made her own terms, and so better ones as far as local conditions were concerned. After the Union of course Kennedy disappeared. I saw Governor Seymour a few times in Victoria, but I do not think he had any affection for Victorians—indeed he could not have—seeing that he had lost the battle of Westminster. He was a gentleman anyhow in manner and appearance—probably of more than average intelligence, but had his faults—who has not? Mrs. Seymour was very much liked at

---

[1]JSH appears to be in error here. It was not Seymour but his successor, Governor Anthony Musgrave, who was told by Lord Granville on 14 August 1869 that the British government now conjectured the prevailing opinion in British Columbia to be in favour of union. Granville added: "I have no hesitation in stating that such also is the opinion of Her Majesty's Government" (*Papers on the Union ... with ... Canada*, pp. 20-31). Seymour "was given no instructions on the matter" (Ormsby, "Frederick Seymour," p. 20); for as Musgrave had been informed when he was told of his appointment on 17 June, Her Majesty's government could take no practical steps until the territory of the Hudson's Bay Company had been annexed to the Dominion of Canada (Granville to Musgrave, 14 August 1869, *Papers on the Union ... with ... Canada*), and this transaction was not completed until 1870 (Rich, *Hudson's Bay Company ... Vol. III*, p. 933).
[2]See above, p. 223.
[3]By the proclamation of 25 May 1868.

Westminster—she being hospitable and agreeable. I once was called in at Westminster to see Governor Seymour for some acquired illness, but on subsequently calling I found the Church of England Minister, had supplanted me, and so I was not admitted. This parson—I forget his name [blank in MS: Rev. W. E. Hayman][1]—used to doctor and take care of the Governor.

During the year [blank in MS: 1869] Governor Seymour took a journey to the North in H.M.S. [blank in MS: *Sparrowhawk*]. He was not well at starting—he became worse, I believe troubled with dysentery and died on the passage, his remains being brought to Victoria and buried in the Naval Cemetery at Esquimault.[2]

Now Governor Musgrave takes his place[3]—Confederation is the great question of the day, but Musgrave had not declared himself.

There cannot be a question but that the death of Governor Seymour had a great effect on the immediate future of B. Columbia. I do believe that Seymour thought Confederation premature and indeed at this time but few if any had any idea beyond Confederation—in many instances without or at any price. Governor Musgrave indeed was in a like predicament—he at first did not see how it could be advantageous under present conditions. I need not refer here to De Cosmos and the "Yale

---

[1]William Edward Hayman, M.R.C.S., Edin., and L.A.C., became a deacon in 1866 and succeeded the Rev. Percival Jenns as incumbent of St. Mary's, Sapperton in June of that year (Rev. Frank Plaskett, *70th Anniversary of St. Mary the Virgin, Sapperton, 1865-1935* [souvenir booklet, PABC]; and *Colonist* 18 June 1866). He was ordained to the priesthood on 17 March 1867 (ibid., 14 and 18 March 1867), and in July 1868, after the capital had been removed to Victoria and St. Mary's had in consequence lost nearly all its congregation, he was appointed assistant minister at the cathedral in Victoria (ibid., 23 July 1868). Since he was "himself a physician" he was called back to New Westminster when the governor became "seriously ill" (ibid., 30 October 1868). He was clearly an intimate of the Seymour household: when the news of the governor's death reached Government House at 2:00 A.M. on 14 June 1869, "Rev. Dr. Hayman was aroused and by him the heartrending intelligence was broken to Mrs. Seymour" (ibid., 15 June 1869). At the lying-in-state Dr. Hayman and his wife supported the widow as she "gazed for the last time upon the features of the dead" (ibid., 17 June 1869). At the funeral the Rev. Dr. Hayman read the service; and when the governor's widow returned to England she was accompanied by the Haymans (ibid., 21 June 1869). In 1874 Hayman became the vicar of Tudeley-cum-Capel, Tonbridge, Kent.

[2]Seymour died on 10 June at Bella Coola aboard the *Sparrowhawk*. He was buried on 16 June (*Colonist*, 17 June 1869).

[3]Anthony Musgrave (1828-88) succeeded Seymour as governor of British Columbia in 1869 and served until the colony entered Confederation. For further details see the *DNB*.

Convention."[1] It excited a good deal of ridicule, because a coloured man was one of the members—an American of course. He afterwards held the office of [blank in MS] in the United States.[2]

How much influence this Convention had, save and except in stirring up people, it is hard to say—probably little—the platform I forget—but of course De Cosmos made one—he and Robson were decidedly the only two men of note at this time in re Confederation.

After the arrival of Governor Musgrave a general election was ordered;[3] Confederation being the burning question, everyone rampant on one side or the other; of course the American element being against the Union. At this time no distinct terms had been proposed, but if I

[1]On 24 April 1868 De Cosmos had moved an address to the Queen, asking her to approve British Columbia's desire to enter Confederation. Instead, the Legislative Council passed, by twelve votes to four, an amendment proposed by T. L. Wood, affirming the principle but suggesting that no action be taken for the time being. De Cosmos "strongly animadverted the conduct of the Council" in thus reversing their vote of 1867. He had already (in January 1868) organized the Confederation League in Victoria, and when the session closed he saw to it that branches were formed in other parts of the colony. Delegates from the Confederation League met in convention at Yale in September 1868. A full account of the proceedings will be found in the *Colonist* supplement of 29 September 1868. See also the *Papers on the Union ... with ... Canada,* pp. 16-28; and *British Columbia & Confederation,* passim.

[2]Mifflin Wistar Gibbs (1823-1915), born free in Philadelphia, was the most distinguished member of the group of Negro pioneers who came from California to Victoria in 1858. A very successful businessman, he served on the city council, 1866-69 (*Colonist,* 12 November 1866 and 22 July 1869), but he was never a member of the Legislative Assembly, contrary to JSH's assertion on p. 247 below. In 1870 Gibbs went back to his native country and graduated in law. Subsequently he was city judge, registrar of the Land Office, and receiver of public moneys at Little Rock, and he served as U.S. consul in Madagascar, 1897-1901. For further details see the *Colonist,* 31 August 1870; his autobiography, *Shadow and Light* (Washington, 1902); and J. W. Pilton, "Negro Settlement in British Columbia 1858-1871" (M.A. Thesis, University of British Columbia, 1951), pp. 73-88.

[3]There is some confusion in the next few pages of the MS. The election mentioned on p. 246, fought on the issue of Confederation and described on pp. 248-49, took place before, not after, the arrival of Governor Musgrave on 23 August 1869 (*Colonist,* 24 August 1869). It was called on 17 October 1868, and the voters for District no. 1 (Victoria City and Esquimalt Town) went to the polls on 3 November. There was a by-election late in 1869 for Victoria District, when De Cosmos took the seat formerly held by Dr. John C. Davie (ibid., 3 December 1869), but there was no general election until November 1870. In the 1868 election JSH and M. T. W. Drake defeated De Cosmos and Dr. Powell on an anti-Confederation platform; in 1870 JSH and Henry Nathan Jr. defeated the anti-Confederation candidates, in a far less colourful election. In 1868 the *Colonist* (4 November 1868) devoted nearly two columns to a description of election day in Victoria, "wherein was manifested more excitement than in the contest some three years since over the Free Port and Tariff question."

recollect rightly De Cosmos and the colored man Gibbs and [blank in MS: John Gustavus Norris] had been to the "Yale Convention"; a Convention for the purpose of an organization for Confederation purposes. The Convention was ridiculed and lampooned by opponents[1]—the colored man [blank in MS: Gibbs] having a good share. Bye the bye I had been a means of getting the coloured man elected to the House of Assembly and really he was in some measure a superior man and very gentlemanly withal. I think he claimed being a West Indian.

I came out against Confederation distinctly, chiefly because I thought it premature—partly from prejudice—and because no suitable terms could be proposed. The tariff was a sticking point: altho we had at this time a tariff but could change it to suit ourselves. Our income too would be diminished and there at this time appeared no means of replenishing it by the [British] North America Act. Our population was too small numerically. Moreover it would only be a confederacy on paper for no means of communication with the Eastern Provinces existed, without which no advantage could possibly ensue. Canada was looked down on as a poor mean slow people, who had been very commonly designated North American Chinamen. This character they had achieved from their necessarily thrifty condition for long years, and indeed they compared very unfavorably with the Americans and with our American element, for at this time and previously very many liberal-handed and better class of Americans resided here, many in business—some on account of the Civil War necessitating their remaining even after the frightful internecine killing had ceased. Our trade was either with the U.S. or England—with Canada we had nothing to do. Of course my being an Anti-confederationist, led to my being dubbed an Annexationist, but really I had no idea of annexation,[2] but merely wished the Colony to be let alone under HM Govt

---

[1]See, for example, Plate 22. There was also a more dignified protest in the shape of "A Card" signed by some three hundred people headed by JSH, stating that the convention, which purported to represent the opinion of the citizens of Victoria, had received no authority to represent the opinions or desires of the signers (*Colonist*, 22 December 1868).

[2]Yet A. G. Dallas had advised him from London on 15 November 1866 "to keep up a cry for annexation to stir up the Home Government to do something for them" (HC) and in the Confederation debate JSH said: "I deny that I uttered any such thing as that the choice would be put to the people by the Government between two issues of Confederation and any other union. But if the Canadian Government refuses to agree to terms equivalent to these, but chooses to offer some mean terms for consideration, when it comes to the polls the people themselves will raise the issue between Confederation and the only other change which offers itself for

and to fight her way unhampered. I had nothing whatever to do with annexation petitions, and do not know who signed them—tho I have heard that some who now hold or have held official positions had done so.[1] This petition doubtless went to the President of the U.S. but no one has ever been able to see a copy of it since, altho it is said to exist in Victoria somewhere. There is no doubt the Americans had a contempt for Canada and this feeling extended to the colonists.

I suppose the election was one of the fiercest ever fought in Victoria, everyone seemed crazy, I among the number—these were the days of great excitements. I had the British and American elements and Jewish element on my side and after a time the election came on. Numberless ladies wore my colours, red, white and blue,[2] in shape according to their taste, the men likewise. Ladies were at the windows waving their handkerchiefs, every hack in the place was frightfully busy. The polling went actively on, but there were no rows, or if there were, they were insignificant. Various committees had districts under control; they had to get the voters up and were responsible therefore. The cry went round that both sides had a number of voters locked up and were feeding them with whisky, to get them into proper trim; altho this accusation was not strictly true, still voters came to the polling place, where the Courts of Justice now stand, in files. Notwithstanding all this there were no rows outside the polling places, the matter was too serious for this. At length 4 o'clock struck—the polls closed; everyone tired—thirsty, hoarse and expectant. The Anti-confederations had won handsomely—but I think I was second—I fancy Nathan was first, but am not certain.[3] After the declaration came the elation of the

---

consideration" (*Government Gazette Extraordinary,* March 1870, p. 6, cited by Tim Truesdell, "From Sea to Sea," in *British Columbia & Confederation,* p. 127).

[1]See above, p. 182.

[2]The *Colonist* (3 November 1868) assigns these colours to his opponents: "Both parties seemed to muster strong, and the supporters of De Cosmos and Powell were so thoroughly mixed up with those of Helmcken and Drake that for some time it was impossible to tell who headed the poll. We thought, however, that the red, white and blue, the De Cosmos and Powell colours, mustered strongest before the polls opened."

[3]Here JSH is referring not to the 1868 election he has just described, but to the contest in November 1870, after the Terms of Union had been made known and after the passage of the Act to make further provision for the Government of British Columbia, 9 August 1870, under which there were to be nine members elected and six appointed. "All elected members have been returned in favor of Confederation," Musgrave reported to the British government on 22 December 1870 (British Columbia, Governor Musgrave, Despatches to London, 11 January 1868—24 July 1871, PABC). On this occasion JSH was, as he thought, sec-

victors—speeches &c.—I was carried in a chair and felt afraid all the time of being dropped—as the men were a little unsteady—the streets filled with excited people, the windows lined with ladies likewise. The end was I was carried to the Colonial I think—made a speech on a table before the bar and at length got home, but having a strong remembrance of the road being like a heaving sea—so I reeled worse than a sailor!!! The next morning. Oh. My.

After a while of course things settled down—but the expenses had to be paid, these being pretty heavy—partly paid by the Committees in part by myself—but I knew precious little about what the Committees did. In these days we had for the most part to pay our own expenses, heavy enough to be sure, but on the other hand, the voters themselves were open-handed and excited, and paid treats and so forth out of their own pocket. I had the expensive side—the Canadians were canny and thrifty. We knew little of Canadian politicians then!! There were few restrictions in these days about hacks, colours, expenses and so forth, but the rules against bribery were pretty strict. I do not think bribery had much to do with the event on either side—anyhow there was little or none of it, save tobacco and whisky on both sides— excitement enough without this.

About this time too I wrote a series of letters to the newspapers— the *Chronicle*[1]—anent and opposing Confederation, in fact I must have had the subject on the brain. I have never seen these long-winded letters since—but one of them wrecked me, as will be seen bye and bye —it caused Confederation!!! I preached to curse but had blessed!!

At this time B.C. was of course under Crown Government—Musgrave Governor. The Governor appointed me, (elected) a Member of the Executive Council; and so I accepted, and thus became aware of the ins and outs of the Executive Government.[2] The Governor and Executive had frequent meetings at which various subjects were discussed, each Member being for the nonce equal, and gave expression to his

---

ond; the poll was headed by Henry Nathan Jr. (1842-1914), an importer and commission merchant in Victoria since 1861, who was dubbed "The Mercantile Candidate" (*Colonist*, 1 November 1870). He later sat as M.P. for Victoria City, 1871-72.

[1] The Victoria *Daily Chronicle*, founded in 1862, had been amalgamated with the *Colonist* on 23 June 1866. For JSH's letters "anent and opposing Confederation" and the replies to them, see the *Colonist*, 14 November to 1 December 1869.

[2] He was appointed, along with R. W. W. Carrall, on 31 December 1869 (*Government Gazette*, 1 January 1870) and was sworn in on 10 January 1870 (Executive Council, Minutes).

own opinion. The Council was a large one, included Trutch—O'Reilly
—Hamley—Crease—and several others—but as in all matters, some had
more weight and some only followed. There were no long-winded orations,
but mere conversations or debates—everyone's opinion being condensed
into a comparatively few sentences.

At this time Governor Musgrave in getting on his horse, broke his
leg—a compound fracture about the ankle, the upper fragment (tibia)
protruding. I think I was first to see him, but Powell, Ash and other
doctors soon arrived. I did not want the case, and so Powell stepped
in somehow or other. I gave the Governor chloroform and after some
trouble, Powell and some others got the bones into pretty good apposi-
tion. Ash was sulky and grumpy—I think I ought to have proposed
him, but Powell had come in earlier.[1]

At this time the antiseptic treatment by means of carbolic acid had
come in and from Edinburgh had come reports of most extraordinary
successes.[2] I did not propose or oppose the treatment, I knew too little
of it to do either. Powell however determined to use it—according to
what he had read. So the wound was covered with carbolic oil and
lint &c., bandaged and there the thing ought to have rested. [Blank
in MS] undertook to watch Musgrave during the night, but having
the carbolic oil at hand, he thought he ought to apply it frequently—
and so he did liberally! There was some misunderstanding about this—
anyhow the treatment was very disappointing—made things worse in-

---

[1]The accident happened on 2 November 1869. Two days later the *Colonist* reported that the Governor had "passed a quiet night on Tuesday [the day of the
accident] and yesterday his condition was easy. The bone was set by Dr. Powell
assisted by Drs. Helmcken, Ash, Trimble and Davie. The extent of the injury may
be surmised when we state that the broken bone forced its way through the leg of
the boot." Musgrave's recovery was slow. Miss Sophia Cracroft, who with her aunt
Lady Franklin stayed at Government House on her way to Alaska in May 1870,
says: "The fracture was so dreadful that the bone protruded thro' the skin,
exfoliation is going on, but the progress is now considered satisfactory. He was
entirely confined to his bed for *4 months*, & at best, has been during the day in a
lay chair in which he cd be wheeled about" (*Lady Franklin Visits the Pacific
Northwest*, ed. Dorothy Blakey Smith, Archives Memoir no. 11 [Victoria:
Queen's Printer, 1974], p. 117). In July 1870 Mrs. Crease wrote to her husband:
"I was told it was *very* bad, but is doing better again now. Poor man! I feel so
sorry he has such confidence in that Canadian doctor [i.e., Dr. Powell]" (quoted
in Ormsby, *British Columbia*, p. 234).
[2]Joseph Lister (1827-1912), the founder of antiseptic surgery, was appointed
to the Glasgow Royal Infirmary in 1861, and in the wards there he first used the
carbolic acid treatment on a compound fracture in 1865. A year later he reported
a very successful case, but finding that carbolic acid irritated the tissues he later
devised other preparations such as carbolic oil for the prevention of suppuration.

stead of better. The wound and bones did not go on favourably—the Governor lay in his bed for weeks—and was crippled for life—this would probably have happened under any treatment—for a portion of the tibia died. Under these trying circumstances the Governor kept his equanimity—was always pleasant and gentlemanly to visitors and the Executive Council. He was a very pleasing man—gentlemanly in manner—had a fine appearance—clear intellect—and of persuasive tho rational conduct. He wished to do the best for the Colony—and gave reasons for his ideas and measures, which however he never forced down our throats—and apparently were never brought forward without previous deliberative thought. Anyhow he and the Council got on uncommonly well together—there was nothing approaching jobbery—the country and its benefit had to be considered and nothing or very little else.

It became pretty evident that Confederation dozed but snored—we knew it to be there and come to stay—but it had not come plainly and distinctly to the front.

At length one day I went to see the Governor, whether he had sent for me, or I made a sympathetic call, I do not remember. I found the Governor, of course, in bed, but pleasant and cheerful, with the *Chronicle* [*Colonist*] before him. "I have been reading your letter. Do you know you have made Confederation practicable? You have solved a difficulty that I could not get over, i.e. the financial part.[1] Our population is so small, that our income from Canada would be insignificant, but you show in your letter that our population pay fully three times as much per head as the Eastern Provinces and so ought to receive three times as much per head as the Eastern Provinces per capita. You say this would give us accordingly three times the population or to put it your own way the per capita of the Eastern Provinces would give us a population (I forget the number) of [blank in MS]

---

[1]In three letters in the *Colonist*, 14, 16, and 27 November, 1869, JSH presents a bewildering mass of figures. At one point he estimates the actual population of British Columbia at 30,000, each paying $12.00 per annum to the customs, whereas in the Canadian provinces each person pays only $3.50. Since the revenue for customs in British Columbia is $349,500.00, it would take 105,570 Canadians at $3.50 per head to supply the same amount. In another set of figures he says that the income of British Columbia from customs duties amounts to $320,000.00. At $3.35 per head it would take 95,500 persons to make up that amount. By the time the delegation was sent to Ottawa the fictional population figure had been set by the government of British Columbia at 120,000. The Canadian government refused to accept this, and the final figure of 60,000 was agreed upon. See below, p. 262.

according to the Customs Returns—but you say there is no Census, and so this number must be considered the population for the time being—and this Province must be paid accordingly and its representation also based thereon." I answered, "I did not write these things to favour, but to oppose, Confederation—for public reform here, and I feel that I am right in my argument-facts." "What you intended to do and what you have done are two different things—instead of cursing you have blessed the Union—I tell you, you have made Confederation possible—the financial part I could not get over until I read your letter." "Well Governor I have been elected to oppose Confederation and I mean to do it." "Do be reasonable: do you mean to tell me if the Canadian Government would give all that you want or can reasonably ask, that you would still oppose Confederation?" "Governor you are placing a mere supposition before me—but you know that I cannot be caught by suppositions—the financial terms are only one part, it would not make our isolation less." "Now," says his Excellency, "between ourselves, mind, Doctor, HM Govt wish B.C. to come into the Confederation, but desire that this shall be brought about by the desire of B. Columbians—HM Govt desire that no force shall be exercised in the Council or the Legislature, all are to be left free and untrammelled. On the other hand the Canadian Government want B.C. to join—these are afraid that B.C. may, if left alone, choose to join the U.S. and the annexation cry makes them anxious. So please think over the matter —and see whether you cannot turn, what you consider a bad job, the question, to the benefit of B. Columbia, depend upon [it] I will assist to the best of my ability, for I would think it wrong to sacrifice the interests of the people of B. Columbia for a mere theory. Mind, this conversation is confidential." After a little more talk on general subjects I left—not a little troubled and anxious. What had to come?

There is no doubt I had "Confederation on the Brain"—a regular nightmare—I was always thinking about it, for it was in the air, everywhere. We got the Terms of Union of the other Provinces and from these I jotted down what B.C. ought to get and carried a pocket full of these always with me.

The American arguments were but few, both political and pecuniary, they seemed to care very much for V.I. but little for the Mainland—V.I. was and is the keystone of the whole. They pointed out that as a State of the Union, we should have a free government instead of a Crown Colony rule—be close to the centres of population—that the Americans would soon fill the country—Victoria and Esquimault be great commercial cities—property would rise in value—dollars be abundant—be members of a rich country, with plenty of capital to back any enterprises, instead of being members of a poor confederacy with[out] capital and who could do nothing for the Island or country. That we should still be an isolated people, worse off than ever if we remained independent. That American nation and colonists were all one—there was no distinction of race or language—and so on and so on. As far as dollars were concerned their arguments were captivating, but we were British and had the Navy at Esquimault. Undoubtedly a good many placed the dollar before loyalty or patriotism and somehow or other I got the character of being an annexationist—I suppose because I opposed Confederation and talked—but I never had any idea of annexation,[1] yet the character became advantageous to the Province—for it extended to Canada. Anyhow at this time or previous to this, the Cobden and Bright school were in the ascendent, they looked on Colonies as children—only to grow to become independent—an expense to the Imperial Government in the meanwhile. These in fact had said to go to Canada in hidden language, go if you please. The Tories did not hold this view; but the Americans made use of the argument, shewing it not to be disloyal to quit the Empire and join the U.S., it being looked for by HM Govt. What a change has come over Governments and people since this!!!

At length the Governor rises from his bed, a cripple still. At an early meeting what had been in the air—a ghost, assumed a form, the Governor came out in favour of Confederation.[2] Altho it was a mere preliminary discussion, I knew—we all knew—that the Union had to come. So I told the Governor—"I have been elected to oppose Confederation, and so I beg leave now to resign my position in the Executive." He answered, "This cannot be—it would be very unjust to us. You have been made and become acquainted with the doings of this Council and so of course would make use of them. I cannot and will not accept your resignation—think over the matter: my observations have only been as to the principle—the Terms are another matter altogether and you can assist very materially in this." All the Members

---

[1]See above, p. 247n2.

[2]On 28 January 1870 Governor Musgrave laid before the Executive Council the despatch from Lord Granville, secretary of state for the colonies, 14 August 1869, which had been published in the *Government Gazette*, 30 October 1869. The council met at Government House for the discussion of Confederation from 31 January to 12 February, although no minutes were recorded at some of the meetings (see British Columbia, Executive Council, Minute Book, 30 April 1869—7 July 1871, PABC).

echoed aye strenuously. A man who hesitates is lost—I did not insist at the moment. After a day or two I called my political friends and chiefs together and hinted to them the condition of affairs: they were not very much surprised. The pretty general consensus of opinion was that I should not resign but remain in the Council, they believing I could be of more influence there and have more power in regard to the Terms than outside. In private my friends gave the same prudential advice. A few of the Members of the Council came to gossip with me on the situation, and urged me not to be hasty—they supposed I knew more of the subject than most of them and they would lend their assistance—in argument at all events. I did not resign my position— governed by the advice of my political and other friends—tho I did not actually tell them of the position of affairs, they comprehended my position and the whole surrounding conditions—they felt that Confedera- tion had to come—but the interest now centered in the conditions or Terms.

The Governor had advised his Council to think well over the matter and to help him to frame Terms that would be of benefit to the Province—he being for the time being one of ourselves. There cannot be a doubt that some of the Councilmen had ideas about "Terms" and were earnest in the matter, but we had little to guide us, save the Terms granted to other Provinces. Of course, being a little crazy on this sub- ject, I jotted down my opinions of the Terms. The day soon came for expression—then as now I carried numerous papers in my coat pocket. Few had anything to say, the Governor remained a listener—putting in a few words now and again. Trutch—Carrol [Carrall][1] were amongst the earnest, and I gave my ideas. At last Hamley said, "Why, Helmcken has his opinion of the Terms in his pocket—they are sticking out and no one can help seeing a heading or two." The cry arose, "Out with them—let us see what they are! Let us have another of his surprises." Well, I read my notes from a rumpled sheet or two of foolscap—full of erasures and interlineations. They contained the most of the "Terms" afterwards agreed to, in fact became the object of discussion open for amendment or the addition of new ones, so a great step in advance

---

[1]Robert William Weir Carrall (Carroll) (1837-79) received his M.D. from McGill in 1859, practised briefly in his native Ontario, and served as a surgeon in the Union forces in the Civil War before coming to British Columbia. He sat in the 1869 Legislative Council as member for Cariboo and was an ardent advocate of Confederation, corresponding at some length with Sir John A. Macdonald on the subject. For further details see the article by Dorothy Blakey Smith in *DCB* 10.

had been gained. Of course in these "Terms" I insisted that the Customs Revenue should be at $3.50 (I think) per head by the number of the population. This would justly give us treble income,[1] and would likewise carry with it, the representation as well in the Commons as the Senate. The Dry Dock at Esquimault—and Naval Station there also were there and some others, but notably one that the Dominion Government should build a railway and operate it from the lower Fraser to Kamloops! and a waggon road from Kamloops across the mountains to Canada proper. The general scope of these rough terms were thought very favorably of, and so the Council adjourned to meet a few days after, for further discussion and development.

At the next meeting or so after we adjourned to luncheon—(in Government House as usual), and after lunch Trutch met me in the hall, and said, "Helmcken, your idea of a waggon road and railroad are good, but on thinking the matter over I think Confederation will be valueless without a railway to the Eastern Canada!" Trutch and I were friends! he almost took my breath away. "Heavens, Trutch, how are they to build it?—and as to operate it—well I do not see the way." "Well," says Trutch, "but I think I do." "Well you know more about railways than I anyhow." "Then," says Trutch, "suppose I propose, that there shall be, not your little tho difficult road, but a railroad all the way to the East, will you assist me?" "Yes Trutch with both hands." Now in the above few words was the embryo of the Canadian Pacific R.R.

When the Council assembled, after a while Trutch proposed his scheme—it looked like a bombshell—everyone stared, some laughed, others smiled, but Trutch stuck to his point, that without this Road there would be neither physical nor sentimental Union—but that B. Columbia would be isolated and might as well be in Timbuctoo or elsewhere. That B.C. had to look for business and population from the East and without the R.R. this would not happen. The Governor seemed to favor the idea, but the Council adjourned without action having been taken.[2]

---

[1]See above, p. 251n1.
[2]According to the Minute Book, on 9 February 1870 the Executive Council adopted Resolution No. 8 in the following terms, as indicated here by JSH: "Inasmuch as no real Union can subsist without the speedy Establishment of Railway Communication connecting the Sea-Coast of British Columbia with Canada, The Govt. of the Dominion shall engage to use all means in her power to complete such communication at the earliest practicable date, and that surveys to determine the proper line for such Communication shall be at once commenced, and a sum of not less than one million dollars expended, in every year from, and after

As I have stated before, there were two apparently great reasons for Confederation, viz. the expense of government—entirely incommensurate with the income. The Union of the Colonies had not rendered this relation of cost of government and income more equable. Again, the Colony was in a state of depression—so poverty became a cry for Confederation, altho in reality our indebtedness did not exceed a couple of years' income—but the old folk had a horror of debt! In the next place, there was a hurrah for Responsible Government: this would make government cheaper and better—get rid of what was called the iron heel of despotism!

Anyhow Council meeting after meeting were held—the Terms licked into shape by degrees and Crease I think had the legal work assigned to him, but this is really all he did before the Council or outside in his office. The Terms were really proposed by Trutch—myself and of course the Governor—debate altered them a little but added nothing material to them.

At length the Terms came before the Legislative Assembly [*sic*: *for* Council]—they were fully discussed—and being printed they may be consulted.[1] For the Railway the Ottawa Government were to have the land for nothing. I remember laying great stress on the fact that the tariff was the great question, and other things connected therewith, that they were far less suitable than our own and our own ought to be retained until after the R.R. were built—this according to the Terms

---

three years from the date of Union, in actually constructing the Initial sections of such line from the sea-board of British Columbia to connect with the railway system of Canada." On 12 February, however, "upon discussion of the Minutes of the 9th February, the following amendment was made, That in lieu of Paragraph 8, of the Confederation Resolutions of that date, the following Resolution was adopted, and ordered to be substituted." In this second Resolution, instead of Trutch's Railway, British Columbia asked for a Coach Road and Railway; and it was in this form that the Resolution went to the Legislative Council for debate, and in this form that it was printed in the *Journals* of 17 March 1870 and the *Government Gazette Extraordinary*, May, 1870, pp. 13-14. During the negotiations at Ottawa this term was again revised: the idea of the coach road was abandoned, and, as Trutch had originally suggested, the construction of a railway was guaranteed.

[1]The resolution concerning union with Canada was introduced into the Legislative Council by Attorney-General H.P.P. Crease on 9 March 1870. The terms proposed by the governor and the Executive Council were introduced on 14 March and accepted on 6 April 1870. The entire discussion, 9 March to 6 April 1870, was printed in two issues of the *Government Gazette Extraordinary*, March 1870 and May 1870, the first entitled "Debate on the Subject of Confederation with Canada"; the second, "Debate in Committee of the Whole on the Confederation Terms."

being ten years. Of course as a general principle I had to support now Confederation, and the Terms agreed to in Council I could not object to further than we had full liberty of debate and the Terms were open to amendment. De Cosmos proposed some sliding scale about the subsidy—but the great cry was that Responsible Government immediately had not been put in the Terms. Anyhow in the end the Terms passed without any, or at all events without any material alteration. As the Government had the majority there could not have been any material change.

Before this period, telegraphic communication existed between the Atlantic and Pacific,[1] so doubtless all our proceedings and Terms required, were duly telegraphed to the authorities by the Governor— and doubtless Governor Musgrave took our side. So it may reasonably be believed, that the Terms sent down to the Assembly had in the main been agreed to by the Government at Ottawa. It is quite possible that HM Govt may have had something to do with impressing the Ottawa Government and encouraging them to assent to the Terms, but of this I have no personal knowledge save from friends of the Colony in England. Of course there is no doubt HM Govt wished the Union, but it is very questionable whether HM Govt or the Ottawa Government realised the importance of the railway further than as a local necessity and benefactor. True, trade with the Orient and so forth was freely spoken of and used as an argument and encouragement, but at the time, the trade seemed a long way off as well as regards time as distance.

Of course it was said by many here and elsewhere that the Railway was an impossibility and merely inserted in order to defeat Confederation—that the Canadian Government was too poor &c. &c. to build it. Now I know the Railway terms were not put in to defeat Confederation but in reality to make it a reality. All acknowledged Confederation to be useless without physical union and easy access from one to the other.—At all events the public looked on the Railway as a smart trick—how not to do it. Personally it looked like an inflated balloon— I could not grasp it—did not see how it could be built—or by what means—but having decided upon having it, and making it the *sine qua non*—ideas grew apace, impossibilities seemed to disappear—but the practicability of the undertaking—the means of carrying it out—

[1]Telegraphic communication between New Westminster and the United States telegraph system (which was already linked to Eastern Canada) was established in 1865 (*Colonist*, 20 April 1865) and between Victoria and San Francisco in 1866 (ibid., 25 April 1866).

and the probability of successful working and paying, were in cloud land.

In due course the Terms came back from the Assembly [Legislative Council] to the Executive Council—and of course some communication held by the Governor with Ottawa, of which however he was reticent—but the time being ripe—the question arose who should be the delegates. Trutch, Carrall and myself were proposed by the Governor—there was no demurring by the former two, but I did not wish to go and would not accept—it seemed out of my line and the more that I had been opposed to Confederation and had unfairly been dubbed an annexationist: besides I was poor—my practice would be altogether neglected—I might lose my professional appointment in the HBCo, a thousand dollars per annum: moreover my wife having died, the care of my children devolved on me and providing for the future was ever in my mind. Mrs. Forman, a truly good woman had charge of them, in fact was my housekeeper. In fact I had no liking for the business— was not politically ambitious—did not want any favors or any appointments—and indeed meant to quit my political status as quickly as possible. Now altho I had worked very hard to do my duty to my constituents—to do my duty in fact, still I never liked the position—this may seem strange, but it was a fact nevertheless. It was a plaything at first, but acquaintance with later politics and politicians did not induce a greater liking for them or respect for the people I was thrown amongst.

So I proposed De Cosmos to go in my stead, but this was objected to, and the appointment was deferred, hoping I might change my mind. The whole thing caused me much anxiety and I was bothered in and out of Council by people wishing me to go, Trutch being particularly anxious that I should go with him. He had a great dislike to De Cosmos personally as well as politically. "Well then," I said, "send Robson—he is a clever fellow," but somehow or other Robson was at this time obnoxious. In the end, very unwillingly, I consented,[1] for the Governor

---

[1]Musgrave wrote personally to JSH on 18 April 1870: "You *must* go . . . . Let me have a positive answer—in the affirmative." An official request, promising an allowance of a thousand dollars for travel, was sent by the colonial secretary on 20 April. On the 21st, JSH wrote to the governor, accepting the appointment "if the business will not necessitate my absence from Victoria for a longer period than two months." The next day he withdrew "the hasty assent given yesterday," feeling that he could not give the time necessary for the business; to which the governor replied: "I have put your refusal into the fire; and depend upon you to stand by me now. You must not get me into any more difficulty." (This letter is dated only "Monday," but may reasonably be assigned to Monday, 25 April 1870. For the

said, "There will really be very little to be done, save to defend, demand and adhere more or less closely to the Terms. The Ottawa people can't eat you anyhow—altho they will feed you." The above is how I became a delegate. After debate, we were each allowed a thousand dollars to pay our expenses—including those of travelling as well as others—so we were not and did not go as millionaires. To me was entrusted the financial terms and knowledge of Vancouver Island. Carrall had the Mainland—he was a friend of the Main[land] but not of Victoria. To Trutch was entrusted Railway and Public Works—in fact he was to be the front and general of the whole affair. No one indeed so capable— he being a head and shoulders above us in intellect—and pertinacity —and introduced by the Governor as such, so from the word go, we were not on an equal footing, and soon discovered this at Ottawa. Trutch was everything and everybody—it mattered little in reality, as we all had to stick to the Terms.

I forget the date of the morning we left Victoria in a little steamer whose name I have forgotten also—Mrs. Trutch being one of the party.[1] To make my narrative a little concise, I shall avoid incidents of travel[2] —they may come in bye and bye. The journey from San Francisco by railway opened our eyes not a little, for a railway had been built through a mountainous country quite as bad as that of B. Columbia— if this one could be built so could one through B. Columbia. The balloon grew smaller—the scheme looked now very practicable—but the means? In course of time we arrived at Ottawa, and in due course presented our credentials.[3] The Governor General invited us to dinner

---

whole series of letters see Musgrave Correspondence [HC]; JSH Correspondence Outward [HC]; JSH Correspondence, Colonial Correspondence, PABC; and British Columbia, Colonial Secretary, Correspondence Outward, PABC.) The reasons for the governor's insistence on JSH as a delegate are indicated in his despatch to Lord Granville, 5 April 1870 (cited in W. N. Sage, "The Critical Period of B.C. History, 1866-1871," *Pacific Historical Review* 1 [1932]: 442): "Mr. Helmcken has great influence in the Community. He is far from being an ardent Confederate, but practically with him the question is one of terms, and it will be very desirable that he should have a voice in the discussion of them."

[1] The party, including Mrs. Trutch, left on the *Active*, on 14 May 1870 (*Colonist*, 14 and 15 May 1870).

[2] The journey from San Francisco to Ottawa has been reconstructed in detail from contemporary accounts by Brian Smith, "The Confederation Delegation," in *British Columbia & Confederation*, pp. 200-202.

[3] For a more detailed version of pp. 259-64, see JSH's "Diary of the Confederation Negotiations," ed. W. E. Ireland, *BCHQ* 4 (1940): 111-28. This article is reprinted in Appendix 3. The delegates arrived on 3 June 1870. The negotiations went on until 27 June.

and very quietly said, "They want you and British Columbia in very badly—you understand!"!!! Here was an eyeopener!! Of course there was the usual "cards" from all the officials and others and returns— so there were opportunities for refreshments about Terms as well as other almost equally difficult subjects of digestion. I called on Sir Francis Hincks and explained matters—he soon comprehended, but did not seem a very affable man. I talked to him about Tariff—keeping our own—but he did not see it, but saw lots of difficulties in the way. Trutch saw his men and so did Carrall, in fact in a very short time we saw everybody of official importance and they saw us and were very agreeable.

After a few days, we were summoned to meet the Cabinet—Privy Council—given seats—mine was at the foot of the table opposite the President. My other friends occupied the centre one on each side, and with my usual impertinence, I made the remark to Sir George Cartier, "This is only a prelude to our occupying these seats." The understanding was that we were for the time, part of the Privy Council —part of themselves, and whatever took place was not to be divulged. We agreed to this and acted loyally.

We very soon found that they knew as much of the subject as we did, nevertheless went through the whole of the Terms, giving the reason therefor, and answering objections. Sir G. Cartier—Tilley [blank in MS] were there, but Sir John A. Macdonald was very ill and had secluded rooms in the Parliament Buildings. I may say at once, that the only delegate who saw him was Carrall. Sir John never appeared at the con- ferences, but it was understood, that everyone knew his opinions—that the Council acted according to his views, but for all this Sir G. Cartier was our man in this business—he was the leader in the Council chamber —yet it seemed as tho the whole had been thought over and prear- ranged. Of course I urged my point about the financial affairs—and representation in accordance. I was asked about the Mainland but referred them to Carrall and Trutch. Trutch had his say about Rail- road—Dry Dock &c. Trutch was asked whether a R.R. could be built through the country—and Trutch gave a verbal sketch of a road through Eagle Pass to the Fraser—his experience of the American overland line—Carrall spoke of the value of the interior and its nature— and he and I spoke of the Railway coming to V.I. and produced a sketch. After two or three hours of this the Council adjourned to con- sider the matters and would let us know when they met again. There was no flourish of trumpets in all this—it was a mere business matter— facts and not eloquence were required, desired and had, as far as it lay in our power to give them. After this meeting of course we often met the ministry singly and urged in season or out of season the Terms— both sides had these on the brain. The Dry Dock appeared to be a stumbling block—every Province on the seaboard would require the same thing. Now I think they have them.

Next day we received notice that the Prince [blank in MS: Arthur] at Quebec was to be made or created a K.M.G. [G.C.M.G][1]

I met Tilley walking next day. He said, "I don't see how we are to build or pay for that Railway?" "My dear Sir—make everybody smoke a couple of cigars a day and take a glass or two of whisky, the duties on these will pay the interest on the outlay!" I did not know then that he was an anti-smoker and anti-drinker!! He did not reply but went to something else. I told him to go over the railway to San Francisco, and he would soon come to the conclusion, that as it was possible to build that railway so it was equally possible and practi- cable to build one through B. Columbia—that I had been in doubt until my eyes had been opened travelling through the Nevadas and Rocky Mountains. Anyhow it has to be built for the R.R. is a *sine qua non* —no R.R. no Confederation.

The last day arrived. All assembled in the Council chamber—so now the work had to be wound up—taken up seriatim.

The Railway of course. The question of terminus came up, but the answer was: of what use is it attempting to fix a terminus when the route of the road is unknown and cannot be known until surveys have been made! A sketch of the route by Bute Inlet, before presented,[2] was seen on the floor under the table!

The waggon road was by consent scratched out—useless as the R.R. had to be built in a short time. Trutch in the Council now drew up the Railway clause, which with some little amendment was agreed to by all, and so became part of the castiron terms.

The Dry Dock was a harder matter—not so much on account of the cost as because it was contrary to the policy of the Government— and every Province would after this precedent require the like. At length the Dry Dock clause was licked into shape, but was not liked

---

[1]On 11 June 1870 the delegates attended the ceremony of investiture by the Governor-General, Sir John Young, in St. Patrick's Hall, Montreal (Montreal *Gazette*, 13 June 1870).

[2]For this sketch by Carrall of the Bute Inlet route for the railway see above, p. 260, and below, p. 264.

—but we must have the Dry Dock and so saying they would not consent, consented.

My part about the financial terms caused me a little trouble. Sir Francis Hincks had virtually agreed to my contention in conversation I had previously had with him, so in the Council he said, "B. Columbia is undoubtedly entitled to the money they ask for. Not having a census of the population, the Customs Returns have been made use of, and according to these, the population is 120,000!"!!

Sir George Cartier replied. "Everybody knows that B.C. does not possess this number, and we cannot go to Parliament and say that she does. Why Helmcken himself says the population does not exceed forty thousand—but that each individual consumes of imported goods three times as much as one of 'old Canada.' We'll admit this—admit them to be entitled to the money—but not the population. Say the population may be 60,000—they come in at $3.77 (I think). Now we have to make up the money somehow. Suppose we give them $100,000.00 per annum for the Railway belt." I smiled. "Oh," said Sir George, "I know what you are smiling about, you promised to give us the land for the Railway for nothing! We have read the Debates of your House on these matters, know all your reasons and opinions!! I offer you $100,000.00 per annum —and you shall have all the representation asked for in the Commons and Senate altho it will be out of all proportion to the population, still we can get over this—your population will increase." Well, we had to agree to this. Some wanted the $100,000.00 limited to ten years or some fixed date, but we would not consent to this, and so it was given for ever. We asserted that as B.C. was a mining region—lumber and so forth, without any manufactories and small agricultural resources, that the Customs receipts would always be more than proportionate to those of other parts of Canada. Sir George said that we must help them and modify. He and his colleagues were willing to give all, but we must remember that it was what the Commons would give and he apprehended considerable opposition to the Railroad, without encumbering them with other matters.

I had had many interviews with Sir F. Hincks on the subject of Tariff. Altho he agreed about the population and subsidy, he was unyielding with regard to the Tariff—considered that I wanted a tariff to encourage smuggling to the U.S.!! The Council would not give permission to alter the Tariff. Our Customs revenue was the basis of our income, population, subsidy and representation. To alter the Customs would or might be to diminish the receipts. The Canadian Tariff would not produce more than our own and so was not more oppressive. The policy of the Government was to use the Tariff for revenue purposes only, but to use it so as to encourage home manufactures, allowing other articles to be comparatively free—they were in favour of reciprocity in productions natural and common to both sides of the line. After a long talk there was a tacit understanding that if the B. Columbians chose to keep their own Tariff until the completion of the R.R. or for ten years, they might do so on representation, but that Canadian goods should be free. They agreed to this with great reluctance—and afterwards I suspect they prompted their supporters in B.C. to accept the Canadian Tariff as it would relieve them of the question in the Commons and would not be more burdensome to B. Columbians.

They were glad to learn of our mineral resources—gold—silver—lumber—coal and called B.C. "New Canada" and supposed it would some day be a most important Province—in fact one that could not be done without—Canada must extend from sea to sea. When I told them of the myriads of salmon—that they could be thrown on shore by hand in many places, they were polite enough to listen, and enquire, but ever after when I said anything remarkable (to them) about B. Columbia, "Oh—this is one of Helmcken's great fish stories!!!"[1] They certainly were far from being convinced about the salmon and other fisheries. The truth is comparatively little was known by them of B.C. and to tell the truth, we did not know so very much either, but in some cases had to deal in generalities. Carrall had the Interior and its resources in his hands and made the most of them. So in the end they knew as much of B.C. as ourselves.

It is useless trying to remember anything more about the Terms—they exist still. The Council yielded nearly everything asked for—indeed we told them we had come to get the Terms proposed or nothing. Everyone was courteous and always open in private to learn or discuss.

At length the Council was over—the end had come. There was no uproarious separation, everyone felt a page of history had been written and all felt relieved. It was arranged that I should carry the Terms

---

[1] Cf. the description of the great salmon run in June and July in the Fraser and the Columbia given by John Keast Lord in *At Home in the Wilderness* ... (London: R. Hardewicke, 1867), pp. 258-60. The Indians hang huge wicker baskets in places where the salmon leap and from 250 to 300 salmon are taken out of one basket two or three times a day. "Two Indians go naked into the huge pannier, each carrying in his hand a heavy wooden club, and, utterly reckless of the water dashing over them, and scrambling about among the struggling fish, they seize one after another by the gills, give each salmon a crack on the head with the club, then fling it out upon the rocks, whereon the squaws are waiting ...."

to B. Columbia as Carrall wanted to remain at home for a while[1] and Trutch to go to England. I was likewise kindly urged to support the Terms in B.C.! They seemed to consider me a doubtful character, for the reason as I said before of my having opposed Confederation and by some considered an annexationist!! Well the character stood B.C. in good stead. Of course I said, "I will do my best to get the Terms carried in B.C." What else could I do seeing that the Canadian Government had granted nearly everything asked for!! After a few days I received the despatches and started for home, very quietly and very unostentatiously! Trutch and Carrall had already disappeared.

Appended to this book will be found the few notes I made at Ottawa[2] —they may throw a little light on the matter, which however just now is of no consequence—the Delegation were successful—this is sufficient.

Bye the bye it was Carrall who sketched the Bute Inlet route—he advocated it too, chiefly of course on the ground of benefit to Cariboo and mining regions. What could either of us say as to the practicability of the route, save what we learned from Waddington? I was a shareholder in his Company. I do not think Waddington ever explored to Chilcotin, but Tiedemann did—and gave an account of roughness at all events.[3]

On arriving at San Francisco, many wanted to know the Terms— whether we had been successful or not. I had been cautioned not to say much about them, so simply said: "Everything asked for has been granted." It was curious too even in Montreal—Quebec and Ottawa to find people asking, "What Terms do you want?" as tho we had come on some secret expedition. We told them, there was no secret in the matter—the Terms asked for by B. Columbia had been published far and wide, all we had to do was to get the Government at Ottawa to consent to them. Generally the people, as well Boards of Trade as others, shrugged their shoulders at the idea of a railroad to the Pacific—

---

[1]He was a native of Woodstock, Ontario.

[2]For the discovery of this manuscript see Appendix 3.

[3]Herman Otto Tiedemann (1821-91), surveyor and architect, came to Victoria in 1858 and received an appointment in the Land Office, where he was responsible for designing the first Parliament Buildings ("The Birdcages") and Fisgard Lighthouse. In 1862 Waddington sent him to explore the route from the head of Bute Inlet to Alexandria on the Fraser. For his report to Waddington see W. A. D. Munday, "A Coast Range Pioneer," *Canadian Alpine Journal* 32 (1949): 42-49. See also Dorothy Blakey Smith, "Fort Victoria, 1859," *B.C. Teacher* 38 (1939): 76.

they could not grasp it—and did not think the Government would promise to build it. They were astonished too to learn of (our account) the riches of B. Columbia, and Helmcken's "big fish stories" had reached Quebec!! Yet I did not exaggerate one atom.

On arriving at Victoria—a good many people came to the wharf.[1] "What news—what have you done?" I merely answered, "All you asked for has been granted." They were incredulous—I jumped into a carriage and straightway carried my despatches to Government House, and thus ended my business. Of course I had a long conversation with Governor Musgrave, who was still in bed on account of a fractured leg. He looked over the Terms &c., but evidently knew pretty well everything before I arrived. The telegraph travelled quicker than the delegate.

At home, I found all right, but Mrs. Forman (Jane) wished to go to England—to leave my service, and it was this that brought me home so soon, my intention at starting being to cross the Atlantic and look at my friends in England for a few days.

How did they receive the news in Victoria? As soon as the Terms were made known, very many ridiculed—dust had been thrown in our eyes—no one would ever see the railway built—when built it would not pay axlegrease—the smart ones at Ottawa had been too much for us—why wasn't the terminus placed at Victoria—quite easy to build bridges at Seymour Narrows and elsewhere—the Canadians were too poor and too mean to build the road—they would get out of it someway or other—as to trade with China, this was a sort of Utopia—a fancy, a dream, very nice but impracticable—and so forth and so forth. Of course many Canadians took the opposite ground, but generally speaking there existed an unbelief. There were not any public meetings for or against. I called an assembly of citizens[2]—a great many attended—gave them a sketch of my journey and of Canada—told them the conditions were binding and made in good faith—that the Ministry were enthusiastic about the R.R. and considered it a necessity—would have a hard fight to carry

[1]JSH arrived from Portland on the *Olympia* on 18 July 1870 (*Colonist*, 19 July 1870).

[2]Presumably a reference to the meeting on 10 November 1870 at which JSH and Henry Nathan Jr., his fellow candidate for election to the Legislative Council, expounded their political views. In his "able and discursive speech" (which pleased the electors more than his printed address in the newspapers) JSH dealt chiefly with "the facts and circumstances connected with the Terms and the negotiations of the Delegates"; he conceived it his "duty to meet the public tonight and explain the object and mission of the delegates to Ottawa" (*Colonist*, 10, 11, and 12 November 1870).

it through. As for ourselves we had to insist on the Terms being carried out and fight (politically) for them. This had some effect, but still the general feeling was one of mistrust and ridicule. Of course the newspapers backed us up and in time they had great influence, and people soon began to think that it would be better to accept than keep the country in a state of turmoil, and backwardness, for business was bad and people pessimistic. It has ever been thus. There was now not so much a feeling about the Terms, only they were too good to be true—a sort of conviction had rooted in men's breast that they would not and indeed could not be carried out—but then they gradually came to the conclusion, that a breach of the Terms means a solution of continuity[1]—the Confederation at an end as far as we were concerned.

Afterwards Trutch and Carrall returned. The Terms were considered satisfactory by the Legislative [*sic*: *for* Executive] Council. Of course there were some differences of opinion, but none as to the main principles. It was however generally understood that the Terms had to be accepted as they were, as a whole—a Treaty—unalterable in any of its parts—the two Governments standing in the same position. So it was determined to send them to the Legislature.

I explained to the merchants the condition of the Tariff question— that by agreeing they could have their existing Tariff for ten years or indeed until the R.R. was built—but De Cosmos and others would not accept—let us have the Canadian Tariff and so complete at once Confederation. The merchants said the Canadian Tariff is a little better than our own in some respects. It will be better to have the Canadian Tariff—it will be stable and not altered year after year with perpetual tinkering!!! There too will be difficulties about Canadian goods and so forth, the end was that the merchants looked on keeping the B.C. Tariff as unadvisable, and so the fight I had at Ottawa might just as well have been left alone! The fact seems to be that the Ottawa Government did not like the retention of [the] B.C. Tariff—it was contrary to good policy and a bad precedent and this they managed to let their supporters in Victoria know, hence the action of De Cosmos and others, for it must be plain that the agitation about Confederation caused much communication between partizans here and at Ottawa.

---

[1]Originally a surgical term, meaning separation of tissues by fracture, etc., thereafter more generally the "condition of becoming discontinuous" (OED).

In due course the Terms came before the Legislature—and of course accepted.[1] The debate was a poor affair—no amendments allowed—the Terms were a treaty—but the feeling was even here, that the Canadian Government could not carry out the conditions.

All this may be found in the newspapers of the day, I am only speaking of my personal recollections.

Now then the Terms have been passed, there wasn't any enthusiasm, but a feeling of—thunder in the air—had a prize or blank been drawn?

Let me say here, that no notice was taken of the delegates—no vote of thanks even given them—positively nothing. It is true some half a dozen bankers and so forth gave Trutch a dinner,[2] but neither Carrall nor I were invited! The 'no notice' business may be taken as a proof of there being no enthusiasm in re Confederation.[3]

Subsequently the Federal Government had much trouble and had to use all their power and exertions to get the Terms through Parliament! Trutch was in Ottawa and helped them, by showing the importance of B. Columbia—and bamboozling them a little with diplomatic tact.[4]

[1]For the election of the 1871 Legislative Council in November 1870 see above, p. 248n3. Under the Act to make further provision for the Government of British Columbia, 9 August 1870, there were now nine elected members of the Legislative Council, as against six appointed by the government. On 5 January 1871 the report of the committee of the Privy Council of Canada submitting the terms was presented by the governor to the Legislative Council; the council went into committee of the whole on 18 January; and the terms were accepted unanimously on 20 January 1871 (Legislative Council, *Journals*), after a rather perfunctory debate (*Colonist*, 19 January 1871).

[2]This must have been a private affair, for Trutch declined a banquet "to which all classes of the community were about to join in inviting him," on the ground that "the great work on Confederation which he has in hand is still incomplete" (*Colonist*, 1 February 1871). He left for Ottawa shortly after (ibid., 12 February 1871) and did great service to British Columbia in bringing about the acceptance of the terms by the Canadian parliament without alteration on 1 April 1871. On 10 April he was given a magnificent banquet in Ottawa "in commemoration of the Union of the Atlantic and Pacific Colonies under one Confederation Government" (ibid., 4 May 1871).

[3]Inserted after this paragraph is a note in pencil in JSH's hand: "I suppose I must go on with my career after this."

[4]On Trutch's role see Ormsby, *British Columbia*, pp. 249-50; Brian Smith, "The Confederation Delegation," pp. 214-16.

BIBLIOGRAPHICAL NOTE

The present edition of the five-volume reminiscences of Dr. John Sebastian Helmcken, written in 1892, depends for explanatory and corroborative detail on two main sources: first, on other manuscripts in the Helmcken Collection in the Provincial Archives of British Columbia—correspondence, diaries, notebooks, additional "reminiscences," and memoranda of various kinds; and second, on material in the contemporary newspapers, particularly the *Victoria Gazette*, 1858-1859 and the Victoria *Colonist*, 1858-1899, made available through the invaluable newspaper index in the Provincial Archives.

No comprehensive study of Helmcken has yet been published. The details in J. B. Kerr's *Biographical Dictionary of Well-Known British Columbians* (Vancouver: Kerr & Begg, 1890), pp. 184-87, provide the basis for the account in the biographical section of R. E. Gosnell's *History of British Columbia* (Chicago: Lewis Publishing Company, 1906), pp. 684-86, as well as for Gosnell's article, "Doctor Helmcken," in *Man to Man*, January 1911, pp. 28-30. The articles in H. J. Morgan's *The Canadian Men and Women of the Time,* second edition (Toronto: Briggs, 1912) and in the *Dictionary of Canadian Biography*, ed. W. Stewart Wallace (Toronto: Macmillan, 1926) also derive from Kerr.

Helmcken played so large a role in the development of the political institutions of Vancouver Island and British Columbia that this aspect of the whole man has perforce been revealed in all the general histories of the province, from H. H. Bancroft's highly individual view in his *History of British Columbia 1792-1887*, Works, volume 32 (San Francisco: The History Company, 1887) to Margaret A. Ormsby's balanced and authoritative treatment in *British Columbia: a History* (Toronto: Macmillan, 1958, revised edition, 1971). In the years between, at least two historians of British Columbia made use of Helmcken's personal knowledge of the early period. In 1913 the British Columbia Historical

Association brought out a *History of British Columbia* in two parts: Part I, by the Provincial Librarian, E. O. S. Scholefield, dealt with events before Confederation; Part II, by R. E. Gosnell, brought the record down to the time of publication. Both authors consulted Helmcken. A letter from Helmcken to Gosnell, dated 29 March 1911 and marked *Not for publication*, asks: "What on earth do you want? More! . . . It is impossible for the present generation to understand the condition of the early settlers . . ."; and a memorandum dated 12 April 1911 reads: "This may give Mr. Scholefield some idea as to where he can get the history of the 'Mint' at New Westminster. It is all the mice have left!" The Scholefield and Gosnell *History* was quickly superseded however by the impressive four-volume *History of British Columbia from the Earliest Times to the Present* (Vancouver: S. J. Clarke, 1914), for nearly fifty years the standard history of the province. The first volume was by Scholefield, the second by Judge F. W. Howay; the third and fourth volumes were devoted to biographical information, including an account of Helmcken (Volume III, pp. 1132-38).

The climax of Helmcken's political career was of course his share in the Confederation negotiations in 1870. His particular role has been analyzed by W. N. Sage in "The Critical Period of B.C. History, 1866-1871," *Pacific Historical Review* 1 (1932): 424-43; and his name appears frequently in *British Columbia & Confederation*, ed. W. George Shelton (Victoria: University of Victoria, 1967), especially in Derek Pethick's "The Confederation Debate" and in Brian Smith's "The Confederation Delegation."

Helmcken was active as a politician only from 1856 to Confederation, but he remained a practising physician until 1910. Robert E. M'Kechnie, M.D., who was responsible for the chapter entitled "Medical" in Volume I of Scholefield and Howay's *History*, gave an account of Dr. Helmcken in Part II, "The White Man in Medicine," pp. 606-7. This aspect of Helmcken was dealt with again, some thirty years later, by J. H. McDermott, M.D., in his "J. S. Helmcken, M.R.C.P. [*sic*] Lond., L.S.A.," *Canadian Medical Association Journal* 55 (1946): 166-71, which was reprinted as a thirteen-page pamphlet (Toronto, 1946? PABC). This article was superseded the following year by Honor M. Kidd's "Pioneer Doctor John Sebastian Helmcken," a soundly based and eminently readable study which won Dr. Kidd the William Osler medal and which was printed in the *Bulletin of the History of Medicine* 21 (July-August 1947): 419-61.

The social history of British Columbia has hardly been touched as yet by academic historians. Dr. J. S. Helmcken and his family found

a place in J. K. Nesbitt's *Album of Victoria Old Homes and Families*
(Victoria: Hebden Printing Company, 1956), pp. 59-63, and many newspaper articles in similar vein have appeared from time to time, some
of them based on the "Reminiscences" of 1892, which became available in the Provincial Archives after the death of Helmcken's daughter
Mrs. Edith Louisa Higgins in 1939. A final mention should be made
of Corday McKay's *Helmcken House Historic Museum, Victoria,
British Columbia* (Victoria: Acme Press Ltd., n.d.), a seventeen-page
illustrated booklet that provides for the general reader an accurate and
interesting basis for further investigation of Dr. John Sebastian Helmcken.

Appendix 1

A Note on the Helmcken Family

The present publication is not a biography of JSH, and no deep or comprehensive research into his antecedents has been undertaken. The following information may be of some interest to the reader and may also serve as a basis for some future biographer. This information is derived from parish registers, census records, the records at the General Register Office, London, family correspondence in the Helmcken Collection, the Douglas family tree in the Provincial Archives, conversations with Mr. Ainslie J. Helmcken, and, of course, from the "Reminiscences" themselves.

Nothing is known of JSH's paternal grandparents, except that his grandfather had lands in Bremerlehe and had a daughter named (possibly) Ann. JSH's father *Claus Helmcken* came from Germany as a lad and found employment in the sugar refinery of Messrs. Charles and John Frederick Bowman at No. 27, Great Alie Street, Whitechapel. Later he became "Victualler" and kept the White Swan public house at No. 36, Great Alie Street. He married Catharine Mittler on 17 December 1817 at Christ Church, Spitalfields, and his eight children were all born in Brick Lane, Spitalfields, between 1819 and 1831. Soon after November 1831 he moved the family to No. 36, Great Alie Street. He died there on 7 September 1839 at the age of fifty-eight; he was buried in the graveyard of St. George's German Lutheran Church in Little Alie Street on 15 September 1839.

JSH's maternal grandfather, *Sebastian Mittler*, a Roman Catholic, came from Messkirch, Germany, and was married to a German woman, a Protestant. He appears to have been living in the neighbourhood of Covent Garden when JSH's mother was born, but he afterwards lived in Spitalfields, where he had a "tolerably large house and garden." After his wife's death he lived with JSH's parents at No. 36, Great Alie Street. The 1841 census lists him in the household as "Independent. Born in foreign parts," and he died on 5 January 1849, his age being given as eighty and his occupation as tailor. Sebastian Mittler had four daughters:

Catharine (she signed the marriage register thus; but her letters to JSH, her death certificate, and her memorial card use the spelling *Catherine*). According to the 1851 census she was "born [in the parish of] St. Ann Covent Garden," but her name has not been traced in the register of St. Ann, Soho; St. Paul (the true parish of Covent Garden); the neighbouring parishes of St. Martin-in-the Fields and St. Clement Danes; the German Lutheran churches (registers in PRO); or the Roman Catholic parishes in the area. She married Claus Helmcken in 1817, and after his death in 1839 she remained as licensee of the White Swan until c. 1865, when she became part of the Fincken household at No. 48, Lambeth Street, Goodman's Stile (see below, under *Mary Ann Helmcken*). Dr. Henry I. Fotherby wrote to JSH, 7 August 1866 (HC): "Your mother evidently enjoys a tranquil happy sunset of her days under the roof of your excellent brother-in-law . . . ," and she died there on 5 February 1869 at the age of seventy-four, according to her death certificate. Her memorial card (HC) gives the date as 3 February 1869 and her age as seventy-five; she was buried on 11 February 1869 at Tower Hamlets Cemetery, Bow.

Mary Regina. She married Diederich Lankenau on 20 October 1817 at Christ Church, Spitalfields, and had a daughter named Regina. The family lived near St. George-in-the-East Anglican Church, Ratcliff Highway.

Caroline. According to the 1861 census she was "born London." In 1846 she was living in Southampton, where JSH visited her. By 1861 she had returned to London and was part of the Fincken household. She died there on 8 October 1871, her age being given as fifty-nine and her occupation as sack maker.

Unnamed. She married "a worthless fellow called Nixon" and had a daughter, Elizabeth Sarah, who was looked after by Aunt Caroline Mittler and went into domestic service. She stayed with her cousins the Finckens between positions.

Claus and Catherine (Mittler) Helmcken had eight children, all of whom were born in Brick Lane and entered in the register of baptisms in Christ Church, Spitalfields:

Catharine, baptized 26 March 1819. She married a man named Perry, but by 1851 she was a widow, living in the Helmcken household; her age is given as thirty-two and her occupation as beer shop keeper. Her illness and death, marked by "excessive plethora" and "general congestion of the whole system," were reported by Dr. Fotherby to JSH on 13 September 1857 and 4 May 1858. JSH says she died of renal disease.

Mary Ann, baptized 11 June 1820. She married Ludwig Fincken, born in Hanover but a British subject, the foreman of a sugar refinery at No. 48, Lambeth Street. In the 1841 census his age is given as forty; in 1861, as fifty-five; in 1871, also as fifty-five. Their children were: Rebecca, said in the 1861 census to be thirteen years old, who died on 4 December 1866 (Catherine Helmcken to JSH, 7 August 1867[?]) ; Mary, said in the 1871 census to be unmarried, aged twenty; Thomas, in 1871 a clerk, unmarried, and reported by his sister to JSH in 1869 as apprenticed to a grocer; Frederick, in 1871 aged fifteen, scholar, and said by his sister to be going to an English school, but writing to JSH in German in 1869; John, in 1871 aged thirteen, scholar; and Catherine, in 1871 aged eleven, scholar. Mary Ann (Helmcken) Fincken died of cancer in July 1866 (Fotherby to JSH, 7 August 1866). It appears that the sugar refinery of which Fincken was foreman closed some time before 1871, for Fotherby, reporting in an undated letter to

JSH the death of his aunt Caroline Mittler [which occurred on 8 October 1871], said that she had been depressed by this closure. The Post Office Directory for 1874 lists "Ludwig Rudolph Finken" at the Flying Horse, No. 63, Lambeth Street. [The spelling of the family name varies. It is *Fincken* in the census returns, but Mary and Frederick, writing to JSH in 1869, sign *Finken*, and this is the spelling in the directory. Dr. Fotherby calls the family *Finck*.]

Ann Margaret, baptized 4 August 1822. She married a man named Kane, brother-in-law of one Kusel (who became librarian of London Hospital), and went to Australia. Her mother told JSH on 7 August [1867?] that she was "doing very well"; that her daughter Margaret was also "doing exceedingly well" and had "saved £50 the first year she was married"; and that "Edward Junior is a jokey and very smart young man"—which suggests that Ann Margaret's husband may have been called Edward.

JOHN SEBASTIAN, baptized 13 February 1825, for whom see below.

Henry, baptized 5 February 1826. In 1851 he was still living at home unmarried, his age being given as twenty-five and his occupation as tailor. On 27 November 1866 his mother wrote to JSH: "Your brothers are all doing well except Henry and he is rather slack of work." In [October 1871?] Fotherby told JSH that "Brother Henry and family are much as usual," but that there was "little cordiality between them and the Goodman Stile people [i.e., the Fincken household]."

Claus Frederick, baptized 25 March 1828. In 1851 he was still living at home, unmarried, his age being given as twenty-three and his occupation as carpenter. By 1866 he was married, for his mother told JSH on 23 November 1866 that "Frederick's wife his going to open a shop in the fancy toy and Berlin wool line ... in the Mile End Road, but Frederick is still agoing to keep his situation." The shop was open by the time JSH's mother wrote again, on 23 August [1867?].

William, baptized 25 November 1829. He is listed in the 1841 census as living at home, aged ten, but had apparently left home by the time the 1851 census was taken.

Elizabeth, baptized 18 November 1831. In 1851 she was still living at home, unmarried, her age being given as nineteen and her occupation as dressmaker. On 23 November 1866 JSH's mother reported to him that "your sister Elizabeth cannot let her shop and she as got three of her children ill with a low fever"; by 7 August [1867?] she was "out of business and lost a deal of money in letting it." After the death of Catherine (Mittler) Helmcken in February 1869 Ludwig Fincken (writing in German to JSH through his son Frederick) asked JSH to forgo at least a part of his share of his mother's estate in favour of his sister Elizabeth. She had been left a widow with four boys and would have been in the poor house long ago, he says, if it had not been for the help given by her mother and her brother Frederick. Fincken himself cannot do much, for he has now full responsibility for "die alte kranke Tante" Caroline Mittler. He hopes that JSH and Frederick Helmcken will do the best they can for their sister.

JOHN SEBASTIAN HELMCKEN married *Cecilia Douglas,* eldest daughter of Chief Factor and Governor James Douglas and Amelia (Connolly) Douglas, on 27 December 1852. The full complement of their descendants may be traced in the Douglas family tree in the Provincial Archives; only their children and grandchildren are dealt with here. They had seven children, of whom four survived infancy:

Catherine Amelia (Amy), b. 19 March 1855; m. 4 December 1877, George Archibald McTavish; d. 1 November 1922. Five children:
> John Archibald, b. 1878; d.s.p. 1929.
> Margaret (Rita) Cecilia, b. 1879; m. 1916, David C. Hughes; d. 1964; two children, of whom one survived infancy.
> Duncan Douglas, b. 1881; m. 1911, Emily Lysle Craig; d. 1967; two children.
> Claus Sebastian, b. 1884; d.s.p. 1962.
> Dorothy Olivia, b. 1889; m. (i) 1916, Edwin Heddle; two children; (ii) 1949, Claire Spence Downing; d. 1972.

James Douglas, b. 2 February 1858; m. (i) 19 June 1886, Mary Jane Halliday (d. 1887) ; (ii) 18 July 1888, Ethel Margaret Mouat; d. 2 April 1919. Five children:

> Cecilia Mary, b. 1889; m. 1915, Douglas Bushby Fitzherbert Bullen; d. 1973; five children.
>
> Edith Helen Douglas, b. 1892; m. 1918, George Allen Watson; two children.
>
> Ethel, b. 1893.
>
> John Sebastian, b. 1896; m. (i) 1929, Olive Brethour; (ii) 1939, Julia Mae McGill.
>
> Ainslie James, b. 1900; m. 1924, Edith Richardson; two children.

Henry (Harry) Dallas, b. 23 December 1859; m. [August?] 1895, Mrs. Hannah Jane Goodwin; d.s.p. 6 July 1912.

Edith Louisa (Dolly), b. 24 June 1862; m. 23 April 1889, William Ralph Higgins; d.s.p. 13 April 1939.

Appendix 2

A Reminiscence of 1850

About March, 1850, I happened to spend a day in Victoria. The *Norman Morison* had arrived from England, bringing about eighty immigrants. The ship lay in Esquimalt harbor. The immigrants were busy ashore, scrubbing and washing their clothes, trunks and so forth, and I learned that soon after leaving England, the small pox broke out on board, but that for the past two months it had disappeared. The ship, men and four or five women were in quarantine. Nearly the whole of them whom were under engagement to the Hudson's Bay Co. at £25 per annum.

Upon my arrival, I was soon presented to Governor Blanshard, Chief Factor Douglas, Mr. Finlayson and some other gentleman, and turned over to the care of Dr. A. Benson, whom I had known in England— a well clothed man known by the soubriquet "Commodore." There he lived in "Bachelors' Hall," a gentleman good and kind as ever, but his garments! He had on a pair of "sea-boots" into one of which he had managed to put one leg with the pants on, the other with the pants outside, and other parts of his dress were equally conspicuous by their eccentricity. "Ah," said he, "you laugh, but if you were to remain here a few months you would of necessity become the same!" He had a coffee pot, and such a coffee pot! on the stove. The stove was square, made of sheet iron, bent in all directions by the heat, with a cast iron

Colonist, Holiday Number, December 1887, p. 3.

door, and it was fed with large billets of wood, of which plenty existed in the Hall. It looked mean and dilapidated, but it was soon found capital for roasting native oysters upon.

"Bachelors' Hall" was a portion of a large story and a half block building, having a common room in the centre, and two rooms on each side with a door opening into each. One was occupied by the Doctor, one by J. W. McKay, and a third by Capt. Nevin, the fourth being the "surgery." The latter was unique. It contained a gun case and a few shelves, with drugs in bottles or in paper in every direction. The tin lining of a "packing case" served for a counter; there was a 'cot' slung to the ceiling; to this room I was consigned. The remainder of the building (it occupied the site of the now Bank of British Columbia) belonged to the chaplain and lady, Mr. and Mrs. Staines, who kept a boarding school for young ladies therein—and a splendid teacher and preceptress she was.

Capt. Grant, of Sooke, arrived in the evening and domiciled in Capt. Nevin's room, and I turned into the hammock.

Every room had sporting weapons in it—muskets and rifles of great variety—swords, a saddle and bridle, tobacco and pipes, lots of dust, and the usual utensils, but not all supplied with the necessary articles. I slept well that night, and was awakened in the morning by the loud ringing of a bell, and a concert proceeding from a host of curs— these curs assembled under the bell at every meal, and looking up to it—howled, the howling being taken up by some dogs in the Indian village opposite.

Benson called out, "Get up quickly; that is the breakfast bell."

I did, and so did Captain Grant. Whilst dressing I heard the following dialogue:

"Dear, oh dear, where's the soap? Capt. Grant, have you my soap?"

"Aye, aye," was the response, "You shall have it directly."

"Why, what has become of my razor! Grant, have you my razor?"

"Yes, nearly finished, you can have it directly."

And he got it and shaved, then I heard:

"Where's my shirt? I shall be late for breakfast. Grant, have you taken my shirt?"

"I have, my dear fellow; I want to appear at table decent."

"This is too bad, Grant; it is the only clean shirt I have to put on!"

"Never mind, old fellow, put on your old one. It will be clean enough. Mine hasn't been washed for I don't know how long; more than a week, anyhow. You can get yours washed, and Benson, send mine, too, please."

However, we all got to breakfast and afterwards we returned and the following,

"Bless me, where's my tobacco? I left half a case of 'Cavendish' under the bed."

"Oh, yes," says Grant, "I took it, my good fellow, to pay my Indians with! *We'll* get some more soon!"

After having smoked a pipe of peace, for Grant was a splendid fellow and every inch an officer and a gentleman—he had been a captain in the "Scotch Greys"—Benson insisted upon showing me the "lions" of Victoria. He put on his sea-boots, with legs of pants inside—I had only my London-made thin soled—his were dirty; mine nicely polished—he was cute; I a greenhorn—so the doctor "practiced" a little on my verdancy.

Now the "lions" of Victoria then were the Fort and its contents. It had been built by Mr. Finlayson. The Fort was nearly a quadrangle, about one hundred yards long and wide, with bastions at two corners containing cannon. The whole was stockaded with cedar posts about six or eight inches in diameter, and about fifteen feet in length, which had been brought from near "Cedar Hill," hence its name (now called "Mount Douglas"). There were inside about a dozen large block story and a half buildings, say 60x40, roofed with long and wide strips of cedar bark. The buildings were for the storage of goods, Indian trading shop, and a large shop for general trade. It contained everything required. The mess-room, off from which lived Mr. Douglas and family, was at the corner (of now) Fort and Government streets. The "counting house" was near (now) Wharf street. Mr. Finlayson occupied this post and lived there with his family. A belfry stood in the middle of the yard and its bell tolled for meals, for deaths, for weddings, for church service, for fires, and sometimes for warnings. At meal time it was assisted by a chorus of curs. On Wharf street there existed a flagstaff and near it a well some eighty feet deep, but which contained but little water. The prevailing color of the paint was "Spanish brown," and "whitewash" was abundant. The Fort yard was muddy and the sidewalk to the stores consisted of two or three poles, along which Benson trudged, but off which my boots slipped every few steps! So my boots and my pants were not a little muddy, and the wretch Benson laughed at me, saying, "I told you so! you'll soon be like me, if you remain here." For all this exertion I saw nothing but "furs" and stores. Not very many of the former, as they had been already packed to be sent home by the returning *Norman Morison*, Captain Wishart being her commander.

As I could not very well get much muddier, we went outside the "fort" and there lay the *Beaver*, Capt. Dodd in command, so clean, so nice, so spruce, as well outside as in, with "boarding nettings" all round him, cannon on deck, muskets and cutlasses arranged in their proper places, beautiful cabins and good furniture, with a trading place for Indians, who, I was told, were only allowed a few at a time on board, when on trade. She had a large crew—active, robust, weather-beaten, jolly good-tempered men—fat from not being overworked—some grey, some grizzled, some young; the former had once been similar to the latter in the "service." Outside the Fort there were no houses, save perhaps a block cabin or two. Forest more or less existed from "the ravine," Johnson street, to the north, and the harbor was surrounded with tall pines, and its bowers bedecked with shrubs, many of which were at this early period in blossom. Cultivated fields existed from Government street to the public schools; likewise across the bay, and I was informed the company exported the wheat to Sitka! There were barns up Fort street (this ran through the centre of the Fort) about the site of the Mechanics' Institute, and I think there I saw a few days ago a small shanty which existed then. It is covered with cedar bark. Benson next took me to Beacon Hill. The weather was lovely and warm, the sky bright, the mountains clear, and everything looked paradisiacal—and there we rested, looked at "Dutnall's fields," at the Beacon, which I thought in my ignorance a target; then walked along the beach to near the entrance of Victoria harbor. Benson said: "Now, I will go back by a 'short cut.'" The wretched man came to a swamp (Providence Pond, near Moffat's). Says he, "we cross somewhere about here; come on." He walked along a fallen tree, so did I, not very well, tho'; he jumped from hillock to hillock, so did I; we both jumped to a fallen tree again; it sunk and we both went knee-deep into the water. He had "sea-boots" on; he looked at me and laughed, "I told you so; you will soon be like me. You are pretty well seasoned now, so come along for I have lost the track." So we followed through this swamp, got out somewhere, got to the Fort, I a wiser but not a sadder man. I had been introduced to "roughing it." My cockney boots and trousers were used up, but both of us were hungry.

After making ourselves decent, for I was told that Mr. Douglas was rather particular about this, the "bell and the dogs" told us it was time for dinner, and to it nothing loath we went. The mess room was more than thirty feet long, by say twenty wide, a large open fire-place at one end and large pieces of cordwood burning therein. A clock on the wall, a long table in the middle, covered with spotless linen, the knives and forks clean, decanters bright, containing wine and so forth. The chairs of wood (Windsor) but everything European. I suppose there must have been more than twenty people in the room, when Mr. Douglas made his appearance—a handsome specimen of nature's noblemen—tall, stout, broad-shouldered, muscular, with a grave bronzed face, but kindly withal. After the usual greetings, he took the head of the table, Mr. Finlayson the foot. Captain Dodd, Capt. Wishart, Capt. Grant and myself were guests. There were also present J. W. McKay, Charley Griffin, Capt. Sangster, and numerous others whom I do not recollect at this moment. Grace having been said by Mr. Douglas, (the chaplain did not dine at the mess, but all the other married officers did) on comes the soup, then the salmon, then the meats— venison on this occasion and ducks—then the pies and so forth, and down they go into their proper receptacle, each one ready and willing to receive them. Having done justice to the dinner and taken a glass "to the Queen," many of the junior members left, either to work or to smoke their pipes in their own quarters. We remained; the steward, a Kanaka, (the cook was also a Kanaka) brought on tobacco and long clay pipes of the kind called "alderman." Mr. Douglas took *his* pipe, which I noticed was beautifully colored, showing slow and careful smoking, (the clerks used to like to get hold of his colored pipes) and others took pipes either from the heap or their pockets. Everybody appeared to smoke calmly and deliberately.

During the dinner there was conversation, Mr. Douglas taking the lead. Capt. Wishart was asked to be careful of his men, as the gold fever was raging and the men deserting as often as they found an opportunity, giving great trouble and necessitating spies. California was spoken about, which led to someone asking where Solomon got his gold from, but no one could answer the conundrum. To change the conversation, perhaps, Mr. Douglas asked the Doctor why so many of the Hudson's Bay officers were bald? His answer was "*pro pelle cutem*— they had sent their furs home," at which some laughed, but Mr. Douglas gravely said, "perhaps, having given us the poetry of the thing, you will give the prose—the cause," which nonplussed the Doctor, as this was a conundrum too. By the *Norman Morison* files of newspapers and "The Four Reviews" of latest dates—that is to say nearly six months old—had come out and Mr. Douglas commenced about some Scotch battles fought long ago. This brought out Dodd, an Englishman, well read and well educated, who derided the breechless vagabonds, and ushered in the ten of diamonds—Johnny Cope got his share. Douglas and Dodd seemed to know how many men were engaged in each battle and all at once they tumbled into the battle of Waterloo, the one claiming that the Scotch did best, the other that the English did most execution, whilst a third claimed that both Scotch and English and Irish would have been beaten had it not been for Blucher and his host coming up just in the nick of time to save the lot. This question was not settled. "Old Tod" was chaffed for having fired a salute four years after the victory, *i.e.*, as soon as he heard of it. He was indignant and said it was less than three. His post had been somewhere near the North Pole. I was informed that no frivolous conversation was ever allowed at table, but that Mr. Douglas as a rule came primed with some intellectual or scientific subject, and thus he educated his clerks. All had to go to church every Sunday, the mess-room serving every purpose—baptisms, marriages, funerals, councils, dances, theatricals, or other amusements—and did not seem any the worse for it.

After dinner we went to see the Indian village. Benson just pointed out the bullet holes in the pickets and bastions made by hostile Indians. "But," said he, "Don't be afraid, they are only dangerous when excited, and as a rule they don't get excited without cause given." He procured a canoe, of which I felt dubious, but he taught my tiny feet how to get into it, and so we arrived safely after what I then considered a dangerous passage. There must have been five or six hundred Indians. By far the greater number had a blanket only for clothing, but "King Freezy" had on a tall hat and a long coat and considered himself somebody, as indeed he was, and friendly to the whites. He had a most remarkably flattened head—indeed all the Indians had flattened heads—fearful foreheads, retreating backward. We saw babies undergoing the process, a pad and pressure being the instruments. They did not seem to suffer; perhaps it made them good. The cradles were hung on a flexible pole, stuck in the ground at an acute angle, so a slight touch on the pole put it into an up and down motion. In one house there were a number of people beating tom-toms and chanting. They had a sick child in the centre. The doctor was performing some incantations, such as sucking the child's skin and spitting upon it. The child had a devil, and I suggested he was standing alongside. Benson said no, he is the doctor, a man and a brother Medico. This was very interesting, but our time being precious, we looked at their "woolly dogs" and the dirt and filth and returned in our, what seemed to me then, very frail and treacherous conveyance. Bye-the-bye these "woolly dogs" seem to have become extinct. These Indians used to shear them and made a sort of blanket out of the wool. On this side, on our way to Governor Blanshard's, we saw many Indians walking about. Nearly every one had the same covering, a blanket and dirt, and we saw two examining each other's head, looking for—well, never mind, but they ate them!

We found Governor Blanshard smoking a very thick pipe, with a very long stem. He was a comparatively young man, of medium height, with aquiline, aristocratic features, set off by a large military moustache. He had arrived only a few days previously and had been riding. He said: "Benson, you told me all the trails led *to* the Fort, but you did not tell me they all led away from it. Now I got off the trail to wander about and I lost it, but I found another and it led away from the fort and I should not have been here now, had I not turned my horse's head and tail; as it is I have lost my dinner." He told me he had no salary, but that a tract of land had been put aside for the Governor, out of the rents of which he had to make an income!! and that he, whom the Hudson's Bay Co. told me was to be my private secretary, was under orders for Fort Rupert. Although a very intelligent and affable man, he did not see his way to do it, and thought the 'Wakefield system' a mere theory, sure to fail in practice. He proved to be right. We left him with his pipe-stem still in his mouth.

It being now supper time, we went to the mess room. The company was smaller, and after chatting around the fire and smoking of course, every one went his own way, but most to "the hall."

After adjourning to "Bachelors' Hall," a Frenchman came (all the men were French Canadians) and said to the Doctor, "Pierre has a bad stomach-ache." Doctor—"Bad stomach-ache, aye? Ah! eating too much. Ah, yes! Give him a tablespoonful of salts. Ah, yes! a tablespoonful of salts!" "Oh," said the man, "but he is very bad." Doctor —"Ah! hum, yes, very bad, eh! very bad! eh? Then give him two spoonfuls of salts! Oh, yes, that's the way to clean out the 'salt salmon.'"

There were a good many in Bachelors' Hall—all young men. After a while Capt. Grant began "to entertain the company." He showed how to use the sword. He stuck a candle on the back of a chair, and snuffed it therewith, but I am bound to confess he took off a good piece of the candle with it, and down it went. Again the candle was stuck up. Then he split it longitudinally and this time splendidly. He wanted to "cut" a button off Benson's coat (he had none too many) but Benson said—Oh! Oh! cut a button—no, no—split or spit one too! ho! ho! After a while he wanted to escort Her Majesty to Windsor Castle. All were to be cavalry. So down everybody went Kangaroo fashion. Grant being in command, took the lead, and so we hopped in this style round the room, and made considerable of a racket.

In the midst of which, some naughty school girl overhead, possibly not being able to sleep, poured some water through a crack in the ceiling right down upon the cavalry! This put an end to the diversion, but only resulted in others, for some one wanted a song, and it came, for there were good singers among them. In the midst of this a spy brought word that some of the men had a canoe and were about to depart to the other side, so off McKay went. This broke up the party and away we went to bed, and so ended a day in Victoria.

I stand to-day upon the same spot, but oh! how changed. Of the twenty or thirty met before, but two or three answer to the call. Of the fields, naught remain. The forest has been removed and the bleak winds unhindered now rush in to what was before a genial, sheltered place. The *Beaver* remains, but great Jove! no more like the *Beaver* of former days than a coal barge is like a frigate. Mightier steamers float upon the harbor; the Indians, once half a thousand, have disappeared, homes occupy the fields; telegraph and telephone wires make the streets hideous; there is great hurry and scurry, but I doubt whether there is more happiness and content now than was enjoyed by the few but hospitable and kind-hearted Hudson's Bay Co. residents in 1850. Peace be with them—their works live after them.

In the Early Fifties

Colonist, Supplement, 1 January, 1889.

After sojourning six months at Fort Rupert, orders came for my immediate removal to Victoria. A day or so afterwards, in a canoe manned by northern Indians, and having a few cedar mats, a bottle of brandy, grub, matches, muskets, and so forth, we set off to travel three hundred miles. The weather being bad, stormy, rainy and cold, the usual discomforts, of which, however, a young man thinks but little of, were experienced. Seymour Narrows were found angry and impassable, and perhaps the Ucultas, a wild untamed lot, who lived close by and were a terror to the neighborhood, were angry too, so we encamped for the night on an island, having a very poor beach. The men being tired, I kept watch. Nothing apparently disturbed the night save the calling of ducks and the grating of the canoe on the rocks; to remedy this the canoemen were called up, but soon went to sleep again on the ground by the fires, covering their heads with their blankets. They enjoyed the sleep of the just. Bright and early the following morning the canoe got under weigh, but my musket, which I had close by me all night, could not, after diligent search, be found.

Without mishap, no Indians having molested or troubled us in any way, Victoria, that is the fort pickets, pleasantly appeared, my Indians singing and paddling double quick time. Of course a hearty welcome, and enquiries as to how we had run the gauntlet.

About three months afterwards, Mr. J. W. McKay came into Bachelors' Hall, enquiring—"Do you know this musket?" "Of course I do; it is the very one I could not find when leaving Seymour Narrows." "Well, a chief brought it to me in the trade shop and said—tell the young chief when he encamps, not to let his men sleep around the fire, but put it out and order the men to rest somewhere else, because any enemy can see men near a fire, but those encamped cannot see them. His Indian canoe men must have been fools! I and my men were out that night, and would have killed all his men, but said, the young chief is carrying papers to Mr. Douglas, so we will let him and them alone; but I took the musket from the side of the young chief!" So, the 'noise of the ducks and geese,' were these Indians calling to each other; the grating of the canoe their work also. The Indians were thanked and rewarded.

In those days Indians had a sort of superstitious veneration for written papers. It had been the custom for traders on the coast to give supplies to Indians, dividing their share. These they called "Tea-pots," and were fond of showing them to strangers—and strangers were equally glad to read them, because, as a rule they stated whether the bearer were trustworthy or not. I never heard of these being forged by Indians, who, however, used occasionally to write imitating some order or other, and presenting it for payment.

My friend, Dr. Benson, had been transferred to Fort Vancouver, Columbia river. I took his place, to be my own guide in future. Victoria was now in a transition state, no longer a happy family.

Occasionally a vessel would call, on her way to load with piles in Washington Territory, for the purpose of wharves in San Francisco; and rumors were current that a steamer between San Francisco and the Sound, was about to be put on, but the question was whether Portland or the Sound would be chosen. Governor Blanshard, who had been ill, had recovered without the aid of a doctor; a very improper and not respectable proceeding. The poor man had a fever and ague, which had tenanted him in the tropics, and had occasional tic douloureux, to which he became a martyr. The Governor, who now lived at the corner of Yates and Fort streets, in Government House, and Chief Factor Douglas were not on good terms. The Governor could not get grub, esculents, and other things he required, excepting at what he considered very extortionate prices, and as the governor had not any salary, he deemed this very unkind, and as it pinched his pocket the more so. There were now two parties in Victoria—The Governor's party, which consisted of some dissatisfied company's servants and Mr. Douglas' side. Now Blanshard was *de jure* governor, but Douglas was *de facto*. The former had all the authority, but the latter held all the power! Hence no friendly feeling existed, and as time advanced, the warmth of opposition increased to fever heat; Blanshard was in the toils. I did not see the usual Xmas festivities, holidays with gay and good things, but on New Year's Day, all officers and men presented themselves very respectfully before Mr. Douglas, paying him the usual compliments with the usual chat and enquiries—but the remarkable part was, that on this day, the gentlemen kissed the ladies. They would shake hands and then present as a mere matter of politeness, their cheek to be kissed. It mattered little what position the ladies held, this routine went on for this day only. As the company's servants had originally been nearly all French Canadians, I supposed the custom had been brought with them. As it did not seem a very unpleasant ordeal, I, rather bashfully, though perhaps not unwillingly took my part in the performance of the duty. This day was devoted to jollity— all mixed after a fashion—man and master together, good feeling reigned, all were polite and nothing *outre* took place. If men and masters moved more together now, the feeling between them would be less strained.

The chaplain, Mr. Staines, a great mathematician, had a garden on Fort street, where he grew lettuces and other choice esculents. Finding his lettuces disappearing faster than ordinary, he one morning got up early and as he suspected found a man stealing his pets. "Good morning, Minie!" The culprit looked up and merely unabashed replied, "Good morning, sir." "Whilst you are about it, Minie, you had better take them all!" "Thank you, sir," replied he; "so I will," and went on packing them into his sack! The feelings of the chaplain may be imagined. There being neither law courts nor lawyers, the point is disputed. Was Minie right or wrong? He had been told to take them all and he did so. Minie not understanding English irony, the parson should have been less enigmatic!

The chaplain wanted his lettuce, he being famous for salad suppers, to which, ladies and gentlemen, his cronies were invited. In these days the visitors often had a shake down. On one occasion the salad disagreed with his visitors and himself, and numerous were the lights flitting about the passage all night. In the morning they discussed the matter. They all agreed the salad to have been lovely, so perhaps had partaken too freely. Suddenly, however, Mrs. Staines asked Mrs. B.: "Where did you find the oil?" Reply—"In the old bottle, of course!" "Dear me, dear me. I forgot to tell you. I filled that bottle with castor oil! It is a mercy we were not all poisoned!"

The amusements in those days were not numerous, but as spring advanced and the horses, who had been running at large all winter, became stronger, they, every Saturday afternoon, were brought into the fort, and then, weather permitting, Mr. Douglas, daughters and other ladies, together with the gentlemen of the fort, each got a horse saddled and then they all together had a scamper over the country. No fences, no roads then. Ah! those jolly scampers! You may rely the party sooner or later broke into groups—any how they returned separately to the fort—and some were invited to tea with Mr. Douglas and the young ladies.

On the following morning, all appeared at church, *i.e.*, the messroom. No thought then whether a fellow was a Presbyterian or a churchman—no aesthetic expensive churches, no costly chairs, no plate, no subscriptions!! The people were good and kindhearted, each willing to assist the other in sickness or distress. The company paid for all. Church over—pulpit cleared away, and then dinner. The chaplain used to complain, because the mess-room, which had an aroma of tobacco, a scent he was averse to, and occasionally would be angry because he saw a pipe lying about or stub of a cigar, but no one cared about this.

There existed, however, a Roman Catholic missionary Father, who built himself a house and plastered the walls with clay! When this became dry, it would crack and stick no longer, to the great disquietude of the occupant. This place, nevertheless, served him for chapel and everything else. One day he appeared (not an unusual thing) in the Fort yard, and as usual, Mr. Douglas invited him to the mess. Curiously enough, no fish appeared on the table and it happened to be Friday! Mr. Douglas apologized to the Father for the unusual omission, but he replied, "There is no occasion for any apology. I have lived on dried salmon and fish for the past month! I have no objection to eat meat this Friday, and to tell the truth am very glad to get it too." We did not know the wholesome rule, that in such cases, the letter of the law does not apply, and quite right too.

In these days there were continual wrangles about "grub," particularly with the newly arrived English and Scotch. The former wanted beef, mutton and beer, of which precious little existed. The latter had never used oatmeal, but had always been accustomed to the finest kind of wheaten flour! They could not work on game, salmon fresh and salt, and salt food. It was no easy matter to find food daily for about a couple of hundred fastidious stomachs. Captain Grant took me to Sooke to see a sick man. The captain showed me the beautiful serpentine road he had cut to his residence—a carriage drive? The house was a shanty, but of peculiar shape, and he had two small cannon. He explained to me that this was a perfect fortification, and could be defended by a few men against a large number of Indians! However, it so happened that his room and the men's were near each other, and almost the first words I heard through the boards were: To h—ll with the ducks and the geese and salmon. I'd like to know when and where the town is to be? A city of imposing magnitude was expected by them to arise at Sooke—we all had vapor notions about immigration and cities, but they did not trouble our youth very much, but others were dissatisfied—in fact no one seemed to have realized his expectations or fancies.

During the spring the *Tory* brought more immigrants, but this time for the Puget Sound Company. Occasionally, too, a ship would arrive from which we got some things such as were not at hand. The company did not sell any liquor to Indians, and in fact none to the men. Yet they used to get it occasionally, for plenty of the intoxicating fluid existed. However, all the men were drunk on one occasion, and this having lasted for more than one day, Mr. Douglas set his officers to find out the cause. The chaplain—a good temperance man—assisted, he had armed himself with a sword which he said had belonged to some ancestor who had been hanged in some rebellion or other, but of which he was very proud.

Well, we searched the men's houses, and at last found one with some floor boards loose. No sooner did we want to remove these boards, when the drunken men attempted to come forward to prevent, but the valiant chaplain drew his sword, held it across the room at arm's length, and said "pass me who dare!" The men looked with drunken stupicity at the steel and one said "Parson we don't want to pass it." So the whisky was got out—a whole barrel full—and rolled into the fort yard. Mr. Douglas was biding events. Looking at the cask, he said, "knock the head in, Mr. Finlayson." An axe being brought, the head knocked in, out ran the whisky into the gutter and down the length of the fort yard. The men seeing this rushed to the gutter, some scooped up the liquor with any vessel—some on their knees scooped it up mud and all —others lay on their stomachs and lapped it like dogs or got their fill somehow. Mr. Finlayson said, "Doctor, what's to be done now?" So I rushed to my sanctum and got a bottle of tartar emetic and sprinkled the gutter therewith. In a short time the whole crowd vomited the liquor and lay limp, helpless and pallid alongside of it. Now some fellows called out, "the doctor has poisoned these poor men," and upon my word I was afraid they had taken too much of the antimony whisky—but they all recovered after a while. Spirits was a bane then as now. The cause of poverty, disorder, and ruin of mind and body. The baker was fond of taking too much, and so also at length became his wife. The doctor was asked to see him. He had, as usual, the horrors, worms coming out of the logs and getting down his throat; he had his head covered with the blanket, and was in awful dread. "Well Mrs. you know what's the matter—the old story—worms, all moonshine." "Yes, I know all about it, but do what I will I can't keep him sober, and I'm afraid he will lose his place."

A day or two afterwards, the wife said awfully confidentially—"It's all right telling my husband that the worms are all moonshine, but doctor I have just the same things. I feel them in my throat and see them too. I suppose I must have caught them from him."

About this time a Songish Indian killed a cow. The culprit having been discovered, he took refuge in the village; his tillicums refused to surrender him. The Indian must be had and punished, such was the rule; white man's authority and superiority must be upheld. Mr. Douglas determined to have the fellow, and therefore three boats started from the fort with about a dozen armed men all told, to take him out of the village; Mr. J. W. McKay was chief in charge. I had a boat and three men. We had strict orders not to fire or injure anyone if it could be avoided, for Douglas, brave as a lion, was as harmless as a dove to Indians. The boats pulled on to the village. The Indians turned out to receive us with yells, shouts, guns, axes, spears, and so forth. There must have been five hundred men; some were crouching, armed, behind logs, and among them the outpost with gun pointed! The big boat grounded, but instead of the men leaping out of the boat the Indians rushed into the water, and took the muskets away from the men! I stood up in my boat, and have a very vivid recollection of a knife, on a fishing rod about ten feet long, being pointed at my gizzard, and a lot of muskets looking in the same direction. The men apparently pulled, but I could not understand why I had to turn slowly, to keep my face to the enemy, but happening to look behind, I found only one man pulling as hard as he could, the remainder lying flat in the boat; and so the boat was making a circle! The battle was soon over; no wounded, no lives lost! No prisoner! Boats and men returned to the Fort and met Mr. Douglas, with the horse-shoe frown on his forehead. No need of despatches—he had seen the whole affair. I walked with him afterwards along what is now Wharf street. The Indians were firing across the water, the balls striking round about, which made me madder, so I asked Mr. Douglas to allow us to go back again. "No, no; leave them alone. It will come out all right. You'll see."

On the following day some chiefs appeared with a flag of truce, King Freezy among the number. After consultation, the chiefs decided to pay for the cow, and return all the muskets and accoutrements, but, in good humor now, they said of what use was the muskets? The locks were corroded and the hammers would not move! Some of the men had armed themselves with old American army muskets, preferring them to the H. B. Co.'s flint-locks. "Oh," said Mr. Douglas, "you see no one intended to injure you; but do not do wrong any more or worse will happen." Among the things returned was my cap, but how I lost it, is more than I know. This, I think, was the last serious (?) squabble with these people. Of course there were occasional troubles, but generally speaking the natives were peaceable, and we roamed among them and around the country without dread. It says a great deal for their self-command, that they did not fire upon us, but I suppose the party was too contemptibly small, hence its safety. By this time I was no longer the spruce Cockney—Benson's words had come true. At Fort Rupert my education had been a pretty rough one; Indian rows and troubles having been frequent there.

During this and the following year, the Langfords, Skinners, Mc-Kenzies, Blinkhorns and Coopers arrived, together with many other immigrants, but nearly all the latter engaged to the Puget Sound Company. The three first mentioned were bailiffs of the Puget Sound Company, having a share in the profits of the farms they came to make. All ladies and gentlemen in the English sense of the word, with families, and thus society became more extended and varied, *emollet mores nec sinit esse feros*. A vessel of war or more were nearly always at Esquimalt, which enlivened the place considerably, the officers sociable gentlemen, whilst pleasing others pleased themselves too.

Mr. Langford was placed at Colwood farm; McKenzie had one part of the peninsula between Victoria Arm and Esquimalt, to which he gave the name of Craigflower; Mr. Skinner the remainder. Buildings of various kinds arose on those farms, and so did white babies, a sort of new production. The former still remains as evidence, as also the latter. The Puget Sound Company bought all these lands and spent a heap of money in developing them, but proved a failure. Land at this time cost five dollars per acre. The Puget Sound Company sent out a good breed of cattle and sheep, as also a steam saw mill and machinery for brick making. The Hudson's Bay Co. had Uplands, North Dairy, and the home farm across James' Bay, as well as round about the fort. Altogether things looked flourishing, but for some cause or other every lady seemed dissatisfied—things were not as they expected; were not such as they had been accustomed to. They had now to do their own domestic work—Indians being almost the only, and very poor help; but employed as domestics or in field labor they felt the influence of these best of missionaries and so became docile and more useful. The arrival of such nice people altered matters amazingly. There were English ladies—*rara avis*—very pleasing and nice. No longer had the officers to look to themselves for amusement. Visits—little teas —occasional parties, or amateur theatricals, or a ball in the mess-room took place, so that horses and so forth were called more into requisition; so life became extended, more artificial and more expensive.

Of course it was not long before the usual jealousies among ladies came to the front, who should occupy the front seat and so forth, but as the men liked to be friends with all, they managed adroitly to agree with all. The men, however, ere long became split up into parties too, social as well as political. Mr. Douglas, who acted as agent for the Puget Sound Company, could not grant the new-comers all they desired, which led to ill-feeling. Douglas had to bear the brunt of everything. The Puget Sound Company soon began to complain of the greatness of the expenditure, and likewise of the apparently insignificant results therefrom, and so things became a little disagreeable—at all events to the managers of the farms, who had ideas of progress and outlay the company did not relish or coincide with. They wanted to get many things, in order to make the farms, cattle-raising, and so forth, pay, that they might get their share of the profits!

Bickerings about supplies, grub, and so forth, were not infrequent. The truth is the whole country was in a state of unrest. The California gold fields dazzled the people's minds and senses and caused some recklessness. What was Vancouver Island, with California so close at hand? Probably if this had not existed, things would have gone on smoothly; as it was the companies made a mistake in their scheme of colonization—a scheme formed before the discovery of gold became popularly known. If these people had been sent or come upon their own responsibility as settlers, they would have fared much harder and worked harder and contentedly for their own satisfaction and profit, but as they were servants with rich masters, they acted accordingly. On the other hand, had not gold fields existed, there would not have been the unrest, for immigrants then would not have had a more enticing place to go to, and therefore would have been satisfied. Everybody, anyhow, at this time was taken off his or her equilibrium.

Ragged, dirty, almost bootless, tramp-like creatures, used to come to the company's store to rig themselves out, paying for their outfit in gold dust, which they extracted from chamois leather bags, containing many ounces. How much more they had goodness only knows, yet they looked like beggars when they came in; highly respectable when they departed! Fancy the Puget Sound and Hudson's Bay Companies' servants, whose wages amounted to one hundred and fifty dollars per annum and only bound by an agreement, brought into contact with these! What could happen, but that these would work but little and try to get to where these bags of gold came from, and such in reality did happen, for the men would desert at every opportunity and no end of trouble was given in trying to prevent them, a difficulty greater as now communication with Puget Sound and California became and was rapidly becoming more frequent. Who can wonder at the Puget Sound Company and farming by engaged servants being an expensive and complete failure? Nevertheless, their enterprise formed the nucleus of the future development—and that nucleus was composed of intellectual, intelligent people, strong in mind as well as body. Old things and systems were rapidly passing away; without possibility of prevention, new elements had been introduced, and their consequences. A small shop or so began to be erected outside by private individuals, generally by those who had been in the company's service, or by those who had had permission to retire, and so Victoria became a small village, prosperous and likewise political. Three or four little shops, of course including grog, and a few small residences, now composed the village —a little Peddlington, where all the topics of the day were canvassed—news became plentiful from the outside world, and local subjects and scandal afforded some room for amusement and instruction, then as now. Politics!! were indulged in. The governor's and Hudson Bay Co.'s partizans had increased in numbers, both of men and women.

Soon the currency question came to the front. Blankets, shirts, grey cotton, tobacco, were to be no longer current. The Hudson Bay Co. were to be obliged to import money, silver and gold, their servants to be paid in cash, so that they might spend their money, when they got any, where they pleased. The currency question soon settled itself, the gold diggers, sloops and stray ships bringing gold and also American coin, besides the cash paid to sailors and the men of the navy. Shopkeepers made money and saved it. Extravagance had not yet become rampant. Men wanted five or more dollars per day for work. Lumber was sold at sixty dollars per thousand; flour fifteen dollars per barrel, and other things in proportion. At this time J. D. Pemberton and others formed a company for the purpose of getting a steam sawmill. Shares, five hundred dollars each. Capt. Wishart was deputed to obtain this sawmill in England. It arrived and was erected at the head of the lagoon outside Esquimalt harbor. This enterprise for reasons too many to be mentioned, proved a failure and in the end the mill took fire and died. Sawmills were springing up on Puget Sound.

The governor had little to do, except hearing some petty complaints; but, nevertheless, he was a nice, affable gentleman, kind and socially liked, but out of his element. He was at variance with the H.B.Co. and their agent Mr. Douglas. He could not pull with them but made many complaints against them, some exaggerated by hastiness, say officially; others were unworthy of notice, considering the youthful age of the colony. He wanted a regiment of soldiers to protect the people against the Indians, whom he wrote had too much freedom and were better treated than the whites; a ship of war; a chief justice and the full paraphernalia of an old and populous place, and undoubtedly we would have been glad had Her Majesty's government filled the requisition; but who was to pay the piper? The Hudson's Bay Company or the British government? They did not come, anyhow. The fact is, the Americans gave more trouble. They seized a ship or two in Washington Territory. Owing to bad health, without any prospect of honor, glory or emolument, and what not, Governor Blanshard obtained permission to retire, and left, but before leaving appointed a Council. Mr. Douglas, a man of noble mind and presence, being appointed Governor in his stead. Doubtless Mr. Blanshard was a good sensible man, but owing to bad health, and unaccustomed to establishing a youthful colony, without any officers or assistants and the roughness attendant, he was dissatisfied and among unsuitable elements. He and the Company were not in unison. This made some disturbance in Peddlington, and among the Peddlingtonians. Now there was something to talk about. Mr. Douglas had already built his mansion on James Bay. It stands there still, although a wooden building.

It happened soon, that Governor Douglas wanted to raise a revenue! Whoever heard of such a thing? The councillors were called together. The mess-room called into requisition. Governor Douglas wanted to make the sellers of grog pay an annual license of five hundred dollars. The debate lasted till mid-day, and as at this time the council chamber, table and chairs were required for dinner, the council adjourned and the honorable members joined the mess, and made a very good dinner too.

The subject of discussion, however, having leaked out, great was the disturbance in Peddlington. One man excited ran about shouting: "Beware of the first tax! If this be allowed, others will soon follow. The country will be ruined! No taxation without representation. Down with tyranny—down with the Hudson's Bay Company—down with monopoly— Has not the Hudson's Bay Co. to pay all costs and expenses by charter! The Emperor of Russia dare not do such a thing as this—is Governor Douglas greater than the Emperor?" Lots of this talk about the grocery and bar-room, in fact the opportunity for a little excitement was glorious, but there being but few it could not be kept up very long, and as it only affected the publicans, who were growing rich, some laughed at it as a good joke, which made the other side more rancorous still, and so many got drunk, the groceries reaping the benefit.

However, after dinner the council met again and commenced the thing *de novo*, but one or two continued very inimical to the imposition—they sold spirits. The Governor found it dry work, so he rang. The steward appeared. Bring in the Madeira, pipes and tobacco! Now the grave men smoked—pass the Madeira—don't be afraid, it is good and generous, and so it was—but Gov. Douglas not being a wine-bibber took little, but smoke he could and did.

By degrees the opposition became less and less, and the opponents began to see something in it. The Madeira went round, things looked more pleasant; the tobacco and wine rendered them clear headed, and at length convinced them that the tax was perfectly legitimate, and would do a great deal of good as well morally as industrially, and so the first tax came into being. No reading bills first, second, and third then, nor the modern custom about money bills. The thing was done and could not be undone.

About Xmas 1852, a wedding in high life took place. The day before the time fixed it snowed and it snowed—lord, how it snowed!—so that a couple of feet of snow lay on the ground. The only thing approaching to a carriage was a two-wheeled light cart—the governor's carriage—useless, there not being any roads. The bridegroom goes to church. The bride and her maidens at home, waiting for the carriage. The cart was at the fort, had travelled a hundred yards the wheels no longer would turn and there was a dead stop. The charioteer, a lively, active, good natured French-Canadian gentleman, full of resource, got an idea. He sent to the store for a dry-goods box, cut off the top and one side, put a seat in and threw some scarlet cloth over all. Having hewn a couple of willows growing close at hand, of these he made shaft and runners all in one! The box arriving is fixed upon the willow runners, the horse harnessed, the sleigh hastens for the bride and maids.

The poor bridegroom is waiting impatiently in the mess-room church; the hour approaches twelve! His best man rushes into the mess-room, to put the clock hands back, when he suddenly encounters the chaplain's wife, dismayed he kicks out a dog, to disguise his intentions, and returns disappointed. The chaplain appears, and says, if the bride does not arrive before twelve; it only wants a quarter now, I will not be able to perform the ceremony to-day, it being illegal to do so. Here's a pretty kettle of fish; but just then the tinkle of the sleigh bells are heard, and the bridesmaids and dry-goods box appear. The whole party hurry into the church, the ceremony is proceeding, the clock strikes twelve, just as the ring is put on the finger, etc.: the ceremony over, the bride and bridegroom leave the church to return to their parents' house for a good time, and then the guns roar from the bastions. The bell in the middle of the fort rings—the dogs howl thereunder—the men fire muskets—all hurrah. Grog is served out all round, there is feasting, revelling and jollity, and everybody heart and soul wishes the handsome, favorite, and favored couple very many happy new years.

Fort Rupert in 1850

Colonist, 1 January 1890, pp. 4-5.

"Good bye, Dodd; take care of your charge and deliver him safely at Fort Rupert," said Chief Factor Douglas.

"Aye, aye, sir, this side up."

The steamer *Beaver* starts—armed, boarding nettings all right—clears Victoria harbor and then paddles on and on through Dodd's Narrows, Cowitchin Gap, the Gulf of Georgia, to her journey's end. Seymour Narrows were drowsy, so the *Beaver* passed through without difficulty, although when wide awake ships had to remain until the boiling, seething current and whirlpools subsided, not even a steamer being able to overcome them. Some distance further she came to a small island in the middle of Johnstone's Strait, the current on both sides being sufficiently strong to make her stand still. The power of the *Beaver* and of the current about balancing each other.

"What is the name of the island, captain?"

"By jove! it hasn't any, and so I will give it your name, as it is always in opposition."

Subsequently a detached rock was found by H.M.S. *Plumper* and named "Speaker rock," an office I filled at the time.

The voyage and the May weather were lovely. The scenery grand and wonderful then, is now and may be to eternity! Here then existed a country almost one vast forest of firs, pines and other evergreens, which had grown up naturally, untamed, unsubdued; nevertheless governed by the wonderful inexplicable force which we call natural, constant, inexorable, eternal unchangeable law, a mere name to hide our ignorance of its nature or origin. Are law and God but one and the same?

How many seeds had been wafted or floated from foreign places and taking root here, usurped the place of others, altering perhaps the character of the country, which, if it could speak, would perhaps say, civilizing it. How many lesser plants have been destroyed, slowly, but surely, by these gigantic growths hundreds of years old! Wild and savage, yet wonderfully lovely, the scene, no sail, no ship bedecked the surrounding placid waters; vast, silent solitude; apparently happiness, peace and contentment reigned. Yet if these trees, mountains and rocks could speak might they not tell (as in scientific speech they do) of as many strifes among themselves as amongst human beings?

Here am I and others like seeds floated from a foreign shore, bringing a new philosophy, power and artificial resulting mode of living among these natural men and natural forests. What will be the result?

At Fort Rupert

"Ease her! stop her! move her astern!" The anchor down—the

Beaver is at Fort Rupert, not having during this trip struck or discovered a single sunken rock through, as yet, these unsurveyed waters!

A crowd of Indians; a large number of canoes, great and small, and the officers of the fort, viz., Mr. Blenkinsop, who had charge, and Charley Beardmore, his second in command, on the shore. Landed—by boat; introduced—Capt. Dodd soon falling to the lot of Blenkinsop to talk business, I to Beardmore.

"Ah," says he, "you should have arrived yesterday and you would have seen half a dozen heads on the rocks."

The Quocholds had been out on a marauding expedition, brought back six heads and some captives, now slaves.

"Horrible!"

"Oh, you will get accustomed to it, for after all it is much the same as civilized men do in war against their enemies. These Indians are a precious bad lot, a terror!"

I learned subsequently that these followed a marauding business, made expeditions for the sake of taking heads and captives of their enemies, the latter being valuable either for slaves or for ransom. As a rule these were clandestine expeditions against enemies (for Indians had land boundaries, allies and treaties of friendship, a la civilized) whom they preferred catching unawares, either on the water or land.

On one occasion a band of four hundred men went out in many canoes, leaving a few hundred at home to guard the camp. Returning in due season, not less than seventy-five heads were arranged along the shore. After they had glutted their eyes and filled themselves with ecstatic enjoyment, the heads were taken away, the scalps cut off and dried, pieces of wood being used as stretchers to make them of the desired shape, viz., that of a skullcap. The scalp having been removed by first making an incision just above the eyebrows and carried directly round the head. Of course these caps were kept as trophies, and I dare say may perhaps even now be purchased from some of the old warriors—if any of these exist. How many slaves were captured is unknown, but a large number. But mind, they made havoc among their enemies, or to revenge some wrong. Yet these expeditions were at least annual, so I was told.

Of course the whites thought this all wrong, but the Indians thought quite otherwise. They might have asked how many have been killed in wars by Christians.

The Indian Village

This Rupert village contained at least two thousand five hundred bodies, *i.e.,* men, women and children, for the most part armed either with their rude weapons, spears, knives and so forth, or Hudson's Bay Co.'s flint-lock muskets which they had gradually obtained from traders of the H.B.Co., and were becoming rich and so independent. The Quocholds had a man of mature age, grizzled, with by no means unpleasant expression, for chief. He and followers occupied the north side of the fort. The Queechars had a middle aged man, tall, dark, moustached and bearded, named Whale, for their chief, and occupied the south side, together with the Clewichis under Jachlan, their head man. The lodges abutted on the sides of the fort pickets within a stone's throw thereof, so they were close neighbors. The lodges were of the usual style—long rectangular shed-like buildings, with ridge poles, say from 60 to 80 feet long, and a foot or eighteen inches in thickness, resting upon upright slabs. It seemed difficult to understand how the aborigines lifted these very heavy pieces into their place, but when one of the ridge poles had to be raised the builder had a "bee" and a great feast to celebrate and assist at the occasion. The walls and roof were made of cedar slabs about three or four feet in width and about an inch in thickness. I saw a man reducing one out of a split cedar slab. He used a small rude tool somewhat like a cooper's adze, which he had constructed. He chipped, chipped, chipped towards himself taking off at each stroke very small pieces. Time being of no object the longer and wider the board the grander the lodge and its owner. Not very much unlike ourselves.

A canoe had been brought in in a rough state from the woods, looking like a log very roughly hollowed. A man was working at this with a stone hammer, rough ancient tools, and without line, model or measure. It appears that they shaped the canoe by eye and then stretched it by placing it in a heap of seaweed mixed with heated stones, the moist heat making the wood soft and flexible, the finishing touches being made afterwards. This tribe, however, were not canoe builders. They, as a rule, bought their canoes from other professional tribes and paid therefor from a couple to twenty blankets each, according to size and other qualities. They did the same when they wanted any carved work, for the Ruperts seemed to know nothing of carving, handicraft or ground culture. They were for war, they being of the warrior caste.

The ground around these aristocratic buildings were strewed with heaps of clam shells and fish offal. The fragrance so strong as almost to require an axe to cut it. Inside the lodges could not be said to be dirty; there existed a fire on the ground, the smoke finding its way out through the roof, and around the fire were generally squatted some decrepit, bent, wrinkled, blear-eyed, witch-like old women and men, useless and bad tempered. A raised platform, covered with cedar bark, mats and bunks above served for sleeping places. Muskets, spears, boxes, dried fish and other articles for offense, hunting or storage of food were promiscuously placed, and things coiled up like snakes lay in a corner. These snakes were a seaweed (fucus gigantea) made by some process into very strong, thin, flexible bottles or tubes containing oolachan oil. Taking the tail of this coil, the stinking rancid oil was squeezed out in quantity required to be eaten with dried halibut, salmon or other food, it serving the place of butter; used and enjoyed as such. Fresh oolachan oil (made purposely for white men's use to order), however, I subsequently found to be not half bad and very useful for culinary purposes—Hobson's choice! This grease was an article of Indian commerce (for they had trade and commerce in various articles, such as dried berries in cakes, canoes, ointments and what-not) and had to be brought or bought from northern tribes, who had almost a monopoly of the article, the fish frequenting in its annual migration a choice northern river or two (the Skeena and the Nass) on almost a particular day yearly. Coils of fishing lines of great strength and length, made of prepared seaweed, and wooden fish hooks, mostly used to catch halibut, could likewise be seen.

The Burial Place

Between the houses were very narrow, dirty passages, and outside were a few small huts, in which were sick people, it being the custom to remove the sick from the lodges. The chiefs, when dead, were put into a box as small as possible and placed in a tree. I was shown one perched like an eagle's nest near the top of a pine about a hundred feet high, and the branches below had been cut off as the depositors came down. It is said that this dead(?) chief came to life again, and that he rattled and knocked for some time against the box in vain. No one could get up the tree, and so in process of time the sad and dismal sound ceased. Woodpecker?

The men were a robust set, very dark, their hair tied up in a bunch upon the top of the head; each one, and the women, too, wore little save the everlasting three-and-a-half point blanket. Some had, however, tippets, woven and made of teazed cedar bark. Many had streaks of red paint about the face—all were dirty and of dark dirty brown color and altho' untamed by no means repulsive. All were beggars—and they did not always distinguish between meum and tuum. The young women were a great improvement, they greased their faces and painted themselves with purchased vermilion or red earth, with the aid of a circular or other piece of looking-glass, but were nothing to boast of either in feature or fragrance. The hats of all were made of cedar root beautifully platted and so closely as to be very durable and impervious to rain. Children, nude or half naked, were playing in the sun with bows and arrows, the latter tipped with sharp fishbone or blunt headed, endeavoring to hit birds, shoot at marks or space. Stone arrow heads were common. Indeed these Indians almost remembered the day when they had not any fire arms and but only these primitive weapons. Here then was the stone age almost before my eyes, and almost also natural, if not primitive, man.

Natural Man

Here then were natural men—as natural as the forest surrounding them, both of whom had grown almost untutored, so-called unadulterated savages. If some philosophers had seen these people they would have seen something like the stone age; have seen their almost sudden transition to a supposed higher grade, and had before their eyes an example of how one nation supplants, like trees, a weaker one, and how it happens that in digging, primitive man's implement is the lowest in the soil. Doubtless what was seen at Fort Rupert had appeared in the world before, and perhaps some thousands of years hence, antiquaries and philosophers may dig up a musket and a flint arrow head or stone hammer in juxtaposition a few feet underneath and then propound some wonderful theory about the then unknown iron implement.

The Indians almost recollected the time when their forefathers had not fire arms, but used bows and arrows, clubs, spears with flint heads or stray pieces of iron, in warfare; pits, nets and so forth for catching deer and wild fowls. Amongst such people as these came a few of an aggressive and hardy race. What will be the result? A small mountain of coal lay heaped in the front of the fort. This coal had been mined at Saquash, about five miles south. The coal there lay in a seam about a foot or more in thickness, only a foot or two under the beach and ground, but getting deeper as the land ascended. The mineral was taken out by Indians and whites in the way they thought most convenient, by means of hammers, crowbars, etc., and altho' of good quality contained too much sulphur or sulphurets for many purposes. Everyone supposed a tremendously prosperous future would arrive, and the Hudson's Bay Company reap a big harvest—destined, however, not to be realized.

It is time, however, to enter the fort. This was of rectangular shape with pickets and the usual bastions, like large dove cots at two corners and a battery inside—a minor Victoria. A house was on each side of the entrance for trading. These made a sort of alley, in front and back of which were gates. The Indians were not allowed within the fort yard, as in Victoria, but had to keep within the space between the two gates, Capt. McNeill, altho' attached to Indians, being timid and dubious about these, and indeed Indians generally, and so preferred prudence.

The buildings inside were unfinished, the fort recently erected being more for the purpose of the coal industry than for trading—for defence, not offence.

Inhabitants of the Fort

Mr. Blenkinsop, a courageous, good-natured, active, intelligent Cornishman, the officer in charge, Mrs. Blenkinsop and her mother, Mrs. McNeill, were there, but the captain had left for a time, and so the charge had fallen to Blenkinsop. Charley Beardmore, second in command, was a tall, active, red, curly-haired, fearless, energetic, wiry and a little harum-scarum, good-natured fellow, who always carried a sort of shillelah. The fort had ship discipline, for Capt. McNeill had been in command of opposition ships trading on the coast and elsewhere, noted for his kind-heartedness, courage, activity, impetuosity and strictness of discipline, a discipline in those days as necessary as well ashore as afloat, altho' no one felt it, watchfulness having become a mere habit, or second nature, by reason of being constantly surrounded by real or supposed dangers.

Dwelling in the fort were Mr. and Mrs. Muir, their children, wives and relatives, a good, kind patriarchal Scotch family, and some other

miners and their wives, mostly related, and a Scotch blacksmith likewise. The rest were French-Canadians, Kanakas and a few Englishmen,
who went there and who had come out with me in the *Norman Morison* a few weeks previously. There were about thirty-five all told within
the fort, and a great deal more of French and Kanaka spoken than
other languages.

Some Tsimpshean and Kaiganee northern women, the wives of the
Frenchmen, lived there also, and I could not help being struck with
their superiority over the Fort Rupert women. They could use the
needle, make soap, wash, iron, mend clothes, prepare and tan leather,
make moccasins, and, in fact, were of great domestic use. They were
very clean, plump and comparatively fair, dressed more or less in
European clothes. No wonder the men preferred obtaining wives (by
courtesy) from these than from the rude, uneducated, untamed, unsavory damsels around.

Of the Fort Simpson men I learned that they too, by frequent intercourse with traders, and also affected by the influence of the Hudson's
Bay Co., (Mr. and Mrs. John Work, in particular), had in some measure
become tamed, given up many of their bad practices, did not go out
in war parties (which they were never famous for), but had no objection to seize and rob, when they could, any parties who happened to
be found within their domain, trading at the post, and in this way gave
great trouble to the officers thereof, who had to get their customers
safely away by stealth or stratagem. The Hydas, the boldest and bravest
of warriors, were their enemies and truly called them "old women" and
deceitful sneaks, expressing contempt for their tameness, degeneracy
and pusillanimity, which the white man called improvement—a difference of opinion.

Aboriginal Forgers

When Mr. William Manson lived at Fort Simpson, he had occasion
to buy seaweed of these Tsimpsheans, to manure the potato patch. He
hired Indians and gave them a written receipt for every canoeful
brought. The day of reckoning came. He went on paying the orders
until he thought he had paid for more than he received. On carefully
examining the papers, lo and behold! many of them were found to be
forgeries! The Indians had imitated his writing! On another occasion
he received a letter from Eberts, the chief of the Tongas: "Please

send me some tobacco." This, too, had been copied, but he sent the chief the tobacco nevertheless—a chief's dignity must not be offended. These had picked up these accomplishments by constant association with traders.

It appears, too, that a schoolmaster named Edward Allan, in 1842, had been kept at Fort Simpson, who educated the children within the fort and anyone else who chose to be. What influence, however, he had exerted it is impossible to measure. Anyhow, as a matter of history, he was the first professional teacher on the coast, and no one knows what effect a man's utterances may have, what a fire a little spark may kindle.

Soon afterwards (March 1850) I went to an afternoon party. Found six or eight Tsimpsheans had been invited. They were very nicely dressed externally in European fashion, some reclining on cushions, others on the carpeted floor, in various attitudes, armed with a long handled spoon, made of wood or horn of the mountain sheep or goat, polished and nicely carved. They formed a circle, in the middle of which stood a bowl of pretty stiff froth, into which each one dropped the long spoon, took out a portion, put it into the mouth and swallowed. One or two, however, luxuriated by throwing their heads backward and blowing out the froth from the mouth, drawing it in again, and other conjurations therewith. They were naturally polite and well-behaved, chatting and laughing about the news of the day, and perhaps at me! This in 1850! This favorite syllabub is made by taking some La Brue berries, with some sugar or molasses and a little water, stirring these very actively with the hand or other appliance, until they become worked up with a froth like a syllabub. It is by no means half bad.

Aesthetic Indians

Apropos of this, some years ago, a present of a gaudy earthenware soup tureen was made by the trader to a female chief of note (blood goes by descent on the mother's side among Indians). She used it for a lebrue bowl, and was envied by her rivals. A smart Yankee trader noted this, and subsequently took up utensils the nearest approach in appearance he could get at the time to this much-coveted one. He bartered them to advantage, and the purchasers, proud of their acquisition, showed them off in their lodges and used them for lebrue parties, and were now equal to their rival. She retorted, "Why your bowl has only one handle and mine has two, and, moreover, is prettier." Another trader subsequently came along with the genuine coveted two-handled article, and explained the use of the one-handled tureen, and then— whew!

Meals were, of course, at regular hours, but the rations consisted of such things as could be purchased from the Indians (upon whom we depended), such as wild fowl, and deer, or fish. Flour and some other things were, of course, imported and stored up. Fresh beef, mutton, chickens and so forth did not exist. Mails there were none; money, none; currency, blankets, gray cotton, tobacco and so forth—all barter, "pro pelle cutem."

I was lodged in Beardmore's castle, a round log house, the interstices between clayed, about a dozen feet square, minus a window. Inside, there was a bunk on each side, an altar in the centre, upon which a fire of wood burned; the floor, Dame Nature, covered with a few inches of sea-broken, sea-washed white clam shells. The roof had a hole in the centre, which served the purpose of letting out smoke and admitting air, light and rain—the latter pretty frequently. Altogether, it was very comfortable, although primitive and unfurnished, save with arms. My chum being a good-hearted, racy individual, I never felt better or more active in my life. Ah! there's lots in having plenty fresh air and an open fire of wood!

On Sundays the Hudson Bay Company's flag floated from the mast, as it did at the company's posts from the Atlantic to the Pacific, proclaiming to all civilized or otherwise, a day of rest. No trading or ordinary fort labor was done, and this had considerable influence on the Indians, who, doubtless, inquired why this was thus. Half of Saturday was likewise given to the men, for the purpose of allowing them to do things necessary for their own comfort.

An Early Day Strike

It did not take long to gain the acquaintance and friendliness of the civilized within and the untamed without the stockade. The miners had struck work, being dissatisfied with the wild kind of provender, and, they said, other breaches of "their agreement." In fact, their anticipations had not been realized. They expected and wanted to be their own masters—uncontrolled. On account of striking, two or three of them had been imprisoned by Captain McNeill for a couple of days or so in the bastion and shackled, ship-discipline fashion, but were now in their houses in idleness. The gold-fever contagion had been imbibed; they wanted to leave, and did not mean to submit. They had written Governor Blanshard and would bring an action for false imprisonment. Before this event could come to pass, they had deserted, as will soon be seen.

The French Canadians and Kanakas, all old hands, were satisfied, and at first the Englishmen appeared so, but they, too, raised complaints about their grub and breaches of agreement. They said the Hudson's Bay Company's agent had promised them plenty beef, mutton, beer, grog and new wine! I reminded them of their conduct on board the *Norman Morison*; how they had at first refused to eat canned meats and "soup and bouilli" and had thrown them overboard and raised consequential disturbances, but that before long how they had begged to have the rations of canned meats and soup restored. After a while they would like the provisions they now had, but the grog and beer and new wine—nowhere! They had caught the gold fever at Victoria. It was incubating. After a while they struck work also and wished to get away. Their expectations, real or fancied, had not been realized. The dissatisfaction and gold fever kept rising. Mr. Beardmore was dispatched to Victoria to place a statement of the state of affairs before Mr. Douglas, he being agent and the chief officer of the Hudson's Bay Company.

During his absence the disease became more and more clear and severe, each one inoculating the other, so that virtually all became affected and some insubordinate.

A Dining Incident

These troubles were now destined to be augmented and brought to a climax, for during June 1850, the barque *England*, Capt. Brown (she had called at Victoria) arrived for a cargo of coal. The captain, a very plausible man, was invited to dinner. Wine, etc., placed (pure and precious good liquor too) on the table, an unusual occurrence, and only adopted when strangers arrived, to uphold the dignity of the company and to show off a bit on these state occasions. Brown enjoyed his meal amazingly and remarked he had not for a long while tasted such a good, sweet, tender beef-steak! "Beef-steak: Why, there is not such a thing within three hundred miles. It's bear-steak." Turning

very pallid he suddenly bolted out and put the contents of his receiver, wine, bear and all upon the ground outside!! He did not dine
very often afterwards! He could not Bear it. There not being any decent
wharf the ship took a long while to coal and during this period the
sailors and the captain mixed with the fort people and the former,
anyhow, told them of the riches of California and the gold fields:
wondered why we and they should remain in such an outlandish
place, when fortunes could easily and in a short time, be made at
the mines; life, beer, lovely women and reckless pleasure had. Upon
the officers, ever true to their engagements, this enticing picture had
no effect, but greatly otherwise upon the servants. The men became
peevish, delirious and insubordinate: the condition increasing as the
time for the vessel's departure drew near and more near. The men obtained spirituous liquors from the ship and frequent drunken orgies occurred, during which a French-Canadian would sometimes rush into the
yard, flap his arms, crow like a cock, and challenge any one to fight
for "the cock of the walk." Let them fight if they please and they did
please sometimes—generally fair; discipline became more and more
disregarded as the fever increased. The usual discipline was set at
naught. Men, aye and women, too, openly threatened to leave the fort
in canoes if not allowed to leave in the barque *England*. If these left,
of course the fort would be left very weak and almost defenceless,
and being so the Indians would be tempted to attack it for the purpose
of plunder, especially as some of them had obtained spirituous liquors
also.

The Indian chiefs were spoken to and they promised not to sell them
any canoes, or to take them away; the whole tribe of course became
interested and more or less disturbed. The gates were more carefully
looked after, as well to prevent the eruption of Indians as to guard
against the eruption of the employees. Dangers within; dangers outside;
danger all round.

An Unpleasant Prospect

Such was the miserable state of affairs when the *Beaver* on her way
north (June 27th, 1850) arrived. By her I received a despatch from
Governor Blanshard, who had received information from the miners
and others of the unsatisfactory condition of things, asking me to act
as a justice of the peace in and around Fort Rupert, because it was

highly desirable that there should be a magistrate there, "as the miners and laborers had shown a disposition to riot, which if not checked may lead to serious consequences, the Indians being numerous, savage and treacherous." He enclosed a proclamation "warning all against disturbing the peace," and in an accompanying letter advised "that some of the men on whom reliance could be placed, should be sworn in as special constables!"

Of course, I consented, although it placed me in a very false position, being very like making a ship's doctor justice of the peace in a ship at sea! If the crew became mutinous, who was to act—mate, magistrate or the captain? I was advised to accept, otherwise if anything untoward occurred, it would be put down to my refusal. Blenkinsop and I were young men and I was very green, ignorant of this new business. Accordingly in the evening, supported by Capt. Dodd and Mr. Blenkinsop, I read the proclamation and acting commission before all assembled in the fort yard, and afterwards asked who would volunteer to be special constables? Not one came forward! Afterwards, although I used all the persuasion I could, particularly with the Englishmen who had come to the country with me, not one would consent—they did not wish to be at variance with the others—in fact were all tarred more or less with the same brush! All in the same boat. Yet these men had been under ordinary circumstances good, civil and well-behaved young country lads. The gold fever had changed them. Not a single "law book" save the bible existed within the stockade! And as to "law" in our heads precious little found place there. Anyhow "law" without power to compel obedience thereto is worse than useless.

The governor also wished me to enquire into disturbances which took place on the 7th of May (before my arrival). This referred to the strike and imprisonment of the miners by Capt. McNeill. On the following morning, of course, many came with their complaints. The miners, that their agreement had not been fulfilled and so had struck, and some of them had been imprisoned, poorly fed, and ironed, ship discipline fashion by Capt. McNeill, against whom they intended to bring an action for false imprisonment. Another from A. Muir for libel and defamation of character, in that Mr. Blenkinsop had accused him of being the instigator and ring leader of the disturbers in the fort both then and since.

Capt. McNeill and Mr. Beardmore having gone to Victoria, the enquiry into this case was postponed. This did not satisfy them. They wanted to leave at once, and intended to do so. Nine Kanakas, whose time had expired, complained that Mr. Blenkinsop would not permit them to leave. Mr. Blenkinsop said, the rule was, that the company's servants whose time had expired, had by their agreement to wait until the arrival of a company's ship to take them away. This being explained to them, they were recommended to await the arrival of Chief Factor Work or Mr. Beardmore, but to this they demurred, and plainly said if not allowed to go in the *England* they would take canoes and go to Nisqually (Washington Ter.). They were equally plainly told they would not be allowed to incur the danger. They nevertheless bought a canoe, but Mr. Beardmore returning a few days later, brought orders that they be allowed to leave. Capt. Brown, however, refused to take them as no one would guarantee expenses.

Every man now had a grievance, for the most manufactured to suit his purpose; nearly the whole had the same story, breach of agreement and not the right kind of provender and beer. Indeed to judge from their tale the agent of the H.B.Co. in England had induced them to believe they would emigrate to a land flowing with wine, milk, honey and beer, where they would be nabobs and live like princes. The truth is they all wanted to get to the gold fields of California.

Now events came thick and fast—the story nears its tragic end.

Deserting the Fort

Capt. Dodd soon after his arrival complained that four men had deserted at and from Victoria and were on board the *England*. He wanted them to return to the *Beaver*. I went on board, searched the ship, but could not find them, and, of course, no one could or would tell whither they had gone. Capt. Brown, however, said that as soon as the *Beaver* arrived the men left the ship, either on account of fear of being arrested or from information received of its probability. They had clandestinely stowed themselves away in his ship in Victoria —meaning to get to California. On the following day the *Beaver* left on her trip north. A day or two afterwards I told Capt. Brown and the carpenter to get these men on board, as the *Beaver* having departed the men were no longer wanted, and that to allow them to rove about was attended with great danger as he very well knew. He promised to do so. I have no doubt that these men were afterwards supplied with victuals by the ship's crew; but possibly did not trust to the declaration that they were no longer wanted—the more particularly as I was frequently on board, either looking for deserters from the fort or other purposes. No one would tell where they were. Four or five days (on July 2nd) later the six miners and the blacksmith deserted. Whither they had gone no one would tell. They left their wives behind, who a couple of days afterwards came to me for a permission to take passage in the barque *England*. This being refused as their husbands might return, these wives threatened to go to Victoria by canoe. I offered, should their husbands not return, to send them by the first trip of the *Beaver* south. They were not open to persuasion, and in a couple of days or so they deserted also and were housed on board the *England*. This desertion of miners and blacksmith caused consternation. The miners and blacksmith, the latter the most important of the whole having fled, the mining industry must come to a standstill. The Indians and other men of the establishment could get out coal, but there being no one left to make or sharpen the tools, little could be done. Besides allowing these people to escape did not do any credit to the gentlemen in charge. In fact, the desertion was a very serious matter from every point of view. No one ever troubled me about these deserters, well knowing me to be helpless. If any men had been sent to find out their whereabouts and then arrest them, (an impossibility) the men instead of doing so would have become companions. The Indians were as spies and would often bring word of someone attempting to escape. Of course these desertions increased the insubordination of the other servants. The Indians, too, knowing full well the disturbed state of affairs, became interested, excited and therefore believed to be dangerous. Yet other men attempted to leave. Just about this time Indians brought word that they had seen three white men on an island outside the harbor, but could not recognize them. Considering these men in danger, and supposing them to be some of the deserting miners, Mr. Blenkinsop asked old Whale, a good Quochold chief well acquainted and friendly with the miners, to go and induce them to come back to the fort, promising him some blankets for every one returning with him. The promise was made through the interpreter, a Canadian, in French, using the expression (par tête, i.e., per head) each one. This sentence afterwards became tortured into the sentence "so much per head, dead or alive!" Whale returned after a few hours and reported the men had left the island, he did not know whither. Of course he received a present for his trouble. No further steps were taken.

I wrote Captain Brown about the men obtaining spirits and also requesting him not to give passage to any deserters. In reply he stated first that the liquor did not come (to his knowledge) from his ship. (It could not have been had anywhere else;) secondly, that he would not give passage to any one excepting with a written permission, but as he could not answer for anyone coming on board at night, he advised that officers should be sent on board to arrest any one who came and further, that his vessel was now, July 6th, ready for sea. "Officers!" None existed! So I determined to go and stop in the ship. But whilst there an Indian brought word that a tree had fallen at the mines and injured a great many people. I had therefore to go ashore in the evening soon to find that no one had been seriously hurt.

Murdered by Indians

Early on the following morning (about July 7th) a rumor became current among the Indians that three men had been murdered near Newittee. Mr. Blenkinsop despatched a canoe with Jim, an Indian, to learn the truth. Jim returned in a few hours, he having seen some canoes who reported that the rumor was incorrect. The rumor, nevertheless, becoming stronger, Mr. Blenkinsop felt certain that a murder had been committed, but did not know who the victims might be, so he sent Linecous, the fort Indian interpreter, in a canoe to make enquiries about the dreaded affair, giving him also a letter to me, stating the above, and asking me to advise Governor Blanshard of the matter per barque *England*, destined for which ship, knocking about outside the harbor, I had left the fort, but could not get to her on account of having a small canoe and the weather having become bad. Linecous found me in Quatsi bay, having captured a deserter. I gave Linecous a letter to give any white men, the miners in particular, if he found any, telling them of the believed murder and advising them to return to the fort, where they would receive protection. I returned to the fort, and found profound excitement. The deserter I locked up in the bastion.

Early the following morning (July 10th) the ship being at anchor, but getting under way, again I got on board, and gave Capt. Brown letters to be posted in San Francisco for Governor Blanshard, Mr. Douglas and others, giving an account of the state of affairs to date. No deserters were on board (save the miners' wives). Capt. Brown had not heard of the rumor but said that the day previously when in the straits, word had been brought Nancy, the Newittee chief, who with several of his tribe were on board, that his wife was sick. He and the whole of his people had left. Doubtless the messenger had brought him intelligence of the murder to get him and them away, the sick wife being an excuse. Linecous returned (July 9th) and reported having been to Newittee, a village about 25 miles north from the fort, by which the *England* must pass, where he had seen Andrew Muir. The Indians were very hostile and threatening, but denied having committed the murder, but said that northern Indians had done so. Muir told him all the miners were safe and encamped opposite at Sucharti; that the Newittees were kind to them; that they would not return to the fort, indeed he wrote me a note to this effect. It was now pretty clear that the men murdered were the three sailors, who had unfortunately not returned to the barque—possibly intending to board her in the straits.

Indian Friendship

About 1 P.M. of this same day Mr. Beardmore returned from Victoria, whither he had been on business connected with the fort. He immediately volunteered (July 11th) or was ordered by Mr. Blenkinsop, to go and find all particulars about the murder—and the bodies, and offer rewards for their discovery and the apprehension of the murderers. He left towards evening in a canoe manned with four Indians. The Quocholds offered, almost importuned us to allow them to go and make war upon the Newittees, who they declared had committed the murder, and now offered to go with Charley, but of course the kind offer was declined with thanks. They were told the white men would revenge themselves ere long in their own way, but the warriors could not understand why we should wait, as they were quite ready and eager for the fray—the greatest evidence of friendship they could show!

Of course this tragedy, occurring so soon after the desertion of the miners, increased the dissension within the fort; the desire and attempts to run away more determined and frequent, increased by drunkenness caused by the liquors obtained from the *England*. Anarchy reigned— hell and earth seemed mingled—mutiny within, a couple of thousand excited Indians without and around. The green Englishmen were the most refractory, the Canadians and Kanakas less fevered and delirious, more accustomed to fort life; less so but still rebellious. To add to the trouble, the *England*, having had foul winds tantalizingly continued beating about the straits or anchoring within easy distance of the fort. But before Beardmore left she had disappeared and egress prevented. Blenkinsop and I had to keep watch night and day to prevent an eruption. During these watches an Indian would occasionally appear in the dusk or dawn standing for a few moments on the top of the pickets. This did not diminish our anxiety for the safety of ourselves, the fort and the property therein. The Indians, however, even under this great temptation, kept faithful and true to their friendship! The incident, however, had some good effect, it cowed and compelled the most valiant mutineers to have some dread and regard for their own carcasses. Some reason, therefore, began to take the place of their dread, drunken and gold feverish delirium; nevertheless this hellish anarchy continued until the *England* was out of sight. Mr. Beardmore returned having completed his enquiry in two or three days and reported to me.

The Dead Bodies Found

I left Rupert July 11th, 8 p.m., and on the following day reached Newittee. They told me they, the Newittees, had not shot the men, but that some Hydas or Sebassa men had done so.

The Newittees would not go with me to the place but described its situation. I found it about four miles from Sucharti, and looking around discovered the two men. I pulled them out, straightened them, covering them with brush. I left them thinking the magistrate would like to see the men and the place.

From Mr. Thorne, second mate of the barque *England*, I made them out to be Charles and George Wishart, Fred Watkins being the man drowned. Both appeared shot about the heart. Wishart seemed to have been placed upright in a hollow tree; both had been stripped.

On the following day I took a canoe, went to the island; found the bodies of the poor fellows as described; wrapped them in blankets, brought them to the fort, where they lay during the remainder of the day, being identified by some who had come out from England with them in the *Norman Morison*.

The following morning, July 16th, they were, with Christian rites, buried in the garden at the back of the fort; all the residents were sad and mournful.

I find no record whatever of any complaint laid before me of these men having come to their untimely end on account of the reward offered Whale, the Indian chief, but I learned afterwards that some one had written Governor Blanshard to that effect later on, in fact by a canoe despatched to Victoria, as will be presently shown.

Of course all this cast a gloom and dread over all, but the barque having gone beyond reach, the Indians, who continued faithful and true, would have informed of any attempt at running away. These all rendering desertion now dangerous, if not hopeless. Still the men, though now sober, would not work, but the anarchy had considerably lessened. It being doubtful whether the letters to Mr. Douglas and the governor sent by the *England* would reach their destination within any reasonable period, and the employees being still dissatisfied and restless, Mr. Blenkinsop three or four days after the funeral determined to send Mr. Beardmore to Victoria with copies of these letters and my despatches to the governor, they being extended to the time of his departure, viz., July 18, 1850. Now mark, my despatches to Governor Blanshard contained Beardmore's account and the state of affairs to date. He carried with him likewise my resignation of my acting commissioner as justice of the peace, and at the same time one to Mr. Douglas, requesting permission to retire from the H.B.Co.'s service.

An Unfortunate Error

Governor Blanshard received my reports carried by Beardmore, and letters from some one of the fort men, and based upon the man's report he sent a despatch to the government that many of the men of the fort do not scruple to accuse the officers of the Hudson Bay Co. of having instigated the Indians to the deed by offers of reward for the recovery of the sailors dead or alive, and that in consequence the employees at the fort threaten to leave in a body. He likewise wrote that Dr. Helmcken had sent his resignation, he being powerless—the men refusing to aid or obey. I have already shown how the error of the men originated, and so how the governor was deceived, but it was not until after he had come up in the *Daedalus*, that he corrected it in another despatch to Her Majesty's government, which, as he was by no means in love with the company, was by no means agreeable. No one likes to make an official mistake.

Curiously enough about twelve months ago, my letter to Mr. Douglas was handed to me by Mr. Donald McKay. It had been picked up a short time previously among a heap of rubbish and discarded old papers. The following is an extract therefrom:

I cannot stop here; nothing but trouble day after day; not a moment's peace or quietness and now to add to our misfortunes, everyone is afraid of his life, and the fort, and not without reason, for certainly there is not a sufficient number to defend it against the large tribe of Indians (3000) here, who are becoming very saucy and the men are afraid of them. As far as I could, it has been my endeavour to check or remedy complaints; these have now grown beyond remedy and probably abandoning the fort shortly will be the cure. I was sent here on account of the miners. They have disappeared; so please allow me to do the same in the *Mary Dare*.

This letter will give some idea of the state of things from my point of view at this time, but then I was young, a few months from London, and had no confidence in the Indians, who, in reality, were our best friends and wished to be on good terms with us. We knew this afterwards, but at the time we certainly did not trust them, and had great dread lest they should attack us. If they had their reception would have been warm, for the old hands knew how to defend.

At the end of July Beardmore returned. Unfortunately he found Chief Factor Douglas at Fort Langley, where he had gone "to meet the brigade." Beardmore delivered the letters, including my despatches, to Governor Blanshard, containing among other reports Beardmore's statement, to Mr. Douglas at Langley, by whom they would be forwarded to Victoria. He did not see the governor and therefore did not make his depositions to him. Beardmore was quickly sent back by Mr. Douglas with despatches. Accompanying him back were Mr. Hamilton Moffatt and some men to reinforce or replace those whose time had expired. Mr. Moffatt is now the chief officer in the Indian office at Victoria.

A Startling Incident

On his voyage home his canoe had been fired into. Beardmore's Indians had encamped near an Indian hunter. Suddenly one of them, without apparent cause, stabbed the hunter, who, with belly ripped open and the entrails hanging out, ran up the rocks into the bush. The assassin followed, shot and robbed him. So Beardmore and crew had to run the gauntlet afterwards. The Indian spoken of was subsequently seen at the fort quite well! From Mr. Douglas he brought word that it was impossible to accede to the demands of the men with regard to provisions—what they wanted did not exist. If the men would not work they were to receive a pound of flour per diem and to be confined to the fort.

The men were called together and told of the decision. They, one and all, said they would work no more—the Englishmen adding they could not work on fish, wild animals and wild fowl, without beer. After a while the Canadians were reasoned with; they being old servants, and some concessions being granted by Blenkinsop, they resumed their duties and so did the Kanakas, who were ever found faithful, and upon whom for some time previously we had depended, they being "big house men."

The Englishmen held out longer, but the Canadians and Kanakas having returned to duty, they in process of time and with some after trivial concessions, perhaps a glass of grog, returned also, and really they had mighty little to do or to complain of, their food being similar to our own.

The excited state of the Indians around, and the ripping open of the Indian by Beardmore's canoe man, frightened the men and rendered desertion more dangerous and hopeless. No one would run the risk.

Affairs had thus began to quiet down and became gradually settled, watch and word dispensed with, and the Indians finding things quiet, became less interested, and now being believed to be trustworthy, the gates were unlocked, ingress and egress made free and so things assumed their wonted ship-shape, hum-drum style, and all around were friends once more, for the Indians wished to be, and were as friendly as usual.

Beardmore's Corrected Statement

About the middle of August Mr. Beardmore came to my room wishing to correct his statement made after his return from Newittee. He excused himself by saying that he had not given his previous statement on oath, and that Mr. Douglas being his chief he wished to place the report first before him; that the report he was about to give was true, and that it would reach Governor Blanshard at Victoria and would therefore amount to the same thing as if he had given it before me, as I could not have done anything. His amended report is as follows:—

Had very rough weather: had seen the *England* at anchor, and the mate and part of the crew were sounding the bar off Sucharti, where the deserting miners were encamped, boarded her. Capt. Brown felt certain the murdered men were the three from his ship. Some of the crew had given his (Beardmore's) Indian liquor and made him useless and he afterwards had a fit. Reached the Newittees camp in Bull harbor; the Indians turned out armed and forbade me to land, but by telling them I had only come to enquire and not to fight, they allowed me to go ashore. I slept at night in the lodge of Nancy, the chief, and whilst there learned that about five nights previously some Newittees had been out hunting. On their return they fell in with a canoe containing three white men. Wishing to show them w[h]ere the six other (miners) deserters were, they approached. The white men took to land, the Newittees followed. One of the white men brandished an axe in a threatening manner (they had not any firearms) whilst another took a big stone, flung it at and smashed the Indians' canoe. The Newittees became infuriated, fired, killed one, the others took to the bush, but were followed, shot and stabbed likewise, and then stripped and hidden in hollow trees; one man they sunk in the ocean. The Newittees would not go with me to point out where the poor murdered men were, but gave me instructions as to the locality. I left; went to the barque *England* to get some of its people to assist in finding and to identify the men when found, but the mate and another pointed muskets at me, used very violent and abusive language, and one, a brother of one of the murdered men, threatened to jump down and be revenged, and being prevented said he would sail about for twenty years to be revenged on me and my pals. I set off, and with the aid of the Newittees' directions, espied an island about four miles from Sucharti, but on the opposite side of the straits, where I found the two murdered men, one in a hollow tree, the other at its foot covered with brushwood—both stripped and shot. I did not remove the bodies because I thought the justice might wish to see them. The names of the murderers are Tackshicoate, Tawankstalla, Killonecaulla.

Such was the account of this murder, which (account) has varied very little to this day among the Indians. Doubtless Beardmore heard both reports, but had wheedled the true one out of some Indian either by purchase or a matter of confidence.

Visit of Chief Factor Work

I must here observe that this report was not made to me by Beardmore until August 20th, after he returned from the south. A couple or so days before Beardmore made this statement, viz., August 18th, Chief Factor John Work arrived in a canoe from Fort Victoria. The good man was delighted to find things quiet, for he had imagined a hell, but found a heaven of rest. He brought among other things despatches from Governor Blanshard, including a proclamation to be published, in which was the following:

> Whereas, certain persons have likely been murdered by Indians at Fort Rupert, which murders I am immediately about to enquire into and punish,

and so forth, ending with the order that no one should be allowed to leave the fort without an order from the magistrate.

However, the place having become quiet, I merely called the people together, stating the contents of the document, which, however, as they had become good and peaceable I did not think necessary now to enforce, but would keep it in abeyance. In a private note the governor naively said: "The Queen's name is a tower of strength, but at Fort Rupert it apparently requires to be backed with the Queen's bayonets." Not a word about any blame being attached to the officers either by report or otherwise. Accordingly in October the same year, 1850, H.M.S. *Daedalus*, Capt. Wellesley, arrived, having on board Governor Blanshard (who by no means loved the Hudson's Bay Co., and was not on the best of terms with Mr. Douglas, the governor *de facto*). He had grievances also—his expectations not having been realized. In due season he inquired into the cause of the disaffection of the employees, and the cause of the murder of the white men. The greater number of the fort people being the same as at the time of the murder, including Mr. Blenkinsop, myself and two Muirs, father and son Michael. All evidence was available. Governor Blanshard listened to the conflicting statements. In a despatch from Fort Rupert, Oct. 22nd, he says: "On my arrival at Fort Rupert I found that the officer Beardmore had given a totally false account of the murder (see his first report which the governor had received from me) he had given another report to Mr. Douglas at Fraser river, which I did not receive until after my arrival here. Thus two conflicting statements were in circulation at once, which being traced to the same source, raised the suspicion of foul play and caused the report *formerly* sent to H.M.

government, viz: that the employees openly asserted that the H.B.Co.'s officers had instigated the murder by offering a reward for the men dead or alive."

This despatch of the governor is ingenious, he let himself down easily. No doubt he had been misled by false assertions when he wrote his first despatch. He knew nothing then about *"par tête"* having been translated to mean "per head, dead or alive!" by Muir. The despatch goes on to say: "Depositions that have since been made on oath backed by the evidence of the interpreter, leaves no doubt of the murderers. After consultation it was therefore determined to get possession of and punish the murderers." He might at least have exonerated the officers, but this he did not do—neither did he lodge any complaint against them. He had doubtless been hasty in his first despatch. He should have enquired first before penning such a letter.

Searching for the Murderers

It being decided to arrest the murderers, it was thought wise to attempt the same by civil means—legal means, before resorting to force. Accordingly I was requested to go in a canoe with six Indians and Linecous as interpreter and Bottineau as constable, to the Newittee village. Arriving at the entrance we suddenly found the Indians, a couple of hundred or more men painted and fully armed, already assembled, in a very excited state of motion and commotion, making a great noise and levelling their muskets at us; nevertheless, the canoe kept on until it arrived close to the beach before them, but did not ground. I stood up in the frail vessel; the interpreter explained my errand and I demanded in the name of King George, that they should surrender the murderers. The chiefs said they could not, but were willing to pay the value of the murdered men in blankets, furs or any goods, according to their (Indian) custom. Of course after some talk, they were told this would not do and was not as they knew, in accordance with the law of the white men, and so as they had refused peaceably to surrender the murderers force would have to be used and perhaps many would thereby suffer. We then left, Indians, interpreter, constable and magistrate confessedly glad to get away, not finding it by any means pleasant to have so many muskets levelled at us by these excited and untamed creatures. Bancroft's version of this is a damned, malicious lie, like many others in his work.

In returning the weather became beastly—dense fog, drizzle, high, foul wind and turbulent waves. At length, by good luck, the *Daedalus* was reached late at night, and in accordance with agreement, hailed, but it must be privately confessed, not very boisterously. Not receiving any response (the look out, who could scarcely see the canoe through the drizzle, thought it contained Indians only). Being cold, wet and miserable we pushed on for the fort, where a jolly fire and comfort were waiting to welcome us.

King George Men

Early the following morning Capt. Wellesley, in no good humor, appeared, and putting on the captain dignity austerely enquired why I had not gone on board to report? I told him that I thought H.M. vessels always kept a watch; had hailed but failing to receive an answer, had pushed on. He silently swallowed this unpleasant dose. Hudson's Bay officers required to be treated as gentlemen. My report, as already told, being made, he seemed surprised and seriously said: "King George! Why, he has long been dead! You should have demanded them in the name of Her Majesty the Queen!"

"Oh," said I, "these fellows know nothing about King William or Queen Victoria. King George is still the great chief in these regions and we are all King George men and the *Daedalus* King George's ship!"

The Murderers' Escape

It being determined to send armed boats to seize the murderers if not quietly surrendered, they started, but in the evening, a few miles from the Newittee village they lighted fires and encamped for the night. Early the following morning they were on the way, and entering the village bay they found everything quiet! Desiring to announce their presence to the sleeping foe, a big shot or two were fired, but no one appearing, the men landed in battle array to find the village empty—canoes taken away, only emptiness remained! Not knowing where on earth or water the Newittees had gone, the boats, after having practiced with some shot and shell, and destroyed to some extent the village, returned to the *Daedalus* and she a day or two afterwards left for the south.

We subsequently learned that when nearing Cape Scott, some canoes were seen, supposed to contain Newittees. They fired off their muskets, so the *Daedalus* lowered her boats and sent them in pursuit. The Indians finding themselves about to be headed off, and having had a shot fired to bring them to, returned a volley, wounding three men and an officer. The Indians then suddenly sheered off, entering a channel between some islands, and so got clear off.

It was subsequently learned that these Indians were not Newittees but peaceable Bel-bellas on their way south. They had fired at the ship as a sort of salute—but the muskets contained slugs.

A day or two afterwards Governor Blanshard left in a very large canoe, manned by northern (Kaiganees) Indians, with a voyageur supplied by the fort—having sent his despatches by H.M.S. *Daedalus*. None of us ever heard of H.M. government having have made any complaints to or against the Hudson's Bay Co. afterwards; they had no reason to do so.

To finish the tale. During the following summer (I had left Rupert ere this but Mr. Blenkinsop wrote me, and I also heard from other sources) the following:

Another Attempt

H.M.S. *Daphne*, Capt. Fanshawe, appeared, and again boats were sent to seize the murderers. On this occasion the Indians were found in a new and stronger position. On this occasion Mr. Moffatt had been previously sent to spy out the location. Mr. Blenkinsop this time accompanied the expedition for the purpose of getting quiet possession of the murderers. But the *Daphne*'s boats being fired upon and some of the sailors wounded, they attacked, and soon the Indians ran, by a narrow causeway, into the woods behind. The men-of-war's men wished to get possession of this isthmus, but were too late. Of course the Indians were not followed into the dense forest, but the *Daphne*'s men set fire to the village and then left. It was afterwards learned from the Newittees themselves, that on this occasion only one man, Chief Lookinglass, was killed and three wounded. Before the *Daphne* left for the south Governor Blanshard ordered Mr. Blenkinsop to offer a reward for the capture of the murderers, and thirty blankets were accordingly offered for each murderer. The Newittees determined now to give up the murderers who had caused, and would still cause, them much trouble. They tried to do this clandestinely, but on attempting to capture them they resisted, and so they were coolly shot, but in the scuffle a promising young chief was killed. It is said one with light colored hair escaped, and that a slave was killed and substituted for him and used in his place.

The bodies of the murderers were brought to the fort and buried in the back. The Newittees claimed the reward authorized by Governor Blanshard; Mr. Blenkinsop would not pay it, but gave them an order upon, and a letter to Governor Blanshard at Victoria.

Such is the history of this miserable affair, of which malicious misrepresentations have been told affecting Her Majesty's service, the Hudson's Bay Co., their officers and myself by Bancroft. Being still in the flesh I thought it my duty to give a correct account of the horror. The truth is, the sad tale is merely one added to the hundreds of others about the extraordinary, and often tragic, occurrences caused by the Californian gold fever of 1849, and subsequently also during the Fraser river gold fever of 1860. All attacked with this fever were delirious. I am quite sure that Mr. Blenkinsop never even thought of offering such a reward for anyone dead or alive. The accusation so preposterous disproves itself; but that any man in a passion should say in his position "these deserters must be had (meaning the miners) dead or alive," is probable and human. That the navy acted brutally is a lie.

Order Restored

But to go back. After the *England,* the cause of all our real trouble had left, with the six miners and their wives on board, quiet and order gradually returned, the Englishmen became accustomed to their grub and the kind of life. Now the usual hum-drum and clock-work-like routine of Hudson's Bay company forts appeared. Many of the Englishmen who went with me in the *Beaver* were like myself, greenhorns, and therefore every week were set to practising shooting at a target; tobacco and what-not being the prizes. I knew little about fire-arms, but had used the musket on other voyages at white bears, seals and so forth. Icebergs the musket could hit but the others never. It was very amusing to see the mess the Englishmen made of it—most of them did not know how to load or hold a musket, and more than one fell down when the musket kicked him. In a short time these difficulties were surmounted and the men became very good shots for practical

purposes. Occasionally unpleasant, perhaps dangerous, rows with Indians or some amusing scene occurred. For instance, the *Beaver*
brought some horses and cattle; most of the Indians never having seen
any, turned out as though to see a circus. They squatted all around,
the horses landed, but the lookers-on kept stolid. The Kanakas took the
horses, put a rope around the mouth by way of a bridle, and then
mounting the bare-backed steeds, made them gallop about the shore.
The aborigines could not stand this—union of horse and man. They
jumped up, many scampered away, others applauded the actors, in
fact it was a scene for a circus, and the lookers-on felt sorry when
it closed, altho' the Kanakas had sometimes galloped their horses close
to the sight-seers and so frightened them not a little. What their ideas
may have been goodness only knows.

Indian Law

On another occasion an Indian threw a stone at a Kanaka, who
immediately took a stick and struck his assailant. Immediately there
was an excitement, all the Indians turned out, and would have seized
the Kanaka but he ran into the fort just in time. The gates were closed,
the fort besieged, and as usual watch had to be kept night and day.
This siege having lasted a couple of days, a parley was held with the
Indian chiefs from the gallery. They said, truly the Indian stoned the
Kanaka and so did wrong; if the Kanaka had thrown a stone in return
it would have been all right, (an eye for an eye and tooth for tooth)
but as he took a stick, this, according to their law, was wrong and a
grave insult. Result—the insult paid for by giving a couple of blankets,
after which the gates were thrown open and all were friends again.

Such, perhaps dangerous, episodes were not very infrequent, and as a
rule were got rid of by the administration of the invaluable blankets,
the highest current coin. Trouble was generally occasioned by some
of the fort people being usually the aggressors in some way or other,
but the real danger existed in the fact that in these troubles the two
belligerents were not allowed to settle their quarrels in a fair fight, but
all the Indians took part in it. The offense being apparently considered
against the tribe.

Taking of blankets puts one in mind of the Indian dictum: That
they did not fear the muskets, but had great dread of the blankets of
the white men.

My neighbors used to bother me for medicines, so to please them—I made an infusion of Le brue berries and gave it them by the bottle—it was cheap and unpleasant, but the patients had great faith in it—it did them so much good! Unfortunately on one occasion, in decanting, some of the berries went into the bottle. The Indians found them, learned the secret, and then they lost faith—the medicine did them no more good. My successor did not fare so well. He had to pay because an Indian patient died after having taken a dose of salts.

Everybody knows now, that when an Indian falls ill he is believed to be possessed of an evil spirit or bewitched. Chief Factor Manson had a very useful Indian who became possessed. He took all the medicines, peppermint, Turlington's balsam, jalap, salts and emetics, in the fort, but they did not dislodge the wicked "skokum." Manson had a few Seidlitz powders for his own use, but in despair he determined to give his servant one. He mixed the powders in the usual manner, called the man, then mixed the two tumblers together, and told the Indian to drink quickly, but the latter believing it to be boiling and bubbling looked aghast! Drink, said Manson sternly. The Indian obeyed, astonished to find it cold. After a few minutes, as usual up came a large quantity of the gas he had swallowed. "By jove," says Manson with ready wit, "there's the skokum at last." The Indian believed, was cured from that moment, and Manson and Seidlitz powders became a great magician.

The Indians knew nothing about medicine; their feasts are a different thing, but too long to describe. On one occasion the usual procession of artificially phrensied Indians, with their guards and keepers, appeared imitating bears, wolves, dogs and so forth, a slave having a hook passed through the flesh of his back, likewise being driven about. A bear wanted to hug an Englishman who was looking on, so he up fist and gave bruin a blow between the eyes and felled him. We all took to the fort at this sacrilege, but strangely the Indians did not lock us up this time or take any notice of the occurrence.

Indian Rite and Tradition

I never saw anything cannibalistic at these orgies save perhaps arm biting or tricks imitating the animal represented. I am told that on one occasion a slave was seen to be killed with an axe, his body divided and then men wolves, men dogs and so forth seized the flesh, the warm blood dropping therefrom, biting and tearing the severed parts with their teeth, mouth and face covered with blood and foam, loathsome, harrowing and ghastly to behold. They did not swallow the flesh, (there is no evidence of their ever having been cannibals in the proper sense of the term) and yet these people believed in a hereafter, where they would be at rest, waited upon by slaves and women. On one occasion an Indian observed to me, "see that little boy, he will be a great chief, his great-grandfather (or some ancient relative) was a very great chief and was shot in the hip; this boy has a similar mark in the same place, and we believe the spirit of the old chief to be in him returned to us again."

Whether their belief had any good or evil effect on their conduct in this life is a conundrum, perhaps it made them, if possible, braver. I do not think they had any religious belief, possibly the mysterious medicine feasts and ceremonies occupied its place and the medicine men who exorcised for the cure of disease occupied the place of priests and doctors. Yet these Indians had their own unwritten traditional code of laws; offences were punished, fines levied and a murderer abhored—that is to say any one who murdered one of his own or friendly tribe; war of course not being considered murderous. As a rule these people were orderly; peace reigned in their villages. To friends and friendly tribes, friendly; to enemies no mercy. Yet among these people we walked and roamed and certainly, after having become accustomed to them felt less fear of molestation than I had often experienced when traversing the slums of London. If danger existed some one would let one know. Indeed, these Indians were peaceable and better conducted than many of the inhabitants of mining or frontier towns; we trusted ourselves to them in canoes, on land, on journeys to the interior, whether for hunting or business. They were faithful to the trust! No one ever went a journey without them, partly for safety, partly for guidance. Still I do not think strangers would have been safe. Indians are like other people—some good, some bad, and very many occupy the intermediate grades. Living among natural people one gets naturalized and imbibes a good many of their natural conceptions, in contradistinction to some of our civilized artificial and inculcated social and legal principles of right and wrong. In fact become Indianized! There seems to be in man a tendency to return to a natural state, and its concomitants, when the latter suit his purpose! Missionaries and others had better take note of this and examine themselves and their utterances.

Arrival of Capt. Brotchie

During the summer Capt. Brotchie appeared on the scene. He was a portly, good-natured, even-tempered man. His ship, the *Albion,* had been seized and confiscated by Americans at Dungeness whilst taking out and getting in a cargo of spars, I believe without a license. The Ashburton treaty had been recently signed and probably there was not an organized government in what is now Washington state. At Fort Rupert he commenced getting out spars—splendid ones from 120 feet in length and 40 inches in the butt as well as smaller ones, but after he had them cut and trimmed, a ship could not be had to take them away. He employed Indians and they soon liked him very much. Wishing to build a boat he made a steam chest built of whip-sawn plank and took some time in thinking over and turning to use any stray material he could find for the purpose. The Indians wonderingly watched. At length, the chest completed, plank put in and steamed, and when cooked sufficiently, turned out and bent to suit. The Indians then said, Capt. Brotchie, if you had told us what you wanted, we would have done all this for you. "How?" We would have buried the plank in sea-weed and then put heated stones in and around the same as we do with our canoes to stretch them. You white men know nothing! You can't manage a canoe and you can't fish for your own grub; we have to do it for you, poor things. Considerable truth in this. They considered themselves in many respects superior to the civilized men. Bye and bye the U.S. *Massachusetts* called for coal. Major Goldsborough, a very tall, heavy, jolly sort of man, clearly the offspring of English, walked about with a pine staff nearly as long as a small mast, having a spike at the end, which he planted outside the place he visited. Phillips, the doctor, of course made to me and we bargained and swapped books. I remember in the end telling him I thought far better and differently of the Yankees than heretofore. Fifty years ago the Americans occupied a very different position to what they do now. Ridicule being their lot! Capt. Knox, a heaven-born seaman and pilot, very active and energetic when on duty, a good fellow when off, determined to take the *Massachusetts* to the mine. He had discovered opposite the mine a line of sea-weed which acted as a breakwater, nearly converting the open roadstead into a harbor. After coaling she left and we felt sorry at parting with her genial, unfrilled officers.

The following year Mr. Muir's place was taken by Mr. Dunsmuir, who had come from Scotland for the Hudson's Bay Co.; but after a while Nanaimo came to the fore and Rupert sank.

The Indian Tribes

During my stay I saw natural men from the many wild tribes round about, including the artificially sugar-loaf shaped heads of the West coast. The northern people were more or less tamed and differed strikingly in language, physique and other qualities from those around and south of us. They appeared a different race, partly by cultivation, *i.e.*, associating with traders, and so somewhat effeminated or civilized. The line of demarcation north appeared to commence about Bella Bella, from there to Seymour Narrows, (Ucultas) as well as on east and west coast of Vancouver Island, as the main, wild, untamed people, like those at Rupert existed, some a little worse or a little better, in our and their sense of the term, depending in some measure on the strength of the band. In fact I was led to the conclusion that altho' all belonged to the human family, there were different breeds, just the same as there are different varieties and breeds of dogs, each kind being noted for some particular quality, or being easily trained for domestic, hunting, (even men) or other purposes.

The Ruperts seemed to have more of wolf than spaniel qualities. In a civilized sense they were a shocking bad lot, but after becoming acquainted one found in them much to admire, their manliness, boldness, bravery, war tendencies and aggressiveness being just what we admire in our own countrymen and ancestors. Their conduct to their friends and the peaceful condition of villages, their faithfulness, must come in for a big share of praise. Untamed, they were open and intelligent, not sneaks. They had plenty to eat, homes to live in, fire and clothing; in fact were provident, self-reliant, as so far well to do. Have civilized [men] much more?

They, like the squirrels, laid up stores of dried fish for winter use, but for this there was no very great necessity, being able to obtain fish all the year round, fish being for the most part their provender. They were fine-spirited animals, and as such much to be admired. The missionaries subsequently tried to christianize them but in vain; yet in a measure, by intercourse with the whites, they became tamed. It seems, indeed, that intercourse with the whites is and has been the chief source of primitive civilization; for, doubtless, for some reason or other, profit or belief in their superiority, the Indians liked and loved to associate with white men and to be among them, and do to this day. If this be not the explanation, white men must have possessed charmed lives.

Whites vs. Reds

Whilst, however, this intercourse tamed them, the diseases imported and accompanying the waifs and strays killed them before their religious philosophy had much effect. Smallpox, measles, scarlatina, syphilis being frequently fatal, however much care be taken. All men must die. These Indians obeyed the mandate perhaps a little earlier than they otherwise might. The diseases, however, not only killed many, but likewise made the living diseased, and rendered the women barren or their offspring, if any, incapable, for the most part, of living; and this is the real and true reason of their disappearance. Whiskey may have killed its tens, but imported diseases its hundreds. So it comes that the waifs and strays wafted to these shores, bringing a religion for saving the soul, likewise brought diseases destroying the body; the latter taking effect before the former. This is the result. Socially, probably, their death is of little consequence; politically, it may be of more importance, although it does not seem as though they were intended to set the world on fire; yet for the time being they were the best inhabitants of this wild country, very useful and productive. By technical education, these good properties may be fostered. Now these Indians travel hundreds of miles seeking employment, or are engaged for hop-picking in United States territory, or in lumber-mills, mines and fisheries in our own land, earning as a rule about $2 per diem, when employed. Nevertheless, they are Indians still. The breed remains, and will require a great deal of crossing to make a superior race. The British have been through the process, but the pure breed is doomed.

Recalled to Victoria

In December, 1850, a despatch came to Rupert calling me to Fort Victoria. Dr. Benson had been transferred to Fort Vancouver, and Governor Blanshard was ill.

The next day I started for Victoria in a canoe, with half a dozen

Indians, under charge of a French Canadian, Basil Bottineau, with grub, a bottle of brandy and a few rush mats.

I left, not without many regrets, for everybody had been kind to me, and had become friends with the Indians, and, I think, an adopted chief. By this time, however, Rupert had become a place of secondary importance.

We started. All went well. The weather was dirty, but we arrived safely at Victoria as related last New Year.

Looking Backward

I look back: the fort dismantled. Of the three thousand Indians not three hundred remain; and these, how changed, how fallen! The old men died as they lived, bold, brave, open, dauntless warriors. Efforts were made to plant a civilized soul in them, but it rooted not. May they enjoy their ideal, luxurious bliss, peace and repose, for they knew no sin. Death and desolation stares one in the face where an Indian city of thousands a few years ago stood; who maintained themselves. None of the waifs and strays occupy their place. Civilization crushes ruthlessly all that is natural and plants the artificial; forests and men civilized off the face of the earth, and yet, on looking around, the civilized are found to be but savages; the natural man covered with sheep's clothing. Civilization proceeds upon nature's lines, exaggerated, painted, tinselled and adorned. I see the war canoe become the "ironclad ship of war," the Indian warriors represented by disciplined sailors and soldiers; the camp resembles the Indians at home. These like the Indians are defenders of their country, ready at the same time to invade another's territory. Instead of small tribes I see large nations —instead of small parties I see legions of soldiers. Instead of a few heads and slaves being taken, I learn of thousands upon thousands slaughtered! What hypocrites we are. We call it "glory, honor." I see gorgeous churches with choirs and chants representing the exorcists. Side by side with these warriors blessing their flag and praying for victory are seen Christian ministers. Chiefs are represented too, not covered with a simple blanket, but clad in fancy vestments; Indian feasts and marriages become the gorgeous ceremonies of to-day; murders, lying, cheating, and all other vices are certainly fully represented also. Who represents the honest fidelity of the unsophisticated pure Indian?

Where, then, is our boasted civilization? Is it not in many instances merely an exaggeration of what we blame in the Indian the natural man? Man is still a savage—a professed Christian one; but he has bent and warped the Christian philosophy to suit his savagery, but not changed his savagery to suit the philosophy. Now I look around and numerous are the waifs and strays—the civilized invaders; forests have disappeared, civilized off the face of the land; other kinds of vegetation requiring artificial care have been planted in their stead; the earth has been subdued and robbed ruthlessly, made the slave of man and treated as such.

Such is the result of the advent of the waifs and strays. The answer to the question I asked myself forty years ago, where once the aborigines were omnipotent the civilized man now reigns and will be obeyed: The survival of the fittest.

The First Legislature

Colonist, 1 January 1891, p. 1.

So you want to know something about my recollections of the first Legislative Assembly of Vancouver Island?

Well, about the middle of June, 1856, the few residents of the Island were surprised to learn that a proclamation had been published by Governor Douglas, calling together a legislative body to be called the "House of Assembly." In order to provide for the election of seven members to serve therein, the inhabited portion was divided into four districts, viz: Victoria, three members; Sooke, one member; Esquimalt-Metchosin, two members; Nanaimo, one member. All freeholders having twenty acres of land and upwards to have a vote, the qualification of members being, however, the possession of real property of the value of three hundred pounds. At this time there were very few independent settlers, the greater number of people being in the service either of the Hudson's Bay or Puget Sound Companies, nevertheless their votes were their own and no one illegitimately controlled them in any way. At first it seemed difficult to find people qualified or willing to become representatives. After a while addresses, however, were presented to individuals asking them to "stand" and promising them support, so they had, some unwillingly, to consent, but before doing so, those in the Hudson's Bay Co.'s service had to get permission. There was but little interest taken in any district save Victoria, which included the town and its thirty or forty houses, but most of the townsmen were not freeholders, yet they made all the noise.

Sooke and Nanaimo were mere nomination boroughs. The Victoria campaign after the steam had been gotten up, was carried on in the usual manner, that is to say, everyone was buttonholed, and asked to promise his vote; drinks of course were common, but I do not remember any public meetings being held, save perhaps the assemblage of a few people before the counters. The bewildering fact was that when sober the voters would promise one way; when ebrius or ebriolus, another. How many times the candidates visited every freeholder in the district, how many bottles of whiskey were drunk, how many songs sung, deponent sayeth not. It was a good time for some of the voters and a break in monotony, a small game at fisticuffs did no harm. Who had anything to do at election time? The steam was up, but the barometer rose and fell—one day indications "fair" for a particular candidate and another foul.

The votes were so few, that two or three made all the difference between success and failure. At the polls there was no sneaking behind a fathom of grey cotton to sign a ballot paper, and lie secretly, but everyone had to vote openly like a man, and lie, if he chose, like a man; but his vote depending a good deal upon whether he came *ebrius ebriolus* or sober, had to be carefully looked after and the voter kept in proper trim by both sides. It was rather unpleasant to have an obstinate voter, one who would lounge about all day and not vote until a few minutes before the closing—his vote might or might not be valuable then. There were, however, comparatively few of these or the other class. The elections turned a great deal more on personal than on political opinions for no one had any clear ideas, why the "Assembly" had been called or what it would be empowered to do.

My own election was a very pleasant affair. "Noli me tangere" Kenneth McKenzie proposed me at Craigflower. Of course I made a speech, a sort of schoolboy oration, but destitute of political knowledge, assuredly not political. The oration captivated my Scotch friends (for we all were like friends) who asked me to write it out for them, which I did. Afterwards a few bottles of grog were distributed by Kenneth McKenzie, hale, robust and powerful—and a good specimen of a hospitable warm-hearted "Scotch laird" a kind of whole-souled proper gentleman. His lady gave us a lovely election dinner, which went off splendidly—and so did we.

Oh! the merry days when we were young, Kenneth! How many hard struggles we were engaged in afterwards. A staunch honest friend to me or as he always put it—"the cause." Peace be with you and the genial Tom Skinner.

Before the end of July all the elections had been held and the "House" was called to meet for the dispatch of business about the middle of August. The members assembled at the "mess room" in the Fort, where they took the usual oaths before Chief Justice Cameron. This being done, he informed us, that as soon as we had chosen a Speaker, the Governor would be prepared to open the session. The lot fell to J. S. Helmcken, who being formally presented by the members, the Governor accepted and congratulated him. This must have been ironical, for it turned out that I had all the work and the members the fun. Now came the Governor to the "mess room" and delivered a very long and as usual with him elegantly well composed and well thought out speech, too long to recite. After which the Governor left, and business commenced by the presentation of a petition against the return of Mr. Langford for Victoria District, and Capt. Stewart for Nanaimo, they not possessing the required property qualification. In process of time this was proved to be so, and Mr. McKay took Langford's place, and Kennedy took Stewart's. On account of these two unqualified members, the house, not having a quorum, could not do any business, as it took a long time to settle the question of qualification. Probably on this account the Governor's speech was forgotten! and never read.

Behold the seven honorable members seated in the "House of Assembly" this being "Bachelors' Hall," a part of a squared log building situated in the "Fort," about the spot where the Bank of British Columbia now stands.

The "House of Assembly" Hall was a room therein about twenty feet in length by about a dozen in breadth, lined with upright plank unpainted, unadorned, save perhaps with a few "cedar mats" to cover fissures. On each side were two doors leading to as many dormitories. In the centre stood a large dilapidated rectangular stove, its sides made of sheet iron, beautifully and picturesquely bulging. At the end was a wooden home manufactured table, upon which stood a hundred paged ledger, an inkstand, pens, and a small supply of "foolscap," but without a "mace," penknife or postage stamps, although the latter at this time existed for foreign purposes. Around the Speaker's table stood half a dozen very ordinary wooden chairs, for the use of the members, and at a respectful distance a couple of benches, without backs for the audience. This furniture really belonged to Bachelors' Hall, and therefore the "House of Assembly" and country were not put to any unnecessary expense. At the end of the year the accounts indicated that this august body had cost about twenty-five dollars, which occasioned some ironical remarks from the London *Times*.

No Chaplain, no prayers, no "Sergeant-at-Arms," no reporters, no nothing to add grace and dignity to the floor, which could not boast either of carpet or cleanliness; whatever existed of the latter depended on "Dick," the Indian boy, who attended on the Bachelors. Bye the bye I had already been married about four years.

Such then was the crib in which baby "Free Institutions" first saw the light in British Columbia, and the following are the nurses who nourished it, and rocked the cradle of the to be wonderful infant. Mr. James Yates, radical, growler, cantankerous yet earnest, who hated the Governor and the Hudson's Bay Co., although he had come out in their service. Thos. Skinner, a genial gentleman, a sort of liberal conservative, Bailiff of the Puget Sound Company's farm at Esquimalt. He liked the smell of the fox and to follow the hounds; but preferred this to being the fox. Jos. Pemberton, Surveyor General, who always endeavoured to induce both sides to agree! in medio tutissima his motto. Jos. McKay, lively and active, who knew everything and everybody. The patriarchal Muir, one of the led, who had been in the Hudson's Bay service at the coal mines at Fort Rupert—who said Aye or Nay when present. Dr. Kennedy, who voted; and last, J. S. Helmcken, elevated to the position of the "first commoner" verdantly innocent and ignorant of "politics," a London sparrow, too fond of nonsense and cigars. Smoking was not allowed, however, during the session and no guzzle to be had on the premises. The members did not receive any pay for their services—only worked for glory, of which they did not get very much.

One of the first difficulties to contend with, was the absence of any guide book of "Rules and Orders." The only one in my possession was an antediluvian and very learned volume, Horsford's Precedents, so it happened that business was conducted as at ordinary meetings. Motions, adjournments, and so forth not being put in technical language, which led sometimes to difficulties, but no one spent every day in discussing "points of order." Bye-and-bye an American book used by some State legislature was obtained from California, which helped us very considerably, but no one ever heard of "May" until a copy came from England. Imagine, then, half a dozen honest, upright, intelligent, well informed, well mannered gentlemen, meeting to discuss any important or unimportant question, whether in the House or out of it, and you will form a very good idea of the debates in the House of Assembly. Of course there were disagreements, but assuredly these people had honest conviction, a conviction however often governed in one or two by personal hatred to the Governor, the Hudson's Bay Co., fur traders, "*et hoc genus omne.*" Such as human nature is, so were these. One thing is certain, they did not speak "to the galleries," for no audience attended; not for the press, for newspaper and reporter existed not; they did their best for the country, according to their lights.

From the very commencement of the Colony, at all events immediately after the arrival of Governor Blanshard, although not half a dozen *bona fide* independent settlers existed, and these doing well, dissatisfaction and disappointment arose and from that time until the election it had increased, mainly owing to the fact that the number of *bona fide* colonists increased very slowly, supposed to be owing to the Company not inducing any to come, in that it might interfere with their monopoly; and, further, that the Company refused to bring goods from England for the settlers, thus compelling them to buy everything at the Company's store. In reality the settlers feared that they might at any time be oppressed if it suited the Company to act in this manner. In fact a petition had been presented to Governor Blanshard to these effects, but the petition most assuredly bore the impress of a hand not belonging to a colonist.

The singular fact remains, that many of the Company's people in the Colony really believed that the country would be better off, under the immediate control of the Imperial Government, because then they fancied there would in this case be soldiers, judges and all the paraphernalia, grandeur, dignity and attractiveness of a Crown Colony— without any cost to themselves. In this latter they were mistaken, as the Crown would have taken all the revenues to pay the first "Civil List."

All the members agreed that the one thing wanted, was "settlers," and to this end the removal of all obstructions such as the high price of land, and conditions of settlement. Of course everyone had great ideas about bringing out immigrants and other matters. They imagined it to be only necessary to proclaim abroad the wonderful climate and resources of the Island—but they did not realize the expense and difficulty of travellers getting here, and further the probable absorption of the comers by California—the gold and other benefits and excitements there—as had actually occurred. Above all they forgot that in order to carry out *their intentions* and "good resolutions" they must provide the money, the ways and means.

The House proceeded to business and in process of time enquired about the income and expenditure. The Governor sent down the accounts, informing them at the same time, that the only revenue at their disposal was the liquor licences, (amounting to about two thousand dollars), that all other revenues from land and so forth belonged to the Hudson's Bay Company; but although these were for Colonial purposes, the Company expended them as they might deem most fitting for the purpose.

The members knew now pretty well the purpose of the House, viz., chiefly to provide money, *i.e.* levy taxes for the various improvements and purposes they might deem necessary, and to make laws for good government, &c. Well, having all the English laws, we had enough— but to provide money—whew! why the Hudson's Bay Company had been bound by their "charter" to colonize the Island and bear the civil, military and other expenses thereof and incident thereto. These expenses to be repaid them by the British Government, should the Crown at any time wish or determine to repossess the country.

Why the Company can spend thousands of pounds and get them back again, when the charter expires. The more they spend the better; the great complaint against them is, they do not spend anything like enough. What we want and mean to do is to govern the Hudson's Bay Company, the Governor and expenditure! They had the very power in their hands of doing this, but either ignorant thereof or not knowing how to use it, they absolutely threw it away.

The end of this matter was that the House resolved, "it would not grant any supplies until the entire revenues of the Colony were placed under its control, and further that they would not recommend any appropriations for public works, &c., seeing that the House would render itself responsible for the outlay." By letting things alone, the Imperial Government would have to pay the whole when it resumed possession of the Island.

The principle underlying these "resolutions," correct as regards larger and responsible communities, were inapplicable here, inasmuch as the House could not have found the ways and means of making the tiny Colony self-supporting. Anyhow the resolutions were not followed up by offering to take the lands and other revenues and pay all the expenses of government, colonization, &c., the natural sequence. Truly the Colony could neither have existed or progressed without extraneous aid, it is not likely that anyone supplying the aid would have surrendered the "security" without some equal in lieu thereof or suffered irresponsible people to make any use they pleased of the money.

It is thus quite possible, that although the House threw away a very important power and so left the Governor (i.e. H.B.C.) still quasi auto-cratic as regards money, they did the country no injury, but they should not have growled so much when others did what they would not and indeed could not do for themselves. They might have made themselves useful instead of acting the dog in the manger style.

These resolutions rendered the House powerless, kept the Governor autocratic, knocked on the head all the "good intentions" members had about immigration, &c. They would not impose any taxes, in fact they had scarcely anybody to tax directly, would not stand the im-position of Custom dues, even on spirits &c., although they would fall chiefly on the Company, but this matter was never formally brought for-ward. The port of Victoria had been declared "free"—but "free-port" did not necessarily include "free trade." In those days people believed "free trade" to be able to make a second Singapore of Victoria.

The resolutions before mentioned governed the House during the whole of its existence and so in reality the Colony went on exactly as it had done before, save and except that the House growled and growled, but having lost the power of biting became mere obstructionists—a penniless House being about as powerful and useful as a mendicant and as much respected. In this matter I had as little foresight as any, the course seemed best at the time. There was one very great drawback to this Assembly—it had no connections with the execu-tive, no official member to represent it, for Pemberton had nothing to do with the Executive, which, at this time, in reality meant Governor Douglas only.

Any information required had to be asked for and given in writing, this being a very slow and troublesome business, entailing a deal more labor than Mr. Speaker bargained for or expected. At this time no "clerk" existed. After a while the House thought Mr. Speaker had a "right" to interview the Governor, and so save a good deal of time and trouble. So the interviews were not very infrequent and although they made Mr. Speaker a rather more important individual, yet the grandeur was not unalloyed, for members began to have very unjust and uncalled for suspicions that Mr. Speaker knew more than he related, and was a quasi prime minister! All nonsense! Every member was a prime minister; they made me *primus inter pares.* Governor Douglas was a reticent man and did not make confidants. Anyhow, members had to be found to propose the necessary resolutions. Mr. Speaker was present, took no part in the debates, (but always in Committee,) and soon found that more flies could be caught with honey than with vinegar. No one ever complained of his ruling, if he made a mistake he rectified it.

The members met and adjourned to any day suitable, but very often had to be drummed up. Although the Hudson Bay Company was always fair sport, the game had become monotonous. "About prorogation, Your Excellency?" "Give the members plenty of time, Mr. Speaker, plenty time!" Governor Douglas, a man of noble and herculean frame, and of Cromwellian order of mind, necessarily governed. He erected light houses, public buildings, bridges, made roads, etc., and would have done more, had the House, instead of carping, seconded his efforts. He was a far-seeing man, of great intellect, compared with whom honorable members were mere pigmies, yet capable of thwarting and of offering often injurious opposition. He had to deal justly with the Colony, H. M. Government, Hudson Bay and Puget Sound companies, Fur Traders, etc. He felt and knew that the interests of all these in the Colony depended upon its prosperity, and that they were not antagonistic. They indeed *were* the colonists. Conscious of this, he endeavored to use them all for the promotion of the progress of the colony he loved so much. He would have used them more for this purpose, had he not been thwarted by the House and one who only had ideas of making money and narrow streets I know this.

Soon afterwards the "House" removed itself without legal enactment, to a room in the castellated entrance to Judge Pemberton's Hotel, viz: the jail, which served as a lunatic asylum likewise. One Sunday morning we were surprised to see the *Brother Jonathan*, and emerging from her a "shower of black" emigrants, from "the land of the free and the home of the *slave*." These, "like the pilgrim fathers of old" kneeling on the ground, prayed and blessed it as the true land of freedom and their future home. They called for blessings on the flag that floated above the fort, and which, wherever it waves, is the emblem of freedom of body and mind.

> If all unite, as now we should
> To keep this flag unfurled.
> Old England still may fearlessly
> Bid defiance to the world.
> Cheer boys cheer.

Here then the proverb of the "blackest" hour being that just before the dawn, is soon to be exemplified for shortly after, the Fraser river gold excitement occurred, and subsequently the horrible civil internecine war in the States, not forgetting the San Juan imbroglio. Under these Victoria *suddenly* rose to be a city of thousands. Now it was that money was urgently required, but the Legislature had none to give. Governor Douglas proved himself the man for the occasion, and with his own right hand, guided the ship of state safely, fearless of the roughened water made by new political arrivals.

One morning when lighting a fire, an unusual thing, in the dilapidated stove in the House, to my alarm a real expectant audience appeared, i.e. a glossy stove pipe, with a black-haired, dark-eyed, thin visaged, spare and well clothed gentleman under it, who said in measured tones, "If I were Mr. Speaker, I would soon have a decent place of meeting, and someone to light the fire." This gentleman, afterwards, in 1858, published a newspaper called the "British Colonist," a regular spit-fire, which made things lively, and set people by their ears. It roused the dormant energies of the assembly. Being born a little before the gold excitement, it created no little bitter political excitement as well inside as out side the House. In the same year, however, the "Victoria Gazette" made its appearance. Williston, the editor.

Williston, of the "Gazette," had a few months after, an attack of paralysis. He lived with the carrier (H. Riley) and were as faithful good brothers. The house, still standing, near Cathedral Hill, had a wide open hearth, the chimney built of rough boulders encased within wood. Every morning the kind and affectionate carrier, before going his rounds, built a good fire, lifted poor Williston out of bed and placed him in a comfortable chair in front of the fire. In this helpless condition and position, Williston related: "I saw through a chink in the casing, a tiny bright spot, and watched it fascinatedly. It grew larger and more large, and soon a small flame appeared, ran up the casing, set fire to the ceiling and then the roof. Unable to move I speculated how long it would take to make me a cinder, as it was getting most uncomfortably hot, the skin of my hands and face scorching, about to become cracknell. When about giving myself up for lost and wondering what the coroner would find, there came along an early wayfarer, who, seeing the fire, raised an alarm, opened the door, found and carried me out in his arms. This, I think, was the happiest moment of my life. I know I might just as well be dead, but I don't want to be burned beforehand. Not much." A very worthy right minded man, not given to offence, he subsequently left and the "Gazette" died.

Now this is just the point where I could leave off, as the newspapers became history but yet a few more words will not be out of place.

In 1858 a message came from the Governor asking whether the Rev. Mr. Cridge's, the colonial chaplain, agreement should be renewed. The House decided, after beating about the bush, they would have nothing to do with the matter. The appointment was not renewed, and so the union between the Colonial Church and State fell into oblivion. The Hudson's Bay Company, however, gave Church Hill and surrounding property for the support of the incumbent of the church. They had built on the site, with the proviso that any surplus should be employed for the support of a school in connection with the aforesaid church. This occasioned great turbulence at the time.

The House had now been in session three years. It could not be dissolved until provision had been made for its resurrection, for without this provision, there was no power to call an Assembly into existence again. It therefore became necessary for honorable members to make their last Will and Testament.

The drawing of this will, viz: The Franchise and Bills connected therewith, caused me and one or two others an immense amount of work. Of course they did not suit all ideas, and so had to be licked into shape, a conference with the Legislative Council being necessary and held. These "Bills" took up enormous time, but on November 9th, 1859, they passed their final reading, and Mr. Speaker declared "there was no more work to do."

So decently and decorously we awaited dissolution, having bequeathed to our heirs, executors and assigns, a full grown up Franchise Act, a large population, an empty exchequer, and best wishes for their "progressive development," and enjoyment of many prosperous and happy New Years.

Appendix 3

Helmcken's Diary of the
Confederation Negotiations, 1870 *

On May 10, 1870, a delegation of unusual importance left Victoria for San Francisco, *en route* to Ottawa. It was composed of three of the leaders of the political life of the colony of British Columbia: the Hon. J. W. Trutch, Chief Commissioner of Lands and Works; the Hon. R. W. W. Carrall and the Hon. J. S. Helmcken, elected members of the Legislative Council for Cariboo and Victoria City, respectively. To them Governor Anthony Musgrave had entrusted the task of negotiating with the Canadian Government suitable terms for the entry of the Pacific colony into the newly federated Dominion of Canada.

Federation with Canada had been mooted in the colony since 1867, but the supine administration of Governor Frederick Seymour had done little to secure its accomplishment. It remained for his successor to initiate the official action which alone could bring the matter to a successful issue. Upon the opening of the regular session of the Legislative Council on February 15, 1870, Governor Musgrave, referring to the projected union with Canada, had said: —

> For my part I am convinced that on certain terms which I believe it would not be difficult to arrange, this Colony may derive substantial benefit from such an union. But the only manner in which it can be ascertained whether Canada will agree to such

*BCHQ 4 (1940) : 111-28.

arrangements as will suit us, is to propose such as we would be ready to accept.[1]

Consequently the Governor, after consultation with his Executive Council, had drawn up a series of proposals for presentation to the Legislative Council. Long and careful consideration by that body resulted in certain amendments to the terms and the addition of some supplementary recommendations. Thus armed, the three delegates travelled to Ottawa to sound out the Canadian Government.

Hitherto a veil of secrecy has shrouded the negotiations which followed. The various occasions upon which the delegates met with representatives of the Canadian Cabinet were, of course, noted in the press; but no details whatever of the proceedings were made public, either then or later. Moreover, careful search in the Archives of the Dominion, and in other collections, has failed to produce any minutes or memoranda, and after a lapse of almost seventy years it still appeared that not one of the participants had left any record of the discussions which took place.

Such a record has now finally come to light. Amongst the papers belonging to the late Dr. J. S. Helmcken, recently transferred to the Provincial Archives by the heirs of his daughter, Mrs. Edith L. Higgins, is a concise, day-to-day account of the eventful negotiations between the British Columbian and Canadian delegates. The diary was kept in an ordinary exercise-book. When Dr. Helmcken refused a senatorship and retired from politics in 1871, he seems to have placed it in a drawer of his secretaire and ignored it thereafter. Possibly he regarded it as a personal and confidential document, as no reference to it has been noticed in any of the reminiscences he contributed in later years to the press.

The historical importance of the diary is obvious. Though relatively brief, it reveals clearly both the general course of the negotiations and the questions upon which discussion centred. Two points are of special interest. The sincerity of Canada's desire to secure the adherence of British Columbia was made patent by the generosity of the final terms offered by the Dominion. Helmcken's journal makes the interesting suggestion that the concessions Canada was prepared to make were limited only by the necessity of carrying the terms through the federal parliament. The reader cannot but be struck by the number of times this matter is referred to in the diary. In the second place, the journal

---

[1]Victoria *Daily British Colonist*, February 16, 1870.

enables us, with some degree of certainty, to account for some of the most important differences between the proposals which the delegates took to Ottawa and the terms of union offered later by the Dominion. It is not necessary here to detail all the changes made, but Helmcken's notes throw much light upon three of the most important alterations— those in the terms relating to subsidies, to communications, and to the form of government. For the sake of clarity these are reproduced in full.

BRITISH COLUMBIA'S
PROPOSAL.[1]

Subsidies.

FINAL TERMS OF UNION.[2]

3. The following sums shall be annually paid by Canada to British Columbia, for the support of the Local Government and Legislature, to wit:—

An annual grant of $35,000, and a further sum equal to 80 cents a head per annum of the population, both payable half-yearly in advance, the population of British Columbia being estimated as aforesaid at 120,-000. Such grant equal to 80 cents a head to be augmented in proportion to the increase of population, when such may be shown until the population amounts to 400,000, at which rate such grant shall there-after remain.

(Amendment proposed by the Legislative Council:—

That the Governor be respectfully requested to strike out figures "$35,000," and insert in

3. The following sums shall be paid by Canada to British Columbia for the support of its Government and Legislature, to wit, an annual subsidy of 35,000 dollars, and an annual grant equal to 80 cents per head of the said population of 60,000, both half-yearly in advance; such grant of 80 cents per head to be augmented in proportion to the increase of population, as may be shown by each subsequent decennial census, until the population, amounts to 400,000, at which rate such grant shall thereafter remain, it being understood that the first census be taken in the year 1881.

---

[1]British Columbia, Legislative Council, *Debate on the subject of Confederation with Canada* (Victoria, 1913), pp. 162-64.
[2]Scholefield and Howay, *British Columbia*, 2: 696-97.

lieu thereof "$75,000."
That the figures "400,000" be
altered to "1,000,000.")

Communications.

8. Inasmuch as no real
Union can subsist between this
Colony and Canada without
the speedy establishment of
communication across the
Rocky Mountains by Coach
Road and Railway, the Do-
minion shall, within three years
from the date of Union, construct and open for traffic such
Coach Road, from some point
on the line of the Main Trunk
Road of this Colony to Fort
Garry, of similar character to
the said Main Trunk Road;
and shall further engage to
use all means in her power to
complete such Railway communication at the earliest
practicable date, and that
Surveys to determine the
proper line for such Railway
shall be at once commenced;
and that a sum of not less
than one million dollars shall
be expended in every year,
from and after three years from
the date of Union, in actually
constructing the initial sections
of such Railway from the Sea-
board of British Columbia, to
connect with the Railway system of Canada.

(Amendment proposed by the
Legislative Council:
That the word "and,"

11. The Government of the
Dominion undertake to secure
the commencement simultane-
ously, within two years from
the date of the Union, of the
construction of a Railway from
the Pacific towards the Rocky
Mountains, and from such
point as may be selected, east
of the Rocky Mountains, towards the Pacific, to connect
the seaboard of British Columbia with the railway system
of Canada, and further, to secure the completion of such
Railway within ten years from
the date of the Union.

And the Government of
British Columbia agree to con-
vey to the Dominion Government, in trust, to be appropriated in such manner as the
Dominion Government may
deem advisable in the furtherance of the construction of the
said Railway, a similar extent
of public lands along the line
of Railway, throughout its entire length in British Columbia,
(not to exceed, however,
Twenty (20) Miles on each
side of the said line,) as may
be appropriated for the same
purpose by the Dominion
Government from the public
lands in the North-West Terri-

between "construct" and "open," be erased, and words "and maintain" be inserted after "traffic." That this Section be altered so that the section of the Main Trunk Road between Yale and New Westminster may be included in the Coach Road which the Dominion Government is to be asked to construct within three years from the date of Union.)

tories and the Province of Manitoba. Provided, that the quantity of lands which may be held under pre-emption right or by Crown grant within the limits of the tract of land in British Columbia to be so conveyed to the Dominion Government shall be made good to the Dominion from contiguous public lands; and, provided, further, that until the commencement within two years, as aforesaid, from the date of the Union, of the construction of the said Railway, the Government of British Columbia shall not sell or alienate any further portions of the public lands of British Columbia in any other way than under right of pre-emption, requiring actual residence of the pre-empter on the land claimed by him. In consideration of the land to be so conveyed in aid of the construction of the said Railway, the Dominion Government agree to pay to British Columbia, from the date of the Union, the sum of 100,000 dollars per annum in half-yearly payments in advance.

Form of government.

15. The constitution of the Executive authority and of the Legislature of British Columbia shall, subject to the provisions of "The British North America Act, 1867," continue as exist-

14. The constitution of the Executive Authority and of the Legislature of British Columbia shall, subject to the provisions of the "British North America Act, 1867," continue

ing at the time of Union until altered under the authority of the said Act.

as existing at the time of Union until altered under the authority of the said Act, it being at the same time understood that the Government of the Dominion will readily consent to the introduction of Responsible Government when desired by the inhabitants of British Columbia, and it being likewise understood that it is the intention of the Government of British Columbia under the authority of the Secretary of State for the Colonies, to amend the existing constitution of the Legislature by providing that a majority of its members shall be elective.

It is now generally conceded that the inclusion of the guarantee of responsible government in the terms was largely the work of H. E. Seelye, the diligent special correspondent of the Victoria *Daily British Colonist.*[1]

Willard E. Ireland.

DIARY OF THE CONFEDERATION NEGOTIATIONS, 1870

Friday, June 3rd.[2]

We arrived at Ottawa City at 1 o'clock to day from Prescott;

---

[1]See W. A. Harkin, ed., *Political Reminiscences of the Right Honorable Sir Charles Tupper* (London, 1914), p. 128.

[2]Contrary to the general acceptance of June 4th as the date for the arrival of the delegates (see Scholefield and Howay, *British Columbia*, 2:293), the date here mentioned is correct. Compare telegraphic message in the Victoria *Daily British Colonist*, June 5, 1870.

would have been in yesterday had we not missed the train.[1] Mr. Trutch
sent in a note stating we had arrived. The Governor General summoned us to his presence at 3 o'clock.[2] We were received courteously;
after a few minutes Sir G[eorge] Cartier made his appearance and
we were introduced to him and very shortly after conducted and
inducted by him to the Privy Council and presented to all the Members
—a Council being at that time held.[3] After an ordinary conversation,
we were informed that we should be made acquainted with the time
when our presence would be required and then the Hon. J[oseph]
Howe [President of the Privy Council] volunteered to shew us the City.
He did so and we dined with him in the evening, Sir F[rancis] Hincks
[Minister of Finance] being present and Honble. Mr. Tilley [Minister
of Customs]. We subsequently learned that on Monday next we were
required to meet the [Privy] Council at 2 P.M.

Monday. [June 6.]

According to appointment we proceeded to the Govt. Buildings and
met Sir G. Cartier, whom we found in his shirt sleeves, hard at work.
He, as usual, was exceedingly pleasant, gave us sherry, and introduced
us into the Privy Council, Mr. Trutch being told to occupy the Gov.
General [*sic*] seat, I upon his right and Carrall the left.[4] We were
informed that the Council had agreed to appoint a deputation from
their body to confer with the delegates and discuss the various points
submitted by/from the Govt. of B.C. Mr. Tilley explained to the Council,
that the Delegates considered they were here to give every information
and explanation required or desired, 2nd to support the terms of their

---

[1]The Toronto *Globe*, June 10, 1870, states quite definitely that the delegates
arrived in Ottawa on the 28th of May, and H. E. Seelye, special correspondent
of the Victoria *Colonist*, in Toronto on the 27th. Presumably they made a short
visit out of the capital before undertaking to contact the Government, for this
same issue of the newspaper quotes at length from a speech made by Dr.
Helmcken at a dinner in honour of R. W. W. Carrall, in his native city of Woodstock, Ontario.

[2]Sir John Young, later Baron Lisgar, Governor-General of Canada, 1868-72.

[3]The reference here is to a meeting of the cabinet. It is to be remembered that
the Prime Minister, Sir John A. Macdonald, was seriously ill at the time. Consequently the responsibility for the negotiations fell upon Sir George Cartier, Minister
of Militia and Defence, the acting prime minister.

[4]This was in reality the first business meeting of the negotiation. An endorsation
by Sir John Young on the dispatch of Governor Musgrave introducing the
delegates reads: "6 June, 1870. Acknowledge receipt and say I have placed
these gentlemen in communication with the Council of the Dominion. They are
to have their first meeting this morning." Musgrave to Young, May 7, 1870.
Canada Public Letters Received, G series, no. 1493 (Public Archives, Ottawa).

own Govt., 3rd That they had no power whatever to bind the Colony
to any terms, but that the terms as agreed upon would be submitted
to the people as proposed and already determined upon by the Governor
of B[ritish] Columbia. From the remarks of various members of Council,
it appeared as tho the Govt. of Canada would grant everything they
possibly could or that they could get the parliament to agree to. Sir
Francis Hincks thought the 120,000 population clause a very ingenious manipulation of figures, and advised that we should bring all the
information upon which it was based. After conversing generally and
pleasantly it was agreed that we should meet the committee at 3 o'clock
to-morrow to proceed to business. The Committee being Sir George
Cartier, Honble. Mr. Tilley, and Sir Francis Hincks. We have every
reason to be pleased with our reception—the cordial feeling exhibited
towards us—the plainness & simplicity of manner and the studied
endeavour to be agreeable and to conduct the business in a fair, plain
and upright manner.

Tuesday. [June 7.]

We attended at 3 o'clock but found Sir G. Cartier engaged and
continued so for half an hour longer. He then excused himself in a
most merry way, took us to wine and himself to a sandwich likewise,
he not having had time to take anything before. It is astounding how
Sir G. works—morning, noon, night, brings no cessation. Of course the
first thing entered upon in Council was the 120,000 population. The
ministry knew of course this to be a fictitious number and stated they
could not propose it to parliament,[1] but Sir Francis Hincks observed
that he saw that we must have the $150,000. Yet the puzzle was how
to get it. It could not be done by real population and real debt even
supposing the allowance for the debt to be increased. We made no
objection to our population being put down at its real number provided that the money could be obtained. We consented too that our

[1]Governor Musgrave explained the method of computing the population at
120,000 as follows: "It is proposed therefore that for the purposes of an arrangement with Canada our Population should be estimated from the amount of
Revenue contributed to the general fund of the Dominion, from the sources
which would be transferred. On a moderate computation the Customs and Excise
duties are estimated for this year at $350,000. This sum is more than is raised
from 120,000 of the population of Canada.... British Columbia claims accordingly to come into the Union with the privileges, as she relinquishes the
Revenues, of 120,000 of the population of the Dominion." Musgrave to Young,
20 February, 1870, *Canada Public Letters Received, G series*, no. 1359.

Tariff should remain in force, but suggested that it might be improved for B[ritish] Columbia as well as themselves. Sir F. Hincks believed that under present circumstances the tariff could be different in the two countries for some time to come to all events. Tilley differed, but bowed to Sir F. Hincks. They both saw that if they did not maintain the B.C. Tariff the income of the Dominion would not be the same as that set down. However much they could get over our fictitious population they could not support our mode of calculating the debt.[1] It was not logical and could not go down. When we were at a non-plus as to how it was to be done, viz., the money we demanded, obtained, Sir George conceived the brilliant idea of our giving up lands for the Railway and for the Govt. to compensate the colony therefore and in this way make up the sum specified. Every one was taken by surprise and all conceived the idea to be good. The ruling idea was however that they must obtain as much money from the B.C. tariff as B.C. now does, that they could not go to Parliament without that, because all the other Provinces would oppose or all would require to be put upon the same footing as B[ritish] Columbia. They could understand our wish to gain as much as we could, but at the same time it must be recollected that they could not give us more than parliament would allow. They would give us everything they could possibly ask of parliament.

Wednesday. [June 8.]

I saw Sir F. Hincks to-day upon the subject of the Tariff and recommended that our tariff should be altered so that Silks, Satins and such articles should be admitted duty free. He replied that there would be a loss of Revenue and what they had granted had been granted upon the condition of our Tariff being maintained. He asked would we allow our duty upon Sugar to be increased equal to that of Canada? I told him that a reduction of from 12 down to 5 per cent. would not be a loss to the Govt., because the trade in those articles with foreign parts would increase to that extent. He did not believe

---

[1] The debt clause of the terms proposed by British Columbia read as follows: "British Columbia not having incurred debts equal to those of other Provinces, now constituting the Dominion, shall be entitled to receive, by half-yearly payments in advance from the General Government, interest at the rate of 5 per cent. per annum on the difference between the actual amount of its indebtedness at the date of Union and the proportion of the Public Debt of Canada for 120,000 of the population of Canada at the time of Union." British Columbia, Legislative Council, *Debate on the subject of Confederation*, p. 162.

it. I told him, if he would allow us to alter our tariff to that extent, we could then go in under that tariff. He would not go in for Free Trade in V[ancouver] I[sland]¹ because in the first place the same amount of Revenue could not be obtained from direct taxation; secondly, smuggling could not be prevented; thirdly, it was doubtful whether people wanted it. I pointed out to him that the B.C. tariff and the Dominion Excise Laws could not go on together, that if we kept our Tariff we could not have the Dominion Excise at the same time, that it would be increasing our taxation and giving apparently a larger revenue than we proposed, but at the same time it would not be really so because the introduction of the Excise Laws would prevent brewing altogether and ruin the Brewers and react upon the farmers. It is true that more beer might be imported but that would not be beneficial to the country. Sir F. Hincks would maintain that my proposition would diminish the revenue. He did not believe in the increase by increased trade. He would think over the matter. Other people came in to see Sir Francis and then I had to leave.

Wednesday afternoon. [June 8.]

Had to wait as usual for half an hour. The ministers seem overworked.² Sir G. said the same thing occurred with every province, but the peculiarity of our case was that our tariff was in reality higher than theirs. After due consideration there seemed to them two simple courses to pursue, either to take the Canadian Customs Act and Excise or to keep our own Act and Excise. To make a special tariff for B.C. would look very bad and indeed they could hardly face the Commons with it, because each province would then want something for itself specially and lead to great trouble, besides they could hardly propose a diminution of the revenue, because our whole scheme was based upon possessing so much revenue. After some general debate, the conclusion come to, seemed to be, to allow our own tariff to continue until the Railway was built or until the legislature petitioned for the adoption of the Canadian Tariff and Excise. With regard to the Rail-

---

¹At the time of the union of the colonies of Vancouver Island and British Columbia in 1866, Victoria had lost the free port privileges granted to her by proclamation in 1860. The restoration of that system was frequently mooted and assumed considerable proportions in the editorial discussions of the Victoria *Daily British Colonist* during February and March, 1870.

²It should be remembered that the Red River difficulties were approaching a crisis at this time. The expeditionary force under Colonel Wolseley sent to suppress Riel and his associates was *en route* to Fort Garry.

way the Committee were enthusiastically in favor thereof. They do not consider that they can hold the country without it. It was a condition of union with the provinces[1] and they could not see any reason why if agreed upon it should not be made a condition with us. They agreed that a railway was necessary to Red River, ours or that of B.C. would only be an extension of the Railway from Red River. The Committee seemed to agree to put the railway in as part of the terms. They then had a long conversation about the Railway and country and Mr. Trutch proposed a plan for advertising, so as to obtain tenders for the construction of the road. With regard to the Dry Dock[2] [at Esquimalt] they did not see much difficulty in that, it was to guarantee interest upon a certain sum. It was a purely local work and Quebec and Ontario would object, but in such a case a similar guarantee might be given to those provinces for a similar work. The Committee thought they now had all the information required and they would report to the Privy Council. In the meantime we were to go to Montreal to see the Prince installed into various orders,[3] having received an invitation from the Gov[ernor] General so to do. Mr. Tilley said he would go with us by steamer down the St. Lawrence to Montreal, and probably we would be asked to go to Quebec.

[Negotiations were not resumed until June 25, and in the interval the delegates visited Montreal and Quebec. The following paragraph in the dispatch by H. E. Seelye which was printed in the Victoria *Colonist* for July 8, 1870, is of interest: —

"At the investiture of the Prince at Montreal our Delegates were honored with seats among the Cabinet Ministers of the Dominion. Hon. Mr. Trutch dined with the Prince, and in the evening the three Delegates attended a party given by His Royal Highness, by whom they were treated with marked attention, the Prince assuring them that he would visit Victoria as soon as the railroad was completed to the Pacific over British soil."

Presumably the Canadian Cabinet next proceeded to consider the question of union in the light of the information garnered from

---

[1]The idea here conveyed is that as the Intercolonial Railway had been a *sine qua non* of union between the Maritimes and Canada, so the Pacific Railway should be the *sine qua non* for the admission of British Columbia.

[2]The fourth term proposed by B.C. asked the guarantee of 5 per cent. on a loan of £100,000 to build a dry-dock at Esquimalt.

[3]H.R.H. Prince Arthur of Connaught, third son of Queen Victoria, was then serving in Canada. The ceremony mentioned was his investiture as G.C.M.G.

the discussions with the representatives of British Columbia. The visit made meanwhile by the delegates themselves to Montreal and Quebec seems to have assumed the character of a "stumping tour" in the interests of confederation and the construction of the transcontinental railroad.

The two paragraphs which immediately follow are clearly an interjection into the regular diary. Upon his return to Ottawa, Dr. Helmcken evidently jotted down, in the notes which follow, his recollections of certain conversations relating to the question of union which he had had in the course of the journey.]

Proceeded to-day by steamer to Montreal, Mr. Tilley and Mr. Mitchell [Minister of Marine and Fisheries] accompanying. We had long conversations upon the subject of our mission. Mr. Tilley said the Govt. wished to grant all they possibly could, but we must recollect that they had the Parliament to deal with and that they could only grant such things as they were able to carry through the House. He spoke very favorably about steamboat communication with Puget Sound,[1] but he could not advise to allow the Govt. of B.C. to alter the tariff. He made various enquiries about the colony. Mr. Mitchell said that he would do all he could to promote our wishes. At Montreal we saw various Senators, Governors and other influential people to whom we talked railway and confederation. All appeared to be impressed with the necessity of a Railway to connect the Colonies.

From Montreal we went to Quebec and there saw many influential people likewise. The general character of our conversation was the same, and the wishes and desires of the people there in regard to Railways and other matters seemed to be about the same.

[The narrative diary resumes.]

Saturday. [June 25.]

Met the Council to-day. The Honble. Mr. Tilley read over the draught of the Resolutions which the Government were prepared to adopt. The population to be 60,000, they could not give the 120,000 for reasons before asked. The debt to be allowed to be at the rate of $27.77 per head, 5 per cent to be allowed upon the smaller amount of indebtedness of the Colony.

---

[1]Assistance in maintaining communication with Puget Sound and San Francisco was another of the requests included in the proposed Terms of Union.

The Council would not agree to increase the rate of $35,000. If they did the other colonies or provinces would require the same, besides we, they conceived, had a very good bargain without, always remembering that we were to have $100,000 per annum for roads.

The Council would not accede to the desire to increase the 400,000 to 1,000,000 people. There was no reason why they should do so, if they did the other provinces would complain, and the Govt. could not probably carry it through the house.

With regard to the Dry Dock, they did not wish to grant it, because it was purely a local work. If they granted it to B.C. every other province would require the same thing. It was not the amount they dreaded so much as facing parliament with so unusual a demand. They understood the whole subject of the benefit to be conferred upon the Colony and through it upon the Dominion. After long argument on both sides and cold determination on ours, a modification of the clause was agreed to, making the limit of the guarantee ten years, and that being considered preferable to the indefinite period "the completion of the Railway."

Court of Appeal was struck out because the Judges must be paid by the General Government, but the local Government establishes the Court.

A very long discussion took place about the Telegraph service but Sir George Cartier decided it, by saying the Telegraph would be valuable and fall in with the plan of the Govt. to build a Telegraph to Red River, from there to B.C. would follow, so the Telegraph was taken over.

With regard to Steamboats we reminded them that they had previously agreed to allow us mail communication with Puget Sound; so they consented to put it in altho at the same time demurring very much.

Of course the Railway had been previously agreed upon by the Govt., who still seem enthusiastic upon the matter. The resolution was drawn up by Mr. Trutch to-day, and was considered the best that could be had under the circumstances.

The Waggon road could not be allowed, could not be carried either in the Council or the House. Having granted the Railway the other must be considered a local work. We should not attempt to press the govt. too much.

The erection of Lunatic Asylums did not belong to the Dominion, but they had no objection to a ward of the hospital being appropriated thereto if found advisable, but with regard to the Marine Hospital they did not wish to stipulate to build one specially, as the organic act.[1] provided for it. They might put their seamen in an ordinary hospital and pay for them. We told them this was the very thing we did not want, but exactly vice versa and moreover we wished to establish a Med[ical] and Surgical school in connection therewith. It was promised that a resolution should be drafted conveying the obligation to build. The penitentiary was also in a similar category. They had to build it in accordance with the terms of [the] Organic Act and no doubt would do so.

Coast mail service, after various explanations, granted.

Sec[tion] 11 not considered applicable to B.C. altho it was to Newfoundland, therefore expunged.[2]

12. The Govt. had nothing to do with immigration, but the Provinces had, the clause must be expunged.[3]

With regard to Senators, it was agreed that they might be taken from any place or places in B.C. With regard to the qualifications of members of the Commons it was left to the local Govt., because the General Govt. had no law upon the subject.

Clause about volunteers considered unnecessary.

With regard to Tariff the draught was read and thought to answer, it being in accordance with the Terms previously agreed upon, but it was decided that all domestic productions must be admitted duty free.

The Fishery laws of the Dominion would not apply to B.C. until made to do so by an order in Council.[4]

The laws in force in B.C. would continue until altered by the Govt. cf [the] Dominion.

The subject of tariff I broached again but there is an evident reluctance to grant the request.

Mr. Tilley now informed us that the Council would privately consider the resolutions arrived at. On Monday we should be furnished with a

---

[1]That is, the British North America Act, 1867.

[2]This clause asked that the Dominion Government extend "in similar proportion to British Columbia" whatever "encouragement, advantages, and protection" it afforded to the fisheries of any of its Provinces.

[3]A similar request that British Columbia should participate in any measures or funds appropriated by the Dominion for the encouragement of immigration.

[4]The final Terms of Union stated that Canada would "assume and defray the charges for" certain stated services, including "Protection and encouragement of fisheries." No attempt was made to define either Dominion or Provincial responsibility or jurisdiction, and fisheries questions have since been taken to the Privy Council at least twice.

clear copy and probably on that day we should be called together and the government or rather privy Council would make a minute upon their journal of the whole transaction.

The Council have sat four hours then adjourned, but not before the subject of Govt. Resp[onsibility; i.e., Responsible Government] had been talked over, but we were obliged to wait for telegram from Governor.[1]

With regard to the million dollars for the Railway. The Govt. did not intend to do the work so could not agree to the item, as they could hardly make a contract to that effect even with contractors. The Government of [the] Dom[inion] was quite as much interested in this question and as anxious for the completion of [the] Railway as the Delegates, as something must be trusted to their honor.

With regard to material guarantee of money. The Delegates thought that the first thing to be kept in remembrance was to have the Railway commenced from B[ritish] Columbia. Whilst the agreement considered it would be a breach of honor and of the agreement not to carry it out, if not carried out the people of B.C. had just cause of complaint, even for asking separation, and no doubt the Dominion Govt. would do something for them in compensation for the injury resulting from the non-commencement of the Railway. On the other hand to put in a forfeiture, which, however, the Govt. would not agree to, was to offer an inducement not to commence the road on the Pacific coast, at all events it might so happen that a few thousand dollars forfeiture per annum would be rather borne than carry out the agreement. On the other hand it would be very easy to commence the work on the Pacific and do very little. What is a commencement and continuous working. It might mean anything. Considering then that the first object to be held in view was the commencement of [the] Railway on [the] Pacific, we considered it more advisable to rely upon the honor of [the] Govt. to fulfill the treaty and secondly if for some cause it was not, to leave it to the people of the time to decide for themselves what demand they would make or what steps take in the matter.

June 27th. [*Monday.*]

Met the council at 4 o'clock. The subject of Railway and Dry Dock was again gone over and Railway and Dock resolutions finally agreed to. Of course much of the old ground was gone over again. The Govt.

---

[1]No explanation of this reference seems to be available.

wanted to diminish the amount for dry dock but had to give in, which they gracefully did but considered that it was the hardest thing they had to swallow as it would open so many questions in the House.

The whole of the Resolutions were gone over again. Clause 5. The District Judges would be paid by Govt. but their services would be also utilized in other ways, probably as Indian agents and so forth. With regard to Court of Appeal the Council promised not to oppose a Bill to that effect in any way.

A promise was made to build the Marine Hospital at Victoria and to admit other patients upon making reasonable allowance. Langevin could not make any stipulation as to the time. He would probably visit Victoria beforehand.[1]

With regard to penitentiary. The Govt. could not take in prisoners sentenced for short periods. It had been tried and people had very much complained that small criminals should be mixed up with great ones. Such had been the case in Nova Scotia, where the Govt. had now to build a penitentiary or make arrangements with the local government. We must remember that the local govt. could oblige the Dominion to build a penitentiary, because when there were any prisoners sentenced for long periods the general govt. must have a place to keep them in and therefore the local government could if it thought fit compel them to do so.

Lunatic Asylums the Govt. has nothing to do with.

With regard to Pensions.[2] The resolution was agreed to, but the ministry said they meant to make such arrangements as would suit and be agreed to by Gov[ernor] Musgrave. Perhaps give them appointments or get appointments for them from H.M. Govt. With regard to Attorney General [the Hon. H. P. P. Crease] he might be made a judge and thus settle [the question of a] court of appeal and an official at once. Pensions they did not like to go before parliament with, they did not like them and were afraid of them. As few officials as possible would be interfered with.

---

[1]The reference is to H. L. Langevin, Minister of Public Works. He visited British Columbia in 1872 and his *Report* appears in the *Canada Sessional Papers*, 1872, V., no. 6, paper 10.

[2]Under the terms proposed by British Columbia, pensions were to be provided for those executive officials of the colony whose services were dispensed with as a result of confederation. The inclusion of this clause had influenced not a little the change in attitude of the officials towards the question of confederation.

With regard to the Addresses to be presented to the Queen,[1] the forms would be found in the journals of the House of Commons, copies of which would be sent to Victoria.

The section about Responsible Govt. would be put in and speaks for itself. The Govt. are not particularly anxious about Responsible Govt. but will put no objection in its way. It would perhaps be advisable to let confederation come first and settle the responsible govt. afterwards.

The clause about Indians was very fully discussed. The Ministers thought our system better than theirs in some respects, but what system would be adopted remained for the future to determine. I asked about Indian Wars and Sir G. Cartier said that it depended upon the severity, as a rule the expense would have to be borne by the Dominion Govt.

The Laws of B[ritish] Columbia would remain in force until altered by the Dominion Parliament.

There was some probability of a Reciprocity Treaty,[2] in which case B[ritish] Columbia would have to be included. This was considered certain.

It was likewise determined that all produce and manufacture of the Dominion or of B[ritish] Columbia should be admitted free from Customs Dues, each being a portion of the same country. It was decided that the clause mean this.

Mr. Tilley likewise said that if the Governor determined to or desired the Tariff to be slightly modified, if he would show the alterations, the Dominion Govt. would consider and most likely agree to them, but the Dominion could not invite such a request.[3]

The Council desired the Resolutions to be kept quiet until the Gover-

---

[1]The reference is to the Addresses necessary in the admission of a new Province as laid down in the British North America Act, 1867.

[2]The original reciprocity treaty of 1854 had been abrogated in 1866 although considerable opinion favourable to the negotiation of a new treaty existed. The signs were particularly hopeful at the close of 1869 and during the early months of 1870. See L. B. Shippee, *Canadian-American Relations, 1849-1874* (New Haven, 1939), pp. 304-21.

[3]Such a request for tariff adjustment was made early in 1871 (see Musgrave to Lisgar, February 10, 1871, *Canada Public Letters Received, G. series*, no. 1879), but it was not acceded to, for it was considered inadvisable to make any changes prior to the consummation of the union.

r.or choose to make them public,[1] the fact being that a Minister was about to proceed to Ontario to get lands there for the Railway and if Sand[field] McDonald [Premier of Ontario] got wind of it beforehad, he would not give up the land.[2] This was understood to be the reason.

Sir G. Cartier considered that Lower Canada and B.C. would be the most important of the divisions of the Dominion, that the former would be the manufacturing part of the Dominion, B.C. had a great commercial future before it. That in the Dominion Parl[iamen]t the Maritime Members of the Atlantic would always be with the B.C. Members in matters relating to shipping, &c., whilst the interior would also have a policy for its own interest supported by its own Members. That the Dominion would ever act kindly by B[ritish] Columbia and that her Members would be as much listened to as those from other places. That all the provinces would act for the public good and the greatest goodwill existed among all.

I am to tell from Sir George Cartier that it is necessary to be Anti-Yankee. That we have to oppose their damned system—that we can and will build up a northern power, which they cannot do with their principles, that the Govt. of Ontario or rather of the Dominion is determined to do it.

[1]The reference is to Governor Musgrave. A postscript marked private to Young to Granville, July 5, 1870, reads as follows: "Sir G. Cartier desires me to add that it was understood between the Canadian ministers and the delegates from British Columbia that the publication of the terms of the agreement should first be made by Governor Musgrave in British Columbia." *C.O. 42/687.*
[2]The terms were made public in British Columbia on August 31, 1870. It is interesting to note that the Toronto *Leader*, July 7, 1870, mentions the arrival of a deputation of the Canadian Privy Council, composed of the Hon. Sir Francis Hincks, the Hon. Alexander Morris, and the Hon. J. C. Aikins, to wait on Sandfield McDonald to secure his assistance in building the Pacific railroad, a scheme which is heartily endorsed by the newspaper. From a previous article on July 4, 1870, it is apparent that while the newspaper was aware that British Columbia was making a grant of land, it did not know of the indemnity awarded for that grant.

Index